THE OFFICIAL®
IDENTIFICATION AND
PRICE GUIDE TO

POSTERS

With best wishes —

Tony Fusco

Poster by Maxfield Parrish, 1896. Courtesy of Hirschl & Adler Galleries. See chapter on *American Art Posters of the 1890s*

THE OFFICIAL®
IDENTIFICATION AND
PRICE GUIDE TO

POSTERS

BY TONY FUSCO

With Special Guest Contributors:
ROBERT K. BROWN, JOSEPH GODDU,
KATHERINE HARPER, BERNICE JACKSON,
AND MARY ELLEN MEEHAN

Photographs by Robert Four

FIRST EDITION

HOUSE OF COLLECTIBLES • NEW YORK

HC This is a registered trademark of Random House, Inc.

©1990 by Tony Fusco

All rights reserved under International and Pan-American Copyright Conventions.

Published by: House of Collectibles
201 East 50th Street
New York, New York 10022

Distributed by Ballantine Books, a division of Random House, Inc., New York, and simultaneously in Canada by Random House of Canada Limited, Toronto.

Manufactured in the United States of America

ISBN: 0-876-37797-5

First Edition: October 1990

10 9 8 7 6 5 4 3 2 1

TABLE OF CONTENTS

ACKNOWLEDGMENTS

A guide such as this is just not possible without enormous help, and we want to acknowledge here the many individuals who have provided that help.

The poster field is lucky to have attracted many talented writers and scholars who have devoted years and even lifetimes to studying and writing about the field. We are indebted to writers such as Richard Allen, Victor Arwas, Lucy Broido, Robert K. Brown and Susan Reinhold, Joseph Darracott, Bevis Hillier, David Keihl, Patricia Franz Kery, Jack Rennert, Alain Weill, and many others who have made significant contributions to the body of information available today on posters. We will have to thank some of these same individuals again below, as many of them were also of direct assistance in providing information for this volume, referrals, and resources which proved invaluable.

We also welcome and thank most sincerely our Special Guest Contributors to this first edition: Robert K. Brown, Joseph Goddu, Katherine Harper, Bernice Jackson, and Mary Ellen Meehan. Each of them has specially written a chapter for this volume focusing on an area of specialization. We know of no other book where you can get this kind of direct information on collecting from such knowledgeable individuals in the field.

Today more and more auction houses are expanding their general sales, Art Nouveau/Art Deco sales, Arts and Crafts sales, and fine print sales to include posters. We have received a wealth of background information, photographs, and prices realized from numerous auction houses around the country, and are extremely grateful to Carol Hay, Cynthia Stearn, and Laura Horn at Butterfield & Butterfield;

Barry and Melissa Vilkin at Camden House Auctioneers; Nancy McClelland at Christie's; Kathleen Guzman and Peggy Gilges at Christie's East; Richard Barclay at Christie's South Kensington, England; David Bloom and Leslie Clinton at Freeman Fine Arts; Barbara Mintz and Arlan Etinger at Guernsey's; Michael Grogan and Martha Richardson at Grogan and Company; John Delph, Melissa Abdendroth, and Susan Haley at Oliver's; R. Neil and Elaine Reynolds at Poster Mail Auction Company; Benita Nowland-Smith and Claudia Florian at Phillips; Brian Riba at Riba Auctions; Jane Prentiss and Alicia Gordon at Skinner, Inc.; Gary Garland, George Lowry, and Caroline Birenbaum at Swann Galleries; Abigail Furey, Gavin Young, Mary Alice Adams, and Stephanie van Alyea at William Doyle Galleries; and Regina Madigan, Linda Stamm, and Linda Smolack at Winter Associates.

On a subject-by-subject basis, we would also like to thank the following individuals who generously contributed their advice, collecting information, and photographs:

Preserving and Displaying Your Collection: Andrea Pitsch and Laurance Gillaspie, both paper conservators in New York City.

French Posters: Anca Colbert, Anca Colbert, Ltd., Los Angeles; Robert Jacobs and Ilene Horowitz, Arts of the Floating World, Wayland, Massachusetts; Jaques P. Athias, Club of American Collectors, New York; Steve Harris and Sarah Stocking, Harris Gallery, Berkeley, California; Pat Kery, Pat Kery Fine Art, New York; Lucy Broido, Lucy Broido Graphics, Bryn Mawr, Pennsylvania; Nicholas Bailly, Nicholas Bailly Fine Arts, New York; Laura Gold, Park South Gallery at Carnegie Hall, New York; Silvia Pratt, Pasquale Iannetti Gallery, San Francisco and New York; Judith Posner, Posner Gallery, Milwaukee; Steve Ganeles, New York; and Chris Yaneff, Yaneff Gallery, Toronto.

Dutch and Swiss Posters: Bernice Jackson, Bernice Jackson Fine Arts, Concord, Massachusetts.

American Posters: Craig Flinner, Craig Flinner Gallery, Baltimore, Maryland; Stuart and Roberta Friedman, An American Collection, Yorktown Heights, New York; Joseph Goddu, Hirschl & Adler Galleries, New York; David Gartler, Posters Plus, Chicago; and Thomas Boss, Thomas G. Boss Fine Books, Boston.

English Posters: Arthur Lindo, Cooper Hewitt Museum, New York.

Italian Posters: Kate Hendrickson, Gallery Kate Khristianne, Chicago.

Contemporary Posters: Marcie Devaney, Communications Workers of America; Arthur Bernberg, Graphic Expectations, Chicago; Angela Warren, Graphique de France; Thomas Lollar, Lincoln Center, New York; Robert K. Brown, Reinhold-Brown Gallery, New York; and Joel Garrick, School of Visual Arts, New York.

World War Posters: Mary Ellen Meehan, Meehan Military Posters, New York.

Travel and Transportation Posters: Gary Borkan, Gary Borkan Antiques, Melrose, Massachusetts; Marc Choko, Montreal, Canada; and Nancy Steinbock, Nancy Steinbock Fine Posters and Prints, Albany, New York.

Magic, Circus, and Theater Posters: George Goodstadt and Rachel Salzman, The Antique Poster Collection, Ridgefield, Connecticut; and Steve Ganeles, New York.

Cinema Posters: Katherine Harper, private collector, Cleveland, Ohio; Jose Carpio, Cinemonde, San Francisco; Mike Hawks, Larry Edmunds Bookstore, Hollywood; Morris Everett, The Last Moving Picture Company, Cleveland, Ohio; Ira Resnick and Lauren Radler, Motion Picture Arts Gallery, New York; and Bill Luton, Theatre Poster Exchange, Memphis, Tennessee.

We also extend our thanks to the following individual collectors and resources who provided assistance and referrals: Richard Allen, Merrill Berman, Pryor Dodge, Gino Francesconi, Martin Gordon, Ross Scott, and Mark Wise; and to the dozens of individuals at galleries, museums, societies, clubs, and publications who provided information to make the Resource Guide section of this book a truly valuable tool for collectors.

Last, but definitely not least, we wish to heartily thank our Research Assistant Janet Nelson. As many of the individuals who worked with us on this project know, Janet was instrumental in assembling the information compiled here. This book would simply have not been possible without her assistance.

When we started out to create this volume we told those who might be interested in participating that our real goal was not to create just a price guide, but to create a network of poster enthusiasts from all over the country. We have accomplished the first step of that goal, and now, we invite you, the collector, to join the network by taking advantage of the resources which we have assembled here.

INTRODUCTION

From the years 1890 to 1900, Europe and America were in a frenzy over a new form of advertising, which was also a new form of art: the illustrated color advertising poster. Gone were the drab streets and boring broadsides. The boulevards of Paris, the tiny streets of Belgium and Holland, the otherwise solemn squares of London, and the shop windows of America proliferated with colorful images—a veritable public poster parade—created by some of the most talented artists of their times.

From what we have seen in researching this guide, the years 1990 to 2000 may be a recreation of the poster craze of the Belle Epoque. The vintage poster collecting market is today exploding.

Only about a decade since the first all-poster auction was held in this country in 1979, some vintage posters are breaking records with six-figure auction results. The collecting field has expanded widely to actively include the creative output of numerous countries and several subject specializations. Even posters of relatively recent origin have seen dramatic increases in attention, scholarship, and prices.

Our research for this volume has taken us through dozens of scholarly volumes, stacks of coffee table books, and numerous catalogs from auction houses, dealers, and museum exhibitions. We have pooled the information you will find here from scores of expert resources all across the country, as well as in Canada and Europe, in an attempt to present as comprehensive an overview of the field today as the pages of this guide will allow.

We hope that this volume will assist both beginning and seasoned collectors as a handy resource to which they can turn. As far as we know, this guide is unique in the poster collecting field, and even more so because of the many individuals who contributed their time and energy to make it happen.

AN INTRODUCTION TO THE FIELD

TODAY'S POSTER MARKET: AN OVERVIEW

POSTERS: POISED FOR APPRECIATION

When a Vincent van Gogh painting can sell for $53.9 million, should anyone be surprised when a Henri de Toulouse-Lautrec poster sells for a mere $220,000?

The art world was shaken in more ways than one when Vincent van Gogh's painting *Irises* sold in 1989 for such a staggering sum, coming on the heels of the previous record set earlier in the same year of $39.9 million for his painting *Sunflowers*. Even though it was later reported that the buyer of *Irises* defaulted on the loan from Sotheby's which allowed him to buy the painting, the estimated value still hangs in the stratosphere.

Also in 1989 a new record for a poster at auction was set at Poster Auctions International in New York for Lautrec's often-illustrated *Moulin Rouge*: $200,000 plus a 10% buyer's premium of $20,000. This record, and many others recently established, have brought renewed attention to the "poor cousin" of the art world—the advertising poster. More than doubling a $95,000 record for the same poster set less than three years ago, *Moulin Rouge* is but the tip of the recent poster speculation iceberg.

"It's craziness," states Martin Gordon, publisher of *Gordon's Print Price Annual*, a massive compendium of fine print auction records. "In the 1960s, many of Lautrec's posters could be bought for a few hundred dollars. In 1963, when they renovated the offices of *La Revue Blanche*, a Parisian literary journal of Lautrec's era, workmen found

3

hundreds of his posters rolled up under the floorboards. In those days, you could pick out the ones in best condition and buy them by the dozen for a few hundred dollars each. Right through the 1970s, one dealer had 100 copies of Lautrec's *Divan Japonais* which he sold at $800 each. These posters now sell for $20,000, $25,000, and more.''

EARLY AUCTIONS AND THE EXPANDING MARKET

People have collected advertising posters ever since their use first became widespread in the late 1800s. More recently, however, posters surged in popularity in this country in the 1960s, reflecting a growing interest in both Art Nouveau and Art Deco styles. The poster market "fever" didn't really catch on until the New York auction house Phillips hosted a series of poster-only auctions starting in 1979.

Unfortunately, a soft economy, overspeculation at those early auctions, and the discovery that some posters were not as rare as originally thought, all led to a "correction" in prices, and the poster market cooled off from 1982 to 1985. Since that time, poster prices have been rising steadily, although in a few instances posters have still not reached the heights of the early 1980s.

Today, the audience for posters, like the market for all art, is expanding rapidly. The market has also become sophisticated, increasingly complex, and more global.

For the most part, the base of support for prices, the foundation for the poster market, is more stable and stronger than ever before. Recognition of their value has taken posters out of general antique and ephemera shows and put them into fine print and art fairs.

Much of the market's early attention in the late '70s and early '80s focused on the work of French artists such as Lautrec (1864–1901), Alphonse Mucha (1860–1939), and Jules Chéret (1836–1932). Posters from these prolific artists, as well as from poster artists of the Art Deco period in the '20s and '30s—notably A. M. Cassandre and Pierre Fix-Masseau—still bring the highest prices overall.

But as the market has grown up, it has also broadened tremendously. Scholarship and museum shows afford new discoveries every year. More books have been written on posters than on any other form of advertising, and several new volumes appear annually. Recent significant exhibitions have been held at the Museum of Modern Art, the Metropolitan Museum of Art, the Walker Art Center in Minneapolis, and elsewhere.

Long undervalued areas have turned into specializations—turn-of-the-century American, Dutch, Avant Garde and Constructivist, Swiss, German, Italian, Hungarian, Russian, Danish—with prices that have risen steadily through 1990, and can expect to continue to rise through the next decade.

Bernice Jackson, a fine arts consultant in Concord, Massachusets, and contributor to this volume, is widely recognized for breaking new ground in the poster collecting field by concentrating on posters from countries other than France: Austria, Holland, Switzerland, Hungary, and others.

"The Modern Dutch Poster," a nine-museum touring exhibition which she helped organize, opened in 1986 and ended in January 1989 at the Cooper Hewitt Museum in New York. The exhibition brought to public attention a large number of outstanding Dutch artists whose names are not yet household words: Jan Toorop (1858–1928), R. N. Roland-Holst (1868–1938), Jac. Jongert (1883–1942), H. Th. Wijdeveld (b. 1885), Joop Sjollema (b. 1900), and others.

"Posters have been my passion for fifteen years," states Jackson. "At the time, my husband and I were operating an antiques shop on Cape Cod and one of our customers offered us a collection of World War I posters. Let me tell you, once you've started with posters, it's a real voyage of discovery!"

"If you are going to collect posters today, you have to have the courage to wander into untrodden fields," she advises. "You may discover that you have a passion for a certain style, and you may become a leader in a certain area. You have to develop an expertise in an area of the field, by subject, by country, or by specific artist or art movement. Bring your artistic and aesthetic experience to collecting as well as your financial acumen."

The highest-priced Dutch poster today, *Pandorra*, created in 1919 by Jan Toorop, has a bold design influenced by the Italian school of Futurism, and retails for about $25,000. Another stunning Dutch poster, *Architectuur*, created by H. Th. Wijdeveld for Frank Lloyd Wright's first exhibition in Holland in 1931, has climbed with Wright's rising prices, going from $4,000 only a few years ago to as much as $19,000 today.

Other Dutch posters have also started to gain high prices, but many are still affordable. Dutch posters generally tend to be smaller than

French posters, and because Holland is a much smaller country fewer were printed, a scarcity that impacts their value.

Swiss posters, both older "vintage" posters and more contemporary ones, have also gained in popularity and price in recent years. Museum exhibitions, such as "The Modern Poster" at New York's Museum of Modern Art in 1988, have brought increased attention to the great talents of Herbert Matter (1907–1984), Otto Baumberger (1889–1961), Josef Müller-Brockmann (b. 1914), and other leading Swiss artists.

"I am particularly fond of the posters issued by the PKZ men's clothing store in Switzerland," says Jackson. "They were designed for maximum impact by several artists, and have the same effect in a home or commercial office."

Though PKZ posters garnered little attention and relatively low prices when they were offered at the early Phillips auctions, today they can sell for several thousands of dollars each.

American turn-of-the-century posters by such artists as Will Bradley (1868–1962), Edward Penfield (1866–1925), Louis Rhead (1857–1926), and others have recently surged in popularity. Some of this renewed interest has to do with the upswing in prices for furniture and decorative arts from the Arts and Crafts period. Posters such as these provide a perfect compliment to a designer's setting of its mission-style furniture and copper and mica lamps.

Many of these posters were designed for magazines of the period such as *The Century, Harper's, Scribner's* and *Lippincott's.* Perhaps because of the vastness of America, magazines, rather than posters, quickly became the preferred advertising medium. Generally speaking, the posters advertising these magazines are small in format, for display in shop windows and newsstands. Nonetheless, the prices they command today are large.

A few years ago, many of these posters could be bought for under $200, whereas today they can command thousands. For example, an 1897 *Harper's June* poster by Edward Penfield which sold for $700 at auction in 1980 doubled that price at auction in 1989, and today's retail price can be as much as four times the 1980 auction price.

In November 1989, an exhibition entitled "American Art Posters of the 1890s" at Hirschl & Adler Galleries in New York, organized by Joseph Goddu, emphasized the poster's only recently acquired position as a fine art print. Hirschl Adler is well known to fine print collectors for museum-quality pieces, and Goddu, who is also a contributor to this volume, selected only those posters in the best condition for the exhibition.

Belgian posters have also gained renewed attention. One artist, Privat Livemont (1861–1936), was a talented and prolific Belgian artist whose Art Nouveau style is similar to that of Mucha. Prolific and becoming better known, prices for his work are continuing to rise, approaching prices paid for Mucha. Art movements in Belgium often closely paralleled those in France, and the talents of many Belgian artists are today being rediscovered by poster collectors who enjoy Art Nouveau, Art Deco, and more modern styles.

British and German poster artists are also increasingly sought after. Works by Ludwig Hohlwein (1847–1949), with his dramatic style and striking color combinations, lead the way, along with posters by artists such as Lucian Bernhard (1883–1972) and Hans Rudi Erdt (1883–1917). E. McKnight-Kauffer (1891–1951), a transplanted American, is the most sought after "British" artist for his posters for the London Underground and Shell Oil, among others.

Most poster collectors who have been collecting for many years didn't begin because they were looking for an investment, but rather a different form of appreciation. Ross Scott, a Vice President in the Private Banking Division of Citibank in New York, has been collecting Lautrec posters since the early 1960s and had no sense at the time that he was "investing" in posters.

"I was working in a law firm at the time, and my vacation schedule got mixed up," he laughs. "I had to try and find things to do in New York instead of going to France, and a friend suggested that I go see some Lautrec posters. I located a Madison Avenue dealer, a gruff character not really suited to meet the public, but he did have some nice Lautrecs for about $300 to $500."

Scott was not in on the bidding for the *Moulin Rouge*, which broke all records. "Luckily, I already have one," he explains. "It is frustrating for a collector today, and hard to explain the appreciation in the relatively short time period."

Some parts of the explanation are simple, in fact. Today, like never before in history, there are more and more "average" Americans who appreciate and seek to own art. In addition, the weak dollar in recent years has made America a better place for foreigners to buy art.

Another part of the explanation is almost surely linked to pure speculation in the market. Whether or not the prices from some posters have been artificially inflated by such speculation is a question that only a few more years will answer. Part of the speculator's success relies on whether or not the people who come after really believe a poster is worth what it has sold for, and whether others have success in selling the same poster or artist at the same price or higher.

The flowery and elaborate Art Nouveau style of Alphonse Mucha appealed to many early collectors of posters. His depictions of beautiful women with long tendril-like hair epitomize the style which was popular until after the turn of the century. Many of Mucha's posters today sell for $5,000 to $10,000 and more, depending on the size and subject. However, auction prices for works by Mucha have gone up and down over the past ten years.

For example, the well-known Mucha poster for *Job* cigarette papers, which can retail today for $8,000 to $10,000, brought $6,000 in a 1980 Phillips auction. Another example of the same poster, though only in slightly less desirable condition, sold for only $5,500 in 1989 at Christie's East in New York.

Mucha's popularity does seem to be on the rise again, and his posters are steadily climbing on both the auction and retail markets. One dealer interviewed raised his prices last year by 20% on all major Mucha posters, mostly because they are more difficult and more costly for him to obtain.

Another artist who has seen continued appreciation is Jules Chéret (1836–1932), often called the father of the color lithographic pictorial poster.

The vast majority of early fine art posters from the 1880s through the 1920s and early 1930s were printed using the difficult and now highly valued lithographic process, in which each color of the image is drawn or painted onto a separate stone or zinc plate and then applied to the paper to create the image. The work was done either by skilled draftsmen, or in Chéret's case, by the artist himself. Posters printed using the offset printing process which took over in the 1930s are intrinsically less valuable. Offset-printed posters can still command high prices if they are rare or by a highly recognized artist, but lithographic posters will always be more sought after.

Chéret was a master of the lithographic technique, creating intricate designs and delicate hues from only four colors. In all he created over 1,000 posters for everything from soap to cough drops to magazines and cabarets.

Not surprisingly, people in advertising are often attracted to collecting posters by Chéret and the other artists of his era, since in many ways the *ateliers* or workshops of the early poster artists were the first advertising agencies.

"We all have to make a living," explains Mark Wise, President of Wise Advertising in Cleveland, Ohio. "Many of these artists created posters just to earn their living. They were displayed on kiosks and boulevards in Paris, and really represent the origins of advertising."

Wise started collecting American advertising items, such as Coca-Cola signs, but switched to fine art posters about ten years ago. Today, many posters from his collection of Chéret, Mucha, Theofile Steinlen (1859–1923), and others are displayed on the walls of his downtown Cleveland agency, and several employees have been bitten by the collecting bug.

"You have to find out first what you like," says Wise. "I like these because many of them have a sense of humor, and they are simply very beautiful."

"I started collecting 25 years ago," says Judith Posner of Posner Gallery in Milwaukee. "My husband and I found a small gallery on the Rue de Seine. It turned out that the owner was the great grandson of the famous poster book publisher Sagot. He had Chéret posters for sale for $25 and $30, and Lautrec posters for about $200. At the time, my husband thought that was just too high.

"People still think they might be able to find the hidden cache of a poster publisher or posters which someone stored in the basement, but it's a dream," Posner sighs. "Only twice in 25 years of collecting have I ever come across a whole collection. It is a national and even international market now, and much harder to find material in fine condition.

"People tend to discover the 'pretty' posters first, until they have developed an intimacy with poster art," she adds. "Then they start to look beyond to other areas, such as Russian posters."

Anca Colbert, a fine arts dealer in Los Angeles, bought her first poster by Chéret over seventeen years ago for $10, a poster which today brings $2,500. In a 1989 auction, two-thirds of the Chéret posters sold for over $1,000, with a third of those selling for over $2,000.

"The historic value of these posters is now uncontested," Colbert comments. "They are recognized masterworks and will always continue to have an investment value. However, there are still many posters, albeit later ones, which can still be purchased for under $100 for those who are adventurous and are willing to collect for the long term. Use your intuition and don't be put off by a low price."

Interest in Chéret increased after the publication in 1980 of a *catalogue raisonné*, or complete listing of known works, by Lucy Broido of Bryn Mawr, Pennsylvania (see Bibliography), who today sells posters only to the trade.

"One of the strongest changes over the last ten years is that today there is a larger and more knowledgeable group of poster collectors," says Broido when asked to identify trends in the poster field. "This is due, in part, to museum exhibitions and increased news about posters. A museum exhibition will always boost an artist's selling power, and this is true with posters as well as with fine art."

The growing interest in posters has led to increased prices based on supply and demand. However, not all early lithographic posters are breaking records. With so many images and posters available (no one really knows how many of each poster were printed), many good designs of early artists are still available at more affordable prices.

"Prices seem unreasonably high in some cases," Broido comments. "But other early poster artists are currently underrated and will grow more popular with time: artists such as Jean de Paléologue (1860–1942), who signed his posters "Pal"; Jules-Alexandre Grün (1868–1934); Georges Meunier (1869–1942); Francisco Tamango (1851–?), and others who had a strong output and were hardworking graphic artists.

"There is a growing scarcity of early posters—both important ones and ones that are just beautiful—so now travel posters from the 1920s and 1930s and other posters right up through the present are coming up in the market. Years ago you could pick and choose, but there has been a lot of buying over the past 20 years. Of course, some posters do recirculate, but many have been bought up and are in museums and private collections. This is true not only in the American market, but all over the world," she emphasizes.

Museums now represent an important market for posters. There are today over 1,200 art museums in the United States alone. Many museums have turned to collecting posters both for their inherent qualities, and as an alternative to even higher-priced works of fine art. Where auctions used to be the province almost solely of poster dealers, today museum curators, archivists, and private collectors have increasingly turned to auctions as a source for posters.

SOME CAVEATS ON BUYING AT AUCTION

Auctions, however, can be a dangerous place for the uninitiated, and most collectors still prefer to purchase posters through dealers. At an auction, a buyer must rely on his own judgment as to the poster's condition and relative value. Also, competition from other bidders can cause prices to rise beyond retail.

"Auction prices can be somewhat misleading," explains Lucy Broido. "Just because a poster breaks a record doesn't mean it will do so the next time it comes up. All it takes to break a record are two people at the same auction who want the same poster. When you do buy, buy posters in the best condition you can find them. Later, if you want to trade up, posters in better condition will have more value. Buy from reputable dealers, and preferably those near enough so you can get back to them if there is a problem. Buy from someone you can really talk to and who will be there tomorrow."

POSTERS OF THE ART DECO PERIOD

Perhaps the best-known Art Deco posterist is A. M. Cassandre (1901–1968). His posters set the tone for a new style in advertising art where typefaces played an important role and the central image of the product gained in importance. His work influenced an entire generation of designers. Many of his posters are now widely known, including his *Etoile du Nord* for the French rail lines, *La Normandie* for the famous ocean liner, and his striking tennis poster *Challenge Round de la Coupe Davis*.

Cassandre's posters took off in the early 1980s but suffered a big dip in prices thereafter, and are only now fully recovering. Still, many of his best images today sell in the range of $8,000 to $15,000 and more, and a few rarer posters by him can and have sold for twice that amount.

Art Deco posters have seen climbing prices recently due to increased interest in modern era design and the impact of widely publicized Art Deco museum exhibitions. Auctions, such as the auction of the massive estate of Andy Warhol at Sotheby's in 1988, have added fuel to the Deco fire.

Other French Art Deco poster artists such as Jean Dupas (1882–1964), Jean Carlu (1900–1963), Paul Colin (1892–1985), Charles

Loupot (1892–1971), and Pierre Fix-Masseau (1869–1937) have established markets for their work but will continue to grow even stronger in popularity.

WHERE CAN A COLLECTOR START?

The field of poster collecting is so broad, and there are so many aspects to it, that the best advice for collectors is to first read about the field in general, and then to focus in on a particular school, artist or genre that most appeals to them. It is best not to buy until one has familiarized oneself with both the posters and the marketplace.

Bernice Jackson emphasizes the same notion: "No one is an expert in everything, and if you do become an expert in an area, you'll always find a 'sleeper'. You have to have the courage to follow your instincts, and keep looking and learning because you won't find a gem every day."

One poster collector who followed his instincts is Merrill Berman, a private investor with the firm Berman-Kalmbach in New York. Berman has assembled what is today recognized as the world's largest and most comprehensive collection of posters of the avant-garde. He focused his collecting on important art movements, artists, and designers which were not sought after by anyone with the exception of one or two museums at the time: Dada, German Constructivism, the Vienna Secession, Russian posters, and others. Today, he often loans his works for exhibitions in museums such as the Walker Art Center in Minneapolis.

"It was a real thrill of discovery," he notes. "I started trying to put together a vast puzzle without even knowing how many pieces the puzzle had. It took almost five years just to get the focus of the collection.

"Ironically, the best money in the field has not been made by speculators, but by judicious collectors with a view of the longer horizon. I was a contrarian, to use investment terminology, and went against the grain of what others were collecting," he explains. "There are still plenty of pockets of opportunity for collectors, believe me, but you have to stay away from what is 'hot'."

Staying away from what is hot in today's poster market may seem at first glance an impossible task, since the recent market explosion seems to encompass so many areas. However, by delving more deeply into the incredibly wide field of poster art, one is sure to find an artist, country or subject which still deserves attention. The investment of time and money will certainly reward the astute collector with both an appreciation of great art and an appreciation in value.

"I don't have a crystal ball," comments Lucy Broido when asked to give an opinion on which posters are most likely to increase in value. "The market is always changing, but today there is a growing demand for posters of the Viennese Secession as well as German, Swiss, and Russian Constructivist posters and Art Deco posters of all countries. In addition, posters of World War II, the 1940s, and 1950s are growing in popularity. People seem to like the airbrushed, streamlined style of that period."

GLOBAL IMPACT: TRAVEL POSTERS AND WAR POSTERS

Travel posters have always been highly popular, whether it is because they are reminders of voyages we have made or glimpses of places we someday hope to see. The market has steadily strengthened for travel posters from the 1920s through the 1940s and 1950s, although they remain an accessibly priced area for a new collector, with many stunning images from well-known artists still selling in the $200 to $500 range.

The Art Deco style, which became widely popular in the 1920s and lasted until about 1939, also coincided with a broad increase in travel by rail, car, and steamship. Many of the travel posters of the era were executed in the sleek new modern style with its emphasis on progress and speed. The posters of A. M. Cassandre were often for the French train lines as well, but Cassandre's prices are often more than ten times what one will pay for a French travel poster by a different artist.

Nancy Steinbock, a show dealer from Albany, New York, specializes in travel posters and noted some of the recent trends. "There seem to be two generations of travel poster buyers," she muses. "The younger buyers are 30 to 45 years old. They have increased mobility and travel a lot, and may also have new homes that they are decorating. They tend to look for posters from places they have been. The older generation may have traveled as well, but seem to buy from a certain nostalgia for ocean liners and old trains. The younger buyers tend to prefer automobile and airplane posters, and it is harder to sell them steamships, unless, of course, it is simply a great design.''

Mel Meehan, of Meehan Military Posters in New York, who contributed the chapter on war posters in this volume, has noted a trend to younger buyers as well. Many World War I and World War II posters sell in the same range of $200 to $500 as travel posters, making it an area in which younger collectors can actively participate.

The numerous designs, countries, different areas of service, and the great quantity of posters that were issued for Liberty Bonds, war loans, the Red Cross, and other war topics ensure that prices will remain relatively low except for notable rare and sought-after designs. However, that is only part of the attraction.

''World War II posters are now coming of age in the market,'' she comments, noting that in 1989 a World War II poster sold for more than $5,000 at auction for the first time. ''But it isn't World War II veterans who are buying them necessarily. Rather, my average customer is 30 years old, and may be looking for a piece of his or her family's history.''

Steinbock identified the same trend towards ''roots'' in travel posters. ''Another reason why people seem to be buying travel posters is that they are looking for their European roots. A customer's parents' or grandparents' roots may have been English, French or whatever,'' she added. ''I have also had Russian and Polish customers, and even one person for whom I helped find a travel poster from Estonia.''

POSTER COLLECTING ROCKS ON

Psychedelic San Francisco rock posters from the 1960s that were selling for only a few dollars three years ago are today valued at $100 and more. American artist Milton Glaser's now famous 1966 poster of Bob Dylan can sell for hundreds of dollars, even though six million of them were offset printed and distributed in Dylan's album.

The collectible value of rock posters was given a major shot in the arm with the publication of Paul Grushkin's 1987 book *The Art of Rock* (see Bibliography). For the first time, assembled in the pages of Grushkin's book, collectors were treated to an overview of a distinctly American modern poster design movement.

It is still a field in which a beginning collector can get a strong foothold with a minimum investment. Many posters can still be bought for under $100, and they can still sometimes be found in flea markets and yard sales. However, as usually happens after the publication of an important book on a poster subject, many collectors have jumped on board and are vying to build large or complete collections. One forward-looking institution, the Library of Congress, has a significant collection of these posters.

CONTEMPORARY ARTISTS POSTERS AND CONTEMPORARY PUBLISHERS

Robert K. Brown of the Reinhold Brown Gallery in New York, who contributed the chapter in this volume on "Collecting Contemporary Artists Posters," offers a wide selection of original posters by noted artists which are still accessible to beginning collectors.

In the field of contemporary posters, dealers and collectors will use the term "original posters" to mean designs that were created specifically for use on a poster. While these may have been created by the artist to publicize an exhibition of their own work, they are much more valuable than those which use an existing work for the poster image: for example, a museum Renoir exhibition that uses one of his paintings in the poster. Artists such as Picasso, Chagall, Miro, and others created works specifically as posters.

This is an exciting collecting area where posters by Picasso can still be obtained for under $1,000 (although some range up to $5,000), and where other modern masters can be collected for under $500.

Poster collectors will never run out of great images to collect, unless someday posters are no longer produced. Certain contemporary poster publishers and patrons today, such as Lincoln Center, the School of Visual Arts in New York, and the Mobil Corporation for its "Mobil Masterpiece Theatre" television productions, are creating outstanding collectible posters by commissioning leading artists. Poster publishers, such as Graphique de France of Boston with its "Aura Design" line of posters, are issuing great designs which are available at the publisher's issued retail price, some as low as $30.

Some people who specialize in "vintage" lithographic posters of the era of Jules Chéret may scoff at posters which can be bought in department stores. However, those who appreciate contemporary graphic design may have the last laugh in the long run. Remember, some posters by Chéret were selling at $30 just 20 years ago. We thought it would be a valuable historical footnote to include some of these contemporary publishers in this volume.

REACHING FOR THE STARS:
CINEMA POSTERS

Fine art posters have risen significantly in value in recent years, but Hollywood and foreign movie posters seem to be reaching for the stars! There is currently rampant speculation in the cinema poster field, with consortiums of investors buying up the most popular titles at any price.

In addition, Hollywood posters are part of a collecting market that also includes memorabilia, costumes, and other Hollywood nostalgia items. This field is often quite separate from other poster collecting fields, with its own clubs, publications, and conventions.

Hollywood developed its own style of poster art, which borrowed on some of the graphic effects of Art Deco but was decidedly different in its use of photographic imagery, multiple imagery, and enormous amounts of text—everyone got "billing." As a key to the art of movie posters, the collector should read Stephen Rebello and Richard Allen's book *Reel Art: Great Posters From the Golden Age of the Silver Screen* (see Bibliography).

The value of Hollywood posters in the market does not depend on the artist, who is most often anonymous, but rather on the film and the star depicted. Perennial favorites include Judy Garland, Marilyn Monroe, and Humphrey Bogart, and films like *The Wizard of Oz* and *King Kong*.

The Hollywood poster market is also a complex one, with posters for reissued films often fooling collectors into buying what they think is an original. Katherine Harper, a collector from Cleveland, Ohio, gives movie buffs sound advice what to watch out for in the chapter she contributed to this volume.

Like many of the other poster fields described above, there is still plenty of room in cinema poster collecting for beginners.

"The cinema poster market has a long way to go," comments Barry Vilkin of Camden House Auctioneers, a Los Angeles firm which specializes in Hollywood and cinema posters and memorabilia. "Many people are just starting to collect, and you can really feel the excitement in the field." At a 1989 Camden House auction, 95% of the posters sold, over 100 people consigned materials for the auction, and nine television stations covered the event. A lobby card for *The Wizard of Oz* sold for $2,700.

"People can lose control at auctions," laughs Mike Hawks of the Larry Edmunds bookstore in Los Angeles. "If it were for sale in a store, that lobby card wouldn't be that expensive. .

"The speculators in the market are buying up lots of material and will hold it for five or ten years, then release it," he adds. "I think the real reason more people are collecting cinema posters is that Americans are rediscovering their own past. They can identify with the films that were a part of their lives." Hawks' own personal collection is lobby cards, and two outstanding volumes have been written about his collection (see Bibliography).

Like any poster collecting field, the more vintage the poster, the better the price, and early lithographed cinema posters will always bring more than photo offset posters of James Bond and Woody Allen, but that doesn't stop the collectors of more recent movie titles.

Cinema poster dealers often issue catalogs to promote their inventory, and the catalogs are themselves worth collecting as reference works in the field. Particularly useful to our research were catalogs from Bill Luton's Theatre Poster Exchange in Memphis, and Jose Carpio's Cinemonde in San Francisco.

"The one question I always ask a would-be collector is 'Why do you want to collect movie posters?'," states Carpio. "If you are collecting for investment you need a dealer to work closely with you. Prices in this field move speedily. If you are buying a poster just because you like it, you may not need or want a dealer's advice. My recommendation, though, is to find posters that meet both requirements."

Carpio sites some of the best vintage poster titles as *Casablanca*, *Gone With the Wind*, and movies that play frequently or annually on television such as *It's a Wonderful Life* and *Easter Parade* with Judy Garland and Fred Astaire.

In more recent titles, Jack Nicholson in *Chinatown* is a good bet, and the James Bond films which starred Sean Connery are the "blue chips" of the Bond flicks. Carpio wouldn't bet on *Star Wars*, as too many were printed and saved from day one, but he can't keep the Beatles' *Yellow Submarine* poster in stock.

As for movie posters with no future, Carpio points to those starring

Ronald Reagan. "People hoarded his posters when it looked as though he would be President, and then they hit the market with them. Today, Reagan posters are at their bottom price . . . even *Bedtime for Bonzo*—you can't give it away!"

A SNAPSHOT OF THE MARKET

Whether it is politics or poster collecting, things never stay the same. Posters of different subjects, artists, eras, and schools of design will come and go out of fashion. "New" artists will be discovered and new records will be set.

For the future of poster collecting one thing is certain: the poster market is now a fully established and increasingly well-respected collecting field, and, as such, now faces new horizons and challenges for both dealers and collectors.

Only a little more than ten years have passed since the first Phillips auctions set the poster market on fire, but we predict the first decade will pale by comparison to the next. The auction catalogs from those early Phillips auctions are excellent resource material for anyone who wants to see just how far the market and prices have come since 1979 (see Bibliography).

In compiling the information for this volume, we set out to overview the poster collecting field as it is today, and to provide a reference for collectors now and in the future. In terms of the poster market, it's a snapshot of a moving target.

HOW TO USE THIS BOOK

Please note: This book is a guide, not a bible. We've set out to report on what we've observed in today's poster collecting market, with the goal of providing an overview and a variety of resources for the collector. We hope that you discover posters which you would like to collect and also get a sense of the range of posters which best suit your pocketbook. Rather than as an end in itself, this guide is intended to be a starting point for delving more deeply into any of the poster collecting areas covered.

IF YOU CAN'T FIND IT HERE

We've introduced each chapter with a narrative, often by a leading authority in the field, to give you a better sense of the scope of each area of poster collecting. Unfortunately, we could not mention all of the talented artists, graphic designers, printers, and others whose contributions have had an impact on poster history.

In other words, if a particular artist or poster you are looking for is not included here, it does not necessarily mean that category or designer is not worth collecting.

We also chose to concentrate on those posters and artists which a collector is most likely to readily find on the market in the United States. Besides the countries we were able to cover in this volume, others, such as Japan, Scandinavian countries, China, eastern European and Soviet nations, and South America, have produced and continue to produce interesting poster designs. As the poster market continues to broaden, and as political conditions change in the years ahead, these posters are more likely to appear on the market. In addition, the rarity or scarcity of posters by certain artists has removed them almost entirely from the trading arena, making market information about them less available.

ABOUT THE RESOURCE GUIDE

For collectors with particular interests, or those who just want to learn more about posters, we created the extensive Resource Guide at the back of this volume.

The Resource Guide gives you the names, addresses, and phone numbers of dealers, auction houses, museums, periodicals, associations, and individuals whom we've consulted in putting this book together. There is also a Bibliography which will help you find other books and periodicals of interest to you.

One great advantage to poster collectors is that the poster field is so thoroughly chronicled. Advertising posters have been written about almost from the first day they were created. Turn-of-the-century magazines and publications informed early collectors of new issues and new artists in the field, and these publications serve today as the earliest written histories of the poster. In addition, dozens of books have been written on specific artists, countries, and artistic movements, providing the avid collector with important source information.

If you would like to find out more about any aspect of posters, the Resource Guide can help. In addition, the dealers who are listed in this volume are always willing to answer questions and guide you to other sources of information which will enhance your knowledge of posters.

TO FIND A PARTICULAR ARTIST

If you are looking for information on a particular artist and know the country in which that artist worked for most of his or her career, look in the chapter on that country first. However, you should also note that the artist you are looking for may also be included under one or more of the subject chapters. For example, Theophile Steinlen is included both in the chapter on French posters and in the chapter on war posters. Check the Index to find other mentions of the artist you are looking for.

IMPORTANT NOTES ON THE PRICE LISTINGS

Please note: We advise you to read this chapter closely. It includes important information on how the prices in this book were established, and other things to watch for in pricing posters.

As is often true of any collectible, the market value of many posters often depends on what the buyer is willing to pay. We interviewed more than one avid poster collector who will pay higher than retail prices for posters he or she needs for a collection.

Also, some of the prices given in the following pages may seem high to beginning collectors. Posters continue to fetch record prices at auction, and more people seem willing to pay higher prices than ever before in the history of the field. However, many stunning posters are still within your reach no matter what your income.

We have offered a sample of prices in each category we have covered—again, this is not necessarily an exhaustive list. If you do not find the exact poster you are looking for here, the prices given can still be used for comparison. Also, many reputable dealers and auction houses will always be willing to quote what a particular object is worth on the market.

HOW POSTERS ARE DESCRIBED
IN THE PRICE LISTINGS

For each price listing we try to give the following information, where it is known to us:

- Name of the artist.
- Title of the poster.
- Year when the poster was created.
- The printing medium used (lithograph, silk-screen, offset, etc.) and the printing company.
- Description and background on the poster, subject, and/or artist.
- Condition, including any information on restorations (see additional Notes on Condition, below).
- Notes on the collectibility of the poster (whether it represents a good, very good, or excellent example of a particular genre, subject, or artist).
- Mounting information—whether the poster is mounted on linen, Chartex, or some other backing. When no indication is given, the poster is assumed to be "plain paper."
- Size, with width preceding height.
- Retail price range or auction price realized.

For a description of poster printing techniques and for definitions of terms commonly used in the poster field, please refer to the chapter entitled "Poster Printing and Terminology."

NOTES ON CONDITION

For the price listings, we have combined two "condition keys" that you will see used by dealers and auction houses. In the price listings in this book you will see the words "Mint," "Very Good," etc., describing the posters. In dealer or auction catalogs you will sometimes see conditions described as "A," "B," "C," etc. Below are the definitions of these terms:

Mint	A+	Flawless; no repairs; new.
Fine	A	Fresh colors and no paper loss; only extremely minor or unobtrusive repairs or tears; folds not apparent.
Very Good	A− B+	Fresh colors overall; minor or slight paper loss, but expertly repaired and not in image or critical area; very light staining, dirt, fold, tear, etc., but not in image or critical area.
Good	B B−	Good colors and lines overall; some paper loss, but not in image or critical area; some light staining; high quality restoration, but not immediately evident or only one or two noticeable repairs; folds somewhat apparent.
Fair	C	Image clear, but colors and lines somewhat faded; some paper loss or noticeable repairs in image area; light staining, dirt or folds more pronounced.
Poor	D	Image not intact or colors and lines faded or marred beyond appreciation of artist's intent; overly pronounced light staining; overly visible or poorly executed repairs; dirt or folds obvious.

HOW GIVEN PRICES WERE ESTABLISHED

The bulk of price listings in this book were observed by us or reported to us primarily by dealers and auction houses during 1989 and the beginning of 1990. We also gathered information about pricing anonymously at exhibitions, poster fairs, and fine art shows.

PRICE RANGES

The price ranges given represent the retail price at which you are most likely to find the listed poster. The retail price may vary greatly depending on the condition of the poster, the dealer from whom you are buying, whether or not the poster has been restored, and many other factors. These price ranges are based on highs and lows reported to us by collectors, dealers, and others and on estimated values from all over the country.

AUCTION PRICES

When the price given for a poster is followed by the word "Auction," it means that this price was reported to us by one of the auction houses listed in the Resource Guide. These prices represent the final bid, not the purchase price. That is, they do not include the "buyer's premium" charged by most auction houses, which is usually 10%.

Where there have been notable differences between two auctions or between the auction and the retail price range, we have noted both prices. In some instances you will see that an auction price exceeded the retail price at which the poster is generally available on the market.

PRICES IN THE POSTER MARKET ARE CHANGING DAILY

Dealers with whom we have spoken are stunned by the rapid changes in poster prices in the last few years. As we mentioned in the chapter on today's market, some of it has to do with a general rapid upswing in the price for all art, and some of it has to do with the greatly increased participation of foreign buyers in American art markets.

However, a lot of the increases are simply the result of a booming audience for posters, brought about by higher exposure, publicity for auction prices, museum exhibitions, and the increased use of posters in interior design and decorating on both a residential and commercial scale. Use the prices given in this volume as a starting point, then go out and check what is happening in the market.

PRICES FOR POSTERS HAVE NOT "NATIONALIZED"

Poster prices are not standard across the country, and there can be great variations on the retail price of any given poster depending on where and from whom it is bought. Generally speaking, New York and California tend to have the highest retail prices for posters, with other major metropolitan areas not far behind: Chicago, Washington, D.C., Philadelphia, Boston, Miami, Atlanta, etc.

The poster market, though, is becoming increasingly "self-conscious." Information on the "going price" and on prices realized at auction is more readily available than ever before. There are still bargains to be found in out-of-the-way shops, smaller towns, and through dealers who do not specialize in posters. However, this is changing as the field matures.

SELLING TO OR BUYING FROM A DEALER

The prices in this guide do not necessarily represent the price at which a particular dealer will either buy or sell a poster. If you are looking to sell your poster to a dealer, do not expect to get the retail price range represented here. Dealers can't pay retail prices because they are in the business of "brokering" posters and need to mark up the price to make a profit.

When using this guide to buy a poster from a dealer, you should also be aware that a dealer has other costs which add to the price of a poster—overhead, shipping costs, and more. With posters, dealers very often incur costs for restoration and cleaning. High-quality material is getting more and more difficult for dealers to find, and many report having to spend increased amounts of time at auctions and elsewhere to obtain it, including travel to distant parts of the globe. As with any service, the price you will pay reflects these costs as well.

SOME CAVEATS ON AUCTION PRICES

More individual collectors are attending auctions, but many still do not understand the auction process. First, each auction is a unique event that will never be recreated.

The price realized at auction depends largely on who is bidding. Remember, if there is just one person in the room who wants a certain poster, he or she will perhaps get it at a price much lower than retail. If there are two individuals in the room who desperately want a poster for their collection, you can bet the price will soar.

Prices realized can also depend on how the auction is promoted. For example, one dealer complained that a major poster auction had not been advertised broadly enough, and that those most likely to buy the posters which were offered were not in attendance. Of course, this was great news for those who were at the auction, but for those who consigned the posters, the results were disappointing.

In addition, when the bid runs very high at an auction, it is more than likely a collector, not a dealer, who is willing to go the distance. Dealers often can't compete at auctions with determined collectors. If it is a dealer who places a retail-level bid or higher, chances are that he or she has gotten the go-ahead from a specific collector who will purchase the poster.

Auction prices in a guide such as this are generally lower than retail prices because dealers acquire inventory at auctions for resale. So don't expect to purchase a poster from a dealer at the auction price listed here. Remember, too, that the auction prices included here at auction do not necessarily always represent the best or most important work of any given artist, designer, or school.

A final note on hunting for posters at auctions: because posters were and are so popular and widespread, often an out-of-the-way country or estate auction will feature a few posters. Generally speaking, not as many poster collectors or dealers will attend these auctions, preferring those which offer a wider selection of posters for sale. In these instances, if you are confident about your ability to judge a poster and buy at auction, you can still acquire some real bargains.

A KEY TO POSTER VALUES

What's the difference between a $3,000 Chéret and a $7,000 Chéret? Why did Lautrec's *Moulin Rouge* sell for a record-breaking $220,000 at auction? How big of a difference can condition make to value? How are poster values different in the cinema poster market?

Many factors determine the value of a poster in today's market. Below are the key factors which shape price, in order of importance.

ARTISTIC ACHIEVEMENT

Posters by recognized artists and graphic designers—Lautrec, Cassandre, Penfield, Chagall, Toorop, Hohlwein, Warhol, Picasso, and others—will always have a higher value than lesser known artists or posters designed anonymously.

For example, Henri Boulanger, who is not well known, designed posters under the pseudonym H. Gray and produced only a few great designs. His breathtaking *Petrole Stella* poster, even in the best condition, only sells for about $2,500 (see color center section).

The signature of a well-known artist can make a difference of thousands of dollars. For example, what one might consider one of the least interesting Toulouse-Lautrec posters, *Bruant au Mirliton*, in which Bruant is simply standing with his back to the viewer with his hands in his pockets, still sells for as much as $15,000 (see price listings for "French Posters").

Also, within an artist's *oeuvre* or body of work, there will always be some pieces that are prized more than others for their artistic achievement. Not all of Chéret's posters are as great as *Loie Fuller/*

27

Folies-Bergère, a phenomenal work for the famous American dancer, which can sell for $7,000 (see color center section). Many nice but lesser-accomplished Chéret posters still sell for less than $1,000.

Remember, also, that an unknown artist today can become a celebrated "rediscovered" artist tomorrow, so use your artistic instincts.

SCARCITY

A rarely seen poster will attract more interest. Chéret's *Quinquina Dubonnet* poster can sell retail for $3,000, but when a rare proof of the poster before letters came up at auction it sold for $7,000.

The Dutch artist Jan Toorop's poster for the play *Pandorra* sells for about $25,000 not only because of the stunning design, but because so few are known to exist (see color center section).

The Lautrec *Moulin Rouge* which broke auction records at $220,000 in 1989 was the full three-sheet poster. Different reports estimate that as many as fifty and as few as ten of these full-size *Moulin Rouge* posters exist (see color center section). The same *Moulin Rouge* poster without the top sheet, which is only somewhat easier to come by, is valued at only one-half of that amount.

In the vast majority of cases with early (so-called "vintage" or "antique") posters before World War II, nobody really knows how many of each poster was originally printed, let alone how many were saved, and in what condition.

Thousands of vintage posters suddenly and recently became more scarce last year when a major fire completely destroyed the inventory of a major Parisian dealer. There is a real crunch going on in the market today as European posters are harder and harder for dealers to find and more expensive for them to buy.

CONDITION

Cassandre's *La Normandie,* when found in "A" condition, can sell as high as $10,000 or more at auction, but last year one in "C" condition brought only $3,200.

Condition, especially for serious collectors, is an important part of the value of any poster and how much they are willing to pay for it. (See our condition key in the chapter called "Important Notes on the Price Listings," and see also the discussion on preservation in the chapter on "Poster Collecting.")

SUBJECT

Theophile Steinlen's poster for *Le Petit Sou*, a Socialist newspaper, sells for about $4,000, but his poster for the French performer Yvette Guilbert sells for $12,000. Very broadly speaking, posters for well-known performers, artistic events, and important exhibitions sell better than political, war, or product posters.

However, in the poster world there is always an exception to the rule. For example, Steinlen's poster for milk, *Lait pur Stérilisé*, with its charming child and cat, can sell for as much as $15,000 (see color center section).

Poster subjects which somehow capture our imagination and become classics always lead their fields. For example, many World War I posters can still be bought for under $300, but James Montgomery Flagg's classic Uncle Sam *I Want You* poster can sell for more than $2,000, and his *Wake Up America!* poster can sell for $3,000 (see color center section).

PRINTING PROCESSES

The earliest illustrated posters were printed by stone or zinc lithography, a recognized artistic medium. They will always have greater desirability than later, photographic offset-printed posters, although other factors described above can make offset posters soar at auctions. (For more detailed information on printing techniques, see the chapter entitled "Poster Printing and Terminology.")

CINEMA POSTER VALUES

While scarcity, condition, and poster printing techniques play a role in cinema poster values, the greatest impact on value in cinema posters is the star and the film. For cinema posters, even artistic achievement takes a back seat to the most sought-after Hollywood stars. For example, a lobby card for *The Wizard of Oz* with Judy Garland recently sold at auction for $2,700, when many lobby cards can still be purchased for under $100. (For additional information on sought-after posters, see the discussion in "Today's Poster Market" and Katherine Harper's chapter on "Cinema Posters.")

MOULIN ROUGE HAD IT ALL

Why did *Moulin Rouge* break all auction records for posters? Following the key above, it was an outstanding work in the *oeuvre* of an internationally recognized artist; was very rare because it included the top sheet; was in very good condition; was an historically important entertainment subject; and was a lithograph. The poster, quite simply, had it all.

POSTER PRINTING
AND TERMINOLOGY

PRINTING TECHNIQUES

By the late 1700s printers in Europe were looking for new and better forms of printing illustrations. Intaglio printing or printing from an incised plate, such as etchings and engravings, had virtually replaced relief printing or printing from raised surfaces, such as in a woodcut.

However, engravings weren't efficient because the text of a book was still printed in relief, and raised metal type would remain the primary form of text printing until after World War II. So, the illustrations would have to be printed separately from the text.

It was discovered that one could engrave on wood, if the engraving was done across the end grain. Wood engravings, as are often seen in early newspapers such as *Harper's Weekly*, became highly popular, as did steel engravings.

Then, in 1798, a German named Alloys Senefelder created the printing method known as lithography from the word "lithos" or stone. This printing method, and later methods, such as offset printing, are called "planographic." That is, the ink is carried on a flat surface rather than on raised edges or in incised lines.

It was not until the mid-1800s, however, that the lithographic process would be perfected. It was Jules Chéret who would refine the lithographic printing technique and master the creation of color lithography, leading to an explosion of illustrated lithographically

31

printed posters. (See chapter on "French Posters" for more about Chéret's work with lithography.)

In early lithographic posters, the artist or an assistant would draw the image desired onto a slab of limestone using a grease crayon. The drawn surfaces of this semi-absorbent stone would then be receptive to carrying the printer's ink. This printing method proved itself versatile and able to achieve multiple printed effects.

Grease pens and crayons were effective for lines and details, and for achieving the tones and effects of a chalk drawing. When larger strokes were required, a brush could be used to achieve painterly effects by covering larger areas. Spatter technique, in which ink is sprayed randomly onto the limestone by scraping a blade across a brush full of ink, was used in stunning ways by poster artists such as Henri de Toulouse-Lautrec.

Lithography offered printers the ability to do larger runs without wearing down the image, as was the case with relief and intaglio illustrations. Lithography and the many variations of it would become the first viable large-scale commercial printing method.

However, many people still do not realize what a cumbersome exacting process stone lithography really was. It had major drawbacks. The limestone was most often Bavarian limestone which was heavy, fragile, and expensive. In addition, a separate stone was needed for each different color of the poster—sometimes as many as nine or ten stones were used! No wonder why stone lithographic posters from Chéret, Mucha, Lautrec, and others are so highly valued. When the printing run was completed, often the stones were ground down to erase the first image and then used again for another poster.

After the ink was applied to the stone, the paper was laid on the stone, a metal backing was laid down on top, and the entire stone passed on runners under a wooden bar called a scraper, which applied pressure to lift the ink from the stone to the paper. The process had to be repeated for each color.

Commercial printers started using roughened zinc instead of the limestone, and for a while in the 1880s these were called "zincographs." Today, they are most often called lithographs and sometimes "chromolithographs." A lithograph and a chromolithograph are produced by essentially the same process; however, "chromolithograph" was used somewhat pejoratively to refer to more commercially produced works.

The distinctive feature about most lithographs is the evenness with which the ink is applied to the paper. Under a magnifying glass one can see that the colors of a lithographic poster are evenly distributed, and it is one method for identifying a poster as a lithograph. However, in some cases, screens were used to give a lithograph texture, so the presence of a screen alone does not mean that the poster isn't a lithograph.

Before the turn of the century, printers were experimenting with numerous kinds of printing processes including:

Transfer lithographs, where the image is not drawn on the stone but transferred from some other medium to the stone;

Offset lithographs, a method in which the plate never touches the paper. Rather, a rubber roller picks up the ink from the plate and then runs it over the paper. Offset printing allowed for higher speeds, bigger runs, and better registration; and

Collotypes, a delicate printing process without much commercial viability, but which was used until very recently to faithfully reproduce works of art in finely printed editions.

In most cases it is very difficult, even for a specialist, to distinguish between the above kinds of printing, and all of them are today often called "lithographs."

What would happen to dramatically change the way in which posters were created and printed was the advent of the use of photography in printing.

Photography in printing was being experimented with as early as 1850, and the first "negatives" weren't film but hand-drawn glass negatives. After the turn of the century, pioneering poster artists, notably in Holland and Switzerland, experimented with *photomontage* posters. Their creations are posters which are produced as part photo, part hand-drawn illustration. The Swiss ski posters of Herbert Matter are excellent examples of the eye-catching effects of early photomontage posters. (See the price listings for "Swiss Posters" for examples of his work.)

In the poster field one will sometimes hear photomontage posters referred to as *photolithographic* posters, although photolithography actually has a broader meaning. A photolithograph is actually any image which has been created photochemically. Virtually all photolithography is printed on offset presses, and it is the printing process most commonly used by commercial printers today.

While the value of any poster has to do with numerous factors (see the chapter "A Key to Poster Values"), posters which are hand-drawn and printed by stone or zinc lithography will always be more valuable than those reproduced by photographic means. Most illustrated posters before World War II are lithographs.

Most commercial posters since World War II are photolithographs. In the poster field, it is common to hear any poster printed photographically referred to as a *photo offset* or simply *offset* (although as we have seen lithographs can be offset as well).

In photo offset a photograph is taken of the original art and turned into negatives. The negatives are then used to make the plate from which the poster will be printed.

In order to make the plate, the negative must be screened into a series of very tiny regular dots in neat straight lines. Look at any photograph in this book under a strong magnifying glass and you will see the dots and lines of photo offset printing, as compared to the evenness of the ink of a lithograph. This is one way to tell if the Cassandre *Normandie* poster your mother gave you is a lithograph or a later photo offset reproduction.

In this guide we have used the terms *lithograph* for any poster printed lithographically; *photomontage* for the combination of photographic and hand-drawn images; and *offset* for photographically printed posters.

Methods used in poster printing are very complicated and can be confusing. The best resource we've found for approaching these questions in an academic way is the book *How to Identify Prints* by Bamber Gascoigne. (See Bibliography under Care and Identification of Posters and Prints.)

TERMINOLOGY

Aside from printing terms, the poster field has numerous other terms which it uses, and which you will see in catalogs and descriptions of posters. Among the most frequently used are:

Active Market   You'll hear dealers say, "That poster isn't available on the active market." This means that a certain poster doesn't come up for sale or at auction very often, but still might be available privately.

Blindstamp	Some publishers use a blindstamp to identify their editions. The blindstamp is impressed into the paper, leaving a raised image, much like a notary public's seal.
Broadside	The term broadside is used to refer to posters with only small or no illustrations. Text comprises most of the poster image. Broadsides were the advertising forerunners of illustrated posters.
Buyer's Premium	Refers to the commission, generally 10% of the final bid price, paid by the buyer to the auction house.
Catalogue Raisonné	A *catalogue raisonné* is an attempt to definitively catalog the works of a particular artist. Research works such as these are often cited as references for posters.
Chartex	Chartex is a type of synthetic material which has been used to mount posters in the past. Very stiff and inflexible, it is heat-sealed to the paper and next to impossible to remove. Backing on Chartex can significantly reduce the value of a poster.
Date Strip	Sometimes also called a "banner," these were added to posters to announce specific performances, dates, etc. Some collectors like to have date strips with magic, circus, and theater posters.
Folio Folds	Many posters are too big to store flat, and were therefore folded and put into drawers. While it is always better to find posters in perfectly mint condition, traces of folio folds are extremely common in some very desirable posters. However, watch for folds along which there are tears or which are too obtrusive because they are stained along the fold.

Foxing	Foxing is a term used to describe "rusty" colored spots on paper, caused primarily by moisture. Foxing can be reduced, if not eliminated, with proper treatment, but excessive foxing does lower the value of a poster, especially if it affects the image.
Japan Paper	Japanese papers are generally delicate mulberry fiber papers used for mounting fragile posters by many paper conservators. It is generally applied with a wheat paste.
Limited Edition	Generally a limited or numbered and signed edition refers to fine art lithographs, wood engravings, and the like and not to posters, which were printed and sometimes reprinted in great quantities. However, some contemporary posters are issued in limited editions.
Linen-Mounted	This means that the poster has been laid down on cloth, usually using some form of animal glue. Mounting posters on linen was long thought to be the best way to preserve them, although other methods are now also used. In the earliest posters mounted in this way, the linen is a very thin muslin-type cloth. Today, most "linen" on posters is really cotton canvas. Be aware, too, that the term "laid down" can also mean that the poster has been glued to cardboard, wooden panel, or some other backing which is difficult and costly to remove.
Maquette	Refers to the original art from which a poster is made, often either a watercolor, drawing, or some form of graphic design. The common term "mock-up" is derived from "maquette."

Mark
Some artists did not sign their posters with their name, but used a mark to identify their work. This is the case with Toulouse-Lautrec, for example. Other posters are simply "monogrammed" with the artist's initials.

Monograph
A book on a single artist, sometimes overviewing the artist's entire *oeuvre* or "body of work."

One-Sheet, Two-Sheet, Etc.
Some posters are billboard size and are printed in several sheets of paper. One-sheet, half-sheet, two-sheet, and other poster sizes generally are used to refer to standard cinema poster sizes, and are explained in the chapter "Cinema Posters."

On the Stone
Generally posters were not signed in pencil as fine art prints were. Instead, an artist using the lithographic method would sign the poster directly on the lithographic stone. In printing using blocks, such as woodblocks, one might see a signature "in the block." In photolithographic or photo offset printing, the signature will be "in the matrix."

Panel
Panels or "decorative panels," as they are sometimes called, are poster-size lithographs on paper created by several artists during the poster "craze" of the 1890s. These designs are generally without advertising text, and were meant to be used as decorations in the home.

Paper Sign
Generally used when talking about country store advertising, a "poster" and a "paper sign" often differ only in that paper signs often have frames and were considered more permanent than posters.

Proof   Artists often pulled "trial" posters to see how
                        the image looked before the advertising message
                        in type was applied. These are sometimes called
                        "proof before letters" and can be very rare.

Secondary   The term "secondary market" is generally used
Market   to refer to all antiques, because they are not be-
                        ing sold directly by those who created them. In
                        the field of graphics and works on paper, it is
                        used to refer to works by artists no longer avail-
                        able directly from the artist, the artist's agent or
                        the original publisher.

Silk-Screen   Screen printing evolved from stenciling, and at
                        first used a fine mesh made of silk, and thus the
                        name. In this process, the ink is drawn over the
                        screen and prints on the paper wherever the
                        artist has left spaces for it to pass through. Silk-
                        screens appear to the eye almost as lithographs,
                        and many contemporary small-edition fine art
                        posters are made using silk-screens.

Stencil   Stencils are a relatively old form of printing in
                        which the ink is brushed or rolled over the cut-
                        out areas. Only a few posters were printed using
                        stencils, notably some of the Dutch De Stijl
                        posters which are composed entirely of type.

Tin Sign   Also a term from country store advertising, it
                        means what it says. Essentially this is an adver-
                        tising poster, often rendered lithographically on
                        tin.

To the Trade   Dealers who only sell to other dealers are sell-
                        ing "to the trade." At shows you'll hear a
                        dealer ask another, "Do you offer a discount to
                        the trade?", meaning a dealer discount.

POSTER COLLECTING

THE FIRST POSTER COLLECTORS

There was a veritable poster collecting "craze" from the late 1880s until after the turn of the century. The new and exciting advertising medium of the illustrated or "pictorial" poster was quickly seized upon by collectors and enthusiasts.

Luckily for us, some of these zealous early collectors crept through the night to sponge-off posters from the walls of buildings and secrete them away. Poster shows and exhibitions abounded, drawing thousands of visitors, and poster collecting clubs, societies, and publications sprang up all over Europe and the United States.

It was not long before poster artists and publishers realized they could overprint a commercial edition and make it available for sale through print dealers, such as Editions Sagot on Rue Chateaudun in Paris. Early French artists such as Chéret, Mucha, and others issued numerous decorative panels, which were essentially paper posters without type, which people could use in their homes for decoration.

At the time they were issued through Sagot in the 1890s, posters such as Toulouse-Lautrec's *La Revue Blanche* sold for 5 francs, and *Jane Avril* for 10 francs. Sagot also commissioned well-known artists to create posters for his store and his publications, such as Paul César Helleu (see "French Posters" price listings) and George de Feure's captivating poster for *Paris Almanach* (see color center section).

We've not found anyone who can totally explain why such a riotous collecting spree should descend upon the lowly poster, a "poor cousin" of the fine arts, but perhaps it was a combination of several factors.

Cities were burgeoning with the rise of a new merchant class which sought to put art into their homes. Posters were inexpensive, large, and decorative works. In addition, illustrated advertising posters were a new notion and had given the drab streets of Paris the aspect of a public gallery. Each new poster was eagerly anticipated, talked about, and written about.

Numerous publications and periodicals fanned the fires of the poster fad. As early as 1886, publishers were issuing illustrated catalogs and books of posters. Starting in 1896, under the direction of Jules Chéret, a Parisian printing company started reproducing the best posters of Europe and America in lithographic plates. Called *Les Maîtres de l'Affiche,* or "Masters of the Poster," these portfolios of miniature masterworks were issued monthly for about 2½ francs per issue. Each issue contained four posters, the first of which was always a Chéret. In all, by 1900, 256 plates had been issued.

Today, the *Maîtres* are highly collectible, with some of the plates selling individually for hundreds of dollars, especially those by better known artists. (See also the chapter on "French Posters.")

Courtesy of Poster Mail Auction Company

In other countries, the poster craze was just as strong. In London, a monthly magazine called *The Poster* kept collectors up-to-date with the latest news. In Germany, *Das Plakat* or "The Poster" was another

publication which included numerous finely printed tipped-in miniature posters from 1913 to 1921 (see photos).

Other publications and miniature poster issues for collectors included *Les Affiches Illustrées,* and bi-weeklies *La Plume* and *L'Estampe
et l'Affiche.* In the United States, collectors turned to the pages of *The
Chap Book,* printed in Chicago from 1894 to 1897; William Bradley's
Bradley: His Book, printed in Springfield, Massachusetts, from 1896 to
1897; *The Poster,* printed in Chicago from 1910 to 1930, and others.
(See Bibliography for a full listing of Historical References.)

Whatever the reason for the phenomenal rise in the popularity of
the poster, by World War I the poster craze was all but extinguished,
although it flourished once again more briefly between the two World
Wars.

THE POSTER REVIVAL

In the 1960s in both Europe and the United States, there was a
renewed interest in the decorative styles of the turn of the century
through the 1920s, primarily focused on Art Nouveau and Art Deco.
(For more about these design movements, see the chapter on "French
Posters.") Interest was heightened by important museum exhibitions

of these decorative styles, as well as important exhibitions of posters by Aubrey Beardsley and Alphonse Mucha.

Evidence of this resurgence of interest can be seen in the impact early posters had on the designs of San Francisco rock posters of the late 1960s. One San Francisco publisher even took the name "Tea Lautrec Litho." (See chapter on "Rock Posters.") Pop artists such as Andy Warhol, who was a notable collector of Art Deco, popularized the poster.

Posters once again began to be popular collectibles, and the greatest artists could still be found in abundance and at relatively low prices. (See "Today's Poster Market" for more reminiscing over the once low prices of outstanding works!)

For example, a 1966 Sotheby auction realized a price of £580 or about $1,000 for Toulouse-Lautrec's *Divan Japonais,* and a record price of £2,100 or about $3,800 for *Jane Avril.*

More articles and books began to appear about posters by the leading writers on the Art Deco and Art Nouveau styles such as Bevis Hillier and Victor Arwas, and more collectors became aware of the growing collecting value of posters. (See Bibliography.)

By the end of the 1970s, the poster had firmly re-established itself as a collecting field. In 1979, the auction house of Phillips in New York held the first all-poster auction in this country to resounding success. Mucha's *La Dame aux Camélias* brought $16,500, and Toulouse-Lautrec's *Divan Japonais* brought $19,000 in a negotiated sale four days later. A rare poster by Charles Rennie Mackintosh for the Glasgow Institute of Art also brought $19,000 at an auction in France the same year.

After three or four boom years in the poster market, prices began to decline, and in some cases quite rapidly (see "Today's Poster Market" for more information), but the poster had achieved the status of a firmly established collecting field. In the 1980s, that field expanded and changed, and, as of this writing, records are still being broken and the price of vintage posters continues to spiral upwards.

STARTING A POSTER COLLECTION

Like any collecting field, the more you know about posters before you decide what to collect, the better off you will be in the long run.

What you'll hear over and over from experts in the field is that the best way to start a poster collection is not to buy posters. Rather, the best way to start is to read about posters, go and see posters at museums and dealerships, and go to auctions which have posters—just to watch. Go window shopping. Don't spend your hard-earned money until you have a good knowledge of the posters in which you are interested.

With prices on many artists and posters reaching into the tens of thousands of dollars, you may want to invest in today's "blue chips" or you may want to collect in a field that hasn't yet gone out of reach. You will find ample advice on collecting and "investing" in posters in the pages of this guide, much of it directly from professionals in the poster field.

Not all posters are expensive, although you most often read about those which break records. Many areas of poster collecting are likely to appreciate over the next decade but can still be bought at reasonable prices.

Lesser-known European and American turn-of-the-century artists can still be very affordable. Many American and European World War I posters are good choices, but World War II posters may show faster rates of appreciation. As the collecting horizon moves away from its focus on French posters, posters of other countries such as Italy, Scandinavia, and Spain have added appeal.

Also, though many cinema posters are very pricy, hundreds of fine titles exist which can be bought at very low prices. San Francisco rock posters, while not as inexpensive as only a few years ago, are still selling at prices that will look like bargains ten years from now. Modern Swiss posters and contemporary graphic design from many countries are also accessible good bets.

Really the first step is to decide what kind of posters you like and what kind you would like to collect. Flip through the pages of this book and you'll see the wide range of options you have in the poster collecting field.

Some poster collectors decide to concentrate on a particular artist, genre, or subject. For example, some people collect only bicycle posters, magic posters, cinema posters, or World War I posters. Within those fields, people even further specialize in collecting just the films of Humphrey Bogart or in the war posters of Howard Chandler Christy or James Montgomery Flagg. Others collect a variety of different posters simply because they are attracted to the images.

Whichever way you go, you should set standards and try to collect the very best examples you can find, both in terms of quality and in terms of condition.

PRESERVING AND DISPLAYING
YOUR COLLECTION

Ideally, you want to look for posters which are in fine to mint condition. Although posters can be restored, it can be a costly procedure, and it is best to avoid posters with tears in the image, faded colors, excessive stains or dirt, and other visible damage.

However, especially with vintage posters, it is not always possible to find specific posters in fine condition. Remember, for almost one hundred years posters have been treated as "throw-away" advertising and were not always accorded special handling! Many posters you will find on the market have already been restored to some degree, and you may have to look hard to see where tears have been repaired or paint touch-ups have been applied.

Posters are paper, and paper collectibles require special preservation, handling, storage, and framing. Many of the most valuable posters today, such as those by Toulouse-Lautrec, were printed on what is essentially newsprint—wood pulp paper with a high acidic content which can deteriorate the paper over time. Many libraries across the country are facing the same problem today with books which have begun to deteriorate from the acid content of the paper. "Deacidification" has become a specialized field as researchers seek new methods to preserve works on paper.

"In the hands of a specialist, most posters can be cleaned by immersion," explains Laurance Gillaspie, a New York City paper conservator. "The acid, both innate and accumulated, can be removed. The paper is then buffered to slow more acid accumulations from the air."

Acid isn't the only problem in preserving posters. "Each poster must be treated individually with respect to cleaning, mounting, repair of tears and image or color restoration," Gillaspie explains. "One even finds that posters of the same image can be slightly different or react differently because the kind of paper or ink was changed during the print run."

Gillaspie reports that one common problem is that many posters come to him with excessive amounts of paint applied to replace lost color or to cover darkened or dirty paper. In-painting can usually be seen by raking the poster over a light, and collectors should avoid posters with large amounts of in-painting.

Other damage to posters can be repaired by paper conservators. "Filling losses can be done with a matching piece of paper, and tears can be repaired with Japan paper and wheat starch paste," explains Andrea Pitsch, also a New York paper conservator. "In the past people used Scotch tape or masking tape, or Kraft paper with Elmer's glue. These are difficult to remove, especially since they were applied to an already weakened area such as a skinned patch or a fold.

"So-called 'library-tape' (also called museum tape) is less harmful," Pitsch adds, "but still may have to be removed with an organic solvent. It's hard to discourage people from using a commercially available product like library tape. After all, who wants to cook wheat starch and water on the stove for hours to make wheat starch paste?"

Most of the posters that collectors will find commercially available in today's market have been mounted on linen or cotton canvas, which makes the poster lie flat. While this has advantages for handling and framing, it is now known that in the long term it can cause preservation problems.

Now that many posters have attained the high prices of fine art, the poster field is becoming more aware of the complexities of preservation and conservation. The practice of mounting posters on cloth has come under the closest scrutiny recently.

"Paper is incompatible with cloth," explains Pitsch. "When there is moisture in the air, which is inevitable in many parts of the country, cloth contracts and paper expands." "Over time," she says, "this can leave the paper creased and torn."

Pitsch sometimes mounts very brittle posters to Japan paper, but generally prefers to allow posters to hang from hinges. "I'll put on twenty hinges if necessary to support the paper, made from Japan paper attached with wheat starch paste. If the framed poster falls off the wall, the hinge should be weaker than the poster paper. That way, the hinge will tear and not the poster.

"If you see an old mounted poster, don't be too upset," comments Pitsch. "The backing might have prevented some handling damage over the years. In many cases, a linen or cardboard mounting can be removed, depending on the type of adhesive used. Animal glue, which is the older method of mounting, is easier to remove than heat-set tissue, which is often used by framers today."

Gillaspie adds, "There is no 'best way' to mount all posters. If mounting is necessary, the artwork itself will dictate to what it should be mounted. Some of the smaller posters can be mounted to quality papers successfully. Some Japanese papers work for this, but because they are more porous than the poster paper, they absorb more moisture, expand more, and can result in a rippled poster. The larger the poster, the more frequently this occurs.

"I feel that a soft open-weave linen with no sizing presents fewer problems over a period of many years. This is especially true for larger-sized posters. An open-weave linen has no grain, unlike a quality paper. It provides ample contact area for strength, and expands less with moisture, creating less tension with the poster paper. Meanwhile, the openness of the weave allows the artwork more breathing area on the verso and more freedom to move."

In the years ahead, it is likely that more discussion and research will take place over the question of mounting and other preservation issues. There are also conservation issues to be aware of in storing, framing or displaying your posters.

If posters are to be stored, they should lie flat in archival storage boxes in individual acid-free folders so that one poster does not sit directly on top of another.

A framed poster should have a four-ply backing, and be matted with a mat which is 100% rag content and acid free. In the past, framers used mats which were not acid free and the acid from the mat leaked into and stained the print or poster. The mat also keeps the poster from touching the glass.

Exposure to sunlight or light with high ultra-violet content can bleach some colors completely, so don't hang your poster where it will receive direct light. Notice how low the lights are in museums. Never use gallery lights on posters, as they can create hot spots. Ultra-violet-filtering plexiglass is now available as an added way to protect your poster from harmful light.

One valuable and easy-to-understand book on paper conservation is Francis W. Dolloff and Roy L. Perkinson's *How to Care for Works of Art on Paper,* a fifty-page paperback with illustrations, published by the Museum of Fine Arts in Boston.

FAKES AND REPRODUCTIONS

Happily, the poster field has not been fraught with as many fakes and forgeries as the world of painting, but fakes do exist. Now, with the price of posters rising dramatically, the poster field is bound to encounter its share of "Mona Lisas."

The most common deception, whether intentional or not, is the sale of a photo offset poster reproduction as an original lithograph. The copyrights on many vintage posters, if they had them to begin with, ran out long ago. Anyone with a printing press can print and distribute for sale a vast number of poster titles by notable artists or reproduce them on T-shirts, mugs, and other items as has been done. Popular artists for reprinting are Toulouse-Lautrec, Mucha, Cassandre, Pierre Fix-Masseau, Hohlwein, and others.

Fortunately, the stone lithographic process is a difficult and expensive one to recreate, so the reprinted posters are printed using photo offset means. Under a strong magnifying glass it is quite easy to identify a photo offset poster by the regular series of lines and dots that comprise the image. (See the chapter "Poster Printing and Terminology.")

A few posters, such as Albert Bergevin's *Avranches* poster, Paul Colin's *Bal Tabarin*, and Maurice Dufrène's *Rayon des Soieries* opera poster, have been targets of lithographic counterfeiting in the recent past. Word about these kinds of forgeries tends to travel quickly through the trade, and reputable dealers will avoid any questionable poster.

In addition, while the world of posters is quite broad, detailed descriptions of hundred and hundreds of posters now exist in books and auction catalogs. One of the first questions a dealer may ask when someone calls to find out if their Toulouse-Lautrec is real is, "What size is it?" If the *Moulin Rouge* poster in the caller's possession is much smaller than the original, it is probably one of the many reproductions of his work that have been printed over the years.

However, some small "reproductions" of posters have great collecting value, such as the early editions of *Les Maîtres de l'Affiche, Das Plakat, L'Estampe Moderne,* and others mentioned at the beginning of this chapter.

One rule of thumb to follow is this: if you are offered an "original" poster which seems to be an incredible buy, such as a Mucha for only a few hundred dollars, don't believe it. Vintage posters have had

tremendous exposure in recent years, and it is doubtful that any antiques dealer or someone in the trade today would be unaware of their
great value.

If you find a poster at a flea market or a garage sale, where the
seller may truly not be aware of the value, you should take the risk
of purchasing what you believe to be an original 1) only if the price
is what you would pay for a reproduction, and 2) only if you truly like
the poster, because you may have made a find or you may have to
live with your mistake for a very long time!

CLASSIC POSTERS

FRENCH POSTERS

If there was something called The Tomb of the Unknown Designer, Parisians would certainly claim to be the keepers of the flame. Much French energy has been expended over the past one hundred years to convince the rest of the world that it is the absolute center of the designed environment. In some cases, the French even have a legitimate claim to hegonomy, and the early poster is one such case, for if Mesopotamia was the "Cradle of Civilization" then Paris was the "Cradle of the Poster."

Not that all of the outstanding Parisian artists from the beginnings of the poster were necessarily French—far from it. Paris was the magnet for talented designers from Switzerland, Belgium, Italy, Czechoslovakia, Holland, and elsewhere. However, if you are an outstanding artist and live in Paris, you are automatically part of French national heritage.

So it was with Swiss artist and posterist Eugene-Samuel Grasset (1845–1917), who would become the major theoretician of the Art Nouveau movement. When Grasset emigrated to Paris from Lausanne, Switzerland, in 1871, the illustrated poster was still in its infancy. Jules Chéret (1836–1932) was having success experimenting with color lithography. Three years earlier, the French fine artist Edouard Manet had created the first illustrated advertising poster. However, his design for the poster *Champfleury Les Chats*, which advertises a book, was a black and white lithograph pasted to a larger sheet of colored paper.

It wasn't until 1881 that a new bill posting law was finally passed that created official posting places and protected posters from vandalism. In a very French manner, the government set about creating a format for standard sizes based on the *Colombier* (24″ × 32½″) and the *Grand Aigle* (27½″ × 43¾″). In the manner of the French people when faced with a government regulation, these sizes were not always adhered to, and many posters were printed in several different dimensions, reduced in size for collectors' portfolios, and scaled to fit into publications and newspapers.

The importance of the 1881 law was that merchants and businessmen, who by now occupied positions of power in Paris, were free to commission advertising posters to their hearts' content, and talented artists were attracted to the newly sanctioned medium by the droves.

Posters came forth in an explosion and artists' reputations were made seemingly overnight. The first poster exhibition was held in Paris in 1884, with posters pasted from floor to ceiling of the gallery, much as they would appear on the street hoardings. The first ten years of such postings were dominated by the work of Jules Chéret, who had his first one-man exhibition in Paris in 1890. By then, his color lithographic techniques were already legendary, and also by that time the cities of France were overrun with posters.

Special Focus: Jules Chéret (1836–1932)

Jules Chéret is called alternately "The Father of Color Lithography" and "The Father of the Poster," because he is at once recognized for both his mastery of the color lithographic process and his talent as an artist and designer.

His posters, influenced by 18th-century Rococo artists, also captured the essence of an era and a style in the arts which is called "La Belle Epoque" or "The Beautiful Epoch."

The Belle Epoque style was forwarded by numerous fine artists who finally succeeded in establishing the fine art print as a genre to be respected on a par with oil paintings. Artists such as James Tissot (1836–1902), Edgar Chahine (1874–1947), and Paul César Helleu (1859–1927) emphasized an elegant and sophisticated woman who represented all that was civil and good about life in a time of peace. Helleu himself created at least one poster, *Ed. Sagot*, for the famous Parisian print and poster dealer.

Chéret at his most fanciful created parades of personages that always included a "Pierrot" and an allegorical beauty almost floating on air, with a pretty countenance so recognizable she has come to be called "Chérette."

He is today the most popular of French poster artists because of his talent, his ground-breaking lithography, and his prolific production. His posters are everywhere on the market, and range in price from under $1,000 to $7,000 and sometimes more, with most of them bringing $2,000 to $5,000. (See special section in the price listings following this chapter.) Thoroughly chronicled, his work is the subject of a well-known *catalogue raisonné* or complete listing of his work by Lucy Broido. (See Bibliography.)

The Pasquale Iannetti Gallery of San Francisco held a retrospective of Chéret's work in 1987. His biography from the catalog, reprinted here courtesy of Pasquale Iannetti Gallery, gives additional insight into the reasons behind Chéret's towering presence in the world of posters for over one hundred years:

Chéret devoted a long and productive life to the development of color lithography as an inspired art form, integrated with the modern phenomenon of advertising, opening the way for a younger generation of artists including Lautrec, Steinlen, and Mucha to produce spectacular works in the medium.

The artist was born in Paris in May 1836, the son of a typographer. Apprenticed for three years from age 13 to a lithographer whose production tended towards headlines, invitations, funeral announcements, and the like, Chéret's work consisted mainly of drawing lettering in reverse on the heavy, fine-textured slabs of limestone from which lithographs are printed. He worked for various printers, enduring years of mundane, unartful work, though he was able to attend L'École Nationale de Dessin and spent his Sundays sketching and studying paintings in the Louvre, especially the works of Watteau.

During his twenties Chéret made two trips to London to seek work. On the second visit it was his luck to be hired by the French perfume manufacturer Eugene Rimmel, for whom he did design work for several years. While in England Chéret discovered the paintings of Turner, and, traveling with Rimmel to Venice, found "his god," Tiepolo. These painters, with Watteau and Fragonard, had a felicitous influence on Chéret's later works, in their charm, radiant clear color, and sense of cascading movement.

Rimmel became the artist's benefactor. In 1866 he advanced

Chéret the funds to return to Paris and set up his own printworks with the massive presses needed to produce large color stone lithographs. Chéret had conceived the revolutionary idea of transforming the dreary advertising bills that papered walls and kiosks along the streets of Paris, enlarging them to bold dimensions and making them explode with bright color and eye-catching imagery.

Influenced by American circus posters he had seen in England, and by the simplicity and broad color fields of the Japanese woodcuts that so inspired artists in 19th-century France, Chéret designed with expanses of clear, bright color and jagged, energetic, flame-like elements, mellowed in places by a fine rain of splattered inks, creating a sizeable population of dancers, masqueraders, iceskaters, and coquettes whose endless smiles promoted not only star performers, masked balls, music halls, operas, skating rinks, novels, and aperitifs, but also medicinal bitters, bicycles, lamp oil, and cough drops.

Once a succession of commissions gave him exposure, Chéret enjoyed belated but huge success and acclaim among critics, collectors, artists, and people in the streets. His large studio was accessible to friends and visitors who would find the exceptionally good-natured artist leaning against a large lithographic stone, drawing his design, happy to engage in conversation as he worked.

Chéret was awarded a silver medal at the 1878 International Exposition and the gold medal in 1889. In the same year he had an exhibition of posters, pastels, and paintings at the Théâtre d'Application. In 1890 he was made a *chevalier* of the Legion d'Honneur, commended for creating, since 1866, a new art industry by the application of art to commercial and industrial printing.

Though he never bothered vying for acceptance in the official Salons, Chéret produced paintings and pastels which he sold independently. In 1900, after making 1,000 posters over 30 years, he retired to Nice and devoted himself to painting until blindness made work impossible. The Louvre organized an exhibition of his works in 1912; in 1928 The Musée Chéret was founded in Nice. Chéret died in September 1932 at age 96.

In the early 1890s, other fine artists were attracted to designing for the poster, and it is ironic that those best known for painting rather than printmaking made the most significant contributions to the field: Pierre Bonnard (1867–1947) and Edouard Vuillard (1868–1940) both produced posters which are today highly sought after, with prices in the $5,000 to $10,000 range. In 1897, Bonnard created the first poster for the influential journal *L'Estampe et L'Affiche*, which chronicled the print and poster world.

In the year 1890, as the story goes, a friend came to compliment Bonnard on a poster he had seen in the street and asked to meet Bonnard's printer, Ancourt. The friend thought that he, too, might turn his painting skills to poster commissions. Bonnard was more than happy to introduce his printer to his aristocratic friend, Henri de Toulouse-Lautrec (1864–1901).

Toulouse-Lautrec's artistry towers above the world of the French poster in the 1890s. While he created only thirty or so posters, they are considered the highest expression of the art form and command the highest prices on today's market, ranging all the way up to the current record price of $220,000 for *Le Moulin Rouge*.

Much myth surrounds the life of this diminutive giant, whose legs atrophied as the result of childhood accidents. His imagery is full of dynamic movement, and his portraits of the chanteuses of Montmartre are irreverent. He, too, was influenced by Japanese design styles and admired Gaugin, van Gogh, and Edgar Degas. He perfected his illustrative style by working for many periodicals, such as *Paris Illustré*, *Le Rire*, and *Courrier Français* among others. He became a master of the lithographic technique called "spatter," in which ink is sprayed on the lithographic stone by drawing a blade over the brush.

His 1891 poster for *Le Moulin Rouge* is certainly his largest and most artistically complex, but many feel that his 1893 poster for *Jane Avril* is his best, and today it is estimated in value at $40,000 to $45,000.

Ironically, perhaps because of the singularity of his talent, Toulouse-Lautrec did not have a large impact on other French poster artists, unless one counts one or two rare posters by Jacques Villon (1875–1963) and the effect Toulouse-Lautrec may have had on his contemporary, Theophile-Alexandre Steinlen (1859–1923).

Steinlen followed in the footsteps of his countryman Grasset, emigrating to Paris from Lausanne, Switzerland, in 1872. Steinlen was to become one of the most outstanding posterists of the period, as well as being an illustrator for popular journals. A socialist, he worked for the publications *Gil Blas Illustré*, *L'Echo de Paris*, and *L'Assiette au Beurre*. His most popular posters are those in which he depicts cats. He is one of the most widely recognized French, World War I poster artists as well. (See the chapter on "World War Posters.")

Steinlen has a strong and growing following in the poster market today, and prices for his posters range from a few thousand dollars to $15,000. The years ahead will definitely see continued appreciation of his artistic talents.

Another Montmartre artist, Jules-Alexandre Grün (1886–1954), left his distinctive mark on the French poster by the turn of the century, designing for many famous singers of the café-concert. His highly original designs for such posters as *Scala c'est un Raid,* in 1902, have been long overshadowed by his towering contemporaries. His women are not the diaphanously clad beauties of Chéret, but rather buxom fun-loving Parisiannes who laugh the night away in cabarets. His work, which still often sells for less than $1,000, is, for the time being, undervalued.

By the mid-1990s, the poster was firmly established as an important advertising medium and artistic vehicle. In 1890 the United States had its first exhibition of French posters at the Grolier Club in New York. In 1894, the Salon des Cent was established in Paris, organized by Léon Deschamps, editor of the review *La Plume.* Monthly exhibitions featured one artist or several, but no more than 100 items were shown at a time, and thus the name. Deschamps commissioned leading posterists to advertise these monthly exhibitions: Pierre Bonnard; George de Feure (born George van Sluiters in Holland, 1868–1943); the Czechoslovakian immigrant Alphonse Mucha (1860–1939), and others. Toulouse-Lautrec made a poster for the Salon's "International Poster Exhibition" in 1896.

Also in 1896, the fine lithographer Imprimerie Chaix, which had absorbed Chéret's own printing company, began to issue posters in miniature for collectors under Chéret's supervision. Called *Les Maîtres de l'Affiche* or "Masters of the Poster," they were issued in monthly portfolios of four posters each, with a total of two hundred and fifty-six plates issued until 1900. Today, each plate from *Les Maîtres* can sell for several hundred dollars, depending on the artist. The full collection, bound into five volumes with covers designed by Paul Berthon (1872–1909), has brought over $16,000 at auction.

Les Maîtres was only one of several publications that sprung up to supply the poster-collecting market which had been created. (See also the section on The First Poster Collectors in the chapter titled "Poster Collecting.")

Numerous artists who were influenced by Chéret's style at the time are today collected in their own right: Pal (aka Jean de Paléologue, 1860–1942), whose posters are rapidly gaining in the market today; Alfred Choubrac (1853–1902), who created some 400 posters; Henri Gray (aka Henri Boulanger, 1858–1924), who created a few stunning designs, especially for *Petrole Stella*; Georges Meunier (1869–1934), who was employed by Chaix and whose posters are gaining increased recognition on the market today; and others.

Other French artists of this early period who are worth finding and collecting are René Péan (1875–?); Henri Gabriel Ibels (1867–1936); Sem (aka Serge Goursat, 1863–1934); the travel posterist Misti (aka Ferdinand Mifliez, 1865–1923); Frimin Bouisset (1859–1925); Manuel Robbe (1872–1936); Eugene Vavasseur (1863–?); and Francisco Tamango (1851–?).

THE EMERGENCE OF ART NOUVEAU

A strong new movement in the decorative arts, Art Nouveau began to have an impact on the world of posters in the 1890s. It was led by Eugene Grasset, whose posters reflect his taste for the Middle Ages, and who played a role not unlike that of William Morris in the English Arts and Crafts movement. While his theories had perhaps a stronger impact than his posters, he influenced many other artists.

When one thinks of Art Nouveau posters in France, one is most likely to think immediately of the artist who seems to epitomize the style: Alphonse Mucha (1860–1939). Born in Czechoslovakia and trained at the Munich Fine Arts Academy, he came to Paris where he studied at the Académie Julian until 1889. He worked exclusively for the printing firm F. Champenois in Paris, and had a tremendous output, although in fact, it appears that he suffered greatly under Champenois, who did not give him a moment's rest. From the time of his first poster in 1894, his influence spread beyond the borders of France to other countries such as Belgium and Germany where the Art Nouveau style was called Jugendstil.

His posters for Sarah Bernhardt are among the most sought after of all French posters, having designed all of the posters for her plays from 1894 to 1903, as well as sets and costumes for her productions. Today, many of Mucha's posters sell in the range of $5,000 to $10,000 and more.

Other artists who are recognized for their posters in the Art Nouveau style are: Italian-born Manuel Orazi (1860–1934), who designed stunning posters for performers and for La Maison Moderne, one of the leading Art Nouveau shops founded in 1899; Paul Berthon, a pupil of Grasset, who was known for his numerous decorative lithographic panels and whose color palette distinguishes his posters; and the Dutchman Georges de Feure, whose poster for the *Paris Almanach* is a well-known poster image and whose work continues to gain popularity with collectors today. (See color center section.)

Art Nouveau was the predominant style in the decorative arts only for about twenty years, roughly from 1890 to 1910. The style really reached its peak in about 1900, and slowly ebbed during the following decade, flourishing more in Europe than in America. The term itself is said to have originated with a shop called Maison de l'Art Nouveau, owned by Siegfried Bing. Bing exhibited leading artists including Bonnard, Vuillard, and Aubrey Beardsley. René Lalique created many of his best Art Nouveau jewelry designs for Bing's store.

At the end, the Art Nouveau style became so obsessed with the excesses of ornamentation that it became further and further detached from the integration of art and life it claimed to seek.

FRENCH POSTERS FROM 1900 TO WORLD WAR I

After the turn of the century and until the outbreak of World War I, French poster art declined somewhat. Toulouse-Lautrec died in 1901, and Paul Berthon in 1909. Other posterists from the 1890s went on to new professions. In 1904, Alphonse Mucha left France, making several trips to the United States and finally returning to Czechoslovakia in 1912, devoting himself to painting and official designs for Czech bank notes and other government commissions.

One outstanding posterist did emerge in the period from 1900 to the outbreak of World War I: an Italian immigrant, Leonetto Cappiello (1875–1942). Cappiello arrived in Paris in 1898, and by the year 1900 was already well known for his design.

Cappiello's posters are notable for their direct impact: bold, striking color combinations; plain backgrounds which only serve to emphasize the central illustration and product name; and humorous eye-catching images of people and animals, often in close-up. Where poster artists of the previous period often sought to paint an entire scene or an elaborate cast of characters, Cappiello was an ad man's dream—a designer who understood the value of sheer visual impact in delivering a sales message. No wonder he was so often commissioned by an array of products including cars, beverages, cigarettes, corsets, perfumes, soaps, household products, and chocolate. Less frequently he would also be commissioned by cabaret performers and the Folies-Bergère.

Before World War I, most of Cappiello's posters were printed by the firm Vercasson. After World War I, Cappiello would continue to produce posters with unmistakable talent, usually printed by Devambez.

It is now estimated that Cappiello created nearly 1,000 poster designs, not only for French clients, but for advertisers in Italy, Belgium, Spain, England, and other countries. His posters are rapidly gaining increased exposure and new collectors. Many of his posters already sell in the $3,000 to $5,000 range, with some good ones still available for less than $1,000. He will undoubtedly be one of the poster artists who appears frequently on the market in the years ahead.

By the time France entered World War I, a new design style, today called Art Deco, was already emerging. However, the full flowering of the new style would be retarded until after the war, as artists put their talents at the service of their patriotic duties. (See also the chapter on "World War Posters.")

Special Focus: French Opera Posters

In 1976, author Lucy Broido brought new attention to the specialized field of French opera posters, and created a collecting trend that continues to this day.

From the late 1860s until about 1930, the music publishing firms Heugel & Company and G. Hartman commissioned dozens of posters for opera, operettas, and ballets by musicians such as Louis Varney, Jules Massenet, and Richard Strauss.

Many well-known artists were commissioned to create posters including Maurice Dufrène (1876–1955), who headed the specialized boutique La Maîtrise at the department store Galeries Lafayette; Eugene Grasset, Manuel Orazi, Pal (Jean de Paléologue); and Alexandre-Theophile Steinlen. Perhaps the most prolific opera posterist of all was Georges Rochegrosse (1859–1938), whose stunning dramatic posters are highly sought after.

Many of these posters remain affordable to the beginning collector. Smaller than some French posters, many of them can still be purchased for a few hundred dollars, and even the most sought after have not broken the $1,000 mark. We have created a special section in the price listings following this chapter to introduce a selection of these posters to the reader.

DESIGN INFLUENCES

Even before the turn of the century, design movements outside of France were growing up in opposition to Art Nouveau, which, it was felt, was altogether too leisurely a style for the changing world. By 1910, the Art Nouveau style had been replaced completely in France, but the emergence of a new dominant style was not complete until after World War I, when other outside influences also came into play.

THE GLASGOW SCHOOL AND
THE ARTS AND CRAFTS MOVEMENT

Charles Rennie Mackintosh's Glasgow School and the Arts and Crafts movement in England were among the first to look for a more functional style of design in the decorative arts. The Arts and Crafts movement in both England and the United States decried the use of ornamentation for its own sake, and posterists of these countries began to design with simplified shapes and flat colors. (See chapters on "English Posters" and "American Art Posters of the 1890s.")

THE VIENNA SECESSION

In Vienna, architect Otto Wagner insisted on a return to straight lines and geometric forms, and Adolf Loos attacked what he called the "delirium of Art Nouveau." In 1897, architect Josef Hoffmann and some of his students founded the Viennese Secession, a movement which was committed to functionality and geometricism in design.

Viennese Poster by Egon Schiele.
Courtesy of Bernice Jackson

Posters of the Viennese Secession, some of which are very scarce, have doubled and tripled in price since the 1986 Museum of Modern Art exhibition "Vienna 1900." They appear very rarely on the market, and many can bring tens of thousands of dollars. Noted artists include Gustav Klimt (1862–1918); Egon Schiele (see photo); Koloman Moser (1868–1918); Berthold Löffler (1874–1960); and others.

THE BAUHAUS

The German Bauhaus did as much to revolutionize typography as it did architecture. Often elongated and condensed, the new typography lent itself to the sense of speed which characterized modern design and modern life. Many of the new typefaces were *sans serif*, adding to their sleekness. Popular new styles included Paul Renner's "Futura" (1928), Koch's "Kabel" (1927), Eric Gill's "Gill Sans" (1928), and others still widely used today.

A much more modern style was evolving outside of France from these and other influences such as Futurism in Italy, the German

Werkbund, the Dutch De Stijl, and Frank Lloyd Wright and the Prairie School, itself influenced by Arts and Crafts.

FRENCH ART DECO

The French design style which was emerging at the time, now called Art Deco, though more simplified than Art Nouveau, still reflected a spirit of opulence in its use of exotic woods and materials in furnishings and decorations. It was strongly influenced by the lavish sets and costumes of Diaghilev's *Ballets Russes*, which arrived in Paris in 1909. French Art Deco had its roots in the world of fashion, and expanded its impact when the fashion designers became *ensembliers* or "interior designers."

The most outspoken French advocate of a more modern style, architect Le Corbusier, had been influenced by the *Deutscher Werkbund* exhibition in Paris in 1910. However, his more angular Modern style, characterized by the use of materials such as tubular steel, was more Germanic than French. It was in fact this Germanic style which was to have the greatest impact on American Art Deco, although this influence was long overlooked because of our bias against German cultural traditions since World War II.

The early French Art Deco artists, however, were able to keep the new style at bay at least until after the famous 1925 Paris Exposition des Arts Décoratifs et Industriels Modernes. Their desire to ignore the Modernists was evident when a 10-foot-high fence was constructed to hide Le Corbusier's pavilion at the Exposition. They would have nothing to do with a display where furniture was called "household equipment."

The world was changing around them, however. The pressures of urbanization, a growing demand for industrialized production, and economic imperatives would force the adoption of the new style almost universally before the 1929 Wall Street Crash. The grand French style would survive into the 1930s only through commissions for ocean liners and public buildings.

Graphic design, too, would change to fit the times. Advertising became a critical vehicle to attract wider markets to the host of new manufactured goods being offered. Modern posters had to be strong enough to be read from passing cars. They captured attention with typography, the central image of the product, bold lines and colors, short messages, and interesting angles and perspectives. Important "advertising agencies," such as Cassandre's Alliance Graphique, were founded by poster artists.

It has been argued that posters were in fact the vanguard of the new design movement. In many instances, for the general public, the advertising poster was their first exposure to new design ideas.

Happily, fine art printing techniques such as lithography still dominated poster production, offering artists an appropriate medium for expressing their talents while serving commercial interests. Even the photomontage posters of the period were primarily the execution of an artist's, rather than a camera's, vision. In the end, however, the photographic image would overcome the illustrated image, almost completely displacing the fine artist from the world of commercial advertising.

Posters of the Art Deco period by artists such as Jean Carlu (1900–); Paul Colin (1892–1985); Daniel DeLosques (1880–1915); Jean-Gabriel Domergue (1889–1961); Jean Dupas (1882–1964); Charles Gesmar (1900–1928); Georges Lepape (1887–1971); and Charles Loupot (1892–1962) are highly sought after.

Many of the posters of this period were created for performers and cabarets. Well-known stage performers such as Josephine Baker, Mistinguett, Alice Soulie, Spinelly, Marguerite Valmond, and others commissioned new posters frequently. Charles Gesmar, who designed about fifty posters in his lifetime, created almost half of them for Mistinguett!

Paul Colin's posters for Josephine Baker's "Revue Nègre" at the Music Hall des Champs Elysees did as much to promote the world of black American jazz as did her performances. Posters for Josephine Baker have skyrocketed with the publication of a recent biography, and "La Revue Nègre" was recently sold by a dealer for $45,000. Colin also created posters for Loie Fuller, the Casino de Paris, Tabarin, and other performers and theaters. He went on to have a very productive career, creating fine poster designs into the 1950s.

Georges Lepape is best known for his fashion illustrations for *Vogue*, but was also commissioned to create several posters. Charles Loupot and Robert Bonfils (1882–1972) both created posters for the 1925 Paris Exposition des Arts Décoratifs et Industriels Modernes, which are highly sought after for both their design and historic importance.

Jean Carlu was inspired by the Cubists and created stunning Art Deco designs. Carlu later devoted his graphic skills to the cause of

World War II, creating effective wartime Art Deco posters. (See chapter on "World War Posters.")

Jean Dupas developed an original style that is immediately recognizable. His posters for the Salon des Artistes Decorateurs, the influential circle of artists who controlled the world of French design until the 1925 Exposition, and for the English department store Arnold Constable are very popular. Much of his original work came to light when Sotheby's auctioned the estate of Andy Warhol in 1988.

However, by far the most collected and overall highest-priced artist of the Art Deco period is A. M. Cassandre (1901–1968), who created an entirely new style of advertising design, reflective of the later trends of Art Deco and more "modern" than France had seen until that time.

Cassandre's first poster appeared in 1923 and set the tone for a whole new style. He influenced an entire generation of graphic designers, both in France and abroad. An important exhibition of his work was held in this country in 1936 at the Museum of Modern Art in New York, and his influence spread to America. However, it was not until 1951 that the Musée des Arts Décoratifs held a retrospective of his work.

Posters by Cassandre, especially his posters for the French state railways or "Chemin de Fer" and for ocean liners such as "La Normandie," can sell in the range of $8,000 to $15,000. His bold avant-garde style quickly became the standard of French Art Deco design, replacing the early fashion influence with architectural and structural design elements. His 1928 poster, *L.M.S. Bestway*, broke the record for the artist in 1990, bringing $55,000 at auction at Poster Auctions International in New York.

Another French posterist, Pierre Fix-Masseau (1869–1937) had been a sculptor but became a poster artist between the two World Wars. The influence of Cassandre is evident in his poster *Exactitude*, which can sell for as much as $10,000.

Another artist influenced by Cassandre is Sepo (aka Severo Pozzati, 1895–?). Of Italian origin, he came to Paris in 1920, designing first in a style reminiscent of Cappiello, and later in a style that recalls Cassandre. He created many posters and is an artist to watch for on the market as his prices are still reasonable for the quality of his work.

Another French artist who has a distinctive style and whose work is truly still inexpensive is Francis Bernard. Bernard was employed for thirty years as the art director for the Salon des Arts Ménagers, or the "Salon of Household Arts," an annual Parisian "home show."

His posters, which presaged the post–World War II style of the 1940s and 1950s can still be purchased for a few hundred dollars.

A later French artist, Bernard Villemot (1911–1989), has gained attention in recent years for his simple yet effective designs for Bally shoes and other commercial clients. Prices on his posters have increased rapidly in the last few years in recognition of his talent.

As French posters evolved from the Art Nouveau to the Art Deco period, there was a widening gulf between "artists' posters" and those by graphic designers created for commercial advertisers. While we recognize the enormous talents of a Cassandre, he was in fact not a painter and did not gain recognition in the world of fine art in his lifetime. Artists such as Pablo Picasso, Marc Chagall, Joan Miro, and their contemporaries created several fine artists' posters, but mainly for art exhibitions. (See the chapter "Collecting Contemporary Artists' Posters.")

WHERE TO GO TO SEE FRENCH POSTERS

French posters are the ones you will find most frequently at any poster exhibition or sale. For collectors with serious interest in French posters, we suggest that you visit one of the dealers we recognized for their assistance with this chapter in the Acknowledgments or those listed in the Resource Guide. In addition, several museums have fine collections of French posters including the Art Institute of Chicago, which has almost every poster Toulouse-Lautrec created, as well as significant holdings of Steinlen and Mucha; the Baltimore Museum of Art; the Museum of Modern Art in New York; and the Zimmerle Art Museum at Rutgers University in New Brunswick, New Jersey. (See Resource Guide for museum listings.) Never expect to find the entire collection of any museum displayed at the same time. Although special exhibitions of French posters are scheduled fairly regularly, museums with permanent collections tend to rotate the posters that are on display, "resting" the others from the effects of heat and light.

REFERENCE WORKS

More has been written about French posters and French poster artists than the posters of any other country. At the end of this guide we list numerous current and historical references for learning more about the French posters in which you may be interested. (See Bibliography.)

PRICE LISTINGS

FRENCH POSTERS

Note: *See the chapter "Important Notes on the Price Listings" for more information on prices given. Also note that many French artists also have listings in other chapters such as "World War Posters," "Travel and Transportation Posters," etc.*

ANONYMOUS

Armand Guy, ca. 1930. Lithographic poster depicting cabaret performer in black tie sitting playfully on the keyboard of an oversized, orange grand piano. Very good condition, linen-mounted, 39″ × 54″.
$1,000 (Auction)

Automobiles Delahaye. Lithographic poster printed by J. Barreau. One woman holding a torch in red and turquoise, two women in a green automobile. Fine condition, a good example of automobile poster, linen-mounted, 36½″ × 51¼″. $1,400–$1,600

Le Ballet et la Danse, 1942. Lithographic poster printed by Mourlot. Mint condition, linen-mounted, 18½″ × 25¼″. $200–$250

Bonal Gentiane-Quina, ca. 1930. Lithographic poster printed by Lang, Paris. A bottle of Bonal and gold lettering with a red border on a black background. Very good condition, horizontal 21″ × 17″.
$50–$75

All price ranges represent the retail value.

Courtesy of Poster Mail
Auction Company

Cognac Jacquet. Lithograph depicts luxuriant peacock posed beside bottle of cognac. Very good condition, 46" × 64". $375 *(Auction)*
$500–$550

Exposition Maritime Internationale–Bordeaux, 1907. Lithographic poster showing a rowboat and a steamship in foreground harbor, city of Bordeaux in background; Bordeaux landmarks inset in lower left foreground. Mint condition, very collectible, linen-mounted, 29" × 36".
$1,200–$1,500

Familial Radio, ca. 1930. Lithographic poster showing a young boy, silhouetted, sitting in front of a radio highlighted by a warm glow. Good condition, a good example of radio advertising, linen-mounted, 32" × 47".
$500–$600

Liqueur de St. Barbe, ca. 1905. Lithographic poster showing a devilish figure sneaking out a window after stealing a bottle of liqueur from the Convent of St. Barbe. Fine condition, a good example of liquor advertising, 45" × 60". (See color center section.)
$550–$600

Nuits du Théâtre et de la Danse, 1953. Stylized Deco-like image of dancing figures; in blue, red, and black. Very good condition, 15″ × 23″.   *$350–$400*

Sauvion's Brandy, 1925. Lithograph printed by Joseph Charles. Charming white-faced Pierrot in a bright red costume laughingly takes a swipe with his badminton racquet at a green parrot flying off with the bottle of brandy. Very good condition, linen-mounted, 16″ × 23″.   *$235 (Auction)*
$300–$400

Le Trait d'Union, 1880. Lithographic poster depicting a romantic couple in evening dress, decorative border. Mint condition, linen-mounted, approx. 26″ × 36″.   *$2,000–$2,200*

AMAN-JEAN

Beatrix. Lithographic poster in fair condition, 29½″ × 45½″.
$1,600–$1,700

GUY ARNOUX

Les Vins de Bourgogne, ca. 1920–1928. Lithographic poster showing a soldier dressed in a long blue coat and high black boots, sitting on a barrel enjoying a glass of wine and a pipe. Fine condition, 32″ × 47″.   *$400–$450*

LEON ARTRUC

Maria Del Villar, ca. 1925. Lithographic poster in very good condition, linen-mounted, 31″ × 41″. $1,200–$1,300

ALBERT BERGEVIN (1887–1974)

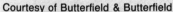

Courtesy of Butterfield & Butterfield

Avranches, ca. 1925. Lithographic poster printed by Imprimerie du Syndicat d'Initiativ d'Avranches. Collectors should be aware that this poster has been forged in recent years. The differences in color can only be observed when compared to the original, so caution is advised. Very good condition, linen-mounted, framed, 23⅝″ × 31⅝″.
$2,500 (Auction)

EDOUARD BERNARD

Alcazar d'Eté, ca. 1910. Lithographic poster. Fair condition, linen-mounted, 31½″ × 62″. $550–$600

Courtesy of Stephen Ganeles

Arlette Montal, ca. 1905. Lithographic poster showing a woman in a Greek-type costume dancing with a garland of flowers. Fine condition, 32″ × 47″. $400–$450

FRANCIS BERNARD (*1900–?*)

Arts Ménagers/Grand Palais/24 Fevrier–20 Mars, ca. 1935. A comical figure carries a painter's canvas in the form of a house, announcing the exhibition of household arts; in tones of blue, yellow, orange, red, and green on a black field. Bernard served as the art director of the Salon des Arts Ménagers for over 30 years. Very good condition, with four-inch tear at top center, 47″ × 63″. $250–$500

Arts Ménagers/Grand Palais/26 Fevrier–23 Mars. Whimsical design of orange figure playing a cello/house to announce annual Paris exhibit. Very good condition, 46″ × 61″. $250–$350

Arts Ménagers/Grand Palais/23 Fevrier–18 Mars. A child-like drawing of a woman in her house putting a flower into a vase; in light blue, green, orange, pink, brown, and black. Very good condition, 47″ × 63″. $250–$350

Arts Ménagers/Grand Palais/26 Janvier–12 Fevrier, 10th salon, 1933. Classic design of silhouetted woman holding a broom; in tones of blue with tan and black lettering. Fine condition, 24" × 39".

$200 (Auction)

Arts Ménagers/Grand Palais/23 Fevrier–19 Mars, 19th salon, 1942. Imaginative design of a head looking down into a house through its lifted-off roof; in yellow, red, blue, black, and pink on a brown field. Fine condition, 14" × 22". $100–$150

Arts Ménagers/Grand Palais/27 Janvier–13 Fevrier, 15th salon, 1938. A woman with a broom stands inside the outline of a house; in red, blue, salmon, pale green, and black with white and green lettering on a black field. Fine condition, 15" × 22". $100–$150

Arts Ménagers/Palais de la Defense/4 au 19 Mars. A clever design of a woman standing in the doorway of a world-shaped house illustrates the international composition of the exhibit; in red, yellow, orange, blue, green, and maroon on a black field. Very good condition, 47" × 63". $200 (Auction)

Arts Ménagers/Palais de la Defense/5–17 Mars. A playful design of a woman in her house, a flower with a globe in its center on her table; in orange, purple, maroon, and black on a crisp yellow field. Very good condition, 47" × 63". $250–$350

Extension de Ciboure, ca. 1925. Lithographic Art Deco-style travel poster printed by Editions Paul Martial for this resort in the south of France, depicting three stylized men in various outfits for relaxing, mountain climbing, and swimming, all set on an angle with sea and mountains as background. Fine condition, a very good example of the artist's style, linen-mounted, 31″ × 47″.   *$1,300–$1,500*

PAUL BERTHON *(1872–1909)*

Almanach d'Alsace et de Lorraine, 1896. Lithographic poster, printed by Chaix for the Alsacian publication, depicting a peasant girl in traditional costume against a background of an Alsacian village. A stunning poster, one of the best examples of Berthon's style. Fine condition, linen-mounted, 14½″ × 22⅛″. (See color center section.)
          $2,500–$3,000

Folies-Bergère/Liane de Pougy, 1896. Lithographic poster printed by Société des Impremeurs, Paris, signed in the stone. Art Nouveau design of Liane dancing as the Spider Woman. Very good condition, a good example of the artist's style, linen-mounted, 23½″ × 59½″.
          $3,500–$5,000

ROBERT BONFILS *(1886–1972)*

Exposition Internationale des Arts Décoratifs, 1925. Printed by Imprimerie de Vaugirard, Paris. Depicting a woman and a gazelle in Art Deco style; one of the official posters for the 1925 Exposition. Very good condition, linen-mounted, 15¼″ × 23½″.   *$1,500–$2,000*

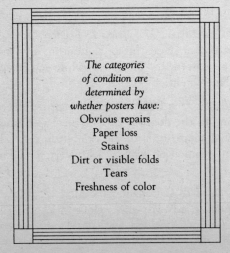

*The categories
of condition are
determined by
whether posters have:*
Obvious repairs
Paper loss
Stains
Dirt or visible folds
Tears
Freshness of color

PIERRE BONNARD (1867–1947)

L'Estampe et l'Affiche, 1897. Lithographic poster advertising the influential publication for turn-of-the-century poster collectors; depicts an older woman putting on her glasses to watch a younger one go by, carrying a large portfolio out of which drawings are falling. Good condition, linen-mounted, 24″ × 31″. $5,000–$8,000

La Revue Blanche, 1894. Lithographic poster printed by Ancourt, Paris. Depicts a woman in a ruffled cape and large hat holding a program for "La Revue Blanche." Mint condition, outstanding design by a leading fine artist, linen-mounted, 24¼″ × 31¼″. $7,500–$8,000

FIRMIN BOUISSET (1859–1925)

Les Specialités, Maggi, Profitens à Tout Ménage. Lithographic poster printed by Camis, signed in the stone. Young girl in reddish-orange dress holding an advertisement, a blackboard with prices; tan background. Mint condition, linen-mounted, 38¾″ × 50⅞″.

$950–$1,000

ROGER BRODERS (1883–1953)

Antibes, ca. 1930. Lithographic Art Deco-style travel poster printed by Lucien Serre. Broders is one of the best-known Art Deco travel poster artists in France. (See additional price listings for this artist under "Travel and Transportation Posters.") Very good condition, linen-mounted, 30″ × 42″.

$1,400–$1,800

BURRETT

Enghien, Les Bains. Lithographic poster printed by Bourgerie. Lady in white dress with swans, background yellow, blue, green. Very good condition, linen-mounted, 36½″ × 50¼″.

$500–$650

LEONETTO CAPPIELLO (1875–1942)

Bitter Campari, 1921. Lithographic poster printed by Devambez showing a clown-like figure with a bottle of Campari, surrounded by an orange peel. Very good condition, a very good example of the artist's style, linen-mounted, approx. 27½″ × 39″.

$4,000–$6,000

Café Martin, 1921. Lithographic poster depicting a genie rising on a cloud of steam from a colorful coffee cup. Very good condition, linen-mounted, 51″ × 79″.

$3,000–$3,500

Cognac Monnet, 1927. Lithographic poster, signed in the stone. A girl frolics barefoot with an oversized glass of brandy from which a swirling sun is rising. Mint condition, linen-mounted, 51″ × 79″.

$1,500–$2,500

Grand Chais du Medoc, 1901. Lithograph printed by Vercasson, signed in the stone. "Vins Authentiques"—a man pours wine into the glass of a woman in a flowing dress and large black hat seated at a table. Mint condition, mounted, approx. 39½″ × 55″.

$2,500–$3,800

Maurin Quina, ca. 1910. Lithograph printed by Vercasson, signed in the stone. Green devil, gold printing, black background. Fine condition, linen-mounted, 46″ × 61″. $600–$800

Same as above. Good condition, with small tears. *$450 (Auction)*

Mossant, 1938. Lithographic poster for Mossant hats. A clever design showing only three men's arms with hats in hand apparently as they doff them in a greeting. Mint condition, a fine example of the artist's product advertising, 47″ × 63″. *$1,200–$1,500*

Courtesy of Butterfield & Butterfield

Réglisse Sanguinède, 1902. Lithograph printed by Vercasson. A woman in a blue hat and maroon dress walks through a winter landscape, about to take the advertised cough drop. Fine condition, a very good example of the artist's style, linen-mounted, framed, 38″ × 54″.
$3,000–$3,500

Le Thermogène, 1909. Lithograph printed by Vercasson, Paris. Advertises that thermogene will bring you warmth and cure coughs. Good condition, framed, 46⅛″ × 62⅜″. *$800–$1,200*

Vermouth Martini, 1931. Lithographic poster depicting a woman holding aloft two bottles of Martini Vermouth, walking towards the viewer with a sunburst design behind her. Very good condition, a good example of the artist's style, linen-mounted, 27″ × 40″. *$600–$700*

JEAN GEORGES CARLU (1900–)

Exposition Internationale Paris 1937, 1937. Lithographic poster depicting the profile of a woman's face against a background of international flags. Fine condition, 10½″ × 15½″. $400–$600

Pepa Bonafé, 1928. Lithograph printed by Marcel Picard, Paris. Good condition, linen-mounted, 14¾″ × 22⅜″.   *$170 (Auction)*

A. M. CASSANDRE (1901–1968)

Courtesy of Nancy
McClelland, Christie's

Challenge Round de La Coupe Davis, 1932. Lithographic poster published by Aliance Graphique, Cassandre's advertising agency. This strong composition is an outstanding example of Cassandre's Art Deco style. The same image was also used for a poster announcing the "Grand Quinzaine Internationale de Lawn Tennis" in May and June of the same year. Fine condition, linen-mounted, 45″ × 62″.
$10,000–$12,000

Etoile du Nord, 1927. Lithographic poster printed by Hachard, Paris, for the Chemin de Fer. Cassandre's now well-known image of train lines disappearing at the horizon where they converge at the North Star. (For other train and travel posters by Cassandre see the price listings under "Travel and Transportation Posters.") Fine condition, linen-mounted, 30″ × 41″. $7,000–$9,000

Normandie, 1935. Lithographic poster printed by Aliance Graphique. The ocean liner Normandie was a palace of Art Deco design, with commissions by many leading artists. Collectors should be aware that this poster is a favorite for photo offset reproduction. Very good condition, linen-mounted, 25″ × 39½″. $10,000–$12,000

L'Oiseau Bleu ("The Blue Bird"), 1929. Lithographic poster for the Chemin de Fer du Nord, printed by L. Danel, Lille, advertising the Pullman trains from Antwerp to Brussels to Paris. A good design with a close-up of a stylized blue bird flying alongside the speeding train. Fine condition, linen-mounted, 25″ × 39″. $4,000–$6,000

PUVIS DE CHAVANNES

Centenaire de la Lithographie, 1895. Lithograph printed by Lemercier, signed in the stone. Woman in pink dress holds a lithograph while a cherub at her feet holds open a print portfolio; in greens and blues. Fine condition, linen-mounted, 43″ × 58″. $650–$750

JULES CHÉRET (1836–1932)

Jules Chéret is considered the father of the modern poster. Approximately 20 years after the new technology of lithography became available, Chéret added a new degree of lightness, movement, color, and style to the art form that opened all the possibilities for poster designers right up to the present day. The reference numbers which follow some of the titles below are posters illustrated in Lucy Broido's book *The Posters of Jules Chéret: A Catalogue Raisonne* (see Bibliography).

Alcazar d'Eté/Lidia, 1895. (Broido #174) Lithographic poster printed by Chaix. An impression with only the name of the performer, without the lettering above for the café-concert Alcazar d'Eté. Fine condition with brilliant colors, no folds, linen-mounted, 34″ × 48⅜″.
                    $3,500–$4,000

Alcazar d'Eté/Louise Balthy, 1893. (Broido #173) Lithographic poster printed by Chaix, depicting the chanteuse. Good condition, linen-mounted, 34½″ × 49″. $1,600–$1,800

L'Argent, 1890. (Broido #664) Lithographic poster printed by Chaix for the Emile Zola novel as serialized in the publication *Gil Blas*. Very good condition, linen-mounted, 34½″ × 97″. $1,500–$2,000

Arlette Dorgère, 1904. (Broido #221) Lithographic poster with a full-length portrait of the young chanteuse in a filmy dress, long red robe, and wide-brimmed hat. A popular entertainer of the day, Arlette Dorgère often performed at the Scala. Fine condition, linen-mounted on two sheets, 35″ × 96½″. $3,200–$3,500

L'Auréole du Midi, 1893. (Broido #975) Lithographic poster printed by Chaix. Advertises a brand of lamp fuel—extra-clear and scentless; depicts a child in a red and white polka dot dress holding up a lantern while another child holds up a can of fuel. With the stamp of Affiches Illustrées Sagot, Paris, in violet ink in lower left corner. Fine condition, brilliant colors, traces of folds, linen-mounted, 34⅛″ × 48½″. $2,600–$3,000

Bal du Moulin Rouge, 1892. (Broido #316) Lithograph printed by Chaix. For the popular dance hall in Montmartre, where besides nightly dances there were masked balls, singers, acrobats, an outdoor garden for dancing, and even donkey rides. Good condition but several splits and tears and some in-painting on the donkey, linen-mounted, 34¼″ × 48⅛″.   *$1,800 (Auction)*

Same as above. Fine condition, linen-mounted, 34″ × 47″. $2,500–$3,000

Courtesy of Club of American Collectors

Same as above. Mint condition, linen-mounted, 34¼″ × 47¼.″ $4,000–$6,000

Courtesy of Park South Gallery at Carnegie Hall

Benzo-Moteur, 1900. (Broido #1031) Lithograph printed by Chaix. Advertising "special gasoline for automobiles." In the foreground a woman drives an automobile, looking back toward a couple motoring along in the background. With the Republique Française tax stamp. Brilliant colors, fine condition, linen-mounted, 32″ × 47″.

$2,500–$3,200

Bigarreau, 1895. (Broido #875) Lithograph printed by Chaix, signed in the stone. A young man offers a taste of wine to a young woman standing on a ladder, picking grapes. Mint condition, a good example of Chéret's product advertising, linen-mounted, 33″ × 95″.

$2,500–$3,500

Casino de Paris/Camille Stefani, 1891. (Broido #212) Lithographic poster in very good condition, linen-mounted, 22″ × 31″. $1,400–$2,000

Closerie Des Genets, 1890. (Broido #666) Lithographic poster printed by Chaix to announce the novel in *The Radical*. Very good condition, linen-mounted, 34½″ × 49″. $1,100–$1,300

Cosmydor Savon, 1891. (Broido #937) Lithographic poster printed by Chaix for Cosmydor soap. Good condition, linen-mounted, 34½″ × 48″. $1,100–$1,200

La Danseuse de Corde, 1891. (Broido #240) Lithographic poster printed by Chaix for the tightrope dancer and mime Felicia Mallet. Here, she crosses the rope in a tutu using a rifle as a balancing pole; wonderful lettering. Very good condition, linen-mounted, framed, 35″ × 49″.
$1,500–$2,000

Expon. Blanc et Noir, 1890. (Broido #442) Black and white lithograph, printed by Chaix, signed in the stone. For a magic lantern show, shows a young woman holding a humorous projection. Fine condition, linen-mounted, 32″ × 47″.
$850–$900

Exposition Universelle Des Arts Incoherents, 1889. (Broido #438) Lithographic poster printed by Chaix depicting the head of a clown juxtaposed with calligraphy. Good condition, linen-mounted, 34″ × 48¼″.
$700–$1,000

La Farandole, 1884. (Broido #56) Lithographic poster printed by Chaix for a ballet in three acts with music by Th. Dubois. Printed in black and white on sea green tinted paper. Very good condition, linen-mounted, 19½″ × 25½″.
$900–$950

Courtesy of Park South Gallery at Carnegie Hall

Folies-Bergère/L'Arc en Ciel, 1893. (Broido #123) Lithographic poster depicting four artists from the ballet-pantomime under a rainbow. Fine condition, a very good example of the artist's mastery of color lithography, linen-mounted, 32″ × 47½″.
$2,800–$3,000

Folies-Bergère/La Loie Fuller, 1893. (Broido #125) Lithograph printed by Chaix, signed in the stone. Commissioned for the Paris debut of the celebrated American dancer Loie Fuller, who invented a new choreography of floating movement, diaphanous costumes, and multi-colored, projected electric lights against a background of darkness, inspiring works by many artists and sculptors, including one of Chéret's finest posters. In green and orange on a dark green background. Fine condition, linen-mounted, 33⅜″ × 48¼″. (See color center section.) $6,000–$7,000

Folies-Bergère/"Le Miroir," 1892. (Broido #122) Lithographic poster printed by Chaix, signed in the stone. Young woman in Dutch peasant dress, Pierrot holding mirror behind her; in white, red, blue. Very good condition, linen-mounted, 33¾″ × 48½″. $1,000–$1,750

Grand Magasins du Louvre, 1896. (Broido #674) Lithographic poster printed by Chaix. For a department store; the cascading, carnivalesque figures beckon Parisians to buy New Year's presents ("etrennes"). From a hole in the clouds, forming a jagged splash in the background, a blue shadow-figure emerges as if to catch up with the frontrunners in a mirthful troupe of comedians, Pierrots, and harlequins. With the Republique Française tax stamp. Fine condition, linen-mounted, 33⅜″ × 48″. $2,800–$3,700

Halle Aux Chapeaux, 1892. (Broido #830) Lithographic poster printed by Chaix. Depicting a little girl and her mother trying on hats. Good condition, linen-mounted, 33¾″ × 48⅜″.

$1,800–$2,000 *(Auction)*

Jardin de Paris, 1890. (Broido #250) Subtitled "Spectacle Concert." Lithographic poster, printed by Chaix, of a young Chérette with a fan dancing with other performers and dancers in the background. Great color. Good condition, linen-mounted, 32″ × 46″.

$1,800–$2,000

Madame Sans-Gêne, 1894. (Broido #670) Lithographic poster printed by Chaix for the serialization of the novel in *The Radical*. Good condition, linen-mounted, 34½″ × 48½″. $900–$1,300

Musée Grevin/Les Fantoches de John Hewelt, 1900. (Broido #471) Lithograph without text printed by Chaix. Issued for collectors to hang in their homes rather than for use as advertising placards, it was retailed through the bookseller Sagot. Depicts a variety of colorful entertainers vividly; mainly in lively yellows, reds, greens, blues, and black. Brilliant colors, fine condition, linen-mounted, 34⅜″ × 48⅞″.

$2,250–$3,750

Musée Grevin/Les Fantoches de John Hewelt, 1900. (Broido #471) The same lithographic poster as above, printed by Chaix, but rarer because it has the text for John Hewelt's puppet show. In most cases, proofs before letters are rarer, but in this case the opposite is true. Fine condition, linen-mounted, 34½″ × 47⅞″. $4,500–$6,000

Musée Grevin/Pantomimes Lumineuses, 1892. (Broido #468) Lithograph printed by Chaix. A curtsying Chérette invites passersby to an "optical theatre of luminous pantomimes." With the Musée Grevin stamp and the Republique Française tax stamp. Fine condition, bright colors, linen-mounted, 33½″ × 48¼″. $2,500–$2,900

Olympia, 1893. (Broido #346) Lithographic poster printed by Chaix and subtitled "Anciennes Montagnes Russes," featuring the performer with cymbals in hand. This poster was also printed in a larger version in 1892. Very good condition, a good example of the artist's style, linen-mounted, 14″ × 19½″. $1,400–$1,600

L'Oncle Sam (Uncle Sam), 1873. (Broido #228) Lithographic poster printed by Imprimereie Chéret for the Théâtre du Vaudeville for a "quadrille Americain." Printed in black on tinted paper. Very good condition, linen-mounted, 10¼″ × 14″. $500–$600

Palais de Glace, 1893. (Broido #263) Lithographic poster printed by Chaix. One of several by Chéret advertising the ice-skating rink; depicts a woman skater in a long red coat with white fur trim, with other skaters silhouetted in the background. Fine condition with brilliant colors, linen-mounted, 33¼″ × 94″. $5,500–$6,500

Courtesy of Park South Gallery at Carnegie Hall

Palais de Glace, 1893. (Broido #362) Lithographic poster printed by Chaix. In the foreground, a woman in a long coat; in the background, a man and several women with one arm raised. Fine condition, linen-mounted, 32″ × 45½″. $3,400–$3,600

Palais de Glace, 1894, (Broido #365) Lithographic poster printed as a supplement to the *Courrier Français* issue of January 28, 1894, for the famous ice-skating rink on the Champs Elysées. Chéret was commissioned both to design posters to advertise the publication and to create special edition posters for its readers. Fine condition, 13″ × 21″. $750–$800

Paris Courses Hippodrome de la Porte Maillot, 1890. (Broido #520) Lithograph printed by Chaix, signed in the stone. For a racetrack in Paris, the lady rides sidesaddle through lettering that announces a grand prize of a "river of diamonds"; her horse exemplifies the angular stylization that so often gives Chéret's imagery its choppy energy. Good condition, linen-mounted, 33⅛″ × 48″. $3,300–$3,500

Pastilles Geraudel, 1891. (Broido #902) Lithographic poster printed by Chaix for cough drops, published as a supplement to *The Courrier Français*. Fine condition, 14″ × 22″. $800–$850

From the author's collection
(Photo by Robert Four)

Pastilles Poncelet, 1896. (Broido #909) Lithographic poster printed by Chaix for Poncelet cough drops, depicting a Chérette in a rainstorm. Fine condition, 16″ × 22″. $800–$900

Les Pays des Fées, 1889. Lithograph from *Les Maîtres de l'Affiche* (see more information on *Les Maîtres* in the chapter on "French Posters") with the blindstamp of the publisher, Chaix. Good condition, framed, 9″ × 12⅝″. $425 (Auction)

Le Punch Grassot, 1895. Lithograph from *Les Maîtres de l'Affiche* (see more information on *Les Maîtres* in the chapter on "French Posters") with the blindstamp of the publisher, printed by Chaix. Good condition, framed, 9⅛″ × 12¾″. $400 (Auction)

Purgatif Geraudel. (Broido #899) Lithographic poster printed by Chaix. Very good condition, linen-mounted, 34½″ × 96″.

$3,000–$3,200

Quinquina Dubonnet, 1895. (Broido #873) Lithograph printed by Chaix, signed in the stone. Spirited young lady in a green dress holds a bottle of the aperitif in one hand, a snifter in the other; a perfect example of "less is more," simple and succinct, mainly in blues and reds. Fine condition, a very good example of a Chéret beverage poster, linen-mounted, 33⅝″ × 45¾″. $2,000–$3,000

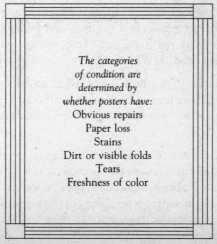

*The categories
of condition are
determined by
whether posters have:*
Obvious repairs
Paper loss
Stains
Dirt or visible folds
Tears
Freshness of color

Courtesy of William Doyle Galleries

Saxoléine, 1895. (Broido #953) Lithographic poster depicting a fashionably dressed woman lighting an oil lamp, from a series for the lamp oil company. Good condition, linen-mounted, 34″ × 49″.

$1,500–$2,000

Saxoléine, 1900. (Broido #958) Lithographic poster printed by Chaix. Depicts a red-haired woman in a red dress and yellow bonnet holding up an oil lamp. With the Republique Française tax stamp. Mint condition, linen-mounted, 32½″ × 46¾″. $2,500–$3,000

Il Signor Pulcinella, 1876. (Broido #245) Lithographic poster printed by Imprimerie Chéret for the Théâtre de l'Athenée-Comique, depicting the actor Montrouge. Very good condition, linen-mounted, 10¼″ × 15¾.″ $600–$700

Taverne Olympia, 1889. (Broido #848) Lithographic poster printed by Chaix. For an all-night restaurant occupying the former site of the Montagnes Russes cabaret; depicts a couple in evening dress seated at a restaurant table making a toast. (See also listing for Chéret's *Olympia*.) With the Republique Française tax stamp. Fine condition, brilliant colors, linen-mounted, 33⅞″ × 48″. $2,400–$2,800

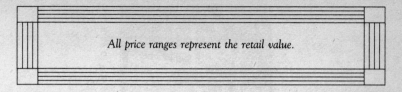

Théâtre de l'Athenée-Comique, 1876. (Broido #244) Lithographic poster by Imprimerie Chéret, depicting the head of the actor Montrouge wearing Puchinello's hat and peering from a cellar window. Very good condition, linen-mounted, 10¼″ × 15¾″.　　　　　$600–$700

Théâtre National de l'Opéra/Carnival 1892: 2e Bal Masqué, 1892. (Broido #284) Lithographic poster printed by Chaix. For the second annual masquerade ball celebrating Carnival at the Théâtre National de l'Opéra; depicts a masked woman in evening dress in front of a man in evening clothes and a clown. Good condition, 33⅝″ × 47⅝″.　　　　　$2,500–$2,900

Viviane/Eden-Théâtre, 1886. (Broido #59) Lithographic poster printed by Chaix for the five-act ballet by Edmond Gondinet. Mint condition, 23¾″ × 31½″.　　　　　$900–$1,000

CLAIRIN

Theodora—Sarah Bernhardt. Lithographic poster in mint condition, linen-mounted, 30½″ × 81½″ .　　　　　$5,500–$6,000

MARCEL CLEMENT

Bi-Borax Oriental. Lithographic poster in very good condition, linen-mounted, 25″ × 33″.　　　　　$900–$1,000

PAUL COLIN (1892–1985)

Falconetti . . . Théâtre de l'Avenue, 1930. Lithographic poster printed by Succes, signed in the stone. Wispy woman in pink floating in a cloud. Good condition, a good example of the artist's style, framed, 47″ × 62″.　　　　　$2,000–$3,000

Haut de Cagnes/Ou la Joie de Vivre, ca. 1950. Bright design for an exhibition sale of the shops and artisans of Haut de Cagnes; in deep green, yellow, red, and black. Fine condition, a fine example of the artist's later style, linen-mounted, 33″ × 48″. $600–$700

Marguerite Valmond, 1928. Lithograph printed by Chachoin, Paris. Wonderfully soft portrait of the French singer. Very good condition, linen-mounted, 47″ × 63″. $700–$800

Paris/1937/Exposition Internationale, 1937. Nicely stylized design in dark blue, red, yellow, light blue, gray, brown, and black. Good condition, linen-mounted, 16″ × 23″. $800–$1,000

Tabarin, 1928. Lithographic poster from the artist's early Art Deco period, Cubist influence is evident in the juxtaposition of the three different images of the same female figure. Very good condition, an excellent example of the artist's work, linen-mounted, 15″ × 24″. (See color center section.) $2,500–$3,500

ERIC DE COULON (*1888–1956*)

Alpes et Jura. Lithograph in very good condition, 24½″ × 39⅜″.
                    $900–$1,200

ANDRÉ DAUDE (*1897–1979*)

Pianos Daudé, ca. 1926. Lithographic poster printed by Publicite PAG depicting stylized image of man at piano seen from above, his bald head gleaming. Very good condition, linen-mounted, 47″ × 63″.
                    $1,500–$1,800

DELLEPIANE

Exposition Nationale Coloniale, 1922. Lithographic poster printed by Moullot, Marseille. Colorful design with three women from Asia, Southeast Asia, and Africa in front of a distant ship steaming into Marseille. Good condition, mounted on Japan paper, 32″ × 47″.
                    $500–$600

DANIEL DELOSQUES (*1880–1915*)

Mistinguett, 1911. Lithographic poster printed by H. Cachoin showing the young performer in a long, slim blue dress with red trim and a blue hat with red flowers standing in a field. (This poster was also printed with the same image except she is in a red dress against a deep green field.) Very good condition, a popular image, 42″ × 76″.
                    $1,000–$1,400

DELVAL

Fap'anis, ca. 1925. A brightly dressed young lady toasts the viewer; in red, yellow, orange, green, blue, and black. Very good condition, linen-mounted, horizontal 63″ × 47″.   *$350 (Auction)*

JEAN-GABRIEL DOMERGUE *(1889–1962)*

Alice Soulie, 1926. Lithographic poster printed by Chachoin of the entertainer with her bare breasts hidden behind a fan of ostrich feathers. Very good condition, linen-mounted, 46¼″ × 63″.

$1,000–$1,200

Galeries Lafayette, 1920. Lithograph signed in the stone. Elegant woman in striped coat with fur collar and cuffs, opening her small black handbag to pay for French savings bonds, which could be bought at the department store. Mint condition, linen-mounted, 47″ × 63″.

$1,500–$2,500

JEAN DUPAS *(1882–1964)*

Arnold Constable, 1928. Lithographic poster with text in English for the department store, depicting three women rendered in Dupas' unmistakable style, each wearing a different fashionable ensemble. Very good condition, linen-mounted, 30″ × 46″.   *$3,500–$4,000*

Xveme Salon des Artistes Décorateurs, 1924. Lithograph signed in the stone. Art Deco design in gray and red; two women, one in profile, one full face. Fine condition, linen-mounted, 15″ × 23¼″. (See color center section.)   *$2,500–$3,000*

GEORGES DE FEURE
(AKA GEORGES VAN SLUITERS, *1868–1943*)

Paris Almanach, 1894. Lithograph printed by Bourgerie & Cie, Paris, signed in the stone. Advertising a book about life in Paris, published by Ed. Sagot; pictures a woman dressed in cape and hat with the book in her hand, a group of men in the background. Mint condition, a highly desirable example of the artist's style, linen-mounted, 24½″ × 31½″. (See color center section.)   *$2,500–$4,500*

PIERRE FIX-MASSEAU (1905–)

Courtesy of Nancy McClelland, Christie's

Exactitude, 1932. Lithographic poster printed by Edita, Paris, depicting a French train in Art Deco style traveling directly towards the viewer. Fix-Masseau worked with Cassandre and was influenced by his style. Fine condition, long recognized as an outstanding poster of the Art Deco period, linen-mounted, 25″ × 39½″. $8,000–$10,000

P. GELIS-DIDOT AND LOUIS MALTESTE

Absinthe Parisienne. Lithographic poster in good condition, linen-mounted, 32″ × 47″. $800–$1,000

GEO-CAP

Parfums Djemie. Lithographic poster in an Art Deco style, showing a woman with perfume bottles sitting on cushion. Fine condition, linen-mounted, 38″ × 52¾″. $800–$1,000

CHARLES GESMAR (1900–1928)

Mistinguett, 1925. Lithographic poster featuring a close-up of the chanteuse with mammoth jewels on her fingers. Very good condition, linen-mounted, 44″ × 63″. $1,800–$2,300

Mistinguett/Casino de Paris, 1922. Lithographic poster depicts the famous performer sitting on a three-legged stool, with a parakeet perched on her bejeweled fingers. It is estimated that Gesmar designed more than 20 posters for Mistinguett. Very good condition, linen-mounted, 30″ × 47″. $2,500–$3,000

GASTON GIRBAL

Lisa-La-Honte, 1925. Lithographic poster for the musical by André and Arco, scene inside a café-concert shows woman at table with bottle, projector throwing light, gents at tables. Fine condition, linen-mounted, 45″ × 61″. $750–$800

EUGENE GRASSET (1845–1917)

Encre L. Marquet, 1892. Lithograph printed by Nouvles Affiches Artistiques Malherbe, signed in the stone. A young woman with flowing hair sits at her desk pondering the letter she is writing; in subdued greens, orange, and black. Fine condition, a very good example of the artist's style, linen-mounted, 32″ × 48″. $1,500–$2,000

Exposition d'Art Décoratif, 1894. Lithograph. Good condition, linen-mounted, 32″ × 51″. $2,000–$2,200

Grafton Gallery Exhibition, 1893. (No text) A flowing, lovely Art Nouveau woman amidst trees and flowers; pastel colors. Although this poster is called the Grafton Gallery Exhibition poster, the version with type, if it exists, has never been recorded. It may have been sold as a decorative panel by the gallery. Good condition, a fine example of the artist's style, framed, 19″ × 25½″. $1,800–$2,500

Jeanne d'Arc. Lithograph advertising Sarah Bernhardt's performance. Good condition, linen-mounted, 30″ × 46½″. $800–$1,200

HENRI GRAY (AKA HENRI BOULANGER, 1858–1924)

Petrole Stella, 1897. Lithographic poster printed by Courmont Frères. A stunning design for lamp oil, with three nude women with butterfly wings soaring in the air above the rays of a rising run. Very good condition, one of Gray's best designs, linen-mounted, 38″ × 51″. (See color center section.) $2,500–$3,000

Pneumatique Continental, ca. 1895. Lithographic poster printed by Courmont Frères. A couple sits on a tire which opens onto a country landscape; in light blue, light green, and pinks. Fine condition, linen-mounted, 12″ × 24″. $375–$450

Le Trefle à 4 Feuilles George Richard, ca. 1890. Lithographic poster for a well-known brand of bicycle. Very good condition, linen-mounted, 47″ × 63″. $750–$850

P. F. GRIGNON

Automobile le Gui, ca. 1900. Early lithographic automobile poster shows hood of the car parked in a glade, the driver showing the marvel to a group of white-robed forest people. Good condition, linen-mounted, horizontal 47″ × 31″. $400–$500

JULES-ALEXANDRE GRÜN (1886–1934)

Bal Tabarin, 1904. Lithographic poster printed by Chaix, Paris. Depicting a gentleman with a monocle, his revealingly dressed companion and their black coachman on their merry way to the nightclub Tabarin. Very good condition, very good example of the artist's style, framed, 34½″ × 48″. $3,000–$3,500

Hotel Du Pacha Noir. Lithographic poster in very good condition, linen-mounted, 49½″ × 34½″. $900–$1,000

L'Opera 2e Bal Masqué, 1914. Lithographic poster in very good condition, linen-mounted, 36″ × 51″. $1,000–$1,200

Paris à Londres, 1899. Lithographic poster in good condition, 27¾″ × 39½″. $800–$1,000

All price ranges represent the retail value.

Courtesy of William Doyle Galleries

La Pépinière. Lithograph depicting a Montmartre woman and an admiring gentleman. Good condition, linen-mounted, 35″ × 48½″.

$850 *(Auction)*
$1,600–$1800

Courtesy of Butterfield & Butterfield

Scala c'est d'un Raid, 1902. Lithographic poster printed by Bourgerie, Paris. Very good condition, linen-mounted, 34″ × 48″.

$750 *(Auction)*
$1,200–$1,800

PAUL CESAR HELLEU (1859–1927)

Courtesy of Poster Mail Auction Company

Ed. Sagot, 1897. Lithographic poster advertising Sagot, the largest print and poster dealer in Paris at the time. A young lady scrutinizes the prints for sale; in shades of sepia. Fine condition, linen-mounted, 29½″ × 41¾″. $600–$800

HENRI-GABRIEL IBELS (1867–1936)

J. Mevisto, 1892. Lithographic poster depicting Ibels' full-length image of the singer Mevisto as a Pierrot. Very good condition, linen-mounted, 25″ × 71″. $800–$1,000

LOUIS ICART (1887–1951)

Monte Carlo. Lithographic poster depicting two women sitting back-to-back on a large beachball, advertising the joys of Monte Carlo in the summer; mainly in bright blues, yellows, blacks, and whites. Fine condition, one of very few Icart posters, linen-mounted, 30¼″ × 44½″. $2,500–$3,000

KALISCHER

Au Ras d'Amhara, ca. 1935. Lithograph printed by Réunies de Lyon. Shows a large coffee bean set in a blue background with a Turk rising from the bean holding a cup of coffee; in red, yellow, brown, and blue. Fine condition, a good collectible, linen-mounted, 47″ × 62″. $350–$450

CHARLES LEMMEL

Bonal, ca. 1930. Lithographic poster showing a bottle of Bonal standing in front of a fir tree and a snow-covered mountain. Fine condition, nice example of a liqueur advertisement, 47″ × 60″.   *$300–$350*

Bonal–l'Ami des Sportifs, ca. 1930–1935. Lithographic poster showing football player reaching for the ball as another tackles him. Mint condition, 22″ × 32″.   *$125–$150*

Bonal–l'Ami des Sportifs, ca. 1930–1935. Lithographic poster showing one boxer delivering a knock-out punch to another. Mint condition, 22″ × 32″.   *$150–$200*

LE MONNIER

Valmya–Grand Vin Généreux Doux, 1937. Lithographic poster showing a dark-haired woman in a long, red-and-white striped dress holding a glass, seated behind a large bottle of Valmya. Fine condition, 45″ × 60″.   *$450–$500*

GEORGES LEPAPE (1887–1971)

Spinelly, 1914. The famous Lepape image of the singer, smiling behind her lace fan, an Art Deco classic. Very good condition, linen-mounted, 33″ × 45″.   *$1,400–$2,000*

L. LOPES-SILVA

Nouveau Théâtre, 1893. Colorful Belle Epoque design of diaphanously clad beauties rising from the ashes of the old theater. Very good condition, linen-mounted, 39″ × 58″.   *$700 (Auction)*

CHARLES LOUPOT (1892–1962)

Courtesy of Anca Colbert
Fine Arts, Ltd.

Exposition Internationale des Arts Décoratifs–Paris 1925. Lithographic
poster signed in the stone. Very good condition, a very collectible
poster from the 1925 Exposition, linen-mounted, 15″ × 23″.

$2,250–$3,000

Mira, 1929. Lithograph. Mint condition (best quality), linen-mounted,
9½″ × 12¼″. $1,275–$1,375

PIERRE LOUYS

Citroën, ca. 1925. Lithographic poster printed by Chaix. Four ladies
in 1920s' fashions in their sedan; in the background is the Loire valley
with a 13th-century castle. Colorful, large format, rare. Very good
condition, linen-mounted, 59″ × 86″. $2,250 (Auction)

A. LUPIAC

Artistes Méribienaux. Lithographic poster printed by B. Sirven, Toulouse, Paris. Good condition, framed, 38½″ × 53¾″.

$400 (Auction)

PIERRE MARRAST

Cherry Kobler, ca. 1930. For Columbia Records, France, stylized portrait of the cabaret performer seated at her piano. Very good condition, linen-mounted, 31″ × 47″. $600–$800

GEORGES MEUNIER (1869–1942)

À la Place Clichy, 1896. Lithograph printed by Chaix advertising Christmas gifts and showing a jester and little girl on a rocking horse. Good condition, linen-mounted, 34½″ × 49″. $800–$1,200

L'Excellent/Consommé de Viande de Boeuf, 1895. Lithographic poster printed by Chaix, signed in the stone. A young woman dressed in red, white, and black, with red flowers in her hair, offers a cup of beef bouillon. Mint condition, an excellent example of the artist's style, linen-mounted, 35″ × 49″. $1,600–$2,500

Jardin de Paris. Lithograph printed by Chaix, signed in the stone. Girls at an amusement park; in red, green, yellow. Good condition, linen-mounted, 33¾″ × 49″. $800–$900

Presse Parisienne/Les Soldats de Madagascar, 1895. Lithographic poster. Good condition, linen-mounted, 34½″ × 49″. $700–$800

MISTI (AKA FERDINAND MIFLIEZ, 1865–1923)

Berthelot. Lithograph. Fine condition, linen-mounted, 37″ × 51″.
$900–$1,000

Cottereau & Dijon, ca. 1900. Lithograph. Very good condition, linen-mounted, 45″ × 61″. $2,200–$2,300

Fête de Neuilly, 1909. Lithograph printed by la Lithographie Nouvell, Asnieres. Good condition, linen-mounted, framed, 36¼″ × 52″.
$1,000 (Auction)

Fête de Neuilly, 1912. Lithographic poster in good condition, linen-mounted, 39½″ × 54½″. $1,275–$1,350

Fête de Neuilly, 1913. Lithographic poster in good condition, linen-mounted, 39″ × 55½″. $1,150–$1,250

Rouxel & Dubois, ca. 1895. Lithographic poster in fair condition, linen-mounted, 37″ × 51½″. $550–$600

Bières de la Meuse, 1897. (No text) Lithograph with dark olive green outline, signed in the stone. A Mucha beauty with long flowing tresses adorned with green hops, poppies, and barley stalks (ingredients used to produce this 1890s French beer); in purple, red, yellow, blue, and orange pastels. Fine condition, rare proof before letters, linen-mounted, 40⅝″ × 60″.   *$7,000–$9,000*

Biscuits Lefèvre Utile/Flirt, 1900. Lithographic poster printed by F. Champenois to advertise cookies, depicting a gentleman and lady "flirting" in an enticing greenhouse full of flowers. Very good condition, linen-mounted, 10½″ × 24½″.   *$2,800 (Auction)*
$3,500–$4,000

Exposition Universelle & Internationale de St. Louis, 1903. Lithograph printed by F. Champenois, Paris. For the 1904 St. Louis World's Fair, showing an elaborately dressed woman holding the hand of an American Indian with full headdress who sits behind her. Very good condition, linen-mounted, 29¾″ × 41¼″.   *$5,000 (Auction)*
$7,000–$10,000

Job, 1898. Lithograph printed by F. Champenois, Paris, signed in the stone. This well-known Art Nouveau poster for Job Cigarette Papers shows a young woman with long hair sitting within a totally designed space; in greens, yellows, reds, browns, and black. Fine condition, a very good example of the artist's style, linen-mounted, 39″ × 61″. (See color center section.) $8,000–$10,000

   Same as above. Framed, 39¾″ × 58¾″. $6,000 *(Auction)*

   Same as above. Good condition, smaller size, with creases, framed, 15¼″ × 20¼″. $6,500 *(Auction)*

Lance Parfum Rodo, 1896. Lithographic poster printed by F. Champenois depicting a maiden using a "new" spray perfume. Good condition, framed, 12″ × 17″. $4,000 *(Auction)*

Lorenzaccio, 1896. Lithographic poster printed by F. Champenois. Smaller format for the Théâtre de la Renaissance performances of Sarah Bernhardt, in which she played a man's role. Fair condition, linen-mounted, framed, 14¾″ × 41⅛″. $2,250 *(Auction)*
                                                                    $3,500–$4,500

Courtesy of William Doyle Galleries

Salon des Cent, 1897. Lithograph printed by F. Champenois for an exposition of works by Mucha in Paris, June 1897. Good condition, repaired tear, mounted on Japan paper, 18¼″ × 26⅛″.
                                                                    $4,000 *(Auction)*

   Same as above. Linen-mounted, larger format 43″ × 63½″.
                                                                    $4,800 *(Auction)*

Courtesy of William Doyle Galleries

La Samaritaine, 1897. Lithograph printed by F. Champenois for the Théâtre de la Renaissance. Sarah Bernhardt, the play's star, stands leaning on a large water jar; behind her head are a halo and gold stars. Fine condition, linen-mounted, 23″ × 68″.

$8,500–$9,000

Sarah Bernhardt/American Tour, 1895. Lithographic poster printed by Strobridge, Cincinnati, announcing Sarah Bernhardt's 1896 American tour; a recreation of Mucha's *Gismonda* poster, considered one of his finest. Fine condition, an excellent example of Mucha's style, linen-mounted, 29⅛″ × 77⅝″.

$7,000–$9,000

All price ranges represent the retail value.

Courtesy of Freeman Fine Arts

Vin des Incas. Lithographic poster printed in two parts by F. Champenois advertising a medicine for "convalescents" made from coca or cocaine and depicting a female Inca god refusing to give coca to an Indian. Good condition, laid on Japan paper, linen-backed, a very large version of the poster, horizontal 80⅝″ × 32½″.

$7,500 (Auction)

Same as above. Smaller format, framed, 13¾″ × 4¼″.

$2,000–$2,500

OCHOA

Orient Express, ca. 1898. Lithographic poster in good condition, 34″ × 47″. $1,500–$1,850

MANUEL ORAZI (1860–1934)

Palais de la Danse, 1900. Lithographic poster printed by Bourgerie. Shows the Greek goddess of dance in pastel colors, advertising the dance palace at the Paris Exposition Universelle of 1900. Very good condition, framed, 23″ × 61″. $3,500–$4,500

PAL (AKA JEAN DE PALÉOLOGUE, 1860–1942)

La Belle Otero, ca. 1895. Lithographic poster showing the dancer Otero in Spanish dress with castanets. Mint condition, linen-mounted, 38½″ × 55½″. $1,200–$1,700

Cléo de Merode. Lithograph printed by Chardin, depicting a lady dancer in ballet costume; in yellow and turquoise. See other price listings for Pal under French Opera Posters in this chapter. Good condition, a good example of the artist's style, linen-mounted, 35⅜″ × 49¼″. $950–$1,200

Humber Cycles, ca. 1900. Lithographic poster in very good condition, linen-mounted, 41″ × 55″. (See other price listings for Pal under Cycle Posters in "Travel and Transportation Posters.") $800–$1,300

Palais Royal. Lithographic poster in fine condition, linen-mounted, 39½ × 54″. $1,400–$1,600

Rayon d'Or. Lithographic poster depicting a diaphanously clad beauty hanging from a star, lit by her new gas lamp. Fine condition, linen-mounted, 37″ × 47″. $1,100–$1,300

RENÉ PÉAN (1875–?)

Le Figaro. Lithograph printed by Chaix, signed in the stone. Man in bull-fighter costume, women reading paper *Le Figaro;* in red, pink, green, yellow. Fine condition, a very good example of the artist's style, linen-mounted, 33¼″ × 48½″. $800–$1,000

Mlle. George. Lithographic poster in very good condition, 25″ × 35½″. $275–$350

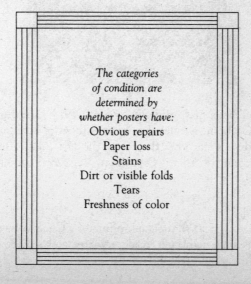

The categories of condition are determined by whether posters have: Obvious repairs Paper loss Stains Dirt or visible folds Tears Freshness of color

Moulin Rouge, 1905. Chéret-like quintet of fashionably dressed Parisians riding the turn-of-the-century roller-coaster. Good condition, linen-mounted, 33″ × 48″. $800 *(Auction)*

Shakespeare, 1899. Lithographic poster in good condition, 24″ × 31½″. $450–$500

HENRI RAPIN

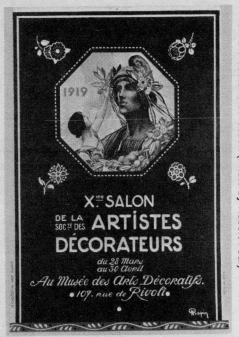

From the author's collection (Photo by Robert Four)

X.me Salon de la Soc. des Artistes/Décorateurs, 1919. Lithographic poster printed by Cachoin. Rendered in various tones of blue and red with white lettering, a patriotic theme for the first salon after the war, which led to the 1925 Paris Exposition. Very good condition, linen-mounted, 31″ × 46″. $600–$650

RENE RAVO

Mazda Perle, ca. 1930. Lithograph printed by Champrosay, signed in the stone. A huge lightbulb inside a yellow and red jewelbox. Fine condition, linen-mounted, 45″ × 61″. $600–$700

MANUEL ROBBE (*1872–1936*)

L'Eclatante, 1895. Lithographic poster printed on two sheets by Bourgère et Cie., Paris. Good condition, linen-mounted, framed, 37″ × 51½″. $2,500–$2,750

ROBYS

Premier Fils, 1936. Lithographic poster showing three horses racing a woman in a flowing drape who rides a winged wheel holding up a liquor bottle. Fine condition, horizontal 75″ × 50″. $700–$800

GEORGES ROCHEGROSSE (*1859–1938*)

Automobile-Club de France, ca. 1901. Lithographic poster printed by L. Barreau, Paris. (Several posters by this artist are under the price listings for French Opera Posters in this chapter.) Good condition, linen-mounted, framed, 33½″ × 37″. $850 (Auction)

G. ROCHETTE

L'Art à l'École, 1931. Lithographic poster for children's art exposition show. Stylized, three children work in a garden. Mint condition, 26″ × 35″. $200–$250

J. ROSETTI

La Raphaelle–Liqueur Bonal, 1908. Lithographic poster showing a waiter reaching up after his bottle of Bonal as it is lassoed by a man flying by in an airplane. Fine condition, 47″ × 60″. $550–$600

ST. LORELL

Adoptez le Bonal—Comme Dolly Davis, ca. 1925. Offset-printed poster showing a black and white photo of Dolly Davis, with a bottle of Bonal in one hand and a glass in the other, with a border of orange and black. Very good condition, 45″ × 60″. $350–$400

SEM (AKA SERGE GOURSAT, *1863–1934*)

Paulus, 1891. Very fine lithograph printed by Chaix from the early Sem design of the entertainer full-figure with top hat in hand. A lovely Belle Epoque entertainment poster in a large format. Very good condition, linen-mounted, 33″ × 71″. $1,200–$1,800

SEP (AKA SEVERO POZZATI, 1895–?)

Anic Cigarettes, 1938. Lithographic poster printed by Creation Idea, St. Ouen. Cassandre-like depiction of a dove to promote the mildness of filtered cigarettes. Good condition, linen-mounted, 38″ × 58″.

$800–$900

THEOPHILE-ALEXANDRE STEINLEN (1859–1923)

Courtesy of Arts of the Floating World

Ambassadeurs/Yvette Guilbert, 1894. Lithograph signed in the stone. Shows Yvette Guilbert, one of the greatest singers of the period, on stage in her typical attire, with long black gloves; audience in the background; in orange, black, tan, red, and blue. Fine condition, an excellent example of the artist's style, linen-mounted, 31½″ × 71¼″.

$9,000–$12,000

Chat Noir, 1896. Lithograph printed by Charles Verneau, Paris. A black cat as the central part of the design; used to announce the forthcoming entertainment programs for the famous cabaret Chat Noir. Steinlen's fascination with cats is evident in many of his posters and paintings. Fine condition, an excellent example of the artist's style, linen-mounted, 15¼″ × 21″.

$4,500–$5,500

Exposition de Peintures, 1903. Lithographic poster printed on tan paper, by Ch. Wall and Cie., Paris. Good condition, with some creases along the margins, linen-mounted, framed, 37⅛″ × 54⅛″.

$1,100 (Auction)

Lait pur Stérilisé de la Vingeanne, 1894. Lithographic poster. One of Steinlen's most celebrated works, charming in its candid simplicity and humor. This popular image secured Steinlen a position as a premier illustrator, along with his famous *Chat Noir* and *Mothu et Doria*. Good condition, linen-mounted, framed, 36″ × 52″. (See color center section.)

$7,500–$15,000

Lait pur Stérilisé, 1897. Lithograph from *Les Maîtres de l'Affiche* (see more information on *Les Maîtres* in this chapter under Special Focus: Jules Chéret) with the blindstamp of the publisher, Chaix. Very good condition, framed, 9″ × 12½″.

$500 (Auction)

Le Locataire, 1913. Lithographic poster depicting a sympathetic strong social statement about a displaced family. Fair condition, discoloration, creasing, and soiling, 18-inch stain along edge 1 inch into image, linen-mounted, 47″ × 63″.

$2,000 (Auction)

Courtesy of Arts of the Floating World

Le Petit Sou, 1900. Lithographic poster for the socialist newspaper *The Little Penny.* Depicts Marianne with broken shackles, leading a group of workmen to storm the Bastille of capitalism and the position of the church; in shades of black, reds, oranges, and yellows. Fine condition, a very good example of the artist's social style, linen-mounted, 39½" × 54¾". $3,500–$4,000

Courtesy of Arts of the Floating World

La Traite des Blanches, 1899. Lithographic poster for *The White Slave Trade,* a novel serialized in *Le Journal,* a late 19th-century Parisian magazine. Shows three victims reacting to their situation in different ways; in greens, reds, oranges, browns, and blues. (See additional works by Steinlen under "World War Posters.") Fine condition, an excellent example of the artist's style, linen-mounted, 48" × 73¼".
$7,000–$8,000

TAMAGNO FRANCISCO (1851–?)

Cachou Lajaunie. Lithograph printed by B. Sirven. Woman in foreground, six men in background, in green and orange. Mint condition, linen-mounted, 38¾″ × 51¼″. $850–$900

Terrot & Cie. Lithographic poster printed by la Lithographie Parisienne, Robin de Paris. Man and woman biking in the mountains; in blue, green, brown, and red. Mint condition, linen-mounted, 38½″ × 54″. $1,200–$1,500

HENRI THIRIET

Courtesy of Arts of the Floating World

Exposition de Blanc à la Place Clichy, 1898. Lithographic poster in fair condition, linen-mounted, 37″ × 51½″. $1,800–$2,000

Omega Cycles, ca. 1897. Lithographic poster in good condition, linen-mounted, framed, 24¼″ × 37″. $1,400 (*Auction*)

HENRI DE TOULOUSE-LAUTREC (1864–1901)

Bruant au Mirliton/Bock 13 Sous, 1893. Lithographic poster advertising entertainer Aristide Bruant for shows in his Montmartre night club Le Mirliton; in black and red. A rear view shows him in boots, a suit, and a large-brimmed hat. Fine condition, linen-mounted, 23⅝″ × 32⅜″. $10,000–$15,000

Courtesy of Arts of the Floating World

532

The Chap Book, 1896. Lithographic poster commissioned by Stone & Kimball, the Chicago publisher of *The Chap Book;* illustrating "The Irish American Bar" in Paris, depicts a bartender serving two customers, one of whom is thought to be a well-known coachman of the aristocracy. In vibrant tones of blue, tan, yellow, mauve. Fine condition, a very good example of Lautrec's work, linen-mounted, horizontal 23¾" × 16⅛". $25,000–$35,000

Jane Avril, 1893. Lithographic poster printed by Chaix, depicting the performer dancing on stage in a yellow and orange dress, framed by a design proceeding from the neck of a cello. Very good condition, an excellent example of the artist's work, 36½" × 51". $40,000–$45,000

Moulin Rouge, 1891. Lithographic poster printed by Ch. Levy. The juxtapositioning of "La Goulue" with her swirling petticoat, Valentin le Desosse in his high-hat, the floorboards and lamplights of the famous Montmartre night spot, the patrons, the intriguing calligraphy, as well as the bold use of spattered blacks, yellows, reds, purples, and blues made for a poster that defied challenge by the great poster artists of his time. Fine condition, the most sought after of all Lautrec's works, linen-mounted, 48½" × 77½". (See color center section.) $200,000–$250,000

La Revue Blanche, 1895. Lithographic poster for an artistic and literary periodical published in Paris between 1891 and 1903; depicts a well-dressed Parisienne with muff and plumed hat ice skating. One of the best known of Lautrec's posters. Fine condition, a very good example of Lautrec's style, linen-mounted, 36″ × 50″. $25,000-$30,000

A. TRINQUIER-TRIANON

Griffon. Lithograph printed by Imp. du Griffon, signed in the stone. Man on motorcycle, race in the background. Gold background. Fine condition, linen-mounted, 41½″ × 55½″. $500-$650

EUGENE CHARLES PAUL VAVASSEUR (1863-?)

Compagnie des Wagons-Bars, 1898. Lithographic poster in mint condition, linen-mounted, 35″ × 48½″. $1,100-$1,300

BERNARD VILLEMOT (1911-1989)

Arts Ménagers/Grand Palais. Design features a snail with a chimney on its back; in red, blue, yellow, orange, green, and gray on a black field. An early pupil of Paul Colin, Villemot has emerged as the premier poster artist in Paris today. (See additional listings for Arts Ménagers posters by French artist Francis Bernard.) Very good condition with the top left corner chipped, 47″ × 63″. $350-$400

Bally, 1975. Offset poster with elegant design featuring golden-haired girl whose black dress blends with the black background while her long legs show off her pink Bally slippers. Fine condition, 47″ × 63″.
$800–$1,000

Bally. Offset poster with sensuous design in yellow, blue, black, and two tones of deep red. Good condition, linen-mounted, 46″ × 62″.
$700–$900

C. VILLOT

Au Grand Pasteur/Meubles Decoration. "Late Deco" design combining Constructivist and Deco lines with pleasing, soft pastel colors; in dark blue, light blue, mint green, orange, yellow, brown. Fine condition, 47″ × 62″.
$400–$600

EDOUARD VUILLARD (1868–1940)

Album d'Estampe Originales, 1899. Lithograph designed as the cover for a proposed collection of prints to be published by Roger Mars and Andre Marty which was never published. Very good condition, 17⅜″ × 22¾″.
$4,000–$6,000

FRENCH OPERA POSTERS

Note: *See the chapter "Important Notes on the Price Listings" for more information on prices given. The reference numbers which follow some of the titles below are posters illustrated in Lucy Broido's book* French Opera Posters *(see Bibliography).*

ANONYMOUS

La Fille de Fanchon, ca. 1880. Sepia-tone lithographic poster with images of characters from the four-act comic opera with music by Louis Varney (1844–1908). Very good condition, 22″ × 31″.

$175–$225

Le Papa de Francine, ca. 1900. (Broido #49) Charming lithographic poster, possibly by Alfred Choubrac (1853–1902), for the four-act Louis Varney operetta at the Théâtre Cluny. Depicts a gay crowd of clowns, dancers, an equestrienne, and others. Very good condition, linen-mounted, 24″ × 31″.

$200–$250

Courtesy of Poster Mail Auction Company

Surcouf, ca. 1915. Lithograph printed by Edw. Ancourt & Cie. Depicting a scene from the three-act comic opera with music by R. Plancette. Good condition, linen-mounted, 23″ × 31″.

$250–$300

Suzanne, ca. 1880. Delicately rendered black and white lithograph for romantic opera with music by E. Paladilhe. Very good condition, with minor foxing at edges, 22″ × 30″. $200–$225

Vendée, ca. 1900. Sepia-type image for lyric drama in three acts with music by Gabriel Pierne. Very good condition, linen-mounted, 25″ × 35″.   *$150 (Auction)*

EMILE BERTRAND

Cendrillon, 1899. (Broido #35, used on the cover of the book) Lithograph printed by Devambez for an opera with text by Henri Cain and music by Jules Massenet (1842–1912). Stunning Art Nouveau design for the "conte de fées" or "fairy tale" of Cinderella. One of the best French Art Nouveau opera posters of the era. A wide range of prices was reported on this poster, some as high as $1,400. Below, a more general price range, mint condition, 24″ × 31″. (See color center section.) $500–$700

JACQUES BLOUIN

Girofle-Girofla, ca. 1890. For the Light Opera by Charles Lecocq at the Théâtre de la Gaité, a vignette of a medieval court scene. Good condition, restorations evident, linen-mounted, 35″ × 47″.

                    $200–$250

GEORGES DOLA

La Chauve-Souris (Die Fledermaus) (1872–?), ca. 1910. (Broido #47) Lithograph for the Strauss operetta (text by Paul Ferrier) at the Théâtre des Variétés. Shows a crowd of elegant people at Prince Orloffsky's ball in the second act. Very good condition, 23¼″ × 31½″.

                    $650–$750

All price ranges represent the retail value.

MAURICE DUFRENE

Courtesy of Bernice Jackson

Rayon des Soieries (Silk Department), 1930. (Broido #17) Art Deco-designed lithograph printed by Chaix for an operetta with text by Nino and music by Manuel Rosenthal (1904–?), which takes place in a department store. Stylized woman with arm outstretched, draped with bolts of silk. Original printed in black, white, and shades of gray with a single fold of pink silk and one in green. Unfortunately, many forgeries were released on the market a few years ago. The easiest way to notice is that in the forgery there is more than one green-tinted fold of silk. Fine condition, mounted on linen, 31″ × 46″.

$800–$1,000

HENRI GRAY (AKA HENRI BOULANGER, 1858–1924)

Mam'zelle Boy-Scout, 1915. (Broido #29) Lithograph printed by Delanchy et Fils for a three-act operetta with text by Paul Bonhomme and music by Gustave Goublier (?–1926). Depicts a woman in Boy Scout uniform and heeled pumps saluting, surrounded by sketches of scenes from the production. Fine condition, linen-mounted, 27″ × 35″.

$250 (Auction)

MAURICE LELOIR (1853–1940)

Courtesy of Poster Mail Auction Company

Cigale, 1904. (Broido #37) Lithograph printed by Devambez for a ballet with music by Jules Massenet. The image and colors convey the icy-cold feeling of the scene in which generous Cigale, having given away all her worldly goods, begs to be let in from the cold. Fine condition, 22″ × 36″. $450–$550

P. MAVRON

La Femme de Narcisse, ca. 1890. Lithographic poster for the three-act operetta with music by Louis Varney and text by Fabrice Carré. Full-length figure of a woman in 1890s' costume standing in front of a flower-bordered screen. Good condition, 22″ × 32″. $200–$250

PAL (AKA JEAN DE PALÉOLOGUE, 1860–1942)

Les Fetards, 1897. (Broido #44) Lithographic poster after a design by Pal, printed by E. Delancy, Paris. For the operetta *Les Fetards*, text by Antony Mars and Maurice Hennequin, music by Victor Roger (1854–1903), at the Théâtre du Palais Royal. Depicts a voluptuous woman dancing in a revealing pink dress. Very good condition, linen-mounted, framed, 23″ × 30¾″. $600–$800

Sapho. Lithograph printed by F. Hermet for the opera by Jules Massenet starring Emma Calvé at the Théâtre de l'Opera Comique. Woman with black hair in black dress; in red, black, blue with yellow background. Good condition, linen-mounted, 39½" × 55½".

$600–$800

RENÉ PÉAN (*1875–?*)

Le Fiancé de Thylda, ca. 1910. (Broido #51) Lithograph printed by Chaix. For the Louis Varney operetta with text by Victor de Cottens and Robert Charvay at the Théâtre Cluny. Depicts a pensive man seated in front of a party scene. Very good condition, linen-mounted, 23" × 33".

$275 (*Auction*)

GEORGES ROCHEGROSSE (*1859–1938*)

Antar, 1921. (Broido #23) Lithograph printed by Maquet. For a four-act opera about the 6th-century warrior-poet Antar, the Arabian embodiment of chivalry, text by Chekri Ganmen with music by Gabriel Dupont. Shows a helmeted Antar on his horse in front of a mountain range. Fine condition, linen-mounted, 27" × 35".

$400–$500

Don Quichotte, 1910. (Broido #41) Lithograph printed by Ed. Delanchy. For the opera by Jules Massenet with text by Henri Cain. Depicts Don Quixote and Sancho Panza riding up the mountain against a backdrop of blue hills and a colorful sky. Fine condition, cited by Broido as an excellent example of the intense crayon-like character of lithography, 27" × 35½".

$600–$750

Louise, 1900. (Broido #22) Lithograph printed by Ed. Delanchy & Cie. For the opera by Gustave Charpentier (1860–1956) at the Opéra Comique. Shows two lovers embracing with the lights of Paris in the background. Mint condition, 25" × 35½".

$400–$500

THEOPHILE-ALEXANDRE STEINLEN (*1859–1923*)

Le Rêve, 1890. (Broido #28) Lithograph printed by Gillot, Paris, published by G. Hartmann and Cie., Paris. For the ballet, choreography by J. Hansen, music by Leon Gastinel. A giant fan with the goddess Isanami, who leads the heroine into a dream experience, at the top; in rich grays, green, ochre, and orange. A wide range of prices was reported on this poster, some as high as $1,100. Below, a more general price range, mint condition, linen-mounted, 25" × 35".

$450–$600

BELGIAN POSTERS

The tiny country of Belgium holds an important niche in the history of the poster, but before 1890 it had few notable illustrated posters. However, tied to France both culturally and commercially, Belgium would soon discover the talents of Chéret, who exhibited in Brussels in 1890.

The art world in Belgium was flourishing in the 1890s, and most of the artists belonged to one of several "circles" or artists' societies. One of the most influential of these circles was called "The Twenty." This group would later change their name to La Libre Esthetique (The Free Esthetic). In 1894 they started a magazine under the same name which promoted posters as a new art form.

Other publications and other circles were springing up as well, including *Pour L'Art* (For Art, 1891); *Le Sillon* (The Furrow, 1893); and *l'Art Idealiste* (Idealistic Art, 1896). Posters for these publications are among the most sought-after Belgian posters today. Many leading artists, including Theodore Van Rysselberghe (1862–1926) and Fernand Toussaint (1873–1956), created posters for these publications.

Toussaint was really a painter, and actually created only a few posters. In this way, he was like Henri de Toulouse-Lautrec in France. His posters were usually printed by the master lithographer O. de Rycker in Brussels. His first poster for *Le Sillon*, created in 1895, has a finely executed painterly feeling and Art Nouveau hand-lettering, and can sell for more than $20,000. His 1897 poster for *Café Jacqmotte* is a strikingly colorful work, and also sells in the same price range.

Starting in this cultural arena, Belgian posters would soon spread to other more commercial fields, as merchants began commissioning artists to execute posters. Despite its small size, Belgium was a very rich country, and had a colonial empire in the Congo and elsewhere. Large quantities of ivory were imported from Africa and used in luxurious bronze and ivory statues of the time.

If Toussaint was the Belgian Lautrec, Privat Livemont (1861–1936) is often considered to be the Belgian Alphonse Mucha. It should be noted, however, that his style, though similar in many ways to Mucha's, was not an imitation. In fact, the two artists were developing their art and their reputations almost simultaneously. Each was influenced by the Art Nouveau style, which reached its height of popularity around 1900. The style is characterized by its sinuous free-flowing lines, drawn mostly from nature. Women with long tendril-like hair, dragonflies, and vine-like plants were all popular Art Nouveau motifs, not only in graphics, but in furniture, glass, and other decorative arts.

Livemont studied in Paris, where he painted architectural decorations and stage designs. Although he started only in 1896, he was a prolific posterist and by 1900 he had created over 30 posters. For the most part, Livemont's posters use the female form (most often in profile), elaborate ornamentation, and a variety of color combinations to attract the viewer's eye. Unlike many artists who had skilled draftsmen render their work onto the lithographic stones, for the most part Livemont drew his designs on the stone himself, like Chéret. He often used the talented firms of J.-L. Goffart in Brussels or Van Leer in Amsterdam for printing his posters. Like Mucha, he also created decorative panels, printed like his poster images, but with little or no advertising text, for use as decorations in the home.

Livemont's work is very popular today, and he has a strong following of collectors. Many of his posters sell in the range of $3,000 to $8,000, but can sell for as much as $15,000 and higher. He created posters for numerous products, resorts, and manufacturers, including the liqueur Bitter Oriental, Cacao Van Houten, colognes, corsets, perfumes, and more.

Belgium is a country whose culture is really half Flemish and half French. The Flemish, until relatively recently, have been primarily the working classes, whereas the French tended to be the more highly educated and urban merchant classes. The proximity of Holland had an impact on artists whose roots were in Flanders or Zeeland.

The most outstanding Flemish artist of the period was Hendrick Cassiers (1858–1944). His best-known works promote shipping companies such as the Red Star Line (which became the Holland America Line) and the American Line, as well as for beach resorts and other subjects. He developed several favorite themes, and his scenes often include peasants in their traditional costumes. Favorites among collectors of Cassiers include his series of works for the Ostende-Dover Line in 1900, showing the early steamers that crossed the channel linking England and Belgian rail lines. In many of these, Flemish workers, smoking pipes and wearing fishing gear, stand on the shore watching the steamers arrive. His posters can often be found for under $1,000.

Henri Meunier (1873–1922) was another outstanding Belgian Art Nouveau artist. He participated in the Sillon exhibitions after about 1897, and developed a reputation for his posters for concerts and cultural events. His posters always have a quietness about them, and are almost meditative.

One of his most striking and desirable posters is from 1897 for Rajah coffee, which depicts an exotic-looking woman sipping her coffee against a plain background where only the steam makes lazy Art Nouveau swirls in the air. The colors reinforce the overall feeling with flat shades of tan, flesh, brown, and accents of green and red, applied in a manner reminiscent of Japanese prints.

Other Belgian artists of this early period to look for are: Emile Berchmans (1867–1947), Gisbert Combaz (1869–1941), Adolphe Crespin (1859–1944), Auguste Donnay (1862–1921), James Ensor (1860–1949), George Lemmen (1865–1916), Victor Mignot (1872–1944), Armand Rassenfosse (1862–1934), Felicien Rops (1833–1898), and Henry van de Velde (1863–1957).

After World War I, Belgian posters, like the French, had to change to fit a faster and more complex world where advertising was designed in a different manner. However, Belgian artists did not seem able to make the change. Posterists of the previous period continued to produce, but many created in styles that were less than progressive. Belgium did not even have a pavilion at the 1925 Paris *Exposition des Arts Décoratifs et Industriels Modernes*, from which the name "Art Deco" is derived.

The best "Belgian" posterist of the new era, and the leading exponent of the Art Deco style in Belgian posters, would come from Switzerland: Léo Marfurt (1894–1977). Moving to Belgium in 1927, he created an advertising agency, Les Créations Publicitaires, which he ran until 1957.

Like Cassandre's agency Alliance Graphique in France, Marfurt's agency created posters for many clients, products, and services such as Belga Cigarettes, Chrysler and Minerva automobiles, the English LNER, resorts, and a host of others.

In addition to Marfurt, some good poster designs of the period came from Francis Delamare, who also founded an advertising agency; Auguste Mambour (1896–1968); Milo Martinet; Lucien de Roeck (b. 1915); and others, including the country's leading surrealist painter, Rene Magritte (1898–1967).

From the 1930s until now, many of the best Belgian posters are for travel, fairs, and festivals. The Art Deco style continued to be used in Belgium through the 1950s, and posters from this period are now increasingly seen at shows. In addition, as the Flemish population increasingly entered the middle classes and the political and economic mainstream, more posters in Flemish were produced. Posters in the above categories generally cost $200 to $500.

WHERE TO GO TO SEE BELGIAN POSTERS

Look for Belgian posters anywhere there is a collection of French posters. Often, Belgian Art Nouveau posters by artists with French names have been included in poster collections of the period. One museum we identified that has a comprehensive collection of Belgian posters from 1890 to 1910 is the Zimmerle Art Museum at Rutgers University in New Brunswick, New Jersey. (See Resource Guide.)

REFERENCE WORKS

In 1970, during the resurgence of interest in Art Nouveau, a touring exhibition of works by Belgian artists entitled "La Belle Epoque" traveled to ten museums in the United States, featuring many of the early artists noted above. The catalog, with text by Yolande Oostens-Wittamer and published by International Exhibitions Foundation, serves as an excellent guide to early Belgian poster art. (See Bibliography.)

PRICE LISTINGS

Note: *See the chapter "Important Notes on the Price Listings" for more information on prices given.*

ANONYMOUS

Arlon Villeqiature Agréable, ca. 1895. For the Belgian State Railways; shows the town, at 460 meters of altitude in the Ardennes, where one can take the "cure from the air." Very good condition, linen-mounted, 25″ × 38″. $300–$350

Courtesy of Poster Mail
Auction Company

Binche-Mardi Gras, 1910. Richly colorful lithographic festival poster. Fine condition, 23″ × 39″. $300–$350

Courtesy of Poster Mail Auction Company

Bruxelles/Foire Internationale, 1950. Art Deco image of the Grand Palais which has housed the international exhibitions since 1935; in deep blue, gray, light blue, and orange. Good condition, linen-mounted, 24″ × 39″. $200-$250

Chemins de Fer et Paquebots de l'Etat Belge/Red Star Line, ca. 1907. Lithographic poster printed by O. de Rycker. Depicting a woman looking out to sea at the channel-crossing steamer, with full information given on ticket prices. Very good condition, linen-mounted, 19½″ × 20″. $800–$900

Exposition Internationale de Bruxelles, 1897. Lithographic poster in Art Nouveau style, subtitled "Science Art Industrie"; in quietly muted tones of blue, yellow, red, green, and black, very good condition, linen-mounted, 28″ × 39″. $400–$600

Jaarbeurs der Vlaanderen, ca. 1948. Offset-printed poster in Flemish for Belgian Industrial Fair; in red, orange, black on a green field. Good condition, 22″ × 32″. $200–$250

Le Destructeur/Le Meilleur Papier/Tue-Mouches, ca. 1895. Lithographic poster depicting an elegant lady and her maid admiring the effectiveness of fly paper. Good condition, folio folds, 26″ x 37″.

$450–$500

Le Zoute/Jardin de la Mer du Nord. Early photomontage poster with graphic design for the Belgian sea resort. Stylized lettering and a flag fluttering overhead with a huge "Z." Very good condition, plain paper, 25″ × 39″. $250–$300

L'Impérforable Belge, ca. 1900. Lithographic poster of man in bathing suit pointing to the bicycle tube product. Red, blue, black, and flesh tones on a yellow field. Very good condition, 25″ × 33″.

$250–$300

29e Foire Internationale de Bruxelles, 1955. Offset poster depicting a colorful international display of flags against a white field with a large hand holding up one finger, indicating that the Brussels Fair is #1. The Grand Palais tops the design. Very good condition, 45″ × 62″.

$200–$250

EMILE BERCHMANS (1867–1947)

La Lampe Belge/Fourneau Belge, 1897. Lithographic poster printed by A. Besnard, Liege. Depicting a mother and two children enjoying the light of their new "inexplosible" gas lamp; in yellows, light red, orange, blue, and browns. Very good condition, linen-mounted, 27¾" × 40⅜". $1,000–$1,500

HENRI CASSIERS (1858–1944)

Red Star Line, ca. 1917. Lithographic poster depicting two men in traditional fishing outfits looking out to the channel where a steamer is heading into shore. Very good condition, horizontal 44½" × 60".
$1,000–$1,200

Red Star Line, ca. 1915. Lithographic poster depicting a woman and two children walking along the sea. In the distance, two steamers pass one another. Rich colors, good condition, 24" × 28". $900–$1,000

GISBERT COMBAZ (1869–1941)

La Libre Esthétique, 1899. Chromolithographic poster printed by J.-L. Goffart. Announcing the annual salon at the Musée Moderne. An elaborate design, reminiscent of Will Bradley, of a fruit tree, leaves, and a rising sun with patterned rays. Fine condition, 17⅔" × 29".
$2,800–$3,000

ADOLPHE LOUIS CHARLES CRESPIN (1859–1944)

Exposition d'Art Ancien Bruxellois. Lithographic poster printed by Ct. Gouweloos & Cie. Good condition, 33¾" × 49½". $1,200–$1,400

Paul Hankar Architecte. Lithograph, originally printed by Ad. Mertens, from *Les Maîtres de l'Affiche* (see more on *Les Maîtres* in the chapter on "French Posters") with the blindstamp of the publisher, Chaix. Depicts the architect smoking, working at his desk; elaborate patterned background in bistre, gray, red, and greens. Very good condition, framed, 9" × 11¾". $450 (Auction)

Same as above, but the original poster. Fine condition, mounted on Japan paper, 16" × 21⅝". $7,000–$8,000

JULIAN KEY

36e Internationale Jaabeurs Brussel, 1963. Offset-printed poster striking in its use of bold flat colors in green, yellow, red, and black. Depicts the profile of a man with a globe of the world as his eye and the Brussels expo center in his hat brim. Very good condition, plain paper, 23″ × 39″. $150–$200

PRIVAT LIVEMONT (1861–1936)

Absinthe Robette, 1896. Lithographic poster in yellow, flesh, reddish-brown, light blue, and dark green. Showing a young woman in a see-through veil holding up a glass of absinthe. This was a very successful poster, published in an edition of 500. Ten years afterwards, in 1906, Belgian law forbade the sale or use of absinthe. Very good condition, 33″ × 44″. $4,000–$6,000

Courtesy of Butterfield & Butterfield

Bitter Oriental, 1897. Lithographic poster printed by J.-L. Goffart in ochre, red, blue, and black. Advertisement for a liqueur made from herbs and gin. Fine condition, linen-mounted, 33½″ × 44″.
$2,500–$3,000

Cabourg, 1896. Lithographic poster printed by P. Lemenil, Asnieres. A railroad poster to lure Parisians to the seaside resort of Cabourg. Good condition, minor creases, linen-mounted, framed, horizontal 43⅛″ × 29½″. (See color center section.) $3,250 *(Auction)*

Cabourg, 1896. Lithograph from *Les Maîtres de l'Affiche* (see more information on *Les Maîtres* in the chapter on "French Posters") with the blindstamp of the publisher, Chaix. Good condition, framed, 7½" × 11¼". $650 (Auction)

Cacao Vanhouten, 1897. Lithographic poster printed by L. Van Leer, Amsterdam, subtitled in French "The best chocolate to consume as a liquid." Maiden with elaborate flowered headdress enjoys her steaming chocolate; in yellow, blues, gray, and flesh. Very good condition, linen-mounted, 25⅛" × 60" (this poster also was printed in smaller versions). $5,000–$6,000

Rajah, 1899. Lithographic poster for Rajah coffee. An elaborately dressed woman shown in profile with her long hair holds up a tiny cup of coffee from which steam curls up to form the word "Rajah" in the air; in reds, blue, olive green, yellow, and black. Very good condition, linen-mounted, horizontal 17" × 29". $6,000–$8,000

MAJORELLE

Tanger, 1924. Lithographic poster showing people in North African costume, sailing vessels in the harbor, and a stylized town in the background. Very good condition, linen-mounted, 29" × 41". $800–$900

LEO MARFURT (1894–1977)

Bruxelles Exposition Universelle, 1935. Lithographic poster using Belgian national colors—black, red, and aqua—as the backdrop for Atlas carrying the world. Designed for the 1935 World's Fair. Good condition, linen-mounted, 46" × 62". $1,000–$1,500

MILO MARTINET

F/N, ca. 1930. Lithographic poster for Fabrique Nationale, the Belgian auto maker. Depicts a speeding dark blue limo, with the F/N emblem in black and red. Very good condition, linen-mounted, 32" × 47". $800–$1,000

HENRY MEUNIER (1869–1942)

Amueblements, 1897. Lithographic poster printed by Renette, Brussels, for a furniture company. Good condition, minor creases, linen-mounted, 22¼" × 13½". $700–$800

Rajah, 1897. Lithographic poster for Rajah coffee, printed by J.-E. Goosens, Brussels. Depicting an exotic-looking woman drinking coffee while the steam rises in lazy Art Nouveau swirls. In browns, tan, flesh, red, and green. Very good condition, linen-mounted, horizontal 30″ × 24″. $4,000–$5,000

THEODORE VAN RYSSELBERGHE (1862–1926)

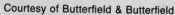

Courtesy of Butterfield & Butterfield

La Libre Esthétique, 1897. Lithographic poster printed by Vve. Monnom, Bruxelles, in yellow, red, orange, and blue. Designed to announce a salon, depicting a woman reading the arts publication. Very good condition, 26½″ × 36¾″. $3,500–$4,000

All price ranges represent the retail value.

FERNAND TOUSSAINT (1873–1956)

Bruxelles, 1931. Colorful street fair scene with people in Renaissance costume, announcing the 12th Commercial Fair. One of his less interesting post–World War I designs, Toussaint's image of the herald ringing the bell was nonetheless used for many posters advertising the annual fair from the 1920s up to the present. Very good condition, linen-mounted, 47″ × 63″. $400–$500

Le Sillon, 1895. Lithographic poster printed by O. de Rycker in pale blue, pink, yellow, and black. A young winged girl personifies Glory, standing in a field holding a shaft of wheat and a sickle. Very good condition, one of the most sought-after Belgian posters, linen-mounted, 32⅛″ × 42⅛″. $23,000–$30,000

DUTCH POSTERS

By Bernice Jackson

Bernice Jackson is a Fine Arts Consultant, offering a wide range of posters, and specializing in posters of several countries such as Austria, Holland, Switzerland, Hungary, and Poland. She is the author of numerous articles on posters, and is the U.S. Representative of The Print and Publicity Foundation of Amsterdam. Call or write: P.O. Box 1188, Concord, MA 01742. (508) 369–9088.

While many aspects of Dutch arts are known, appreciated, and collected throughout the world, Dutch poster art, while of the same quality and distinction, has remained relatively unknown until recently. Dutch art from Rembrandt to Van Gogh has always been a staple of museum shows. However, it was not until November 1986 that a comprehensive collection of Dutch posters was assembled for exhibition in the United States.

The exhibit, entitled "The Modern Dutch Poster," was organized by the Print and Publicity Foundation (Stichting Prent and Publiciteit) of Amsterdam, and supported by the Royal Dutch Government and a few major Dutch corporations.

This rich and diverse show of vintage Dutch posters was on loan primarily from two Dutch collectors, Werner Löwenhardt and Martijn Le Coultre. Their painstakingly assembled, comprehensive collections allowed viewers to witness the great range of styles, subjects, and techniques that make Dutch posters a captivating subject of study.

Curated by Stephen Prokopoff, Director of the Krannert Art Museum at the University of Illinois, it toured nine U.S. museums through January 1989, closing at the Cooper Hewitt in New York. It was met with critical acclaim by both the art-viewing public and the press. The accompanying book, *The Modern Dutch Poster: The First Fifty Years*, was published by MIT Press and provides an excellent overview (see Bibliography).

The result of this exhibition was a major increase of interest in lithographic Dutch poster art. The positive response indicated that the enormous contributions of Dutch poster art are beginning to take their rightful place in the history and chronology of great posters of the world.

The Netherlands was, and still is, frequently crisscrossed by travelers from many countries. From the 1890s through the 1940s, it was a meeting ground for important European design movements which are reflected in its poster art. Art Nouveau, Arts and Crafts, Futurism, Expressionism, and Art Deco all had their heyday and their artistic champions in Holland. In addition, the De Stijl design movement, an important precursor to the Modern style, found its expression in posters designed with typographic elements.

In Holland, the earliest leading poster artists were Jan Toorop (1858–1928) and R. N. Roland-Holst (1868–1938). These artists were akin to Renaissance men, working in many different art forms.

Both Toorop and Holst studied at the Riijksakademie, Amsterdam, and had interests including painting, architecture, furniture design, city planning, and print making, as well as in poster art. One of Toorop's most memorable pieces is a 1919 color lithograph, promoting a play entitled *Pandorra* by Arthur van Schendel. This theater poster, whose design is influenced by Cubism and Futurism, today can sell for as much as $25,000.

Theatrical posters are often more highly prized than those promoting products or other services. Another distinctive Dutch poster created for a theatrical event is *Chaliapine* by Joop Sjollema (b. 1900). Designed in 1932 for Boris Godounov and the Wagner Society of Amsterdam, it is highlighted in gold ink, and today sells for over $8,000.

An important artistic movement evolved in Holland that would affect Dutch poster art and the entire field of typography: the De Stijl design movement, which was influenced both by the Vienna Secession and the Deutscher Werkbund. High prices are being realized today for De Stijl posters which make use of typography to achieve design goals.

For example, the poster *Architectuur—Frank Lloyd Wright*, by H. Th.

Wijdeveld (b. 1885), sold for as little as $4,000 a few years ago but today can bring as much as $19,000. This is due to both the reputation of Wijdeveld as one of the leading exponents of De Stijl design in graphics, and to the growing popularity of its subject. Created in 1931, it is lithographed in red, white, and black, and was created in 1931 for the first Frank Lloyd Wright exhibition in Holland. J. J. Hellendoorn (1878–1959) and Antoon Kurvers (1889–1940) are two other Dutch artists influenced by Wijdeveld.

Art Deco also had its heydey in Dutch poster art. Jacob (Jac.) Jongert (1883–1942) is a notable poster artist whose works evolved from an earlier style to commercial Deco-style advertising. Wim ten Broek (b. 1905), who created posters for Holland-America Line ocean liners, was influenced by the French poster artist A. M. Cassandre, who was himself commissioned by Holland-America and other Dutch companies. Other Dutch Art Deco artists include Jan Wijga (1902–1978) for KLM (Royal Dutch Airlines), and Johann von Stein (1896–1965) for Lloyd Lines.

Photomontage posters, created through a mixture of lithography and photographic printing processes, also had their champions in Holland. One fine example is Willem Gispen's (1890–1981) poster for Giso lamps.

In 1923, Jongert wrote the following: "Advertisement is the desire for growth that is in us all, the desire for continually different development and ever more perfect form in society. And because it is so at one with the supreme will to life, it surges up in ever new places and in continually different forms. . . ."

Advertisement is certainly, in part, the desire for growth. However, if Jongert's sublime optimism is no longer ours, he nevertheless put his finger on one of the reasons why art posters have exerted their great attraction: they satisfy our simple delight in visual images, but also afford teasing glimpses into the daily life, desires, and ideals of an epoch. At their best they can have the complexity of paintings, and they can communicate an infectious sense of the artist's pleasure in his task as it was expressed by Jongert in his paean to advertising.

Posters, by definition, are part of the general advertising medium, but the scope of their subject matter is enormous. In the earlier years of Dutch poster art, posters were created for the theater, musical events, exhibitions, and fairs, as well as product advertising. In later years, the social consciousness of the Dutch was also expressed in their poster art. Some of the social issues depicted in Dutch posters include campaigns against alcoholism, announcements of rehabilitation programs for ex-convicts, solicitations of funds for orphaned children, and drives to eradicate various diseases, including syphilis, tuberculosis, and cholera.

Political posters were also a potent force in the fabric of Dutch society, primarily those by Alfred Hahn, Sr. (1877–1918), and Alfred Hahn, Jr. There are also many examples of travel and transportation posters showing the Dutch countryside, or superb examples of KLM Air Travel, or Rotterdam-Lloyd Steamship Line to Sumatra-Java and other destinations of equal romance and interest.

Dutch cinema posters also have several rare movie posters. Extraordinary examples are of Marlene Dietrich in the *Blue Angel*, done in 1937, and a very rare poster for the Russian movie *Potemkin*, by Dolly Rudeman.

For someone wanting to begin a collection of Dutch posters, there are so many stunning examples of Dutch poster art that, once familiar with them, it will be hard to believe these posters have been overlooked.

Generally speaking, Dutch posters are smaller than their French counterparts. French posters were meant to be read at a distance on wide boulevards, whereas Dutch posters were often displayed in tiny streets or in the shop windows themselves. Like Art Nouveau posters, the earlier Dutch posters are harder to read at a glance than those that evolved in the Art Deco style, but are often visually distinctive in their complexity.

Vintage Dutch posters were lithographed in smaller editions than the posters of many other countries, making them less available and more subject to price increases as demand for them grows. Also Dutch poster artists are gaining more recognition and their names are becoming more familiar to the collecting field.

There are a host of artists worth collecting, some well known and many lesser known. While some of the best have captured the imagination of the collecting world and are already fetching high prices, many fine examples of Dutch poster art representing product advertising, fairs, theatrical entertainments, exhibits, and the like are still available for under $1,000. The prices of posters such as these will undoubtedly seem modest ten years from now, as the number of collectors continues to expand.

PRICE LISTINGS

Note: *See the chapter "Important Notes on the Price Listings" for more information on prices given.*

ANONYMOUS

Architectuur en Kunstnyverheid, 1927. Lithographic poster in a strong De Stijl typographic style, with letters against a central column of contrasting color; in cream, red, and blue. Fine condition, 23″ × 39½″. $800–$900

Architectuur Leerdam, 1927. Lithographic poster of a stylized castle, standing over a typographic design; in cream, red, and blue. Fine condition, 23″ × 39½″. $800–$900

Bond Voor Kunst in Industrie, 1935. Lithographic poster featuring a vase, bowl, and painting against a background of factories; in red, orange, green, and black. Fine condition, 19″ × 26″. $550–$650

Hulstkamp's, 1930. Lithographic poster featuring a gentleman walking away from a coach, its occupant, and two footmen; in red, blue, green, and beige. Good condition, 19″ × 29½″. $225–$350

Jaarbeurs Utrecht, 1923. Lithographic poster featuring Mercury climbing a stairway which recedes into a distant building; in orange and purple. Fine condition, 37″ × 41″. $1,400–$1,600

Kant Tentoonstelling, 1926. Lithographic poster utilizing typography within geometric forms; in cream, blue, and gray. Very good condition, 12″ × 21″. $450–$600

Lustrum-Leiden. Dramatic design with two figures standing atop a typographic design; in cream, black, and gray. Condition not noted, 33″ × 42¼″. $1,200–$1,300

Oud's Kinawijn Aperitif, 1919. Lithographic poster featuring a round liqueur bottle with a long neck, inside a square frame with an elaborate border; in gold, black, and white. Very good condition, 32″ × 43¾″. $900–$1,000

WILLEM ARONDEUS (1894–1943)

Den Hollandske Udstilling/Kobenhavn, 1922. Lithographic poster for the Dutch Exhibition in Copenhagen; in cream, browns, and black. Very good condition, 24¼″ × 33¼″. $700–$800

Kerst-Zegels, 1919. Lithographic poster with stylized figures, printed in gold, brown, and purple. Mint condition, 14″ × 23″. $650–$750

MEIJER BLEEKRODE (1896–1943)

De Roden Roepan, 1929. Lithographic poster depicting a worker rendered in a Cubist style against an equally angular factory building. Printed in red, brown, and white. Very good condition, 28″ × 37″.
$900–$1,000

CHARLES C. DICKSON

Royal Dutch Air Lines, 1928. Lithographic poster depicting a small airplane flying under the RDAL crest, with the subtitle "See twice as much of Europe in half the time"; in blues, red, and yellow. Condition not noted, 25½″ × 40″. $1,400–$1,600

AART VAN DOBBENBURGH (1899–1985)

Nationale Reclasseeringsdag, 1937. Lithographic poster with dramatic image of man's hands grasping the bars of a prison window while, beyond his reach, a tree blossoms; in gray, cream, and white. Very good condition, 31½″ × 43½″. $800–$900

ARJEN GALEMA (1886–1974)

Nationale Opera, ca. 1926. Lithographic poster featuring portraits of a Wagnerian Viking and a woman with a fan; in green, purple, and black. Fine condition, a very good example of opera advertising, 31″ × 42½″. $650–$750

FRANS TER GAST

Kunstkring, 1920. Lithographic poster. The bold stylized face of a man in close-up rendered even more striking by the typography, stacked in layers below the image. Printed in yellow and black. Very good condition, 29″ × 50″. $2,200–$2,400

LEO GESTEL (1881–1941)

De Flucht Uit Belgie, 1914. Lithographic poster depicting a host of refugees fleeing Belgium; in buff, black, and red. Good condition, 32″ × 41″. $1,500–$1,750

Jaarbeurs Utrecht, 1922. Lithographic poster, the head of Mercury, symbol of the Utrecht Fair, in close-up. Rendered in a stylized Art Deco manner and printed in beige, black, and gray. Very good condition, an excellent example of Gestel's work, 31″ × 42″.
                                        $2,700–$2,900

WILLEM H. GISPEN (1890–1981)

Courtesy of Bernice Jackson (Photo by Robert Four)

Giso Lampen, 1928. Stunning early photomontage poster for Giso lamps, rendered in eye-catching colors of red, black, and white. Fine condition, highly desirable, 27½″ × 39½″. $9,000–$10,000

ALBERT PIETER HAHN (1877–1914)

Hamlet, 1912. Lithographic poster depicting The Prince of Denmark standing between two pillars, clad in an ermine cloak, pondering his fate; in black and orange. Fine condition, 26″ × 39″. $900–$1,000

S.D.A.P., 1930. Lithographic poster depicting a large flag waving from a tower, echoed by four small figures waving small flags; in black, red, and cream. Very good condition, 27″ × 40″. $600–$800

S.D.A.P., 1930. Lithographic poster showing a large gentleman in a bowler standing at the door of an old woman's house with his hand out; in black, red, and cream. Very good condition, 25″ × 38″.

$600–$800

PIET VAN DER HEM (1885–1961)

Courtesy of Bernice Jackson (Photo by Robert Four)

Spyker Autos, 1910. Lithographic poster depicting a fashionable couple dressed for motoring and followed by their butler, carrying a suitcase, preparing to get into their automobile; in cream, black, and pink. Very good condition, 20″ × 28″. $1,600–$1,800

DAN HOEKSEMA

Tentoonstelling, 1920. Lithographic poster showing a worker pulling on a rope, in front of him a large lantern; in beige, brown, and purple. Fine condition, 25″ × 38″. $1,200–$1,400

PIETER A. H. HOFMAN (1885–1965)

Exhibition of Garden, 1927. Lithographic poster depicting a design of Art Deco letters against two different background colors; in cream and white. Very good condition, 24″ × 32″. $2,800–$3,000

Genealogisch Heraldisch, 1933. Lithographic poster depicting a lion rampant, sword in hand; in cream, gold, blue, and red. Fine condition, 25" × 35¼". $800–$900

Courtesy of Bernice Jackson
(Photo by Robert Four)

Jaarbeurs Utrecht, 1930. Lithographic poster showing a stylized figure of Mercury with abstract design and factories in the background; in red, black, and blue. Fine condition, 24" × 31". $3,800–$4,000

RAOUL HYNCKES *(1893–1973)*

Regatta, 1925. Lithographic poster of a stylized naked woman sitting with her back to the viewer, resting a pad on her knee and holding a pen in her hand; in yellow, purple, and orange. Very good condition, 31" × 43". $1,700–$1,800

H. JONAS

Tentoonstelling Maastricht, 1921. Lithographic poster showing a series of four stylized figures of varying sizes, each one being protected by the next larger one; in black and white. Condition not noted, 28" × 41½". $550–$650

JAC. JONGERT *(1883–1942)*

Apricot Brandy, 1920. Lithographic poster of a bottle of apricot brandy sitting within a stylized frame; in white, blue, black, and tan. Fine condition, 30½" × 39½". $3,500–$3,600

International Gas Exhibition, 1912. Lithographic poster depicting a muscular man holding a child in his arms within a detailed border, each of them holding a sphere in his hand; in red, orange, and black. Very good condition, 29″ × 59″. $6,000–$6,500

Volks, 1920. Lithographic poster depicting a stylized man striding purposefully forward, carrying a bag in his left hand; in cream, black, and gold. Fine condition, 34″ × 49″. $8,000–$9,000

OTTO VAN JUSSENBROEK

Museum van Kunstnyverhed, 1919. Lithographic poster with a design centering on a flower, with layers surrounding it and monograms at top and bottom; in cream, orange, black, and gray. Very good condition, 23″ × 33½″. $750–$850

ALBERT KLIJN

Regatta, 1919. Lithographic poster depicting a man working within a circle made of two trees whose roots and branches weave together; in black, tan, and brown, 34″ × 49″. $1,400–$1,500

WILLEM KLIJN

De Kunst in Nood, 1920. Lithographic poster of a candle burning in front of an artist's palette that has two paintbrushes through the thumbhole; in sepia, brown, and black. Fine condition, 37″ × 41″.
                    $750–$800

Regatta-Feest Park, 1919. Lithographic poster with a design featuring a harlequin; in blue, red, and yellow. Fine condition, 30″ × 42″.

$900–$950

HILDA KROP

Tentoonstelling Architectuur, 1935. Lithographic poster depicting three silhouetted workers in the center of the poster, above them a flying figure, below a block of text; in white, gray, and red. Very good condition, 25″ × 38″. $750–$850

CHRISTIAAN (CHRIS) LEBEAU (1878–1945)

The Wizard, 1914. Lithographic poster depicting a human form, its back to the viewer, facing an otherworldly form, their arms joined to form a large circle; in cream and black. Lebeau is one of the most sought-after Dutch artists. Very good condition, 35″ × 49″.

$14,000–$16,000

CAREL A. LION-CACHET (1864–1945)

Jaarbeurs/Utrecht, 1917. Lithographic poster of a very stylized figure with arms upraised, integrated into a complex design; in cream, blue, and red. Fine condition, 27″ × 40″. $1,800–$1,900

HUIB LUNS (1881–1942)

Recla, 1924. Lithographic poster of an angel blowing on her horn; in gold, white, and black. Fine condition, 30½″ × 47″.

$1,400–$1,500

MARTIN MONNICKENDAM

Collectie Goudstikker, 1918. Lithographic poster depicting a man in old-fashioned costume sitting at an easel, holding paintbrush and palette; in buff, black, and red. Very good condition, 33″ × 49″.

$650–$800

LOUIS RAEMAEKERS (1869–1956)

Jaarbeurs Utrecht, 1928. Lithographic poster of a naked Mercury pointing aloft; in white, gray, and red. Very good condition, 25″ × 42″.

$1,200–$1,300

Tegen de Tariefwet, 1919. Lithographic poster of a large hairy spider sitting in its web; in cream, black, and rust. Fine condition, 30″ × 39″. $1,800–$1,900

ARN. V. ROESTEL

Robert Bertram and Co., 1925. Lithographic poster depicting two men in evening dress, including top hats; in orange, beige, and burgundy. Very good condition, 31" × 42". $450–$600

Stoutertjes, ca. 1930. Lithographic poster depicting two comic figures, one a tall thin man with his clothes too small, the other a short squat man with bow legs and baggy clothes; in cream, greens, and black. Fine condition, 31" × 43". $400–$600

R. N. ROLAND-HOLST (1868–1938)

Baden Arbeid (Labor Boards), 1920. Lithographic poster picturing a worker inside the geometric borders is often found in Roland Holst's designs; in oranges, blue, and black. Very good condition, 31½" × 43¼". $3,800–$4,000

Electra, 1920. Lithographic poster depicting a girl sitting, gazing down, on a couch in front of a window; in sepia, brown, and black. Very good condition, 27" × 39". $2,600–$2,750

Lucifer, 1910. Lithograph. A dramatic theatrical poster of a man hanging above the fires of Hell; in sepia, rust, and black. Roland Holst designed the decor and costumes for the play as well as the poster. Very good condition, one of the best examples of the artist's work, 29" × 48½". (See color center section.) $14,000–$15,000

JOHANNES (JAN) ROS (1875–1952)

Blooker's Cocoa, 1895. Lithographic poster of two women, one seated, one standing, getting ready to enjoy some cocoa; a very elaborate border runs down the left side of the poster; in blue, white, yellow, and green. Fine condition, 23¾" × 34¼". $3,700–$3,800

GEORGE RUETER (1875–1966)

Bijbel Tentoonstelling, 1937. Lithographic poster of a detailed design centering around a fountain, above the words "Statenvertaling 1637–1937"; in cream, blue, and gold. Mint condition, 23" × 36". $1,100–$1,200

South Holland, 1918. Lithographic poster depicting a naked youth kneeling in profile, holding a pole; in red, beige, and blue. Fine condition, 31" × 45". $1,600–$1,800

Stevnt Het Werk, 1927. Lithographic poster of the head of a young girl surrounded by the wings of two angels standing on either side of her; in gray, white, and black. Very good condition, 25″ × 39½″.
$550–$700

WILLEM J. H. B. SANDBERG (1897–1984)

Aalot-Calder, 1955. Offset typographic poster, with "Gemeente Musea" running along the side; in ochre, green, and orange. Fine condition, 25″ × 39″.
$850–$900

Van Gogh Hondered Jaar, ca. 1955. Offset poster features a van Gogh painting, with text above and below; in cream, blue, and green. Fine condition, 28″ × 39″.
$650–$700

PAUL SCHUETEMA

Tentoonstelling Architectuur, 1972. Offset poster with a large "C" and "A" dominating, with the subtitle "CCCP/USSR 1917–1933"; in white, black, and red. Mint condition, 28″ × 39″.
$300–$350

SAMUEL LEVI SCHWARZ (1876–1942)

Arti et Amicitiae, ca. 1920. Lithographic poster depicting a female statue, headless and armless, standing in front of a picture frame and artist's palette; in white, black, blue, and yellow. Fine condition, 25″ × 32″.
$1,500–$1,600

Arti et Amicitiae, 1930. Lithographic poster of a strong graphic design, including a flower in the lower left and a bird in the center; in blue, yellow, red, and white. Very good condition, 24″ × 32″.
$1,100–$1,200

Kon, Ver, Ned, Tooneel, 1920. A stylized lithographic poster with a jester's cap in the foreground and waves in the background; in blue, orange, and cream. Very good condition, 31″ × 43″.
$1,600–$1,800

JOHAN (JOOP) SJOLLEMA (B. 1890)

Chaliapine/Boris Godounov, 1932. Lithographic poster designed for the Wagner Society of Amsterdam. A man in a long coat, his head in his hands, leans against a doorway, in the lower left corner the head of a violin; in white, black, and gray. Very good condition, one of the best posters by this artist, horizontal 48″ × 36″. $8,000–$9,000

Mozart, 1900. Lithographic poster for a Mozart concert conducted by Bruno Walter, depicts a bird in flight against a blue background; in blues, white, and gold. Very good condition, 32″ × 46″.

$1,600–$1,800

WILLY SLUITER (1873–1949)

Courtesy of Bernice Jackson
(Photo by Robert Four)

Laren Exhibition, 1915. Lithographic poster depicting a flirtatious, fashionably dressed woman standing between a painter and a violinist, all stylized figures; in black, white, flesh, and orange. Very good condition, 30″ × 43″. $3,800–$4,000

Naar Keulen, 1914. Lithographic poster of a fashionably dressed couple, the man carrying an overcoat and bag; in yellow, black, and green. Very good condition, 25″ × 33″. $2,500–$2,750

Pleines Zeepeu de Duif, 1910. Lithographic poster depicting an old woman in a checked cape and plumed hat holding open her shopping basket; in green, red, blue, and yellow. Fine condition, 28″ × 37″.

$1,800–$2,000

JAN SLUYTERS (1881–1957)

Dejordan, 1925. Lithographic poster depicting a stylish woman gazing into a young man's eyes, while in the foreground an older man smokes a pipe; in cream, blue, and yellow. Fine condition, 31″ × 47″.

$1,800–$1,900

JOHANN VON STEIN (1896–1965)

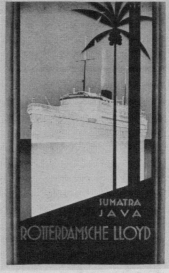

Rotterdamsche Lloyd, ca. 1930. Lithographic ocean liner poster advertising Sumatra and Java. White steamship with long reflection in water echoes elongated typeface. Very good condition, 18″ × 28½″.
$2,400–$2,800

J. TENHAVE

Gitob, 1925. Lithographic poster for the International Growers' Fair, a man carries a load on his shoulder, in the foreground a huge stalk of wheat; in blue, red, and green. Very good condition, 20″ × 33″.
$700–$800

JAN TH. TOOROP (1858–1928)

Arnhem, 1900. Lithographic poster depicting a standing woman giving her hand to a kneeling woman, both of them in long dresses; in yellow and brown. Very good condition, 32″ × 40″. $4,800–$5,000

Delftsche Slaolie (Delft Salad Oil), ca. 1895. Lithograph with stunning Art Nouveau-inspired design of two women in long flowing robes and tresses of hair that fill the image area; in yellow, purple, and white. Delft Salad Oil was one of the first great patrons of poster art in Holland. Very good condition, 27″ × 39″. $12,500–$14,000

Pandorra, 1919. Lithographic theatrical poster for the play by Arthur van Schendel, printed by S. Lankhout & Co., The Hague. A distinctive design with Cubist and Futurist influences. One of the most sought-after Dutch poster designs. 33″ × 44″. (See color center section.) $22,000–$25,000

IS VANMENS

Jarbeurs, 1927. Lithographic poster features portrait of a man in old-fashioned costume; in white, black, and olive. Fine condition, 30″ × 39″. $850–$900

Tentoonstelling, 1919. Lithographic poster depicting an artist, smoking a pipe, intently mixing paint on his palette; in cream, gray, and black. Fine condition, 31″ × 43¾″. $900–$1,000

GERARD VROOM

Moissi, 1930. Lithographic poster of a sinister face/mask with empty eyeholes looking out over a block of text; in black, gray, and gold. Very good condition, 34″ × 47″. $2,400–$2,500

WAGEMAKER

National Disarming, 1945. Lithographic poster with a stark design featuring a skull and a stylized man bound by rope; in gray, white, and black. Very good condition, 22″ × 33″. $550–$600

WIEGMAN

Herwonnen Levenskracht, 1920. Lithographic poster depicting the faces of two girls looking out from a field of flowers; in yellow and orange. Very good condition, 24″ × 36″. $900–$1,000

H. TH. WIJDEVELD (B. 1885)

Architectuur—Frank Lloyd Wright, 1931. Typographic poster in red, white, and black for the first Frank Lloyd Wright exhibition in Holland. Fine example of the De Stijl design influence in graphics and even more sought after because of the subject matter. Very good condition, 20″ × 30″. (See color center section.) $17,000–$19,000

International Theater, 1922. Very long lithographic poster depicting an actor on stage, arms outstretched, and a shaft of light rising into the form of a bird. Very good condition, 23″ × 55″. $4,500–$5,000

JAN WIJGA (1902–1978)

Royal Dutch Airlines, 1933. Lithographic poster cleverly subtitled "The Flying Dutchman—Fiction Becomes Fact." Depicts a four-propeller plane flying over the Dutch countryside while in the background a ghostly galleon sails; in purples, blues, and greens. Very good condition, 24¾″ × 39″. $1,400–$1,600

WILM WOUTERS

Boefje, 1935. Lithographic poster of a young man in tattered clothes, wearing a hat that is too large for him; in cream, black, and gray. Fine condition, 31″ × 46″. $900–$1,000

PIET ZWART (1885–1977)

Voeding in Dezen Tud, 1942. Lithographic poster of a plate, utensils, glass, and covered dish placed together to create a design on the right-hand side of the poster; in beige, red, and green. Very good condition, 26¾″ × 38¼″. $1,200–$1,300

AMERICAN ART POSTERS OF THE 1890s

By Joseph Goddu

Joseph Goddu is an Associate in the Department of American Prints, Hirschl & Adler Galleries, Inc., New York. A member of the American Historical Print Collector's Society, he is an avid collector who has written and lectured on American 19th-century prints. In addition to his background in fine art and art history, he has also worked as an offset press operator and acted as a liaison between contemporary artists and fine art presses in the production of artists' limited edition prints. Portions of this chapter are condensed from his American Art Posters *of the 1890s, a catalog that accompanied an exhibition held at Hirschl & Adler Galleries in the fall of 1989.*

Nearly a hundred years ago America was gripped by a collecting frenzy that would come to be dubbed the poster craze of the '90s. For a brief yet glorious period art posters advertising the literary publications of the day, by Will Bradley, Edward Penfield, Ethel Reed, John Sloan, Arthur Wesley Dow, Louis Rhead, and others became the most popular art form to collect and write about.

Collectors and museum curators today are rediscovering the attraction of the posters from this remarkable era and the secret to the appeal of this unique art form. Posters are designed to communicate forcefully with an economy of means. In this way they distill the aesthetic and philosophical aspirations of the artists who take up the medium, resulting in works of immense power and beauty. American poster designers of the 1890s are now being accorded the attention and acclaim that, until recently, had been reserved for their more familiar French counterparts, Chéret, Lautrec, Steinlen, and Bonnard. The collectors' market today for the American art posters of a century ago reflects this upsurge in interest.

THE BIRTH OF AN ART FORM

The father of the art poster was the Frenchman Jules Chéret (1836–1932), who in the 1870s single-handedly transformed the streets of Paris with the introduction of picture posters brimming with color. Businesses soon scrambled to find artists and lithographers who could provide them with posters equal to Chéret's. Where the sponsors of poster art in France had been the entertainment industries, however, American poster art would be championed by a burgeoning magazine and book publishing industry.

In 1890, the Grolier Club in New York held the first poster exhibition in America, comprised primarily of French posters. In September 1892, an article by Brander Mathews on "The Pictorial Poster" appeared in *The Century Magazine* and helped legitimize the art form in this country. Six months later, following the success of a Christmas poster designed by Eugene Grasset, *Harper's* decided to issue a new poster for each monthly issue of the magazine. But instead of commissioning another French artist, they turned to an art director on their staff.

Edward Penfield (1866–1925), who was born in Brooklyn and studied at the Art Students League, provided the inaugural poster for the April 1893 issue. The design was worked up at the last minute as "an experiment," in Penfield's words, and contained the basic elements that would characterize the more than sixty *Harper's* posters that followed from his hand. A single figure or pair of figures, unmistakably upper class, were carefully integrated with the letters spelling out *Harper's* and placed, very often, against a flat plane of color. Penfield's subjects were usually engaged in a leisure activity associated with the season of the particular issue, or a witty reference might be made to the weather associated with a particular month.

Penfield's 1893 designs for *Harpers*, widely considered the first American art posters, represented a radical departure from the old-style magazine advertisement, which was often simply a listing of the table of contents. His bold, colorful, and clever images gave an oblique testament to the sophistication and social status required of the *Harper's* reader and were most appreciated by precisely the segment of the public the magazine hoped to attract. Penfield also provided a number of fine designs advertising the books of Harper and Brothers, and his later calendar designs for R. H. Russell & Co. are among the masterworks of his mature style. After 1901, he continued a successful career as a commercial artist.

A CRAZE FOR POSTERS

By the end of 1893, other major publishing houses were jumping on the bandwagon, including J. B. Lippincott Co., Charles Scribner's Sons, and The Century Co. Some periodicals, such as *Lippincott's*, followed the lead of *Harper's* by hiring a single artist to provide their series of monthly posters. Will Carqueville (1871–1946) designed the posters for *Lippincott's* from December 1894 through 1895. Carqueville grew up in Chicago amid the smell of printer's ink and the din of the family printing presses. His poster designs for *Lippincott's* and the magazine *International* achieve bold effects with a limited number of colors, a facility born of his experience in commercial printing. Although in America his achievements were overshadowed by those of Edward Penfield and J. J. Gould, he earned considerable attention abroad. In 1896, the year he went to Paris to pursue his studies, ten of his works were included in a major poster exhibition held in Rheims. He returned to Chicago a few years later to continue a career in illustration and design.

In 1896 J. J. Gould (ca. 1875–ca. 1935) succeeded Carqueville at *Lippincott's*, and for the next two years he created monthly poster designs in direct competition with *Harper's*. Gould, who studied at the Pennsylvania Academy of the Fine Arts, made effective use of crayon texture effects and bold diagonal compositions. After 1900 he continued his commercial design work and provided a series of covers for the *Saturday Evening Post.*.

Other mainstream periodicals preferred to commission their advertisements from a number of different artists working in a variety of styles. Louis John Rhead (1857–1926) provided designs for *St. Nicholas*, *Scribner's*, *The Century Magazine*, and for the publications of Louis Prang & Co. He also designed posters for a number of newspapers, some of which reached billboard proportions. Born in England, Rhead received his training at the South Kensington Art School in London, where he was introduced to the philosophy and aesthetics of the English Arts and Crafts movement. He met Eugene Grasset in Paris in the early '90s and saw an exhibition of his work at the Salon des Cent, which proved a lasting influence upon him. Both men shared an admiration for the pre-Raphaelites and the artists Walter Crane and William Morris. Rhead was the only American to be honored with solo exhibitions in London (1896) and in Paris (1897, at the Salon des Cent). After 1900, he pursued a career in book illustration.

Maxfield Parrish (1870–1966), whose father was the painter-etcher Stephen Parrish, studied at the Pennsylvania Academy of the Fine Arts. He received many awards for his poster designs, most of which featured an androgynous figure type that became the trademark of his work. He executed commissions for a variety of publications, including *Scribner's*, *St. Nicholas*, *Harper's Weekly*, *The Century Magazine*, and the *Ladies Home Journal*. He went on to become one of the most popular illustrators and commercial designers of the early 20th century.

Two other notable artists provided outstanding designs for the larger publishing firms of the day. Elisha Brown (E. B.) Bird (1867–1943) earned a degree in architecture from M.I.T. in 1891, but then embarked upon a career as a commercial designer. In addition to his illustration work, he produced at least 16 posters for publications such as *The Century Magazine*, *The Chap Book*, and *The Red Letter*, and also executed designs for book covers and bookplates. The influence of Will Bradley is apparent in much of his work. Joseph Christian (J. C.) Leyendecker (1874–1951), who would come to be best known for his commercial design work between the wars, received immediate acclaim for his prizewinning entry in the 1896 poster contest sponsored by *The Century*. Following his training at The Art Institute of Chicago and the Academie Julien, Paris, he settled in Chicago for the closing years of the decade and provided designs for covers and posters for the *Inland Printer* and *The Chap Book*. In 1899 he decided to leave Chicago for the more favorable commercial opportunities in New York City.

The poster fad was in full swing by 1895, with many publishers printing extra copies of their monthly placards for sale to a burgeoning collector's market. *The Modern Poster*, the first American book about the new medium, was published in that year, and there were poster exhibitions in New York, Boston, Chicago, Denver, and elsewhere. The following year saw the birth of two periodicals, *The Poster* and *Poster Lore*, designed to cater to collectors in America and Canada. *The Poster*, in its inaugural issue, estimated the number of collectors at 7,000.

Magazine publishers were not the only ones to recognize the commercial possibilities of the art poster. The new form of advertising was also enthusiastically adopted by a host of private literary presses and "little magazines" that appeared in the early 1890s as an outgrowth both of the rise of literacy and the spread of the Arts and Crafts movement. The publication in 1891 of *The Story of the Glittering Plain*, by William Morris and his Kelmscott Press, along with the subsequent appearance on American bookstands of art journals such as *The Studio* and the *Yellow Book*, renewed interest in the printing arts and provided the inspiration for the founding of hundreds of small publishing ventures all across America. Most were started by idealistic young men who hoped to fulfill the Arts and Crafts ideal of integrating art and literature into everyday life by producing finely printed, affordable books and literary magazines. The use of artistic posters fell squarely within their philosophical aims and quickly became the primary means of advertising in an increasingly competitive market.

This sponsorship of poster design created a marriage of art and commerce which, at times, yielded spectacular results. Florence Lundborg (1871–1949) provided seven poster designs for *The Lark*, a San Francisco humor and literary magazine during 1895–1897. Her poster for the November 1895 issue is one of the masterpieces of American poster design and reveals the influence of her teacher, Arthur F. Mathews, a leader of the Arts and Crafts movement in California. Lundborg composed and cut most of her own designs in wood, achieving a satisfying unity of medium and Japanese design. After 1900 her career embraced mural painting, book illustration, and portraiture.

The Chicago journal *The Chap Book* was the best known of the little magazines, or "dinkey books," as they were also called. It was started in 1894 by a pair of Harvard students, Herbert Stone and Ingalls Kimball, on the eve of their graduation. Intended originally as a simple newsletter to advertise the books they published, it grew to include observations on contemporary literature and the arts scene. Unlike establishment magazines such as *Harper's*, *The Chap Book* could afford to be bolder in the designs used for advertising, and the posters Stone and Kimball commissioned for *The Chap Book* are among the most aesthetically daring works of the period.

Will Bradley (1868–1962), perhaps the most talented and original American artist to work in the poster medium, designed seven placards for *The Chap Book* during 1894–1895. Bradley's introduction to the printing arts came at the age of eleven, when he became a printer's helper for a weekly newspaper in the northern Michigan town of Ishpeming. He left for Chicago to apprentice as a wood engraver in 1885, but quickly outgrew the position and moved on to work in printing and design as well. By 1889, at the age of twenty-one, he had established himself as a freelance designer and illustrator. His early work, a series of posters for *The Inland Printer* and *The Chap Book*, reveals English influences, in particular that of Aubrey Beardsley. Bradley's posters, in their use of flowing line, asymmetrical compositions, and flat contrasting planes of color, represent one of the most potent expressions of Art Nouveau by an American artist.

In late 1894, Bradley moved to Springfield, Massachusetts, to set up his own Wayside Press, in the tradition of William Morris' Kelmscott Press. His work of the next two years reflects the various stylistic idioms of the Arts and Crafts movement, which he adopted to the mechanized pressroom with an ease that could only come from complete mastery of the printer's trade. In January 1897, at the age of twenty-eight, he collapsed from overwork and sold his shop to the University Press of Cambridge. In the first decades of this century, Bradley was among the best-paid commercial artists in the country, making significant contributions to the fields of illustration, typography, and commercial design. After his departure from Chicago in 1894, *The Chap Book* posters that followed included some daring designs by Frank Hazenplug (1873–after 1908) and Claude Fayette Bragdon (1866–1946).

Along with the magazine publishers, book publishers large and small depended on posters as the most effective way to publicize new titles. Ethel Reed (1874–after 1898) was only twenty-one years old when she produced a striking series of designs for Lamson Wolffe & Co., Copeland & Day, and Louis Prang & Co. These works earned her immediate acclaim and established her reputation here and abroad as the preeminent female poster artist in America. Like Bradley and Rhead,

she worked within the Boston publishing world, and her posters reflect the same English precedents.

Another figure from the Boston arts scene, Arthur Wesley Dow
(1857–1922), was an influential painter and teacher at the turn of the
century, and is best known for his theory of art education based upon
Japanese principles of design. His remarkable poster advertising the
journal *Modern Art* provides powerful testimony both to his mastery
of color and to the extraordinary talent of his lithographer-translator
Louis Prang.

Also among those commissioned to provide designs for book advertisements, binding designs, etc., were a number of young commercial artists who would earn recognition later in their careers as
painters, including John Sloan, William James Glackens, and Maurice
Brazil Prendergast. Other artists whose work graced bookshop windows were Blanche McManus (1870–?), H. M. Lawrence (1852–1937),
and John Stewardson (dates unknown).

Few industries outside of those related to printing and publishing
took to art posters as a means of advertising—with one major exception. The craze for posters was eclipsed by another fad during the
'90s—the craze for bicycles. Two technological advancements of a
rather fundamental nature resulted in what was dubbed, relative to
its predecessors, the "safety bicycle." They were the introduction of
pneumatic tires and the replacement of the towering front wheel with
front and back wheels of matched radii. Bicycling became the rage
overnight, and by 1894, 30 publications devoted to bicycling had
appeared. Bicycle manufacturers shrewd enough to recognize the appeal of the art poster to those wealthy enough to afford their wares
commissioned designs from the best artists in the medium, including
Will Bradley, Edward Penfield, and Charles Cox. The scale of these
posters was usually larger than those produced by the publishing industry, in keeping with the amount of display space likely to be available on the walls of bicycle shops.

Coverage of American poster artists in contemporary newspapers
and magazines of the day was extensive, and before long many publications were offering posters to collectors and earning handsome
profits from the trade. By 1896, posters designed for *The Chap Book*
were being sold by that journal for ten times the newsstand price of
five cents. It is fitting testimony to the American entrepreneurial
spirit that a magazine could earn money by promoting the advertising

designs that promoted the magazine in the first place. Yet, in the long-run, the relationship between collector and advertiser was not symbiotic, even at the height of the poster's popularity.

THE DECLINE OF A COMMERCIAL ART FORM

By 1896 booksellers had discovered what publishers would later learn—that the money the public spent on posters was often at the expense of book sales. By the late '90s, publishers had resolved the conflict by moving the coveted designs from the posters to the book jackets and magazine covers. Now the potential poster collector would, of necessity, have to become a book collector as well.

Many artists managed the transition from poster design to cover design and book illustration with little trouble, including Edward Penfield, Will Bradley, Will Carqueville, Maxfield Parrish, and Louis Rhead. Some artists, such as John Sloan, Maurice Prendergast, William Glackens, and Claude Fayette Bragdon dedicated increasing amounts of time to painting or other disciplines, gradually leaving commercial art behind altogether. Yet others, among them Ethel Reed and J. J. Gould, seemed to vanish from view as quickly as the posters themselves.

Claude Fayette Bragdon recognized in the poster movement the potential for "a renaissance in which the spirit of the century, which is so largely a commercial one, will find an utterance in beauty instead of ugliness." For a brief yet glorious period nearly a century ago those aspirations were realized in works whose legacy provides a rich addition to the history of American art.

STARTING YOUR OWN COLLECTION

The best advice for the beginning collector is to acquaint yourself with the standard reference books in the field, and then look, look, and look at as many works as you can before making an acquisition.

Fortunately, it does not take talent, superior intelligence, or luck to develop a connoisseur's eye for American art posters. One need only begin with the excellent catalog by David Kiehl of the poster collection at The Metropolitan Museum of Art (see Resource Guide for ordering information). This invaluable reference tool illustrates and describes in great detail nearly three hundred different posters by seventy artists of the period. This book and other helpful publications on the subject are listed at the end of this chapter (see also Bibliography).

Next you should examine firsthand as many posters as possible by visiting commercial galleries and public collections with holdings of American posters (see the Resource Guide). In this way a collecting focus will suggest itself as you are drawn naturally to a particular artist or subject matter. You will also begin to develop an eye for how a given poster ought to look. The nuances of color and condition reveal themselves quickly to those with patience and perseverance.

The hours spent at this stage will pay off down the road when you are ready to begin a collection. The posters that retain their value are those which are considered to be the most important works by the most notable artists of the day. Scarcity also adds to the value of a poster, and the best way to judge the relative importance and rarity of an item is to be out in the field looking for works and asking questions of the experts. There is no mystery to the old saw "collect only the best by the best"—simply do the homework.

Condition should also play an important role in the acquisition process. Once you have decided that you would like to buy a particular poster, be prepared to turn down examples of that work in poor condition. In most instances, there is no reason to put up with tears into the image, paper losses, a fading of color, in-painting (touching up by hand), or the backing of a poster with linen or any other material when considering the purchase of an American turn-of-the-century poster.

The backing of posters on linen has long been considered a conservation method, but it has become a somewhat controversial issue (see the section called Preserving and Displaying Your Collection in the chapter titled "Poster Collecting"). Some large or extremely delicate works may require an archivally sound backing for their preservation, but, in the opinion of this writer, this will be the exception rather than the rule.

Poster dealers primarily back posters on linen to make them easier to transport, handle, and display. If you are told that the backing of a poster has been done to archival or museum specifications, then it will also hold true that the process is reversible. You may want to ask the dealer to have their paper conservator remove the backing. There is not a museum curator in the country who would consider paying top dollar for a Whistler etching backed with linen. Why should our standards, as collectors of fine art works on paper of that same period, be any different?

When considering a poster, you also need to see it out of the frame or mat it is displayed in. Some tears may be so skillfully repaired that they are visible only if the back of the poster is examined or when the poster is held up to a strong light. In-painting will show best in a raking light as a different finish or gloss than that of the surrounding original color.

You might lower your standards of condition if the rarity of a given work suggests that you might not find another example. But there are a very few posters that fit in this category. You will be better served by forming a small collection of choice examples, rather than proving, as all too many seem willing to do, just how much people are willing to pay for mediocrity. Accordingly, the price guide that follows to "American Art Posters of the 1890s" (all created between 1890 and 1900) assumes that the poster in question is in "fine to mint" or "A" condition. There is no reason to settle for less.

WHERE TO GO TO SEE
AMERICAN ART POSTERS

Because of their immense popularity in their own day, many notable collections of American art posters were formed at the turn of the century and have since passed into the hands of museums and libraries around the country. Call the institutions nearest you and ask for the curator of prints or graphic art. Major American poster holdings can also be viewed at the Metropolitan Museum of Art, the New York Public Library, the Boston Public Library, the Delaware Art Museum, and the Santa Barbara Museum of Art. Call ahead to make the appropriate arrangements. (See Resource Guide for museum listings.)

All price ranges represent the retail value.

REFERENCE WORKS

Note: To conserve space and list as many posters as possible in the price listings following this chapter, Mr. Goddu has provided reference numbers to two important works which illustrate the posters:

"Kiehl"   *American Art Posters of the 1890s in The Metropolitan Museum of Art, including the Leonard A. Lauder Collection,* by David W. Kiehl;

"DFP"   *Das Frühe Plakat in Europa und den USA,* Vol. I, by Ruth Malhotra, Christina Thom, et al.

Other books and articles of note are: *The American Poster,* by Edgar Breitenbach and Margaret Cogswell; *American Poster Renaissance,* by Victor Margolin; *American Posters of the Nineties* (exhibition catalog), by Roberta Waddell Wong; *American Posters of the Turn of the Century,* by Carolyn Keay; *Designed to Persuade: The Graphic Art of Edward Penfield,* by David Gibson; *Will H. Bradley: American Artist and Craftsman (1868–1962)* (exhibition catalog), by Roberta Waddell Wong; "Will Bradley and the Art Nouveau Poster," by Richard Koch in *The Magazine Antiques* (October 1988); *Will Bradley: His Graphic Art,* by Roberta Waddell Wong and Clarence P. Hornung. (See Bibliography for complete references on the above.)

PRICE LISTINGS

Note: See the chapter "Important Notes on the Price Listings" for more information on prices given. See the section on Reference Works in this chapter for information on references given.

EDWIN A. ABBEY

The Quest of the Holy Grail, by Edwin Abbey, 1895. Signed in the block. Advertising the book published by R. H. Russell & Son. 16½" × 23". Kiehl No. 1. $600–$800

ELISHA BROWN BIRD (1867–1943)

Courtesy of Poster Plus

The Chap Book, 1896. Signed in the block. 13″ × 18½″. Kiehl No. 10. $2,000–$2,500

WILL H. BRADLEY (1868–1962)

Bradley: His Book, 1896. Woodcut and lithographic poster published by The Wayside Press, Springfield, Massachusetts, unsigned. *The Kiss*, as this poster was known, was Bradley's first design for a series advertising his periodical *Bradley: His Book*, and is one of the masterpieces of the American poster movement. 27¹/₁₆″ × 39¹³/₁₆″. DFP No. 174; Kiehl No. 30. (See color center section.) $20,000–$25,000

Bradley: His Book/June 1896. Color relief published by The Wayside Press, Springfield, Massachusetts, signed in the block. This was the second poster for Bradley's magazine and is known also by the title *The Queen*. 8³/₈″ × 18³/₄″. DFP No. 171; Kiehl No. 31.
$2,000–$2,500

The Chap Book, 1894. Lithograph published by Stone & Kimball, Chicago, signed on the stone. This poster is also known by the title *The Blue Lady* and was Bradley's second design for the Chicago literary magazine *The Chap Book*. 12⁷/₁₆″ × 18⁵/₈″. DFP No. 157; Kiehl No. 14. $4,000–$5,000

The Chap Book, 1895. Lithograph published by Stone & Kimball, Chicago, signed on the stone. This poster is known also as *The Pipes* and was Bradley's fifth design for *The Chap Book*. 13½″ × 20⅝″. DFP No. 156; Kiehl No. 20. $2,500–$3,500

The Chap Book, 1895. Lithograph published by Stone & Kimball, Chicago, signed on the stone. Also known as *Pegasus*, this was Bradley's sixth design for *The Chap Book*. 13⅛″ × 19¹¹/₁₆″. DFP No. 153; Kiehl No. 22. $2,000–$2,500

The Chap Book Thanksgiving, 1895. Lithograph published by Stone & Kimball, Chicago, signed on the stone. 13³/₁₆″ × 19⁹/₁₆″. DFP No. 151; Kiehl No. 23. $3,500–$4,500

May/The Chap Book, 1895. Lithograph published by Stone & Kimball, Chicago, signed on the stone. 13⁵/₁₆″ × 20″. DFP No. 154; Kiehl No. 18. $2,250–$3,000

The Modern Poster, 1895. Lithograph published by Charles Scribner's Sons, signed on the stone. A numbered poster, #724, of an edition of 1,000. 11⅝″ × 19¼″. DFP No. 158. $4,500–$6,000

Victor Bicycles/Overman Wheel Company, 1896. Lithograph published by Overman Wheel Co., unsigned. 36¾″ × 57⁷/₁₆″. DFP No. 176 (related); Kiehl No. 35. $21,000–$28,000

Courtesy of Hirschl & Adler Galleries

When Hearts are Trumps, by Tom Hall, 1894. Lithograph published by Stone & Kimball, Chicago, signed on the stone. 13³/₁₆″ × 16⅜″. DFP No. 150; Kiehl No. 15. $2,500–$3,500

Whiting's Ledger Papers, 1895. Lithograph published by Whiting Paper Company, signed on the stone. The border design for this poster generated its nickname, "The Acorns." The first issue of *Bradley: His Book* notified readers of the availability of copies at 75 cents each. 9¼″ × 19⅞″. DFP No. 168; Kiehl No. 26. $1,500–$2,000

CLAUDE FAYETTE BRAGDON (1866–1946)

The Chap Book, 1896. Lithograph published by Stone & Kimball, Chicago, signed on the stone. Bragdon's second poster for *The Chap Book* was the tenth in the series advertising the magazine and is also called *The Carriage*. 12″ × 16¹⁵⁄₁₆″. DFP No. 185; Kiehl No. 37.

$1,100–$1,500

R. J. CAMPBELL

Courtesy of An American Collection

Victor Cycles: Ride a Victor, 1898. Black and white lithograph published by Overman Wheel Co., Massachusetts, signed on the stone. 19½″ × 28″. (Not in DFP or Kiehl.) $3,500–$4,500

WILLIAM L. CARQUEVILLE (1871–1946)

Lippincotts's/July, 1895. Lithograph published by J. B. Lippincott Co., Philadelphia, signed on the stone. 12″ × 18½″. DFP No. 201; Kiehl No. 51. $1,100–$1,500

Lippincott's/October, 1895. Lithograph published by J. B. Lippincott Co., Philadelphia, signed on the stone. 11¹³/₁₆″ × 18⅜″. DFP No. 204; Kiehl No. 54. $900–$1,200

Lippincott's/November, 1895. Lithograph published by J. B. Lippincott Co., Philadelphia, signed on the stone. 12″ × 18⁷/₁₆″. DFP No. 205; Kiehl No. 55. $1,100–$1,500

CHARLES ARTHUR COX

Bearings, 1896. Lithograph published by Bearings, signed on the stone. 11″ × 16″. DFP No. 215; Kiehl No. 60. $450–$600

LAFAYETTE MAYNARD DIXON

Overland Monthly: December, 1895. Lithograph signed on the stone. Bold poster of Indian and bear; in green, tan, black, and white. 12″ × 14″. (Not in DFP or Kiehl.) $1,500–$2,000

Sunset Magazine, 1902. Lithograph signed on the stone. Proud noble Navajo wrapped in a red blanket with geometric designs; in red, brown, beige, and blue. (Not in DFP or Kiehl.) $2,250–$3,000

ARTHUR WESLEY DOW (1857–1922)

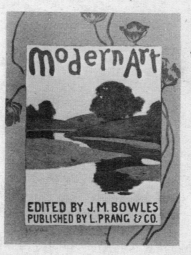

Courtesy of Hirschl & Adler Galleries

Modern Art/Edited by J. M. Bowles, 1895. Lithograph printed by Louis Prang & Co., Boston, signed on the stone. 13¹¹/₁₆″ × 17¾″. DFP No. 217; Kiehl No. 66. $7,500–$10,000

CHARLES DANA GIBSON

Two Women and a Fool, by *Chatfield-Taylor*, 1895. Original poster designed for the Peacock Library Series published in Chicago by Stone & Kimball; in black and white. 12½″ × 19″. Kiehl No. 75.

$225–$275

WILLIAM GLACKENS (1870–1938)

Scribner's/August, 1899. Lithograph published by Charles Scribner's Sons, New York, signed on the stone. 13⅝″ × 21⅜″. (Not in DFP or Kiehl.) $2,000–$2,500

ALICE GLENNY

Women's Edition (Buffalo) Courier, 1895. Lithograph printed by Courier Litho, Buffalo, signed on the stone. One of only two known posters by this skillful designer. 22″ × 29″. Kiehl No. 78.

$1,500–$2,000

JOSEPH J. GOULD, JR. (CA. 1875–CA. 1935)

Courtesy of An American Collection

Lippincott's/August, 1896. Lithograph printed by J. B. Lippincott Co., signed on the stone. 14½″ × 18½″. DFP No. 251. $800–$1,200

Lippincott's/December, ca. 1896. Lithograph signed on the stone. 8⅛″ × 12⅜″. Kiehl No. 87. $1,350–$1,800

Lippincott's/February, 1897. Lithograph published by J. B. Lippincott Co., Philadelphia, signed on the stone. 11¼″ × 19″. DFP No. 258; Kiehl No. 89. $1,500–$2,000

Lippincott's/July, 1897. Lithograph published by J. B. Lippincott Co., Philadelphia, signed on the stone. 11⁹⁄₁₆″ × 16⁷⁄₈″. DFP No. 265.
$2,000–$2,500

Lippincott's/May, 1896. Lithograph signed on the stone. 10⁷⁄₈″ × 15⁷⁄₈″. DFP No. 248. $700–$900

FRANK HAZENPLUG (*1873–AFTER 1908*)

The Chap Book, 1895. Relief published by Stone & Kimball, Chicago, signed in the block. Also known by the title *The Red Lady*, this was the seventh in the series of posters for *The Chap Book*. 7⅞″ × 13¼″. DFP No. 269; Kiehl No. 97. $1,200–$1,600

Courtesy of Hirschl & Adler Galleries

The Chap Book, 1896. Lithograph published by Stone & Kimball, Chicago, signed on the stone. The twelfth *Chap Book* poster, this is also known by the title *The Black Lady*. 13½″ × 19¹³⁄₁₆″. DFP No. 268; Kiehl No. 99. $2,000–$2,500

The Chap Book, 1896. Lithograph published by Stone & Kimball, Chicago, signed in the block. This poster, also called *The Green Lady*, was Hazenplug's third for *The Chap Book*. 13½″ × 20⅜″. Kiehl No. 100.   *$1,500–$2,000*

L. F. HURD

The Bow of Orange Ribbon, *by Amelia E. Barr*. Published by Dodd, Mead, New York. 13″ × 18″. Kiehl No. 106.   *$150–$250*

HERBERT MYRON LAWRENCE (1852–1937)

The Century/October, 1895. Relief published by The Century Co., New York, signed in the block. 11¼″ × 18¾″. DFP No. 281; Kiehl No. 111.   *$1,500–$2,000*

FLORENCE LUNDBORG (1871–1949)

The Lark/August, 1896. Woodcut published by William Doxey, San Francisco, signed in the block. 12⅞″ × 16″. DFP No. 298; Kiehl No. 121.   *$2,000–$2,500*

The Lark/February, 1896. Woodcut published by William Doxey, San Francisco, signed in the block. 11⅜″ × 19⁵⁄₁₆″. DFP No. 297; Kiehl No. 119.   *$1,500–$2,000*

The Lark/May/The Oread, 1896. Woodcut published by William Doxey, San Francisco, signed in the block. 13⅞″ × 23¾″. Kiehl No. 120.   *$2,000–$2,500*

The Lark/November, 1895. Woodcut published by William Doxey, San Francisco, signed in the block. The landscape depicted features Mt. Tamalpais, which is visible across the bay from San Francisco. 19¹³⁄₁₆″ × 16⅜″. DFP No. 296; Kiehl No. 118.   *$3,000–$4,000*

The Lark/What is That Mother? 1895. Woodcut published by William Doxey, San Francisco, signed in the block. 17½″ × 11″. DFP No. 295; Kiehl No. 117.   *$900–$1,200*

HENRY McCARTER (1865–1945)

Scribner's/August, 1899. Lithograph published by Charles Scribner's Sons, New York, signed in the block. 13¾″ × 22¹¹⁄₁₆″. (Not in DFP or Kiehl.)   *$1,500–$2,000*

BLANCHE McMANUS (1870–?)

The True Mother Goose, 1896. Lithograph published by Lamson Wolffe & Co., Boston, signed on the stone. 14¼″ × 20⅜″. DFP No. 301; Kiehl No. 127. $2,000–$2,500

H. MCVICKAR

Harper's Bazaar, ca. 1980s. 16″ × 22″. DFP No. 304. $150–$250

MAXFIELD PARRISH (1870–1966)

The Century/Midsummer Holiday Number/August, 1897. Lithograph published by The Century Co., New York, signed on the stone. 11¹⁵⁄₁₆″ × 18⁷⁄₁₆″. DFP No. 317; Kiehl No. 134. $3,000–$4,000

Exhibition of the American Water Color Society, 1899. Lithograph signed on the stone. 13¹⁵⁄₁₆″ × 20⅞″. (Not in DFP or Kiehl.)

$2,500–$3,500

Poster Show/Pennsylvania/Academy/of the/Fine Arts/Philadelphia, 1896. Relief signed in the block. This impression is one of a limited number signed by the artist for the collectors' market, before the addition of a separate sheet of letterpress to the lower margin. 23¾″ × 30″. Kiehl No. 133. (See frontispiece.)

$12,000–$15,000

Scribner's Fiction Number/August, 1897. Lithograph published by Charles Scribner's Sons, New York, signed on the stone. 14″ × 19½″. DFP No. 316; Kiehl No. 135. $4,000–$5,500

EDWARD PENFIELD (1866–1925)

Aetna Dynamite. Lithograph printed by The Poster Press, Chicago, signed on the stone. 14″ × 19″. Kiehl No. 175. $900–$1,200

Harper's/April, 1897. Lithograph published by Harper and Brothers, New York, signed on the stone. 12¹³⁄₁₆″ × 18³⁄₁₆″. DFP No. 377; Kiehl No. 195. $1,500–$1,800

Harper's/August, 1895. Lithograph published by Harper and Brothers, New York. 12″ × 18½″. Kiehl No. 168. $900–$1,200

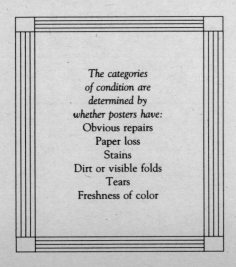

The categories
of condition are
determined by
whether posters have:
Obvious repairs
Paper loss
Stains
Dirt or visible folds
Tears
Freshness of color

Harper's/August, 1897. Lithograph published by Harper and Brothers, New York, signed on the stone. 13³⁄₁₆″ × 18½″. DFP No. 381; Kiehl No. 199. $2,000–$2,600

Harper's/Christmas, 1894. Lithograph and relief published by Harper and Brothers, New York, signed on the stone. 12³⁄₈″ × 18³⁄₁₆″. DFP No. 339; Kiehl No. 156. $1,500–$2,000

Courtesy of Hirschl & Adler Galleries

Harper's/Christmas, 1896. Lithograph published by Harper and Brothers, New York, signed on the stone. 12⁷⁄₈″ × 17³⁄₁₆″. DFP No. 363; Kiehl No. 187. $2,250–$3,000

Harper's/February, 1897. Lithograph and relief published by Harper and Brothers, New York, signed on the stone. 13¹⁵⁄₁₆″ × 19″. DFP No. 373; Kiehl No. 193. (See color center section.) $4,000–$5,000

Harper's/February, 1898. Lithograph published by Harper and Brothers, New York, signed on the stone. 13³⁄₁₆″ × 18³⁄₄″. DFP No. 387; Kiehl No. 207. $1,500–$2,000

Harper's/January, 1898. Lithograph published by Harper and Brothers, New York, signed on the stone. 19″ × 11⅛″. DFP No. 397; Kiehl No. 217. $2,000–$2,500

Harper's/July, 1896. Lithograph published by Harper and Brothers, New York, signed on the stone. Impressions exist in two color variants: with a green or a yellow-beige background. 13¹¹⁄₁₆″ × 18⅝″. DFP No. 350; Kiehl No. 182. $2,100–$2,800

Harper's/June, ca. 1895. Lithograph signed with monogram. 15⅝″ × 9″. Kiehl No. 166. $900–$1,200

Harper's/for March, 1894. Lithograph published by Harper and Brothers, New York, signed on the stone. $11^{11}/_{16}'' \times 15^{7}/_{8}''$. DFP No. 330; Kiehl No. 148.   *$1,200–$1,500*

Harper's/March, 1896. Lithograph published by Harper and Brothers, New York, signed on the stone. $10^{13}/_{16}'' \times 18^{3}/_{8}''$. DFP No. 354; Kiehl No. 178.   *$1,500–$2,000*

Courtesy of Hirschl & Adler Galleries

Harper's/March, 1897. Lithograph published by Harper and Brothers, New York, signed on the stone. Horizontal $19'' \times 13^{15}/_{16}''$. DFP No. 376; Kiehl No. 194.   *$2,700–$3,600*

Harper's/March, 1898. Lithograph. $10^{3}/_{8}'' \times 14^{7}/_{8}''$. Kiehl No. 208.   *$900–$1,200*

Harper's/May, ca. 1895. Lithograph. $11^{1}/_{2}'' \times 17''$. Kiehl No. 165.   *$900–$1,200*

Harper's/May, 1896. Lithograph published by Harper and Brothers, New York, signed on the stone. $11^{13}/_{16}'' \times 17^{9}/_{16}''$. DFP No. 356; Kiehl No. 180.   *$2,000–$2,500*

Harper's/May, 1898. Lithograph published by Harper and Brothers, New York, signed on the stone. 9$^1/_{16}$" × 16". DFP No. 390; Kiehl No. 210. $900–$1,200

Harper's/November, 1896. Lithograph published by Harper and Brothers, signed on the stone. 13$^3/_8$" × 17$^{13}/_{16}$". DFP No. 362; Kiehl No. 186. $2,250–$3,000

Harper's/November, 1898. Lithograph published by Harper and Brothers, New York, signed on the stone. 18$^3/_{16}$" × 11$^1/_8$". DFP No. 396; Kiehl No. 216. $1,500–$1,800

Harper's/September, 1894. Lithograph and relief published by Harper and Brothers, New York, signed on the stone. 10$^5/_8$" × 16$^1/_4$". DFP No. 336; Kiehl No. 153. $1,500–$2,000

Harper's September, 1896. Lithograph published by Harper and Brothers, New York, signed on the stone. 17$^7/_{16}$" × 13$^{11}/_{16}$". DFP No. 360; Kiehl No. 184. $2,000–$2,500

Harper's/September, 1898. Lithograph signed on the stone. 9" × 13$^1/_4$". Kiehl No. 214. $2,000–$2,500

The Northampton/The Northampton Cycle Co., ca. 1899. Lithograph published by The Northampton Cycle Co., signed on the stone. 26$^5/_{16}$" × 39$^3/_4$". Kiehl No. 225. $10,000–$14,000

Poster Calendar, 1896. Lithograph and relief published by R. H. Russell & Son, New York, signed on the stone. Poster advertising a poster calendar. 10" × 13$^1/_2$". DFP No. 373; Kiehl No. 191.

$2,400–$3,200

Ride a Stearns and be Content, 1896. Lithograph published by Stearns Manufacturing Co., signed on the stone. 40" × 54$^5/_8$". Kiehl No. 190. $9,000–$12,000

Western Lawn Tennis Tournament, 1896. Lithograph signed on the stone. Perhaps the rarest of Penfield posters. 18$^3/_8$" × 26$^7/_8$". DFP No. 371. $6,000–$8,000

MAURICE BRAZIL PRENDERGAST (1859–1924)

On the Point/Nathan Haskell Dole, 1895. Relief published by Joseph Knight Co., Boston, signed in the block. 8" × 12$^{15}/_{16}$". Kiehl No. 230. $1,200–$1,500

ETHEL REED (1874–AFTER 1898)

Courtesy of An American
Collection

Arabella and Araminta Stories, 1895. Lithograph printed by Geo. H. Walker & Co., Boston, signed on the stone. Reed illustrated this book. 14½″ × 26⅛″. Kiehl No. 234. $3,500–$4,500

Behind the Arras, by *Bliss Carmen*, 1895. Lithograph published by Lamson, Wolffe & Co., Boston, signed on the stone. 17¾″ × 27⅛″. DFP No. 418; Kiehl No. 236. $1,500–$2,000

The House of the Trees and Other Poems, by *Ethelwyn Wetherald*, 1895. Relief published by Lamson, Wolffe & Co., signed in the block. 8″ × 16⅞″. DFP No. 419; Kiehl No. 237. $700–$900

In Childhood's Country, by *Louise Chandler Moulton*, 1896. Lithograph published by Copeland & Day, Boston, signed on the stone. 10⅜″ × 23½″. DFP No. 430; Kiehl No. 245. $2,000–$2,500

Jacques Damour, by *Emile Zola*, 1895. For the book published by Copeland & Day, Boston. 11½″ × 18½″. Kiehl No. 243. $600–$800

Miss Traumerei, by *Albert Morris Bagby,* 1895. Lithograph published by Lamson, Wolffe & Co., Boston, signed on the stone. 12⁵/₁₆″ × 21″. DFP No. 417; Kiehl No. 235. $1,200–$1,500

The Penny Magazine/Sold Here, 1896. Relief published by The Penny Magazine, Philadelphia, signed in the block. 9¼″ × 20⅛″. DFP No. 429. $1,200–$1,500

Pierre Puvis De Chavannes: A Sketch, 1895. Very rare, 15½″ × 21″. Kiehl No. 244. $1,700–$2,200

The White Wampum, by *E. Pauline Johnson (Tekahionwake),* 1895. Relief published by Lamson, Wolffe & Co., Boston, signed in the block. 16½″ × 22″. DFP No. 424; Kiehl No. 241. $1,200–$1,600

LOUIS JOHN RHEAD (1857–1926)

The Century/for Xmas, 1895. Lithograph published by The Century Co., New York, signed on the stone. 13½″ × 20½″. DFP No. 448; Kiehl No. 259. $1,500–$1,800

The Century Magazine/for June, 1896. Lithograph published by The Century Co., New York, signed on the stone. 10½″ × 20¾″. DFP No. 461; Kiehl No. 265. $700–$900

The Century Magazine/Midsummer, 1894. Lithograph published by The Century Co., New York, signed on the stone. 18⁵/₁₆″ × 13⁹/₁₆″. Kiehl No. 249. $2,250–$3,000

Exposition Speciale . . . de Louis Rhead/Salon des Cent, 1897. Lithograph published by La Plume, Paris, signed on the stone. 14½″ × 23″. DFP No. 468; Kiehl No. 269. $4,000–$5,500

His Lordship, 1896. Lithograph printed by the Ellery Howard Co., New York, signed on the stone. Rhead used himself as the model for this poster. 28½″ × 47½″. Kiehl No. 264. $3,000–$4,000

If You See It in the Sun, It's So/Read It, 1895. Lithograph published by The New York Sun, signed on the stone. 27½″ × 42⅛″. DFP No. 440; Kiehl No. 256. $2,250–$3,000

L. Prang & Co.'s Holiday, ca. 1910. Lithograph signed on the stone. 15⅜″ × 20¾″. Kiehl No. 251. $2,000–$2,500

Le Journal de la Beauté, 1897. Lithograph published by La Plume, Paris, signed on the stone. Originally commissioned by La Plume as a mural panel, this design was given a second life as a poster for one of the company's magazines through the simple addition of text. $58^{7}/_{16}" \times 30^{5}/_{8}"$. DFP No. 454A; Kiehl No. 270.   *$12,000–$15,000*

Morning Journal, 1895. Lithograph printed by Liebler and Maass, New York, signed on the stone. Horizontal $60" \times 48"$. Kiehl No. 257.

$3,500–$4,500

Prang's Easter Publications, 1895. Lithograph published by Louis Prang & Co., Boston, signed on the stone. Beautifully printed, an important poster. $17" \times 24"$. DFP No. 455; Kiehl No. 258.   *$3,000–$4,000*

Read the Sun, 1895. Lithograph printed by A. S. Seer & Co., New York, signed on the stone and pen-signed with dedication. 30″ × 46″. Kiehl No. 255. (See color center section.)   *$3,000–$4,000*

Scribner's/for Xmas, 1895. Lithograph published by Charles Scribner's Sons, New York, signed on the stone. 12¾″ × 17⅛″. DFP No. 449 (variant); Kiehl No. 260.   *$2,000–$2,500*

JOHN SLOAN (1871–1951)

Courtesy of Hirschl & Adler Galleries

Cinder-Path Tales/William Lindsay, 1896. Lithograph published by Copeland & Day, Boston, signed on the stone. 10⅞″ × 20¹¹/₁₆″. Kiehl No. 278.   *$4,000–$5,000*

JOHN STEWARDSON

The Dragon of Wantley/His Tale, by Owen Wister, 1895. Relief published by J. B. Lippincott Co., Philadelphia, unsigned. Book illustrated by John Stewardson. 10″ × 13⅞″. Kiehl No. 280.

$900–$1,200

JOHN HENRY TWACHTMAN (1853–1902)

The Damnation of Theron Ware or Illumination, 1896. Lithograph published by Stone & Kimball, New York, signed on the stone. Rare (the master painter's only poster), 12⅛″ × 20″. DFP No. 486; Kiehl No. 282. (See color center section.)   *$3,500–$4,500*

GEORGE EDMUND VARIAN (1865–1923)

The Century Magazine, June 1898. Features "The Story of the Spanish Armada." 14″ × 22″. DFP No. 488. $200–$250.

The Century Magazine, July 1898. Features "By Order of the Admiral" by Winston Churchill. 14″ × 22″. DFP No. 489. $200–$250

CHARLES HERBERT WOODBURY (1864–1940)

Boston Park Guide, 1895. Lithograph published by Sylvester Baxter, signed on the stone. 12⅛″ × 19¼″. Kiehl No. 286. $1,400–$1,800

The July Century, 1895. Lithograph published by The Century Co., New York, signed on the stone. 10¼″ × 17⅜″. DFP No. 501; Kiehl No. 288. $2,000–$2,500

Society of Painters in Water Color of Holland, 1895. Lithograph published by Chase's Gallery, Boston, signed on the stone. For the first annual exhibition in the United States. 14¼″ × 19⅜″. Kiehl No. 285. $1,700–$2,200

SWISS POSTERS

By Bernice Jackson

*Bernice Jackson is a Fine Arts Consultant offering a wide range of post-
ers, and specializing in posters of several countries such as Austria,
Holland, Switzerland, Hungary, and Poland. She is the author of numerous articles on posters and is the U.S. Representative of The Print
and Publicity Foundation of Amsterdam. Call or write: P.O. Box 1188,
Concord, MA 01742. (508) 369-9088.*

Swiss posters from about 1910 to the present time offer the beginning and advanced collector superb choices from a broad field of design. For several reasons, including a late start in poster design
compared to France, Germany, and other European countries, and a
low-key pragmatic approach to the presence of posters in daily life,
many fine Swiss posters can still be purchased at moderate cost.

While poster design is encouraged by governmental and cultural
institutions in Switzerland with annual exhibitions and awards, national poster production has been somewhat unappreciated. Where
France has always realized that its great poster art was fundamentally
rooted in the work of its fine artists, the Swiss overlooked the profound influence of their great painters like Ferdinand Hodler, Auguste
Giacometti, Max Bill, and others upon the design and development
of their posters.

Because of its geographic position—a small country surrounded by
large and powerful neighbors—it was inevitable that many influences
from the continent seeped into Swiss poster design.

Before 1910, Swiss artists tended to leave Switzerland to pursue
their careers in Paris. Two of the most important of these are Eugene

Grasset (1845–1917), who moved to Paris from Lausanne in 1871 and was to become an important figure in the Art Nouveau movement, and Theophile-Alexandre Steinlen (1859–1923), also from Lausanne.

About 1910 the first important Swiss travel posters started to appear. This is an obvious choice of subject in a country dominated by its mountains and lakes. The beautiful landscape of the country make winter and summer a vacationer's playground. Emile Cardinaux (1877–1936), and Otto Morach (1877–1973) were the first to make notable contributions in this field.

Cardinaux was the first of many Swiss artists to employ the great lithographic printing talents of Johann Edwin Wolfsenberger (1873–1944), based in Zurich. The quality of work from "Wolfsberg," which was the trade name used, and their commitment to this great art form, ensured Swiss poster art a place of predominant excellence in the graphic arts.

Another pioneer Swiss artist who is today widely recognized and collected is Otto Baumberger (1889–1961), who had a prolific career and produced stunning designs in which the object is the focus of the design. His design for the PKZ men's clothing store of a close-up of an overcoat is a true classic and one of the finest examples of color lithography of the 1920s. (See color center section.) Other early Swiss artists worth looking for are Burkhard Mangold (1878–1936) and Eduard Stiefel.

After 1910, almost every aspect of life was depicted in the grand outpouring of posters: art, music, theater, fashion, sports, product advertising, and inevitably politics. In keeping with their national character of tidiness, in 1914 the Swiss established a standard format for posters, which is roughly 35″ wide × 50″ high, and with the exception of very few, all Swiss posters are this size.

Because of its neutrality in World War I, Swiss arts continued to flourish while other countries sublimated their artistic talents to the rigors of the war.

In addition to stylistic influences from other countries that had an impact on poster design in Switzerland, there were two outstanding Swiss schools of graphic design whose influence ultimately extended far beyond its borders.

The first was the rise of the Dada movement, which developed as a literary movement during the war in Zurich in 1916, and lasted for only a short time, until 1923. The founder was the Swiss poet Tzara, but its influence rapidly spread to artists like Picabia, Max Ernst, Marcel Duchamp, and Kurt Schwitters, among others. As the Dadaists embraced photography and film, it undoubtedly was a seminal influence on Herbert Matter (1907–1984), who was among the first to produce a series of great photomontage posters in the 1930s, which combine both photography and hand-illustration. (See also the chapter entitled "Travel and Transportation Posters.")

Another, somewhat later design movement with profound international influence on graphic artists has become known as the International Typographic Style. Jan Tschichold, who was born in Germany but emigrated to Switzerland in the 1930s, brought with him a strong background in the graphic arts which he had experienced through his work with the Bauhaus group and the Russian Constructivists including El Lissitsky.

Influenced by this abstract typographic style are three important Swiss artists whose notable contributions to the art of the avant-garde poster are increasingly recognized: Josef Müller-Brockman (1914–), Armin Hoffman (1920–), and, somwhat later, Wolfgang Weingart (1941–).

Several other artists from the late 1930s through the 1960s produced notable product advertising posters influenced by the object style of Baumberger. They include: Donald Brun, Hans Erni (1909–), Herbert Leupin (1916–), and Niklaus Stoecklin (1896–1982). Travel poster artists of this later period worth looking for include Walter Herdeg (1908–) and Carlo Vivarelli (1919–).

One of the most important early patrons of poster art in Switzerland was the already mentioned PKZ department store. Today, the posters PKZ commissioned from several notable artists are the most collectible and often the highest-priced of all Swiss posters. PKZ used foreign artists such as the German posterist Ludwig Hohlwein and the Frenchman Charles Loupot, but their Swiss roster reads like a history of the Swiss poster: Emile Cardinaux, Burkhard Mangold, Nilaus Stoecklin, Hugo Laubi, Otto Morach, Hermann Blaser, Herbert Matter, Charles Kuhn, and several others. Like the Shell Oil Company in England, it was due to this commercial advertiser and others, such as Bally Shoes, that Swiss poster art occupies an important part of poster history.

The beginning collector may have some difficulty in making choices from the vast array of excellent Swiss posters that are available. An

interesting phenomenon in the novice, making his or her first purchase, is often a preoccupation with the possibilities of appreciation.
Please remember this is not the stock market! Don't buy anything
solely because it is a "good" buy. You may end up hating it.

Posters from 1910 to 1940 will most likely be in higher price brack-
ets because of age and scarcity. Well-known artists command a higher
price than obscure artists. One might well expect to spend from $750
to several thousand dollars for prime examples. Post–World War II
posters can range from $200 to $1,000.

While I certainly would not pick any work of art for secondary
reasons (like matching the wallpaper, etc.), one must certainly visu-
alize the space in which the poster will "live." Two things must be
considered: the size of the room and other art work already hanging.
Each piece of art should have its own breathing space. People are
often more comfortable with a graphic work relating to their interests,
such as sports or music. On the other hand, a completely new visual
experience could well turn out to be an exhilarating and exciting
purchase.

You should be prepared to buy a second and a third, as long as wall
space holds out. Swiss poster collecting becomes a passion!

PRICE LISTINGS

Note: See the chapter "Important Notes on the Price Listings" for more
information on prices given. Also note that some Swiss artists have listings
in other chapters such as "Travel and Transportation Posters."

ANONYMOUS

Acifer, 1960. Poster of an I-beam retreating into the distance; in white,
black, and blue. Fine condition, 35″ × 50″. $350–$400

Bon Genie, 1950. Poster showing a woman in casual attire and sunglasses lounging on the edge of a swimming pool; in yellow, blue, and
white. Fine condition, 35″ × 50″. $450–$500

Kunstausstelling, 1942. Lithographic poster depicting a woman in a
long-sleeved, long gown; in burgundy and cream. Very good condition, linen-mounted, 35″ × 50″. $750–$800

Musiker-Handschriften, 1969. Poster of a musical staff with hand-written notes and notations running across the center of the poster; in gray, black, and red. Fine condition, 35¼″ × 50″.　　　　$400–$450

Plakat, ca. 1950. Poster featuring a design using only letters, many of them receding into the distance at strange angles; in black, white, and red. Fine condition, 35″ × 50″.　　　　$450–$500

Radiotelephono, 1943. Lithographic poster of three crystals, superimposed on each other, floating in the sky; in blue-green and white. Very good condition, 35″ × 50″.　　　　$400–$450

OTTO BAUMBERGER (1889–1961)

Baumann, ca. 1930. Poster printed by Bollmann, Zurich. Impressive Deco design with shiny black topper, sepia letters on white ground. Baumberger was the leading poster designer in Switzerland from the mid-teens to the thirties. Mint condition, 36″ × 50½″.

$600–$1,000

Forster, ca. 1930. Abstract design with the outline of a partially visible rectangle set at an angle on the poster; in black and white. Fine condition, linen-mounted, 35″ × 50″.　　　　$800–$1,000

Grosser Schuh Markt, 1920. Lithographic poster depicting a mountain of various shoes, slippers, and boots; in black, orange, and white. Very good condition, linen-mounted, 35″ × 50″.　　　　$1,600–$1,800

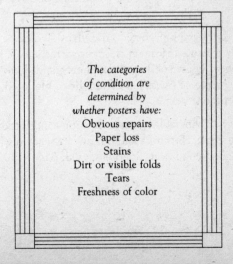

The categories of condition are determined by whether posters have: Obvious repairs Paper loss Stains Dirt or visible folds Tears Freshness of color

Hotel St. Gotthard, 1925. Lithographic poster depicting a lobster, bottle of wine, and an elegant bowl inside a border; in black, red, and green. Fine condition, 35″ × 50″.   *$1,400–$1,600*

Leipziger Gewandhaus Orchester, 1916. Lithographic poster for a concert in which the poster text is surrounded by an elaborate border; in black, red, and white. Very good condition, linen-mounted, 35″ × 50″.   *$1,200–$1,400*

PKZ, 1923. Lithographic poster printed by Wolfsberg, Zurich. Extremely finely executed close-up of a coat with the PKZ label, so exact that many wrongly assume it to be a photograph. Fine condition, an important example of Swiss poster art, linen-mounted, 35″ × 50″. (See color center section.)   *$4,000–$5,000*

Qualitat, 1921. Lithographic poster showing a suit jacket hanging on the back of a chair, the pants laid out on the seat; in white, rust, and green. Very good condition, linen-mounted, 35″ × 50″.

$2,200–$2,400

Zurich, 1935. Lithographic poster depicting a stylized representation of Zurich, with large church, lake with sailboats, and distant mountains; in blue, white, and brown. Fine condition, 35″ × 50″.

$2,500–$3,000

PAUL BENDER

Riri, 1950. Poster depicting unzipped portion of a partially closed zipper, arranged as a design element; in red and gray. Fine condition, linen-mounted, 35″ × 50″. $450–$500

EDOUARDO GARCIA BENITO (1891–?)

Candee, 1929. Lithographic poster printed by Trueb, Aarau, Switzerland. Great Deco streamlined design of fashionable woman walking in the rain in Candee boots; chic cars and buildings in the background. E. G. Benito was a well-known fashion illustrator. Mint condition. 35½″ × 50½″. $3,000–$4,000

BIRKHAUSER

Kunstgewerbe Museum, 1917. Lithographic poster showing a simple candelabra with seven candles; in black, white, and red. Very good condition, linen-mounted, 35″ × 50″. $1,400–$1,600

PETER BIRKHAUSER (1911–)

Osram, ca. 1950. Poster depicts a large lightbulb resting on top of a billfold; in black, red, and gray. Fine condition, 35″ × 50″.

$550–$600

Schweizer Mustermesse, 1941. Poster depicting a wrench with a bow tied around its handle; in blue, black, red, and white. Fine condition, 35″ × 50″. $400–$450

PAUL BRUHNILER

Raymond Chandler/Film Noir, 1979. A stunning poster with a mysterious pair of eyes looking out from under the brim of a hat, peering over the words; in black and gray. Very good condition, linen-mounted, 35″ × 50″. $700–$800

DONALD BRUN

Courtesy of Bernice Jackson (Photo by Robert Four)

Bader, 1928. Poster for the resort spa depicting a stick figure drying his back with a towel, with "Bader" running from top to bottom on the left side of the poster; in black, avocado, and green. Very good condition, linen-mounted, 35″ × 50″. $950–$1,050

Erika, 1960. Poster depicting a close-up of a bee hovering over a molded Erika pudding; in brown, ochre, and off-white. Fine condition, 35″ × 50″. $400–$450

Telephonieren, 1950. Poster depicting a model of a young girl with a telephone in one hand and a small dog under her other arm; in tan, red, and green. Fine condition, 35″ × 50″. $550–$600

EMILE CARDINAUX *(1877–1936)*

Bally, 1935. Lithographic poster depicting a mountain climber holding onto a rope that goes below; in white, red, brown, and blue. Very good condition, linen-mounted, 35″ × 50″. $1,200–$1,400

ALOIS CARIGET *(1902–1985)*

PKZ, ca. 1928. Lithographic poster for the men's clothing store depicting a fox, standing upright, carrying a bag with "PKZ" on it; in green, rust, and buff. Very good condition, linen-mounted, 35″ × 50″. $2,500–$3,000

HERMANN EIDENBENZ

Knorr, 1960. Poster of a package of bouillon cubes sits next to a bowl of soup with a spoon in it; in red, yellow, and white. Very good condition, 35″ × 50″.   *$300–$350*

HANS ERNI (1909-)

Courtesy of Bernice Jackson
(Photo by Robert Four)

VIM, ca. 1950. Poster of a can of VIM cleanser sitting on a shiny tiled surface; in brown and yellow. Fine condition, linen-mounted, 35″ × 50″.   *$450–$550*

HANS FALK (1918-)

Schweized, ca. 1935. Poster showing a man walking with his arm around a boy, their backs to the viewer; in buff and black. Fine condition, 35″ × 50″.   *$300–$350*

HANS HANDSCHIN (1899–1948)

Elco Papiers, 1940. A lithographic poster in Art Deco style shows a stylized woman gazing intently at an envelope she holds in her hand; in red, black, and white. Very good condition, linen-mounted, 35″ × 50″.   *$650–$750*

ROBERT HARDMEYER (1876–1919)

Ovignac Senglet, ca. 1915. Lithographic poster printed by Wassermann, Basel. A flamboyantly feathered proud rooster in a design reminiscent of Will Bradley. Mint condition, horizontal 71″ × 51½″.   *$1,000–$1,500*

ARMIN HOFMANN (1920–)

Moderne Italienische Maler, 1958. Abstract poster in which a large letter "C," with all the text contained inside it, spills off the edge of the poster; in white and black. Very good condition, 35″ × 50″.

$650–$700

Theater, 1955. Poster designed with two large white abstract shapes on a black background. Fine condition, 35″ × 50″. $600–$650

HEINZ JOST

Gustav Mahler, 1976. Musical poster showing a profile of the composer, for his "Symphonie 8"; in white, blue, and black. Fine condition, 35″ × 50″. $350–$400

LEHIN

Toblerone, 1960. Poster depicting close-up of two bars of Toblerone chocolate, one of them opened; in blue, red, and brown. Fine condition, 35″ × 50″. $400–$450

HERBERT LEUPIN (1916–)

Bata Colibri, 1960. Poster shows a woman's shoe with a small heel floating in the air; in white, brown, and blue. Leupin is a master of the modern Swiss product poster. Fine condition, 35″ × 50″.

$300–$350

Bi-oro Creme Soleil, 1942. Poster of a huge tube of Bi-oro Creme Soleil resting on the beach, propped up against a sailboat; in yellow, white, and red. Fine condition, 35″ × 50″. $450–$500

Eptinger, 1940. Poster depicting a prosperous-looking gentleman holding a glass up as if to make a toast, in front of him a table with a bottle of Eptinger; in yellow, orange, and brown. Fine condition, 35″ × 50″. $450–$600

Eptinger, 1960. Poster with the name "Eptinger," the "in" emphasized, filling the center of the poster, with a border of circles around the remainder; in ochre, brown, and green. Fine condition, 35″ × 50″. $550–$600

Eptinger, ca. 1965. Poster depicting a man striding happily along, a hoe and watercan over one shoulder and a bottle of Eptinger in his other arm; in white, red, blue, and black. Very good condition, 35″ × 50″. $400–$450

Jung Mit Dem Alters, ca. 1930. Lithographic poster with a sketch of a collar and tie above the hand-written block of text; in blue, white, and yellow. Fine condition, linen-mounted, 35″ × 50″. $450–$500

Pepita, ca. 1945. Poster depicting a parrot sitting on the handlebars of a bicycle with a drink in its claw, a bottle resting on the bicycle seat; in gray, red, and green. Fine condition, 35″ × 50″.

$600–$650

Pepita, ca. 1945. Poster with the letters of "Pepita" entirely filling the poster area; in gray, red, and green. Fine condition, 35″ × 50″.

$600–$650

PKZ, 1942. Poster of a man dressed in coat, muffler, and hat walking smiling through the snow, a folder labeled "PKZ" sticking out of his pocket; in red, white, and black. Very good condition, linen-mounted, 35″ × 50″. $1,400–$1,600

Courtesy of Bernice Jackson (Photo by Robert Four)

Steinfels, 1942. Poster of a huge clothespin surrounding a box of Steinfels detergent; in white, brown, and green. Fine condition, 35″ × 50″. $500–$600

Tribune, 1955. Well-known poster for the newspaper *Tribune de Lausanne* depicting a coffeepot made out of newsprint; in black, white, and red. Very good condition, 35″ × 50″. $450–$550

HERBERT MATTER (1907–1984)

Courtesy of Pat Kery Fine Arts

PKZ, 1928. Lithographic poster printed by Wolfsberg, Zurich. Classic poster for the men's clothing store depicting a valet showing men's coats. Very good condition, an excellent example of the artist's early Cubist style, linen-mounted, 35″ × 50″. $4,000–$5,000

Courtesy of Bernice Jackson
(Photo by Robert Four)

Suisse, 1934. Photomontage poster of a skier's head with sun visor in the foreground, multiple photos of downhillers and Swiss crosses in the background; in white, red, and green. Fine condition, linen-mounted, 25″ × 40″. $1,400–$1,700

E. MOSSDORF

Turnfest/Luzern, 1928. Lithographic poster for the sports festival in an Art Deco style shows a checkerboard pattern of the angular head of a man, repeated five times; in white, buff, and black. Fine condition, linen-mounted, 35″ × 50″. $1,100–$1,300

JOSEF MÜLLER-BROCKMANN (1914-)

Juni Festsocheu-Zurich, 1959. Poster featuring a design of diagonal lines with colored boxes between them; in gray, blue, red, and black. Very good condition, linen-mounted, 35″ × 50″. $1,200–$1,300

Moholy-Nagy-1922, 1984. Poster for an exhibition of Moholy-Nagy's work is a geometric design in gray, white, pink, and blue. Very good condition, 35¼″ × 50″. $375–$400

B. OLENETSKI

Pablo Casals, 1950. Abstract music poster with the design consisting of the heads of several cellos superimposed on each other; in buff, orange, and purple. Very good condition, linen-mounted, 35″ × 40″.
$450–$500

MARTIN PEIKERT (1901–1975)

Schweiz-Skirennen, 1939. Lithographic poster. Fine condition, linen-mounted, 39½″ × 27½″. $700–$900

P. PERNET

Championnat du Monde 1946 Geneve, 1946. Lithographic poster printed by Atar, Geneva. Red boats, deep blue water, white wakes; for the world championship motorboat races. Mint condition, 25⅝″ × 39⅜″. $600–$1,000

CELESTINO PIATTI (1922-)

Schweizer Kondens-milch, ca. 1955. Poster of a cat standing upright, holding a can in his front paws; in white, gray, and blue. Good condition, 35″ × 50″. $400–$450

VICTOR RUTZ

Walder, 1936. Poster depicting a small dachshund holding a sign in the upper left corner, below it a man's large shoe; in brown and white. Very good condition, 35″ × 50″. $550–$600

NIKLAUS STOECKLIN (1896–1982)

Bell, 1952. Poster is a close-up of a Christmas ham, decorated with a bow and mistletoe; in black, pink, and brown. Stoecklin is well known for his captivating product posters. Very good condition, 35″ × 50″.

$350–$400

Bell, ca. 1960. Poster of a cutting board displaying a variety of cold cuts and meats; in brown and red. Fine condition, 35″ × 50″.

$400–$450

Binaca, 1941. Poster depicting a hand clad in armor holding a tube of Binaca; in black, red, and gray. Fine condition, 35″ × 50″.

$600–$700

E Guete!, 1960. Poster of three fried eggs, sunny-side-up, in a pan; in blue, yellow, and orange. Fine condition, 34″ × 50″. $550–$600

Schweized Eier, ca. 1935. Poster showing a huge egg, cut in half, with a small Swiss flag stuck in it; in purple, orange, and buff. Very good condition, 35″ × 50″. $550–$600

WOLFGANG WEINGART (1941–)

Kunst Gewerbe Museum/Zurich, 1980. Poster for an exhibition featuring a design of abstract shapes with a pen nib at the top; in black and white. Fine condition, linen-mounted, 35″ × 50″. $550–$600

Courtesy of Bernice Jackson
(Photo by Robert Four)

Kunst Gewerbe, 1985. Poster for an architectural exhibition of work by Otto Rudolf (1882–1940) has a photo of building in the upper right corner superimposed on a building design; in black and white. Fine condition, 35″ × 50″. $550–$600

ENGLISH, GERMAN, AND ITALIAN POSTERS

England, Germany, and Italy are recognized for their strong artistic and graphic design for the poster, and offer collectors a wide range of choices that have become increasingly popular over the past ten years.

ENGLISH POSTERS

In England, early pictorial posters were overlooked by the staid business community, and typographic broadsides cluttered the walls of buildings. It was not until Aubrey Beardsley's (1872–1898) poster for *Avenue Theatre* that the advertising poster gained any recognition as either an artistic or commercial medium.

Beardsley, who died when he was only 25, created very few posters, most of which are today held by museums. His graphic design style influenced an entire generation of English and American artists, including the American Will Bradley (1868–1962). (See chapter on "American Art Posters of the 1890s.") We have not seen any Beardsley posters on the market in recent years and his work, when available, sells very high.

Some English artists of Beardsley's era, such as Dudley Hardy (1867–1922), who executed several posters for music halls, performances, and Gilbert & Sullivan's D'Oyly Carte Opera Company (see chapter on "Vaudeville and Theater Posters") and John Hassal (1868–1948), who designed for many publishers and literary magazines, are worth looking for and collecting.

James Pryde (1869–1941) and William Nicholson (1872–1949), who worked together under the name "The Beggarstaff Brothers," are also highly sought after. They established a style using silhouette treatment for figures and flat color fields which affected English poster art for many years, as well as influencing German artists and such American artists as Edward Penfield. Beggarstaff Brothers' posters do surface from time to time on the active market and are quickly snatched up.

THE ARTS AND CRAFTS MOVEMENT AND THE GLASGOW SCHOOL

There is no doubt that the English and American Arts and Crafts movement, with its sparse moralistic tone and its opposition to extravagance, contributed to the popularity of the Beggarstaff style. Today, while the Arts and Crafts collecting field still is primarily focused on Stickley and other furniture, and on decorative arts such as copper and mica lamps, Arts and Crafts auctions have broadened to include graphics.

A much smaller, but equally significant design movement in terms of its long-term impact was Scotland's Glasgow School and its leading artist Charles Rennie Mackintosh (1868–1928). Mackintosh's style combines the design complexities of Art Nouveau with the functional geometric shapes of the Arts and Crafts style.

His few designs for posters, and those of his colleagues Margaret MacDonald and Herbert and Francis McNair, are extremely rare, and it is difficult to put market prices on works which so rarely appear outside of museums.

The Glasgow School had an effect on the design of the Viennese Secessionists and the artists of the Wiener Werkstätte. In fact, one of the leading artists of the Viennese Secession, Josef Hoffmann (1870–1956), eventually married Mackintosh's sister. (See additional information about posters of the Vienna Secession under Design Influences in the chapter on "French Posters.")

ENGLISH POSTER PATRONS

World War I helped advance the acceptance of the poster in England as a means of public communication, and several of England's best artists from the period are also represented in the chapter on "World War Posters." However, just before the war London Transport became the first important patron of posterists in England.

With French posters, one seems to most often talk about the artists, each of whom worked for several clients. With English posters, more often one hears the name of the clients who hired the artists: London Transport, Shell Oil Company, and British Railways. Although some collectors of English posters specialize by artist, more often they seem to specialize in collecting the advertiser. (See information and price listings for British Railway posters in the chapter on "Travel and Transportation Posters.")

Many of the same outstanding artists worked for more than one of the above clients: E. McKnight-Kauffer (1890–1954), an American by birth; Austin Cooper (1890–1964), who emigrated to England from Canada; Charles Pears (1873–1958); Frank Newbould (1887–1950); Tom Purvis (1888–1959); Fred Taylor (1875–1963); J. S. Anderson; John Armstrong; Paul Nash; and several others whose names are becoming better known today.

Edward McKnight-Kauffer, who moved to England from the United States in 1914, is recognized as the most outstanding "English" graphic designer. His work is stunning, simple, and boldly avant-garde. Happily, he was also a prolific graphic designer and received numerous commissions, so his work is widely available on the market today with prices ranging from under $1,000 to up to $10,000.

London Museum, 1922 by E. McKnight-Kauffer.
Courtesy of the Cooper-Hewitt Museum

LONDON HISTORY AT THE
LONDON MUSEUM
DOVER STREET
OR ST. JAMES'S PARK STATION

He received his first commission for London Transport in 1915 and went on to create several outstanding posters for this client, including

his fine *London Museum* in 1922, depicting the flames of the Great
Fire of London, and his 1930 *Power, The Nerve Center of the London
Underground*, depicting a fist emanating from a factory and train wheel,
punctuated by zigzag lighting bolts (see photo). Like Cassandre in
France, McKnight-Kauffer influenced an entire generation of graphic
designers and set the tone and the pace for a new form of advertising
in England.

*Great Western and Southern Railways,
by E. McKnight-Kauffer.
Courtesy of the Cooper-Hewitt Museum*

From November 1989 through April 1990, the Cooper Hewitt Museum in New York, which is the Smithsonian Institution's National
Museum of Design, presented an exhibition of E. McKnight-Kauffer
posters and graphics from their permanent collection of more than
1,225 works by the artist. Among the works exhibited were McKnight-
Kauffer posters for the Great Western and Southern Railways (see photo).

Shell Oil Company posters, most of which were produced with the
slogan "You Can Be Sure of Shell," were also commissioned from
McKnight-Kauffer and other leading artists, and executed in a wide
variety of styles from Cubist avant-garde to painterly landscapes.
These, along with British Railway posters, are increasingly seen at
poster auctions, bringing new attention to many of the artists named
above.

The large, horizontal formats of both the Shell Oil and British
Railway posters have made them popular favorites for decorating large

spaces, both residential and commercial. Along with London Transport posters, they represent the best English graphic design from the period between the two World Wars.

GERMAN POSTERS

Germany has a rich and broad history of poster making, which, unfortunately, is less well known and less available in this country than it should be, given the tremendous output and long list of talented artists. However, numerous factors have combined to make German posters relatively rare and hard to find on the American market.

One reason is that from World War II until very recently, Americans have had a bias against things German. While on one level it meant taking sauerkraut off the shelves during World War II to reappear under the name "Liberty Cabbage," this bias especially extended to German arts. For many years the significant impact that German immigrant artists to America had on the decorative arts in the Art Deco period was ignored. The horrors of the war meant that Nazi posters, which today have surged ahead because of their historical importance, were shunned. (See Design Influences in the chapter on "French Posters" as well as the chapter on "World War Posters.")

Early German posters are also rare because there were strong restrictions against posting in Germany. Even between the two wars, German posters were printed in relatively small quantities. German advertisers, like their American counterparts, tended to rely more on newspaper advertising than on postering to deliver their messages. In addition, under Nazi rule a vast number of posters from master printers such as Adolph Friedlander (1851–1904) and his sons were destroyed. (See the chapters on "Magic Posters" and "Circus Posters.")

Today, efforts to increase the appreciation of German arts and cultural traditions have been greatly forwarded by The Goethe Institute and other organizations in this country. Also, as of this writing, the world is watching the rapid reunification of East and West Germany, a measure bound to increase German cultural exchange in the years ahead.

The market for German posters and German poster artists is now firmly established, and major exhibitions have recognized the important contributions of German artists to poster composition, design, and typography.

THE JUGENDSTIL AND GERMAN SECESSIONISTS

Early poster artists in Germany were influenced by both the Art Nouveau movement in France and the Vienna Secession. Publications such as *Simplicissimus*, *Jugend*, and *Pan* chronicled and promoted the latest trends in the arts. The Art Nouveau movement in Germany, Jugendstil, took its name from the journal, and the posters of Jules Chéret had an influence on some German graphic design.

The artistic movements were centered in Munich and notable poster artists include Thomas Theodore Heine (1867–1948), who was the Art Director for *Simplicissimus*; Bruno Paul (1874–1968) and Peter Behrens (1868–1940), both architects who were strongly influenced by the Jugendstil; Vincez Cissarz (1873–1942), influenced strongly by the Vienna Secession; Otto Fischer (1870–1940); and others.

GERMAN POSTERS AND COMMERCE

Munich may have been the center for posters which promoted artistic movements, but Berlin became the capital of the German product poster, and the most outstanding new posters in Berlin were being created by Lucian Bernhard (1883–1972).

Bernhard was the innovator of something he called the "Sach Plakat" or "Object Poster" as early as 1906, where the product being advertised occupied the main field of the illustrated design. His sense of composition, strong color combinations, and his mastery of typography have made his work highly sought after in the poster market. His "Object Poster" influenced numerous artists in Germany and Switzerland, especially in the Art Deco period.

He moved to the United States in 1923 and taught graphic design at the Art Students' League in New York City. His name lives on in the graphic arts today as the creator of the Bernhard typestyle family. His work does not often appear on the American market, but when it does it can sell in the $2,000 to $5,000 range.

Other Berlin-based artists who are recognized and collected today are Hans Rudi Erdt (1883–1918); Edmund Edel (1863–1934); Julius Klinger (1876–1950); and Ernst Deutsch (1883–1938). Many of these artists relied on the fine work of the Hollerbaum & Schmidt printing company in Berlin.

However, Munich was to claim the greatest and most prolific of all German commercial poster artists: Ludwig Hohlwein (1874–1949). Hohlwein not only created strong and finely composed images for German posters, but was also commissioned in England, Switzerland, the United States, and elsewhere because of his tremendous talents with flat colors, shadows, and interpretation of form and figure.

His strong and stunning poster for the German delicatessen *Wilhelm Mozer* in 1909 is one of the most recognizable images in the poster world. (See color center section.) His work was often printed by the firms of Oscar Consee or Vereinigte Druckereien & Kunstanstaiten, both in Munich. Many of Hohlwein's posters now sell in the $2,000 to $5,000 range, though several sell for more. Some of his travel posters can still be obtained for less than $1,000, and many of his smaller advertising graphics and handbills can be purchased for $100 to $300.

Like McKnight-Kauffer in England and Cassandre in France, his work stands head and shoulders above his contemporaries and he is easily today the single most collected German poster artist. This was not always the case, however, as for many years he was shunned because of his support and the posters he created for the Hitler regime.

It is important to note here that the tendencies towards what is now called Modern design were accepted much earlier in German art than they were in French: simplified line, stylized form, solid bright colors, and geometric shapes. In fact, it was German design innovations from such institutions as the Bauhaus school of architecture that would have the strongest impact on the development of the later 1930s "Moderne" style in France.

Other German artists worth collecting include Fritz Rehm (1876–1950); Jupp Wiertz (1881–1939), known for his posters for German travel and cinema; Walter Schnakenberg (1880–1961); and Hans Koch (1899–1977), who designed with a Hohlwein style.

ITALIAN POSTERS

The history of early Italian posters is really the history of the opera in Italy, for the finest Italian Art Nouveau images were most frequently for opera performances. The Art Nouveau design style flourished in Italy under the name "Stile Liberty" because of the popularity of Art Nouveau goods from the London shop of A. L. Liberty.

Adolpho Hohenstein (1854–?), often called the Father of Italian Poster Art, was actually a German who migrated to Italy. He was hired by the music publisher Ricordi and created what is considered the first important Italian pictorial poster in 1889 for Puccini's opera *Edgar*. He became the first Art Director for the Ricordi company, which was to dominate Italian poster art until after the turn of the century. He also received commissions from Belgium and France and today his posters, with their fine representative style and dramatic colors, can sell for $5,000 and more at auction.

Many other Italian artists generally recognized as important posterists also worked for Ricordi: Leopoldo Metlicovitz (1868–1944), whose finest works now sell in the range of $3,000 to $5,000; Marcello Dudovitch (1878–1962), whose career spanned both the Art Nouveau and Art Deco periods and who went on to be an important product poster artist; Giovanni Mataloni; and others.

Other Italian artists worth finding are Marcello Nizzoli (1887–1960), who worked in an Art Deco style and created some stunning posters for Olivetti; Giorgio Muggiani (1887–1938); Achille Mauzin (1883–1952), who was French but who worked in Italy until World War I; Alearo Terzi (1870–1943); Galileo Chini (1873–1956); Plinio Codognato (1878–1940); Pipein Gamba (1868–1954); and Enrico Sacchetti (1877–1967).

Poster collectors should be aware that many of the finest and most elaborate Ricordi posters for *Madame Butterfly*, *Othello*, *Turandot*, and other operas by Puccini and Verdi are reproduced by Fiesta Arts Company in this country and have been retailed through such publications as *Ovation Magazine*. (See the chapters "Poster Printing and Terminology" and "Poster Collecting" for more information on identifying reproductions.)

Many Italian posters are still very accessibly priced, and except for Hohenstein and Dudovitch, have not received the level of attention that automatically drives the market higher. Kate Hendrickson of Chicago is the only poster dealer in this country we have identified who specializes in Italian posters and who assisted us in compiling the information here. It is a field in which there are bound to be new discoveries in the years ahead.

PRICE LISTINGS

ENGLISH POSTERS

Note: See the chapter "Important Notes on the Price Listings" for more information on prices given. Also note that many British artists also have listings under other chapters such as "Travel and Transportation Posters."

J. S. ANDERSON

Motorists Prefer Shell, 1935. Lithograph depicting a streamlined motorcar as the background with pistons and tubes in the foreground. Fine condition, horizontal 45″ × 30″. $4,500–$5,000

JOHN ARMSTRONG

Artists Prefer Shell, ca. 1935. Unusual lithographic poster from the series depicting a conch shell, artist's palette, and Greek goblet. Very good condition, linen-mounted, horizontal 45″ × 29½″.

$1,500–$1,800

DENIS CONSTANDUROS

Farmers Prefer Shell, ca. 1935. Lithographic poster showing stylized farm implements in a field and birds in flight. Soft pastel colors. Very good condition, approx. horizontal 46″ × 28″. $850 (Auction)

JOHN COPLEY

For London Music, 1935. Lithographic poster for London Transport, green-and-gray charcoal, shows conductor, orchestra. Very good condition, 25″ × 40″. $600–$800

GABAIN

For London Fare, 1935. Lithographic poster for London Transport, in sepia-and-gray charcoal, shows restaurant captain preparing a flambé at tableside. Very good condition, 25″ × 40″. $600–$800

CLIVE GARDINER

At London's Service, ca. 1935. Lithographic poster integrating type and image in an excellent example of London Transport advertising using the noted easel painters of the day. Very good condition, 24″ × 39″. $400–$500

E. Mc*KNIGHT-KAUFFER (1890–1954)*

Actors Prefer Shell, 1933. Lithographic poster which is a McKnight-Kauffer classic. An actor holds a rectangular mask in front of his face. Fine condition, horizontal 45″ × 30″. $2,200–$2,800

Aeroshell Lubricating Oil, 1932. Lithographic poster featuring a yellow race car against a dark blue field and subtitled "The Aristocrat of Lubricants." Fine condition, one of the best examples of the artist's work and the Shell Oil series, linen-mounted, horizontal 45″ × 30″.
$7,000–$8,000

Look! Under That Broad Beech Tree . . . , 1932. From the London Underground series of posters using quotes from English writers (here, Izaak Walton) translated into visual imagery by the designers of the time. Bucolic image of a glen. Good condition, linen-mounted, 24″ × 39″. $600–$800

A Postman in Northern Scotland, 1930. Photomontage subtitled "Outposts of Britain." Fine condition, linen-mounted, 21″ × 26″.
$2,000–$2,500

Power, The Nerve Center of London Underground, 1930. Avant-garde lithographic poster depicting a factory and a train wheel from which a fist protrudes, emanating zigzag lightning bolts. Good condition, an excellent example of the artist's style, linen-mounted, 25″ × 39½″.
$6,000–$8,000

Wherever You Go You Can be Sure of Shell, 1932. Lithographic poster, not as avant-garde as others by McKnight-Kauffer, but a dramatic night scene of Bodiam Castle. Very good condition, linen-mounted, horizontal 44″ × 30″. $600–$900

All price ranges represent the retail value.

PAT KEEL

Many Slip—Get a Good Grip, 1945. London Transport poster depicting double-decker bus and teacher's slate with a shoe and the poster slogan. Very good condition, linen-mounted, 24″ × 37″.

$250–$350

EVE KIRKE

Everywhere You Go, You Can be Sure of Shell, ca. 1940. Lithograph done in a painterly style of the tranquil Strand on the Green, Chiswick. Excellent condition, linen-mounted, horizontal 45″ × 30″.

$500–$600

CEDRIC MORRIS

Gardeners Prefer Shell, ca. 1935. Lithographic poster showing a very painterly and colorful rendering of an English flower garden. Good condition, but with tears into image, horizontal 45″ × 30″.

$750 *(Auction)*

G. R. MORRIS

Judges Prefer Shell, 1935. Lithographic poster showing a justice's wig crowning a stylized owl head. Mint condition, horizontal 45″ × 30″.

$1,500 *(Auction)*

PAUL NASH

Footballers Prefer Shell, ca. 1935. Lithographic poster with stunning design of soccer net, ball, field house, all in shades of brown and blue. Extremely rare, near mint condition, horizontal 45″ × 30″.

$2,000–$2,500

WALTER SPRADBERY

Haresfoot Woods Barkhamsted, 1932. Lithographic London Underground poster for The Green Line shows campers in the woods, dwarfed by the majesty of the great trees. Very good condition, linen-mounted, 25″ × 40″. $600–$700

At London's Service, ca. 1935. Lithographic London Transport poster features Beefield, Farmingham, with superb border design. Very good condition, 24″ × 39″. $400–$500

GRAHAM SUTHERLAND

. . . *From Field to Field,* 1936. Lithographic poster featuring a serene and stunning illustration of two doves, for London Transport's Green Line. Very good condition, rare, 24″ × 39″. $500–$800

GERMAN POSTERS

Note: *See the chapter "Important Notes on the Price Listings" for more information on prices given. Also note that many German artists also have listings under other chapters such as "World War Posters" and "Travel and Transportation Posters."*

ANONYMOUS

Automobile Fabrik Perl, ca. 1930. Lithographic poster in good condition, 36¾″ × 25″.   *$500 (Auction)*

OTTO AMTSBERG (1877–)

Prof. Dr. Friedrich V. Esmarch's Tafelgetrank, 1910. Color lithograph printed by Plakatkunst, Berlin. In muted peach, olive green, brown, black, and white. Very good condition, a good example of the artist's style, framed, 37″ × 27″.   *$1,000–$1,200*

MAX ESCHLE

L'Allemagne/Pays de Bon Accueil. Lithographic poster printed in Berlin for distribution in France; in various tones of blue, bronze, brown, orange. Very good condition, 25″ × 40″.   *$350–$400*

LUDWIG HOHLWEIN (1874–1949)

Bayerische Jagerwoche, 1925. Lithographic poster depicting a Bavarian hunter, rifle, dog, and deer carcass. Very good condition, linen-mounted, 34″ × 48″.   *$4,000–$5,000*

Deutschland, 1936. Small format poster proof for Hohlwein's classic design for the 1936 Winter Olympics; in blue, red, brown, yellow, and black. Fine condition, 9″ × 12″.   *$200–$250*

International Einfurh-Messe (Exports Exhibition), 1919. Lithographic poster in green, red, black, and yellow with dramatic design of a train crossing a bridge. Very good condition, linen-mounted, 23″ × 55″.
$800–$1,000

Lake of Constance, ca. 1930. Lithographic poster depicting the statue of a lion overlooking the lake, flags draped across image. Hohlwein in his watercolor phase. Fine condition, linen-mounted, 25″ × 40″.
$600–$700

Motorenfabrik Oberursel, ca. 1914. Beautifully printed, small format poster design from the German publication *Motor*. Fine condition, 9″ × 13″.   *$150–$200*

Passau, 1929. Lithographic poster in the typical Hohlwein style with bold, flat, sometimes stippled color planes; in brown, green, yellow, and tan. Good condition, linen-mounted, horizontal 34″ × 26″.

$800–$1,000

Wilhelm Mozer, 1909. Lithographic poster for the Munich delicatessen features brightly colored foods and wines with a large lobster in the foreground. (Collectors should note that this poster has been reproduced in recent years by offset printing.) Very good condition, framed, 31″ × 44″ on linen. (See color center section.)   *$1,800 (Auction)*
$1,800–$2,300

LINDENSTAEDT

Kontorbedart Papier-Schultze. Lithographic poster printed by Verlag Ren, signed in the stone. Stylized silhouette figure holding pen and ink, the feather reaching across the composition. Three letter-types, with flat planes of black, white, red, and gray. Fair condition, good example of German poster art, linen-mounted and shrink-wrapped, 36½″ × 26½″.   *$800–$1,200*

CARL MOOS (1878–1959)

Wilhelm Braun & Cie. Lithographic poster printed in Munich, Germany. Fair condition, linen-mounted, framed, 30¼″ × 43½″.

$700 (Auction)

V. MUNDORFF

Horch. Lithographic poster printed by Offsetdruck Brandstetter, Leipzeig. Fair condition, 28″ × 40″.   *$775 (Auction)*

FRITZ REHM (1871–1928)

Suss Stoff Hochst. (Hochst sugar substitute), ca. 1910. Lithographic poster depicting gentleman and lady drinking tea under a stylized tree. Fine condition, 19″ × 29″.   *$700–$800*

WALTER SCHNAKENBERG (1880–1961)

Die Pyramide, 1920. Lithographic poster for the Pyramid Café featuring an Egyptian woman with a tray of food, pyramid in the background. Good condition, linen-mounted, 35″ × 47″.

$8,000–$10,000

FRITZ UHLICH

Courtesy of Poster Mail Auction Company

Hotel am Wank. Elegant poster for Munich hotel features a man and woman in evening dress; open reserve at lower right awaits announcement of the week's highlight. Fine condition, linen-mounted, 23″ × 34″. $350–$400

HANS UNGER (1872–1936)

Courtesy of William Doyle Galleries

Nicodé-Concert, 1897. Lithographic poster depicting a classical figure of a boy playing pipes, excellent colors. Good condition, linen-mounted, 23¾″ × 41½″. $1,500–$2,000

JUPP WIERTZ (1881–1939)

Bayreuth/Festival du Theatre, 1938. The famous Wiertz design for the Festival with the orchestra silhouetted in foreground, Wagner's bust like a medallion glowing above. Very good condition, linen-mounted, 25″ × 40″. $500–$600

Bayreuth/La Ville de Richard Wagner. Poster from this famous German travel-poster artist features elaborate fountains; in blue, yellow, green, and black. Very good condition, 25″ × 40″. $350–$400

ITALIAN POSTERS

Note: *See the chapter "Important Notes on the Price Listings" for more information on prices given.*

ANONYMOUS

Birra doppio malto S. Giusto—Fabrica Dreher Trieste, 1920s. Lithographic poster printed by Istituto Italiano d'Arti Grafiche, Bergamo. Two women holding the beer with an Italian square in the background. Good condition, linen-mounted, approx. 26¼″ × 39″.
$325–$400

Grand Palace Hotel/Lugano, 1930s. Lithographic poster printed by A. Trueb, Logano, depicting the hotel brightly lit with the lake in the foreground. Good condition, horizontal approx. 39¼″ × 27½″.
$300–$400

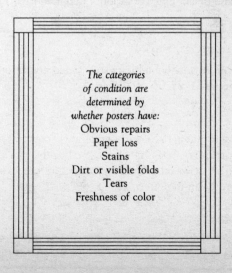

*The categories
of condition are
determined by
whether posters have:*
Obvious repairs
Paper loss
Stains
Dirt or visible folds
Tears
Freshness of color

Courtesy of Poster Mail Auction Company

Liquore del Reno, 1909. A young woman seated at a small table with her legs crossed, beckoning with her liqueur glass; in brown, green, yellow, blue, and black. Fine condition, linen-mounted, 14″ × 22″.

$400–$500

DUILIO CAMBELLOTTI *(1876–1960)*

Incandescenza Auer. Lithographic poster. Good condition with minor tears, linen-mounted, 27¼″ × 77½″. $850 *(Auction)*

G. CAPRANESI

Sotto Scrivete al Prestito, 1915. Lithographic poster printed by Officine dell'Istituto Italiano d'Arti Grafiche, signed in the block. An allegorical figure of Italy fights off a German invader in medieval battle garb. Fine condition, linen-mounted, 28″ × 39″. $350–$500

ERBERTO CARBONI

Automobile Club Diparma. Lithographic poster in good condition, linen-mounted, 25¼″ × 36½″. $1,050 *(Auction)*

GALILEO CHINI (1873–1956)

La Rassegna Internazionale Della Letteratura e Dell'arte Comtemporanea, ca. 1902. Lithographic poster printed by Premto Stabilimto Litografico, A. Gambl., Firenze. Rare Art Nouveau design influenced by Japanese woodblock depicts a woman dressed in flowing white seated on a tree branch of olive green with rust-colored berries. Background is royal blue sky filled with gold clouds. Good condition, very good example of the artist's style, linen-mounted, 39″ × 85″.

$5,700–$6,000

PLINIO CODOGNATO (1878–1940)

L'Itala, ca. 1900. Lithographic poster printed by D. Coen & C., Milano-Parigi. An unusual image of a bare-shouldered woman with rusty red hair in a chartreuse dress riding a bicycle by Atala, set against a plum background. A young Pan holds a garland of white and pale blue flowers that rides around her hips. Good condition, a very good example of the artist's style, linen-mounted, 39¾″ × 59″.

$2,800–$3,000

Maison Talbot Milano, ca. 1900. Lithographic poster printed by D. Coen & C., Milano-Parigi. Two men in a red cart drawn by two horses speed along, sending geese flapping and a boy with a bicycle scurrying out of the way; both the cart and bicycle tires are made of Talbot rubber. Multicolored with gray foreground and forest green background. Good condition, an excellent example of the artist's style, linen-mounted, horizontal 78″ × 55″.

$3,900–$4,200

MARCELLO DUDOVICH (1878–1962)

Distillerie Del L'Aurum/Pineta Di Pescara, ca. 1935. Lithographic poster printed by Edizioni Star Officine Impresa Gen. Affissioni e Pubblicita, Milano. A later close-up version of the 1923 work of a woman in white wearing a conical medieval hat and holding an Aurum liquor bottle up to her cheek; blue background. Rare, good condition, linen-mounted, 39½″ × 55″.

$2,100–$2,300

Esposizione Rhodia Albene Alla Rinascente, 1936. Lithographic poster printed by Off. Grafiche IGAP, Milano-Roma. For Rhodia Albene collection presented at the department store La Rinascente. Two women against a dark blue background, one wearing a red, green, yellow, orange, and black plaid dress, the other a red and white polka dot dress. Rare, good condition, an excellent example of the artist's style, linen-mounted, 54¾″ × 77⅛″.

$4,500–$5,000

PIPEIN GAMBA (1868–1954)

Il Giro del Mondo in 80 Giorni, 1906. Lithographic poster printed by Stabto E. Oliveri e C., Genova. A predominantly red and blue poster filled with vignettes of places and characters from "Around the World in 80 Days," presented by the Italian Comic Opera (Magnani). Fine condition, linen-mounted, 40⅜" × 81¾".   *$2,500–$2,700*

GIOVANNI MATALONI

La Tribuna, Roma, 1897. Lithographic poster printed by Off. G. Ricordi & C., Milano. A woman sprouting Mercury wings from her head wears a burnt orange dress with yellow ochre Art Nouveau detailing. She leans over the earth under a sapphire night sky with a quill pen and paper in hand, waiting for news to send to the Roman newspaper *La Tribuna*. Good condition, a fine example of Italian Art Nouveau, linen-mounted, 57" × 109½".   *$6,000–$6,500*

ACHILLE MAUZAN (1883–1952)

Courtesy of Stephen Ganeles

Divano-Letto Novaresi, ca. 1925–1930. Lithographic poster signed in the block. A woman in a bathrobe gives a huge yawn; behind her is a sofa. Fine condition, 35" × 56".   *$500–$600*

LEOPOLDO METLICOVITZ (1868–1944)

Copertoni Impermeabili, 1933. Lithographic poster printed by Off. G. Ricordi & C., Milano. A horse-drawn cart, done in a slightly Cubist style, carries a large load covered by a tarpaulin made by Ettore Moretti Co. on a flat forest green background. Fine condition, linen-mounted, 55" × 77¾".   *$1,200–$1,400*

Impermeabili Moretti, ca. 1920. Lithograph printed by Off. G. Ricordi & C. A man in a coat and hat stands on top of an open umbrella with rain pelting down all around. Fine condition, a good example of the artist's style, 36″ × 56″. $550–$700

G. G. B. MINONZIO

Borsalino fu Lazzaro (The Pearl of Hats), 1930s. Lithographic poster printed by Moneta, Milano, depicting a gentleman's hat in an opened oyster shell. Very good condition, linen-mounted, approx. 39¼″ × 55″. $800–$1,200

RETROSI

Lotteria di Merano, 1935. Lithographic poster printed by IGAP, Rome, advertising a lottery by depicting currency notes falling from a lucky horseshoe. Linen-mounted, approx. 39¼″ × 55″. $250–$300

ENRICO SACCHETTI (1877–1967)

Verde e Azzurro, Milano, 1900. Lithographic poster printed by Off. G. Ricordi, Milano. On a yellow-green background, a Belle Epoque woman in a white and azure blue dress gaily displays the newspaper *Verde e Azzurro* in each hand. Good condition, linen-mounted, 52″ × 79″. $2,100–$2,300

MODERN MASTERS

COLLECTING ORIGINAL CONTEMPORARY ARTISTS' POSTERS

By Robert K. Brown

Robert K. Brown is co-owner of the Reinhold-Brown Gallery in New York City. He has written extensively on posters and graphic design for several publications and is the author of The Poster Art of A. M. Cassandre *(New York: E.P. Dutton, 1979). Call or write: Reinhold-Brown, 26 East 78th Street, New York, NY 10021. (212) 734–7999.*

When Pierre Bonnard and Henri de Toulouse-Lautrec made their first posters, not only was the modern postern born but the original artist's poster as well. We associate many artists almost exclusively with posters: Jules Chéret, Alphonse Mucha, Ludwig Hohlwein, A. M. Cassandre, and, in more recent times, Herbert Leupin, Bernard Villemot or David Lance Goines. Posters by fine artists, as opposed to illustrators and commercial artists, provide a fresh, innovative, and vital dimension to the history of the art form.

The early period of modern posters is filled with remarkable examples of fine artists' posters coming out of such movements as the Vienna Secession, the Bauhaus, German Expressionism, and Russian Constructivism, and their leading members such as Gustav Klimt, Oskar Schlemmer, Ernst Ludwig Kirchner, and El Lissitzky. Yet because the ability to find these posters and, for most collectors, to comfortably afford them, is so limited, I prefer to devote this chapter to the fertile and exciting area of fine art posters of the past few decades. During this time, there has been a remarkable revival of innovative poster making, mostly for cultural events and attractions. I offer below a road map to a territory that is exciting and appealing in its landscape.

The one most important factor to know in collecting contemporary artists' posters is that it is much like collecting contemporary fine prints. Unlike with vintage posters, there is no tolerance for defects. This means that you must avoid art posters that have tears, soiling, stains, folds, creases or wrinkles, have been mounted on anything or have undergone restoration.

To a large degree, the better the printing process the more desirable the poster. While some original posters printed photographically are sought after, the most desired ones are printed by stone or plate lithography, linoleum cut, woodcut or silk-screen.

The posters you collect must be considered "original" designs. I like to refer to such posters as being designed "from the ground up" because the artist created a work of art exclusively as a poster, as opposed to posters that simply take a work of an artist previously done in another medium and adapt it to a poster. The latter will always remain relatively worthless unless they have some documentary quality, such as being issued for a landmark event or exhibition.

One of the more irksome difficulties you will encounter from time to time is being unable to determine on the spot if a particular artist's poster is an original design. If you are in a gallery or shop in which the owner knows the difference, sometimes the price will be an indication. Other times you may have to look through reference books or monographs about the artist in question to see if the work is documented as an original poster or appears as first being done as a painting, print or drawing.

Just as in the print world, signed and numbered posters are considerably more valuable than those that are unsigned. In instances of posters by the greatest names such as Picasso, Warhol, Rauschenberg or Lichtenstein, a signed or signed and numbered poster can triple or quadruple the price.

As a corollary to this, be alert to the "open-ended" edition. These are posters that are continually being reprinted by their publishers. They are widely available in local art poster/frame shops and, again, you should be able to ascertain such posters by asking the price. Clearly, a poster by a famous artist originally printed several years ago and still available at a very cheap price is one that is probably being reprinted periodically.

In a world abounding with art gallery and museum exhibitions and film, music and dance events, the amount of artists' posters that have been and still are being made is very large. Yet, a wise collector will choose to concentrate his activities on several discreet areas that have emerged in the publication of these posters.

In essence these groups are the "blue chips" of artists' posters and the ones showing the best price appreciation as they move in relative tandem with prints by the same artists. (I use the term "relative" rather loosely because poster prices, while starting to increase as prints become less affordable, still seriously trail print prices both in absolute cost and rate of price appreciation.)

Surely the most ubiquitous or common artists' posters are those published in France by the Foundation or Galerie Maeght. The early posters were printed by Mourlot and from 1964 on by Adrian Maeght, after he acquired his own printing company that he renamed Arte. Even though Maeght published many posters by Miro, Picasso, Chagall, Calder, and many others, for the most part these posters have remained relatively cheap and not much in demand because, with the exception of Miro, Maeght reprints many of his posters.

Indeed the only French-based artists whose posters are truly sought after are Picasso, Miro, and Chagall. Picasso is almost unique in the poster collecting field. Posters have been issued for hundreds of Picasso exhibitions, but only about fifty are considered "original" works of the great master. Even so, many posters published for his exhibitions that were not made by him sell for up to a few hundred dollars.

A collector should avoid these posters and look for, above all others, the Vallauris posters that he designed and printed between 1948 and 1964 for the sale and exhibition of his ceramics.

The Vallauris posters of Picasso can range in price from a few hundred dollars for a late unsigned one to as much as $5,000 for a hand-signed and numbered example from 1954 or 1956. Other Picasso posters worth owning are *Galerie 65-Cannes*, 1956 (about $1,200); *Galerie Leiris: Peintres 1955–56* (about $1,000); the two ceramic exhibition posters for *La Maison de la Pensée Française*, 1958 (about $750 each); the exhibition of his original posters in 1959 held at the same place (about $900); the 1959 Galerie Leiris poster *Los Meines* (about $350); and *Cote d'Azur*, 1952 (about $550).

While not quite matching Picasso in the number of posters designed, Joan Miro created several that are finding increasing demand. Among the more valuable are *Oeuvres Recentes—Galerie Maeght*, 1956 (about $400); *Galerie Matarasso*, 1957 (about $550); *Le Lézard aux Plumes*, 1975 (about $400); and *La Caixa*, 1979 (about $550).

Another European artist of more recent vintage who offers a discreet possibility of poster collecting because of his large output is Joseph Beuys (1921–1986). While not to everyone's sensibilities because he was more a conceptual artist, since his death he has nonetheless been lionized as a kind of latter-day Marcel Duchamp. There are more than one hundred posters by or about him, and prices for his work, while still relatively inexpensive, have skyrocketed.

Several posters that he made himself are already classics. Among them are *24-Stunden-Happening*, issued by Galerie Parness, Cologne, in 1965 (about $200); the Ronald Feldman Gallery exhibition poster of 1974 (about $150); the Munro Gallery 1979 silk-screen (about $400); the Beumans von Beuningen Museum poster done on transparent paper in 1979 (about $400); the *Goldkuchen* poster from Kunsthandlung Menzel, Berlin, in 1982, which is a signed and numbered edition of 100 (about $500); and the *Bonn bracht Kunsthalle*, 1983 (about $75).

In terms of posters, the early masters of 20th-century art may have flourished in Europe, but it is in the United States, especially New York, where most of the activity since 1960 has taken place.

Beginning with the Abstract Expressionists in the 1950s through the Pop Art years of the 1960s, New York was by far the art capital of the world. These years, as well as the ensuing ones, have seen a legacy of artists' posters that are vibrant, energetic, and now earnestly sought after by both print and poster collectors. Two publishers of these posters stand out in particular for commissioning the most famous artists of the day: *The Paris Review* and Lincoln Center for the Performing Arts.

Since the early 1960s, *The Paris Review* has published limited editions of both unsigned and signed and numbered posters, usually not exceeding one hundred and fifty copies. Among the most desirable are those by Robert Indiana, 1963 (about $300 unsigned); Robert Motherwell, 1961 (about $400 unsigned, $800 signed); Claes Oldenberg, 1965 (about $400 signed); James Rosenquist, 1967 (about $850 signed); Willem de Kooning, 1979 (about $600 unsigned); David Hockney, 1981 (about $250 unsigned); Christo, 1982 (about $100 unsigned); and Sol Lewitt, 1984 (about $150 unsigned).

Since the early 1960s, Lincoln Center has commissioned outstanding artists for its annual New York Film Festival, the Chamber Music Society, the Metropolitan Opera, and anniversaries of the opening of the Lincoln Center complex.

Original signed and numbered prints from these series can command high prices: Mel Bochner's *20 Years of Lincoln Center* sells for about $650 and Jennifer Bartlett's 1981 Chamber Music Society poster for about $800. Marc Chagall's posters for the Metropolitan Opera (*Carmen* and *The Magic Flute*) have entered the realm of fine rare prints and can sell for more than $3,000. Lincoln Center continues to offer both unsigned posters and signed prints by the artists it commissions, although many of the early editions have completely sold out. (For more information and price listings on Lincoln Center prints and posters and other contemporary publishers, see the chapter entitled "Contemporary Poster Publishers and Patrons.")

It often seems that the new art of our day falls short of the art of generations just passed. With the disappearance of Pop Art, which was nearly poster art incarnate, and the reluctance of today's great artists to make posters when they are literally making hundreds of dollars per brush stroke, so too may it seem that today's artists' posters fall short of those of twenty years ago.

Even though the opportunities for collecting economically for the long-haul by seeking out the newest posters may seem limited, they still exist. One may have to be assiduous and less casual in seeking them out, however. But there are world-renowned artists such as Keith Haring, Jean Tinguely, and Niki de St. Phalle who still enjoy making posters, while any artists might answer the call to design a poster "pro bono" for a worthy cultural or social cause. Lastly, watch for organizations that make it a point to commission artistically serious posters. (Two that come quickly to mind are the Winter and Summer Olympic Games and the Montreux Jazz Festival.)

As suggested above, the gulf between fine prints and original artists' posters is steadily narrowing, if not in price then certainly in perceived legitimacy and respectability. For the ambitious collector, these posters offer one of the few remaining areas of serious collecting that has not been overexploited.

PRICE LISTINGS

*Note: See the chapter "Important Notes on the Price Listings" for more infor-
mation on prices given.*

JOSEPH BEUYS (1921–1986)

Courtesy of Reinhold Brown Gallery

Maifest im Kunstverein Hannover, 1973. Offset lithograph, signed by
hand, depicting a man sweeping papers off a street while another man
watches. Mint condition, 23⅝″ × 31⅞″.   *$500–$600*

ALEXANDER CALDER (1870–1945)

Courtesy of Reinhold Brown Gallery

McGovern, 1972. Silk-screen campaign poster for the George McGovern presidential campaign. An abstract design with McGovern's name.
Mint condition, 22″ × 29½″. $500–$600

MARC CHAGALL *(1887–1985)*

Marc Chagall . . . Four Seasons . . . Chicago 1974, 1974. Color lithograph printed by Mourlot, signed in the block. Vignette figures against a blue and yellow background. This was the last original poster design by Chagall; for the dedication of a ceramic tile sculpture. Mint condition, an excellent example of the artist's work, linen-mounted, 25" × 36". $600–$800

MARCEL DUCHAMP *(1887–1968)*

Courtesy of Reinhold Brown Gallery

Sur Marcel Duchamp, 1959. Lithograph, for the exhibition "Sur Marcel Duchamp" at La Hune Bookstore, Paris. A silhouetted profile of the artist's face shows up on a light square within a dark border. 14⅝" × 20". $1,000–$1,200

CLAES OLDENBERG (B. 1929)

Courtesy of Reinhold Brown Gallery

Claes Oldenburg/Green Gallery/Sept. 24—Oct. 20, 1962. Lithograph for an exhibition at the Green Gallery. A drawing of an early single-propeller airplane is superimposed over a striped circle. 17½″ × 22½″. $500–$600

ANDY WARHOL (1928–1987)

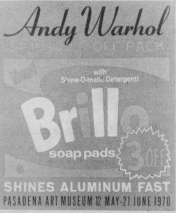

Courtesy of Reinhold Brown Gallery

Andy Warhol/Brillo Soap Pads, 1970. Silk-screen for the exhibition at the Pasadena Museum of Art. A Brillo Soap Pad package with exhibition information at the top and bottom. 26″ × 29½″. $500–$600

ROCK POSTERS

Over the last few years, a growing number of collectors have been attracted to American rock posters of the '60s, '70s, and even the '80s, but with special emphasis on the San Francisco rock posters of the "psychedelic" era from about 1965 to about 1973.

In 1987, Paul Grushkin published a major retrospective work, *The Art of Rock* (see Bibliography), with over five hundred pages of rock history, photos, and documentation of the posters and other ephemera of American rock culture. His book brought both new collecting interest and increased recognition of the major contributions of rock poster artists to the graphic arts. This book is an indispensable resource for anyone wishing to collect the posters of this period.

Today, many psychedelic rock posters of the late 1960s can still be purchased by collectors for under $100, with some still found for $10 to $20 in flea markets, yard sales, and in campus poster shops and second-hand record stores. However, some of the best and rarest examples of rock posters are now selling for $500 and more, a trend which can only continue as more "baby boomer" collectors retrace their teenage roots.

Avid collectors also eagerly hunt for the limited edition silk-screen posters, colored handbills, programs, and other memorabilia of the era.

The most sought-after posters are those created for Bill Graham and for The Family Dog Collective, both important presenters of rock music. Grushkin may have been the most thorough in his approach to the art of rock, but as early as 1980 a collector's guide to these posters appeared. In that year, a small press in Berkeley, California, published Eric King's *Collector's Guide to the Numbered Dance Posters*

Created for Bill Graham and The Family Dog, 1966–1973 (see Bibliography).

These posters were collected from the very first days they were printed. They were created not only to promote concerts but to be sold in record stores and "head shops" of San Francisco's Haight-Ashbury district. For this reason many people who collect vintage posters feel that the posters of this and other modern movements are "self-conscious," but we'd remind them that even Chéret overprinted some of his designs specifically to be sold in Parisian bookstores.

Luckily for today's collectors, both The Family Dog and Bill Graham had numbered poster series, making it possible to retrace the entire history of their production. The Family Dog issued one hundred and forty-seven different posters from 1966 to 1968, and Bill Graham issued two hundred and eighty-seven in his numbered series from 1966 to 1971.

The most outstanding posterists of the period, sometimes called "The Big 5," are Rick Griffin, Alton Kelley, Stanley Mouse, Victor Morosco, and Wes Wilson. Other important artists include Bob Fried, Dennis Nolan, Rick Griffin, Lee Conklin, Greg Irons, and David Singer. As time passes, these names will become increasingly familiar to poster collectors.

The artists who are promoted and the venues that they played are also important components in the collectibility of these posters. The Family Dog Collective produced many shows in the Avalon Ballroom until they were forced to leave in 1968. Bill Graham, who produced shows in the original Fillmore, moved to the Carousel Ballroom which he rechristened Fillmore West. This, along with his New York City venue, Fillmore East, are the two most popular ones to look for in posters.

Groups that were (and some that still are) popular include The Byrds, Fleetwood Mac, Chicago, The Guess Who, Big Brother and the Holding Company, Seals and Crofts, Captain Beefhart, Buffalo Springfield, The Grateful Dead, and so many others who are now part of popular music history.

The Library of Congress, which has one of the most comprehensive poster collections in the world, was given four hundred of these modern masterpieces by Bill Graham in 1970. Though offset printed in great quantities, surprisingly few seem to have survived in mint condition. Like many posters, they were considered inexpensive decorations. Pinned or taped to walls and refrigerators, only to be torn down when a move was made or a college graduation ceremony was over, a great many were lost.

Other distinctive poster designs were created for rock concert producers in cities such as Los Angeles, Detroit, Chicago, and elsewhere. Only the East Coast seemed to have few distinctive native poster designs from the era. Posters of these other cities, too, have some collecting value today depending on the performer, the poster artist, and the overall design. However, they have not yet become as sought after by collectors.

In some ways, the design styles of the San Francisco rock era were influenced by Art Nouveau, which enjoyed a resurgence of popularity at the time. Off-hand homage was paid to great masters, such as in the name of one of the printing companies, "Tea Lautrec Litho." Other early design influences can be seen as well.

However, rock posters are a truly American art form, and, when first produced, were collected all over the world. They represent the dreams, ideals, and revolutionary attitudes of an entire generation at a time when attending a 1969 concert at Max Yasgur's farm for "3 Days of Peace and Music" was considered a radical act.

By the mid-1970s, the counter-cultural aspects of many of the posters disappeared, along with their spark of genius and creativity, as rock music became increasingly a "big business." Today, the creative cutting-edge in posters is in the punk rock scene.

The originality of the early San Francisco rock posters, their innovative use of color and typography, and their ability to evoke an era of history ensures their place in the future of poster collecting.

PRICE LISTINGS

Note: *See the chapter "Important Notes on the Price Listings" for more information on prices given.*

ANONYMOUS

Bill Graham Presents: The Sound, ca. 1967. Fillmore Auditorium concert poster in psychedelic red, green, and chartreuse, printed on stiff board. Good condition, with two or three minor nicks in image area. 14″ × 20″. $100–$125

Leon Russell with New Riders of the Purple Sage and Commander Cody and His Lost Planet Airmen, ca. 1967. Whimsical nonsense design in the style of R. Crumb; very colorful. Very good condition, 14″ × 20″.   *$150–$200*

Western Front: Grand Opening—Blues Band/Big Brother and the Holding Co./Quicksilver Messenger Service . . . , 1967. Intricate three-color design with gypsy wagon. Very good condition, 14″ × 20″.

$75–$100

RICK GRIFFIN

Courtesy of Poster Mail Auction Company

A Magic Show/Big Brother and the Holding Co., 1967. Avalon Ballroom concert poster presented by Family Dog Productions. Mint condition, 14″ × 20″.   *$100–$125*

GREG IRONS

The Western Front: In Concert/Sandy Bull . . . , 1967. Intricate design in dark brown on white paper. Very good condition, 14″ × 20″.

$60–$80

VICTOR MOSCOSO (B. 1936)

Otis Rush, 1967. Printed by Neon Rose. Superbly psychedelic image for a Fillmore concert in San Francisco. Mint condition, 14″ × 20″.

$60 (Auction)

DAVID SINGER

The Byrds/Fleetwood Mac, 1969. Printed by Tea Lautrec Litho. A Fillmore West concert presented by Bill Graham in San Francisco. Mint condition, 14″ × 22″. $175–$200

Chicago/The Guess Who/Seals and Croft, 1969. Printed by Tea Lautrec Litho. For a Bill Graham concert at Fillmore West; depicts a hand holding an ice cream cone out in front of an American flag. Mint condition, 14″ × 22″. $80 (Auction)

Savoy Brown/Sea Train/Ry Cooder/Humble Pie, 1970. Printed by Tea Lautrec Litho. A Bill Graham Fillmore West concert. Mint condition, 14″ × 22″. $50–$75

Ten Years After/Buddy Rich and His Orchestra, 1970. Printed by Tea Lautrec Litho. A Bill Graham, Fillmore West, San Francisco concert. Mint condition, 14" × 22".   *$100–$125*

ARNOLD SKOLNIK

Woodstock Music and Art Fair, 1969. Offset, signed in the matrix. Created at the last minute for the Woodstock Festival when it was forced to relocate to Max Yasgur's farm where it drew 400,000 people for "3 Days of Peace and Music." Colorful, stylized; a dove sits on the neck of a guitar as it's being played. Mint condition, an important poster of the period, 16" × 24".   *$250–$275*

WES WILSON (B. 1937)

The Byrds and the Wildflower, 1966. A Bill Graham presentation in San Francisco at the Fillmore Auditorium; "Fly 3 Miles High with the. . . ." Mint condition, 14" × 24".   *$150–$200*

Captain Beefhart and His Magic Band, 1966. For a Bill Graham, San Francisco, concert. Left half of poster depicts an androgynous quasi-Egyptian figure; right half devoted to poster text in psychedelic lettering. Mint condition, 14" × 19".   *$150–$200*

Chuck Berry—Grateful Dead. Presented in San Francisco by Bill Graham. Intricate two-color design for Fillmore Auditorium concert. Very good condition, 14″ × 21″. $66 (Auction)

Young Rascals, 1967. Depicts a stylized woman whose dress is made up of the poster text. For a Bill Graham concert in San Francisco at the Fillmore Auditorium. Mint condition, 14″ × 24″.

$95 (Auction)

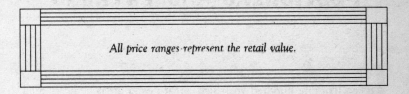

All price ranges represent the retail value.

CONTEMPORARY POSTER PUBLISHERS AND PATRONS

Today, like one hundred years ago, great poster art is being created by talented designers. Certain publishers, organizations, and commercial patrons of the contemporary poster are commissioning some of the best living artists to create posters for a wide diversity of products, events, and organizations. For this chapter, we selected a few of the very best, both to highlight their work and to include in this volume as a historical footnote for future collectors.

We need to note, however, that posters are today a huge business and are the inventory most heavily promoted and sold in thousands of poster shops and frame stores across the country. It takes a lot of time to weed through the hundreds of titles issued each year to find good collectible examples of original poster art.

To emphasize what has already been said elsewhere in this volume, an "original" poster is one that carries a design specifically created for the poster itself. A Renoir painting for a Renoir exhibition at the Museum of Fine Arts is not an original poster.

In the same way, in collecting contemporary posters it is best to collect those which are actually used as advertising or communications campaigns. Many posters are created intentionally to be sold in poster shops and are never really used to actually advertise a product, promote an organization or sell a service.

It is also best to buy posters that are printed in limited editions, and even better if they are signed and/or numbered by the artist. With many posters today, when an edition runs out more are printed, lowering the long-term collecting value. In addition, it is better to look for posters that are printed by silk-screen or some other less mass-produced method than photo offset printing. Some of the posters in this chapter don't meet these last two qualifications, but we'd still recommend them as examples of some of the finest graphic design of our times.

LINCOLN CENTER/LIST ART POSTER AND PRINT PROGRAM

Robert K. Brown has already mentioned Lincoln Center as one contemporary publisher which has commissioned recognized artists to produce limited edition posters. (See the chapter entitled "Collecting Original Contemporary Artists' Posters.")

In 1962, Lincoln Center for the Performing Arts received a generous gift from Albert and Vera List to establish the Lincoln Center/ List Art Poster and Print Program. Since that time, Lincoln Center has commissioned works of art by contemporary artists to commemorate major Lincoln Center openings, festivals, and special events.

Each Lincoln Center edition is created in two versions: a signed print and a poster. With only a few exceptions, the print version is produced without the text used on the poster. The print is signed and numbered by the artist and is usually issued in an edition of seventy-two, one hundred and eight, or one hundred and forty-four with artists' proofs. The poster is printed with the same high standards, with text, and usually in an edition of between five hundred and 1,500.

Virtually all of the posters and prints are silk-screens or lithographs. The printing process is carried out with the utmost care, using the highest quality materials, and under the supervision of the artist. Once the poster and print runs are completed, the screens that are used in the process are destroyed to prevent reprints. In this way, the Lincoln Center/List Art Posters and Prints has earned a reputation based not only on the stature of the artists it commissions, but on the high standards maintained in the printing of the works.

Some posters, mainly from the 1980s, are still available through the Lincoln Center and retail for anywhere from $25 for James Rosenquist's *Eighth New York Film Festival,* 1970, to $100 for Julian Schnabel's *25 Years—Lincoln Center,* 1984 (see Resource Guide).

Most of the early posters from the 1960s and early 1970s have sold out (on a recent list only three pre–1974 posters were still available), and can now be purchased only on the secondary market. Some examples of prices for out-of-print posters for the Film Festival by illustrious contributors are: Josef Albers, 1972 (about $300); David Hockney, 1981 (about $200); Robert Rauschenberg, 1982 (about $150); Niki de St. Phalle, 1973 (about $150); Jean Tinguely, 1974 (about $200); and Andy Warhol, 1967 (about $600).

Collectors should also note that because these artists are so recognizable, during the excitement of an auction prices have often soared past what these posters are available for on the retail secondary market.

COMMUNICATIONS WORKERS OF AMERICA

The "Portraits of Determination Series" was commissioned in 1988 by the Communications Workers of America in commemoration of its 50th anniversary as a special tribute to the accomplishments of the American labor movement and in recognition of the challenges it faces today.

Courtesy of Communication Workers of America

Six posters were commissioned by six leading artists: Fred Otnes, Jerry Pinkney, Bart Forbes, Robert Heindel, Mark English, and Vivienne Flesher. Each poster was designed to illustrate basic values and concerns of the American labor movement with titles such as *We're*

People—Not Machines (see photo), Job Issue No. 1—A Healthy Workplace, and *Standing Strong for Workers' Rights.* The series won top honors in a design competition sponsored by the magazine *Graphic Design U.S.A.*

The posters were printed in one format (18″ × 25″) as a limited edition of five hundred, numbered by hand, as well as in a larger format (25″ × 38″) as posters. The fine art prints sold for $25 each or $100 for the set of six and have sold out. The posters, which are still available, sell for $5 each (see Resource Guide).

The Communications Workers of America poster series is just one example of outstanding poster art being commissioned today by non-profit organizations as special commemoratives. Issued at a price already lower than general retail for fine poster design, these works, especially the limited edition series, will reappear on the secondary market someday.

THE SCHOOL OF VISUAL ARTS

Almost anyone who has ever ridden a subway in New York City has seen the stunning posters created annually by the School of Visual Arts (SVA). From its inception, SVA hired only working professionals to teach art—the first college to do so.

Since 1947 it is these same faculty members who have been called upon to produce the posters, including: Robert Weaver, Milton Glaser, Marshall Arisman, Bob Giraldi, Paul Davis, George Tscherny, Ivan Chermayeff, Marvin Matelson, Robert Giusti, Gene Case, and many talented others whose names you will see over and over again in the contemporary poster field.

In 1987, the college was honored when the Cooper Hewitt Museum in New York hosted "Underground Images," an exhibition celebrating the 40th anniversary of SVA, which is now on international tour. The images have become famous around the world, appearing not only on the subway walls of New York City, but in today's magazines which chronicle the design world: *Print, Graphis, U & lc* (Upper and lower case), and *Advertising Age.*

The posters have done their job as recruitment advertising for the college, but more than that they have become a form of public art in New York where they brighten the otherwise often dismal subway stations and platforms. Many are intended to inspire those who would seek a career in the visual arts as well.

For example, Gene Case's 1968 poster depicts the artist Paul Gauguin behind the bars of a teller's window with a line of copy reading "At 35 Paul Gauguin worked in a bank. It's never too late" (see photo). Paul Davis' 1978 poster of a clown in the moonlight uses a slogan by Dee Ito which has appeared on other SVA posters as well, "To be good is not enough when you dream of being great." (See color center section.)

The SVA poster series has been called "the campaign that built the largest arts school in the country," but their sale also serves to support SVA's student scholarship fund. All posters are offset in full color and measure 29″ × 45″, and each is available for a $32 tax-deductible donation which includes shipping and handling (see Resource Guide).

Because these posters, like others in this chapter, are still available retail from the original publisher, we can't predict their secondary market or investment value, but we can say that they are among the best contemporary posters for their sheer impact.

GRAPHIQUE DE FRANCE: AURA DESIGN POSTERS

Graphique de France of Boston is one of the largest publishers and distributors of posters in the world today, and many of the posters which you will find in poster and frame shops, museum stores, and other locations are created by Graphique de France. For the most part, Graphique de France productions are not original artists' posters and have only decorative rather than collecting value. However, one line of posters created by Graphique de France may be different—Aura Design Posters (see Resource Guide).

These posters, created by some of the most talented graphic designers in America, were commissioned through Aura by a wide range of clients from small businesses to international corporations, and have won numerous awards. In many ways they represent an entirely new direction for the commercial poster industry.

Poster for the Howard Conn Fine Arts Center by Charles Spencer Anderson. Courtesy of Graphique de France

Poster for Limn home furnishing stores by Michael Mabry. Courtesy of Graphique de France

The fifty-two posters in the premier catalog of the company were designed by McRay Magleby, David Lance Goines (B. 1945), Michael Mabry (see photo above, right), Dan Olson, Charles Spencer Anderson (see photo above, left), and Joe Duffy for such clients as Ralph Lauren, the Howard Conn Fine Arts Center in Minneapolis, Gringolet Books, a Minneapolis hair salon, Classico Pasta Sauce, Limn home furnishings stores in California, Ravenswood Winery, and others.

David Lance Goines' name is already becoming well known in the poster-collecting field and his work is in the permanent collections of several museums, including the Museum of Modern Art and the Musée des Arts Décoratifs in Paris.

We have recently seen his work appear on the secondary market, including some of the posters he created for Aura. These posters were printed by the artist and made available only in limited quantities with no option for reprinting.

The printing of the Aura posters is very high quality. Although most retail for no more than $20 to $30, some are printed in as many as ten colors, and others include special varnishes, metallic inks, and special papers.

While long-term collecting value of some of these posters may depend on how many of each are ultimately printed and distributed, in terms of original illustration advertising art they are among the best examples of today's poster designs.

MOBIL OIL POSTERS

In recent years, many fine poster series have been created by large corporations who have commissioned leading artists. In earlier periods of poster art, the same was true of the British Shell Oil series which commissioned E. McKnight Kauffer and other leading artists. Mobil Corporation's sponsorship of the "Mobil Masterpiece Theatre" series on PBS television, as well as other programs, gave rise to the creation of a series of outstanding poster designs and made Mobil one of today's most important commercial patrons of the poster.

Unlike many of the other posters in this chapter, the "Mobil Masterpiece Theatre" posters are not available directly from the publisher, and many are eagerly sought after by collectors on the secondary market.

Arthur Bernberg of Graphic Expectations in Chicago, which specializes in posters of the performing arts, has assembled a large and impressive collection (30″ × 46″). We'll have to repeat ourselves to mention some of the outstanding artists who created posters for Mobil for they include Paul Davis, Ivan Chermayeff, Seymour Chwast, Edward Gorey, Chuck Wilkinson, and others whose names will become increasingly familiar to poster collectors as time goes on.

In the price listing section following this chapter, with the assistance of Arthur Bernberg, we present a cross-section of these fine posters that will appeal not only to collectors of contemporary graphic design but to those who were moved by any one of the numerous television programs that were "made possible by a grant from Mobil."

The publishers and patrons of contemporary poster art in this chapter are by no means the only ones producing collectible images. Those who are interested in contemporary design should look through the pages of some of the publications already mentioned, as well as such magazines as *Communication Arts, Publicite,* and *Advertising Art* to familiarize themselves with the contemporary graphic arts scene.

Today's patrons of outstanding design include opera, symphony and ballet companies, fairs and festivals such as the Spoleto Festival in Charleston, government agencies, museums, visual design publications themselves, the travel industry, and large corporations.

It has been only a little over one hundred years since the advent of the illustrated advertising poster. One hundred years from now, future collectors will look back on our era as a particularly fertile time for posters. Perhaps in the year 2090, if advances in telecommunications and computerized information systems have completely eliminated the need for the printed page (or if we have used up all of the trees), any well-designed surviving poster from our own era will be a treasure to be preserved.

PRICE LISTINGS

Note: *See the chapter "Important Notes on the Price Listings" for more information on prices given.*

LINCOLN CENTER FOR THE PERFORMING ARTS

JENNIFER BARTLETT

Chamber Music Society of Lincoln Center, 1981. Silk-screen poster. Mint condition, 23¼″ × 34¾″. $35 (Retail)

Chamber Music Society of Lincoln Center, 1981. Silk-screen print or artist proof, signed and numbered by the artist from the edition of 144. One of the few Lincoln Center prints issued with text in the limited edition. Mint condition, 23¼″ × 34¾″. $800 (Retail)

ROSS BLECKNER

Courtesy of Lincoln Center for the Performing Arts

Mostly Mozart Festival, 1987. Silk-screen poster. Mint condition, 32¼″ × 43½″. (Signed prints, in an edition of 72, and artist's proofs of this poster have sold out and are only available on the secondary market.)   *$80 (Retail)*

MEL BOCHNER

Twenty-Five Years—Lincoln Center, 1984. Silk-screen poster. Mint condition, 35″ × 45″.   *$50 (Retail)*

Twenty-Five Years—Lincoln Center, 1984. Silk-screen print or artist proof, without text, signed and numbered by the artist from the edition of 144. Mint condition, 35″ × 45″.   *$650 (Retail)*

FERNANDO BOTERO

Mostly Mozart Festival, 1984. Silk-screen poster. Mint condition, 35″ × 46″.   *$80 (Retail)*

ROY LICHTENSTEIN

4th New York Film Festival, 1966. Silk-screen poster in Lichtenstein's strong abstract style. Available only on the secondary market. Mint condition, 30″ × 45″.   *$2,000–$2,200*

ANDY WARHOL

Film Festival/Lincoln Center, 1967. Silk-screen poster designed for the fifth year of the Lincoln Center Festival in the shape of a huge movie ticket. Available only on the secondary market. Mint condition, 24½″ × 44½″. $700–$1,000

NEIL WELLIVER

Courtesy of Lincoln Center for the Performing Arts

TWENTY-FIVE YEARS
LINCOLN CENTER FOR THE PERFORMING ARTS

Twenty-Five Years—Lincoln Center, 1984. Silk-screen poster. Mint condition, 35″ × 46″.   *$50 (Retail)*

Twenty-Five Years—Lincoln Center, 1984. Silk-screen print or artist proof, without text, signed and numbered by the artist from the edition of 144. Mint condition, 35″ × 46″.   *$650 (Retail)*

MOBIL MASTERPICE THEATRE

IVAN CHERMAYEFF

Chermayeff graduated from Yale University. He is a partner in a very successful graphic design firm and the recipient of numerous awards for his work.

Lillie, 1979. Color lithograph printed by Todd Edelman Budeni & Assoc., signed in the block. A popular "Masterpiece Theatre" production shown in many encore seasons; in blues, purples, and turquoise. Mint condition, a good example of both the artist and the series, 30″ × 46″.   *$225–$275*

SEYMOUR CHWAST (B. 1931)

Chwast is a founder of The Pushpin Group and a designer and illustrator of many children's books. Winner of many awards including AIGA gold medal.

Courtesy of Graphic Expectations

Charters and Caldicott, 1986. Color lithograph printed by Todd Edelman Budelli & Assoc., signed in the block. An example of the crisp illustrative style of the artist; in black and pink with blue accents against a white background, type in gray and mauve. Fine condition, excellent example of the artist's work, 47½″ × 68¼″. $500–$750

I, Claudius, 1977. Color lithograph signed in the block. A highly recognizable poster from one of the most popular "Masterpiece Theatre" productions, done in artist's mosaic tile style; in green, blue, red, and gold against white background. Mint condition, 30″ × 40″.

$175–$275

PAUL DAVIS (B. 1938)

Davis heads his own New York design company. His illustrations can be found on posters, book and album covers, and magazines. He is the winner of many awards and is also well known for his Broadway posters.

Courtesy of Graphic Expectations

The Adventures of Sherlock Holmes, 1985. Color lithograph printed by Todd Edelman Budelli & Assoc., signed in the block. The illustrations of Paul Davis are so perfect and so accurately detailed as to sometimes cause the observer to think he is looking at a color photograph. Fine condition, highly desirable, 47½″ × 68¼″.

$1,275–$1,750

King Lear, 1984. Color lithograph printed by Todd Edelman Budelli & Assoc., signed in the block. In blue, gold, and white. Fine condition, an excellent example of Davis' design, 46″ × 64″.

$1,500–$1,800

PHILIP GIPS

A graduate of Yale University, Mr. Gips is the winner of many awards.

Testament of Youth, 1980. Lithograph in various blues, black, red, and white. Mint condition, 30″ × 46″.   *$75–$100*

EDWARD GOREY

A winner of a Tony Award for his work on the Broadway production of *Dracula*, Mr. Gorey is also the author of many books and has done numerous illustrations for theater and dance companies.

Dr. Jekyll and Mr. Hyde, 1981. Color lithograph signed in the block. Only Mr. Gorey can give us such a captivating Jekyll and Hyde; in red, black, and white. Mint condition, a good example of the artist's style, 30″ × 46″.   *$125–$175*

BARBARA SANDLER

Sandler studied painting at the Art Students League in New York. She maintains a dual career as a serious painter and an illustrator.

Sergeant Cribb, 1980. Color lithograph signed in the block. A stunning poster in many colors from one of the most popular series featured under "Mystery! Presents." Mint condition, 30″ × 46″.
$125–$150

DANIEL SCHWARTZ

Schwartz studied at the Art Students League and the Rhode Island School of Design. He has won the Society of Illustrators Gold Medal ten times.

A Town Like Alice, 1981. Color lithograph printed by Todd Edelman Budelli & Assoc., signed in the block. A multi-colored illustration of the main characters against a field of brown, green, and blue; type is in gray. Mint condition, a fine example of the artist's work, 30″ × 46″.   *$100–$150*

NORMAN WALKER

Mr. Walker, a graduate of Art Center College of Design in Los Angeles, has done illustrations for many major magazines.

Quiet as a Nun, 1982. Another key illustration for a popular "Mystery! Presents" series; mainly in black, brown, and burnt orange. Fine condition, 47½″ × 68¼″.   *$350–$550*

CHUCK WILKINSON

Mr. Wilkinson is from Detroit and has won many awards for illustration.

Love for Lydia, 1979. Color lithograph signed in the block. This poster for "Masterpiece Theatre," 1979–1980, has been a favorite in the graphic design community and among collectors; in purple, mauves, and yellows. Fine condition, excellent example of the series, 46″ × 64″. *$500–$750*

Therese Raquin, 1981. Color lithograph printed by Todd Edelman Budelli & Assoc., signed in the block. This poster for a multi-part "Masterpiece Theatre" based on Emile Zola's novel is another favorite of collectors; in dark purples and mauves with copper skin tones. Mint condition, 30″ × 46″. *$200–$250*

Same as above. Fine condition, 46″ × 64″. *$600–$750*

"City for Conquest," 1940 (Cinema). *Courtesy of Motion Picture Arts Gallery.*

"Dames," 1934 (Cinema). *Courtesy of Motion Picture Arts Gallery.*

"Whispering Wires," c. 1930 (Cinema). *Courtesy of Motion Picture Arts Gallery.*

"Gilda," 1946 (Cinema). *Courtesy of Cinemonde.*

"Job," 1898, by Alphonse Mucha (French). *Courtesy of Club of American Collectors.*

"Liqueur du Couvent de St. Barbe," c. 1905, anonymous (French). *Courtesy of Stephen Ganeles.*

"Petrole Stella," 1897, by Henri Gray (French). *Courtesy of a private collector.*

"Cendrillon," 1899, by Emile Bertrand (French opera). *Author's collection, photo by Robert Four.*

"Almanach d'Alsace et de Lorraine," 1896, by Paul Berthon (French). *Author's collection, photo by Robert Four.*

"XVme Salon des Artistes Decorateurs," 1924, by Jean Dupas (French). *Courtesy of Pat Kery Fine Arts.*

"Cabourg," 1896, by Privat Livemont (Belgian). *Courtesy of Butterfield & Butterfield.*

"Tabarin," 1928, by Paul Colin
(French). *Courtesy of Pat Kery Fine
Arts.*

"Nord Express," 1927, by A. M.
Cassandre (French). *Courtesy of Pat
Kery Fine Arts.*

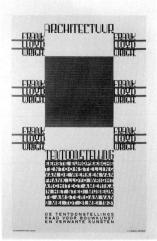

"Pandorra," 1919, by Jan Toorop
(Dutch). *Courtesy of Bernice Jackson;
photo by Robert Four.*

"Architectuur/Frank Lloyd Wright,"
1931, by H. Th. Wigdeveld (Dutch).
*Courtesy of Bernice Jackson; photo by
Robert Four.*

"Lucifer," 1910, by R. N. Roland-Holst (Dutch). *Courtesy of Bernice Jackson; photo by Robert Four.*

"PKZ," 1923, by Otto Baumberger (Swiss). *Courtesy of Bernice Jackson.*

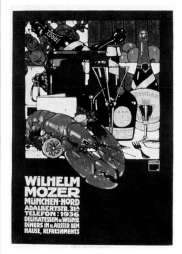

"Wilhelm Mozer," 1909, by Ludwig Hohlwein (German). *Courtesy of Bernice Jackson.*

"Riquewihr," c. 1930, by F. Schultz-Wettel (Travel). *Author's collection, photo by Robert Four.*

"Bradley, His Book," 1896, by William Bradley (American). *Courtesy of Hirschl & Adler Galleries.*

"Harper's February," 1897, by Edward Penfield (American). *Courtesy of Hirschl & Adler Galleries.*

"The Damnation of Theron Ware," 1896, by John Henry Twatchman (American). *Courtesy of An American Collection.*

"Read the Sun," 1895, by Louis John Rhead (American). *Courtesy of An American Collection.*

"Autriche," c. 1925, by Joseph Binder (Travel). *Author's collection, photo by Robert Four.*

"School of Visual Arts," 1978, by Paul Davis (Contemporary). *Courtesy of the School of Visual Arts.*

"Wake Up America!," 1917, by James Montgomery Flagg (World War I). *Courtesy of Meehan Military Posters.*

"Fratricidio!," c. 1942, by Gino Boccasile (World War II). *Courtesy of Meehan Military Posters.*

"Le Moulin Rouge," 1891, by Henri de Toulouse-Lautrec (French). *Courtesy of Club of American Collectors.*

"Lait pur Stérilisé," 1894, by Théophile-Alexandre Steinlen (French). *Courtesy of Pasquale Iannetti Art Galleries.*

"Paris Almanach," 1894, by George de Feure (French). *Courtesy of Anca Colbert Fine Arts, Ltd.*

"Folies-Bergère," 1893, by Jules Chéret (French). *Courtesy of Pasquale Iannetti Art Galleries.*

FROM VILLAGE TO GLOBAL VILLAGE

COUNTRY STORE
ADVERTISING POSTERS

The vast world of collecting country store advertising and memorabilia not only includes paper and cardboard posters, but tin signs, boxes, beer trays, tin boxes, product packaging, store catalogs, and numerous other kinds of advertising emphemera.

Country store advertising, long a "poor country cousin" in the collecting world, has gone through the roof in recent years, setting dozens of new records and justifying years of patient collecting by numerous individuals. Still sought after more by country store and advertising collectors than by poster collectors, American general product advertising posters from the turn of the century to World War I are today entering into the poster collecting mainstream.

Tin advertising signs were early to steal the show away from paper posters, with an early Campbell's Soup sign in the shape of an American Flag setting a record in May 1989 for $40,000, plus 10% buyer's premium. The auction, conducted by Noel Barrett in New Hope, Pennsylvania, was of the collection of Peter Sidlow, a Los Angeles real estate developer who spent almost thirty years amassing his collection of early American product advertising. A year earlier, the same auctioneer offered another outstanding collection by George Haney, setting a previous record of $14,000 for a tin sign of Buster Brown and his dog Tige.

The results of the landmark auction which included the Campbell's Soup sign were reported not only in the antiques press but

in the advertising trade magazine *Adweek*, read by advertising professionals across the country, many of whom are themselves advertising
collectors.

As is typical of country store advertising auctions, the auction included a diversity of items. A complete collection of Hood Sarsapa-
rilla calendars from 1886 to 1922 sold for $2,800 plus premium, and
a set of eighteen Roly Poly tobacco tins sold for $8,200 plus premium.

Paper posters also fared well in the same auction. A lithographed
"paper sign" for Newsboy Plug Tobacco, in its original wooden frame,
sold for $13,000 plus premium. A now famous "Gold Dust Washing
Powder" poster sold for $5,000 plus a 10% buyer's premium, a realized
price that would be repeated in November of the same year at Rivo
Oliver's Auction Gallery in Kennebunk, Maine. (See the price listings following this section.)

The market implications of auctions such as these are almost immediate. Visibility and publicity immediately create new interest and
new collectors. Dealers review their inventory and raise prices of certain items. New auctions appear on the calendar.

Oliver's has created a specialist position for "Advertising and
Country Store Auctions" under the direction of John Delph, who
creates semi-annual auctions which bring to the market interesting
and unusual examples of pre–World War I product advertising posters.

The product posters of the period may never see an elevation to
the status of "artists' posters" mainly because so many of them were
anonymously produced by artists who worked for the printing companies. However, the prices they are bringing in some cases equal
those for a Chéret or a Penfield, and competition among collectors
for rare examples is just as intense.

Many of the posters which were intended for distribution to stores
were "banded" with metal strips at the top and bottom to facilitate
hanging. "Paper signs," as they are called, are posters which are
framed like tin signs and were intended for more or less permanent
display. Cardboard posters and signs were used in windows and on
countertops.

Apart from their value as documents of early American advertising,
these posters recapture an era when even the largest American cities
were really little more than overgrown villages, where life proceeded
at a different pace, and where the middle class was just beginning to
enjoy a full range of "new fangled notions" in clothing, lifestyles,
household products, beverages, and more. They were created with a

humor and innocence that belongs to a time before America was pulled into the "war to end all wars."

After World War I, which drew many into the cities to work in factories, the focus of much American advertising shifted to selling "modern" products to a booming urban population, and the style of the earlier era faded, in many cases giving way to the Art Deco style of advertising between the two wars.

Whatever the reason for the renewed interest in country store advertising, these posters are now hot collectors' items. Long undervalued, though many are extremely rare cultural artifacts, these posters are finally receiving their due as charming images of an era of American life.

PRICE LISTINGS

Note: *See the chapter "Important Notes on the Price Listings" for more information on prices given. Many of the product posters listed below are by anonymous artists, many of whom worked for the printing companies which produced the posters. They are listed in alphabetical order by product name.*

Arbuckles' Ariosa Coffee, ca. 1900. "Getting Her Money's Worth"—a young girl buys Arbuckles' Coffee from a woman shopkeeper. One of two known copies, good condition, 14″ × 28″.

$1,700 (Auction)

The categories
of condition are
determined by
whether posters have:
Obvious repairs
Paper loss
Stains
Dirt or visible folds
Tears
Freshness of color

Courtesy of Oliver's Auction Gallery

Bloomer Club Cigar, ca. 1900. Paper sign of two women in bloomers seated in chairs, one with her bicycle next to her. A tear in upper right-hand corner and left-hand middle, great color, 20½″ × 15″.
$1,250 (Auction)

C. W. Parker, Leavenworth, Kansas, ca. 1900. A merry-go-round with insets of a steam engine and military band organ. Some staining at top, backed with Japanese mulberry paper, framed, 28″ × 21″.
$825 (Auction)

Cognac Cocktails, P. Lorrilard & Co., ca. 1900. Thin cardboard poster of sexy woman advertising Cognac Cocktails, an odd name for what is actually advertised as "Best Chew of Plug Tobacco in the World." Excellent condition and color, 9¾″ × 17½″.
$250 (Auction)

D. M. Ferry & Co.'s Seeds for Sale Here, ca. 1900. City street in background, a variety of vegetables in foreground. Near mint condition, canvas-backed, framed, 32½″ × 22⅞″.
$1,800 (Auction)

DuPont Smokeless Shotgun Powder, 1910. Artist: Robert Robinson. "End of a Good Day"—a hunter returns through the woods with his kill. Fine condition, seldom seen, 27″ × 18″.
$1,600 (Auction)

Courtesy of Oliver's Auction Gallery

Gold Dust Washing Powder. Two black babies bathing in a wooden wash tub next to a box of Fairbanks Gold Dust Washing Powder. Near mint condition, rare, framed, 13½" × 26".

$5,000 (Auction)

Harvard Pure Malt Beverages, ca. 1901. A beacon on top of a building whose columns are topped with beer bottles sends out information about the Harvard Brewing Co. Excellent condition, framed, 9" × 14". $160 (Auction)

Hopkins & Allen Prairie Girl. Beautiful red-haired girl holds gun alongside her cheek, with advertising on her holster. Rare, in original frame, no bands, 10" × 26". $1,150 (Auction)

In a Tight Place, Shoot U. M. C. Cartridges, ca. 1900. A hunter shoots at a charging bear. Good condition, no band at bottom, 16" × 24½". $170 (Auction)

Jacob Hoffman Brewing Co., ca. 1900. Printed by J. Ottman Litho Co., a glass of beer and a cigar stand next to a bouquet of flowers. Fine condition and color, 21½" × 31½". $30 (Auction)

Courtesy of Oliver's Auction Gallery

Jas. G. Johnson & Co., 1897. Paper sign for importers and manufacturers of millinery and straw goods. A beach scene below, some women in bathing dresses, others in full costume including elaborate hats; above are over a hundred different hats. Good condition, matted and framed, horizontal 44″ × 25″.   *$1,950 (Auction)*

Julia Marlowe Shoes, ca. 1900. Lithograph printed by The Milwaukee Litho & Engr. Co. Bust of young woman along with two styles of fashionable shoes. Very good condition, linen-mounted, 24½″ × 41½″.   *$800–$1,000*

Marlin Repeating Rifles and Shotguns. In the foreground two ducks fall into water, shot by hunter in the background—"The Gun for the Man Who Knows." Good condition, 16¼″ × 24¾″.   *$200 (Auction)*

O. B. Joyful Tobacco. Paper poster with bands of a hunter smoking a pipe, taking a thorn out of his dog's paw. Excellent condition, 15″ × 19½″.   *$315 (Auction)*

Ragged Edge Cigars. Cardboard poster of a box of Ragged Edge Cigars. Mint condition, 11″ × 14¾″.   *$35 (Auction)*

Satin Skin Cream, 1903. Lithographic poster of the head of a woman against a yellow background. A common poster, but a good example of the genre. Mint condition, 28″ × 41″.   *$125–$175*

Shamrock Tobacco, ca. 1900. Seated man with knife in one hand, tobacco in the other, advertising "Plug Smoking—10¢ a Cut." Overall very good condition, nice color, backed with canvas and framed, 17″ × 23″.   *$190 (Auction)*

Smoke Gay New York Cigars, 1897. "A Brush on Riverside Drive"—cyclists and a carriage out for a drive. Good condition, horizontal 20¼″ × 14″.   *$750 (Auction)*

Steel Where Steel Belongs—Peters Loaded Shells. Artist: G. Muss Arnolt. A group of ducks flies toward the viewer. Good condition, but with some restoration, dry-mounted, bands have become loose, 19¾″ × 29½″.   *$700 (Auction)*

Use Magic Yeast for Root Beer, ca. 1909. Colorful—a young boy gives a glass of root beer to a man whose head is a globe. Near mint condition, 16″ × 20″.   *$400 (Auction)*

Woonsocket Rubber Boots and Shoes, ca. 1900. A young man in rubber boots carries two young women across a river. Excellent condition, with only minor flaws and touch-ups, 19¼″ × 29½″.

$2,200 (Auction)

WORLD WAR POSTERS

By Mary Ellen Meehan

Mary Ellen Meehan is the owner of Meehan Military Posters, the only poster firm specializing in World War I, Spanish Civil War, and World War II posters. Meehan Military Posters publishes two catalogs annually with over five hundred illustrations and seven color plates. For more information, call or write: Meehan Military Posters, P.O. Box 477, Gracie Station, New York, NY 10028. (212) 734–5683.

By 1914 posters had become such an integral part of popular culture that it was only logical that wartime governments would employ this highly successful medium to influence the attitude and actions of their people.

In an era when the radio or "crystal set" was still a little-heard curiosity, posters assumed an importance as a transmitter of government policy that is hard to imagine in today's media-saturated world.

Although both America and western Europe claimed high literacy rates when the First World War erupted, many people, even in these advanced nations, could not read above the most basic level. Given this prevalent condition, the poster with its visual message, supported by a few well-chosen words of text, was well suited to the conditions of the day and therefore an unusually effective means of communication.

Together with the ability to present many messages simultaneously, posters could also be quickly reproduced and distributed in vast quantities. As World War I engulfed virtually every facet of daily life, even on the home front, this fixation was manifested in the great thematic variety of posters produced.

Recruiting for all branches of the service was a paramount subject, accompanied by posters promoting war loans to finance the conflict. Both wars reached not only into our pockets but into our kitchens, with posters featuring sumptuous displays of food to be conserved for shipment overseas, and even into our trash, and with posters soliciting scrap for recycling into armaments.

Today it is recognized that military poster artists' unstinting commitment to the causes they depicted on posters was felt at such a deep emotional level that many of their military posters transcend their commercial work.

World War I illustrators such as Howard Chandler Christy, James Montgomery Flagg, and Joseph Leyendecker cared so much about the preservation of liberty and freedom that they refused to accept payment for their designs. Most Spanish Civil War artists were themselves combatants in the war, plugging the lines when necessary and returning to their drafting tables at night; many were killed in action. World War II again called upon artists to inspire and direct the energies of the global population with remarkable results. Poster artists working in these violent and crucial times produced an art that directly mirrored the brightest hopes and darkest fears of their countrymen and, as such, were engaged in the battle of ideas.

Military posters are thus in a different, more intense, league than product advertising posters. War posters convey a sense of both urgency and undeniable purpose. The unsullied idealism that informed poster artists during both wars shines through in countless military posters. Looking back in 1948 on his World War II poster production, the great British designer Abram Games commented: "I feel strongly that the high purpose of the wartime posters was mainly responsible for their excellence."

COLLECTING TRENDS

The military poster market has changed radically in the last five years. The achievements of poster artists who applied their full creative energies to the exalted theme of winning global war have at last begun to merit the attention that has long been accorded advertising posters. Serious collectors are now responding to the passion behind the posters. Young collectors in particular are attracted to the sense of idealism and conviction apparent in so many military posters. Unlike advertising posters, whose sole purpose is to sell products, the war poster attempts to save a way of life from perishing at the hands of an implacable foe.

Among World War I posters, James Montgomery Flagg's poster *I Want You*—the vintage Uncle Sam recruiting poster—is certainly the best known poster of all time. It fetched over $2,000 at auction in 1988 and it continues to be acquired as the cornerstone of every prominent World War I collection. Fred Spear's haunting *Enlist* is today one of America's most valuable World War I posters, and would likely command a price of over $7,000—if it could be found. This poster, privately printed for the Boston Committee of Public Safety in 1915, depicts the eerie scene of a doomed mother and child slowly sinking to the bottom of the sea after their ship, the British ocean liner *Lusitania*, was sunk by a German torpedo. Equally in demand is L. N. Britton's poster *Warning!*, showing a Curtiss Jenny bi-plane that crashed as a result of manufacturing slip-ups. It would surely command a price well in excess of $10,000 were it to appear on the market today.

The increased appreciation that museums and collectors are now according military posters is part of the cause of startling recent increases in the prices. As posters enter museums and are permanently taken off the market, scarcity is becoming an important factor. Many posters that were relatively easy for dealers to find ten years ago are now virtual rarities.

Auction houses have recently featured military poster auctions in Boston, New York, London, and Hannover, West Germany. War-related works by exceptionally talented artists are beginning to be considered to be at least as valuable as the non-military posters executed by the same artists.

Ludwig Hohlwein, for example, contributed his considerable talents to Germany's war effort in both world wars. All of his subjects, whether advertising or military, bring high prices at auction today. The 1940 British wartime recruiting poster, *Join the ATS* by Abram Games, fetched over $6,000 in 1988 in London, the highest price yet paid for a military poster at auction.

There is also a conspicuous interest in "elite unit" posters from both world wars. Typically this would include U.S. Marine posters, Waffen SS posters produced both in Germany and German-occupied countries, and recruiting for submarine, airborne, and armored units of all nations.

World War I posters have long been a staple of the military poster market. American and French posters have been heavily collected in the United States since they were first issued, as it has always been recognized that the poster artists were often of the highest caliber. The 1988 publication of Walton Rawls' book *Wake Up America!* with its superb color illustrations, was a revelation to poster collectors (see Bibliography). Regard for German posters, particularly the works of Hohlwein, is burgeoning. Austrian, Italian, and Russian works have also made great gains in popularity as they become better known and as many new European collectors and museums enter the market.

Interest in World War II posters has recently caught up with the enduring interest in World War I posters. The 50th anniversary of World War II has focused enormous worldwide attention on that war. Television, books, and magazines have all contributed to a flood of information, constantly reminding people of the tremendous importance of the war and its outcome.

World War II posters are often sought after not only for their powerful imagery but also for the documentary value that attaches to any original document dealing with crucially important events. Subjects of particular interest to World War II collectors include Pearl Harbor, the Battle of Britain, the Blitz, and D Day. In addition, recent discoveries of the burial places of Polish officers have focused renewed attention on the massacres perpetrated by the Russians in the Katyn Forest.

The most intensely sought-after posters in today's market, however, are works relating to the Holocaust, racially motivated injustices, and wholesale pogroms. Many new museums have devoted themselves to ensuring that the world neither forgets nor repeats disasters like the Armenian massacres or the Holocaust. Due to the reprehensible nature of racially biased or anti-Semetic posters, most have been destroyed. There is fervent interest in the few extant posters that remain to document monstrously aberrant times.

OUTSTANDING ARTISTS: WORLD WAR I

There are legions of talented illustrators that took up the cudgels for their respective governments during World War I. A few of the most outstanding and prolific were Frank Brangwyn and Paul Nash in Britain; Abel Faivre and Maurice Neumont in France; Hans Rudi Erdt,

Fritz Erler, and Ludwig Hohlwein in Germany; and Howard Chandler Christy, James Montgomery Flagg, and Joseph Leyendecker in the United States.

GREAT BRITAIN

Frank Brangwyn (1867–1956) studied with William Morris before becoming one of England's most respected artists. His World War I posters have the authority of an eyewitness account. The bold simplicity of Brangwyn's black and white palette contributes substantially to the emotional power of the images. One poster, *At Neuve Chapelle*, functions on the level of front-line reportage elevated to artistry.

Paul Nash (1889–1946), an official AEF artist assigned to the western front, is perhaps the most daring of all the celebrated World War I artists. He was trained in London as a landscape artist and turned this pleasant training to ferocious use in his intensely felt images of the devastated war zones. His remarkable poster announcing an exhibition of his work at the Leicenter Galleries disguises a rigorous geometric structure behind a shocking view of a battlefield. Nash's visionary posters were recognized immediately as superb, a fact that the poster for his Leicester show makes clear.

FRANCE

Abel Faivre (1867–1945) was a respected painter and cartoonist before turning his talents to war posters in 1914. His famous image for the Liberation Loan is typical of his moving and highly accomplished style. The once truculent Kaiser, his lethal sword now broken, slumps under the crushing weight of the combined Allied forces symbolized by their massed flags. Details, such as the flags wielded by anonymous hands that burst forward out of the field, attest to the energy and originality of the artist.

Maurice Neumont (1868–1930) trained in Paris under the famous Romantic-Classicist painter Gerome and became a well-known illustrator. The apocalyptic realism of his depiction of the ragged "poilu" in *On Ne Passe Pas* resulted from his personal observations on the battlefield of Verdun. Compelling works such as this earned Neumont the Legion d'Honneur.

GERMANY

Hans Rudi Erdt (1883–1918) was a top Berlin graphic designer before the war, whose economical style produced posters of forceful concentrated power. The simplicity of his imagery was combined with a fine sense of texture. His best-known and extremely rare *U-Boote Heraus!* revolved around a plain "U" that functions almost like a magnet, compressing the U-boat captain and his victim into a single sharp focus. Erdt's brief career exemplified the best and most advanced techniques of German poster design.

Fritz Erler (1868–1940) trained in Paris and was a co-founder of the influential Munich art magazine *Die Jugend* that popularized the Art Nouveau movement in Germany. He later developed into an artist of outstanding sensitivity, far from the brutal Hun of World War I fable. Erler's rendering of a lonely soldier peering around the barbed wire of Verdun in his war bond poster *Helft Uns Siegen* is one of the most indelible images of the war.

Ludweig Hohlwein (1874–1949) was the most prolific poster artist of his generation. His characteristic mottled textures, combined with a powerful concentrated style, can be seen in posters that spanned both wars. Hohlwein's *Ludendorff Spende* spotlights a seriously wounded vet intently pondering the tools he'll need to build his future. Rather than look directly at the viewer, Hohlwein's subjects draw us into their world as sympathetic accomplices. Hohlwein's reputation continues to grow both in America and Europe. His posters were accorded an impressive retrospective at the Staatsliche Galerie in Stuttgart in 1985.

UNITED STATES

Howard Chandler Christy (1873–1952) studied under the acclaimed artist William Merritt Chase. He became renowned for his beautiful "Christy girls," who were meant to represent a soldier's dream woman. Christy's muses were wholesome, outdoorsy, and come-hither at the same time. They beckoned prospective sailors to the fleet by announcing on posters *Gee, I Wish I Were a Man, I'd Join the Navy—Be a Man and Do It*. The appealing model for this poster, clad in an oversize middy and snapping imaginary suspenders, typifies Christy's ideal. Christy rivaled James Montgomery Flagg for artistic stardom, later painting wives of U.S. presidents and industrial titans.

James Montgomery Flagg (1877–1960), recognized as a prodigy from his teens, studied in the key artistic centers of New York, London, and Paris. He introduced himself as Uncle Sam in his famous poster *I Want You*. Among his lesser-known images is the exceptional *Wake Up America! Civilization Calls Every Man, Woman and Child!*, and it is now among the most collectible of World War I posters. It features a lovely rosy-cheeked Columbia slumbering innocently while the world beyond erupts in smoke and flames. The poster was commissioned by a patriotic group that undertook to combat Wilson's isolationist policies by issuing posters warning of the grave international dangers.

Joseph Leyendecker (1874–1951), an accomplished illustrator, came to America from his native Germany at the age of nine. After training in Chicago and Paris he drew hundreds of covers for the *Saturday Evening Post*. His best-known military poster, *Order Coal Now*, executed for the conservation-minded U.S. Fuel Administration, is a poster of enduring beauty. The poster was issued to remind home-front homemakers to order their coal out-of-season so that the supplies would be available for the front during the critical winter. Clydesdales are shown standing patiently in the leafy shade in front of a coal wagon off-loading during the summertime. Leyendecker later created the highly successful ad campaign for the Arrow Shirt Collar Man; his gentlemen were taken as models of taste and style throughout the 1920s and 1930s.

OUTSTANDING ARTISTS: WORLD WAR II

Outstanding World War II posters were produced by Abram Games and Pat Keely in Britain; Paul Colin and Jean Carlu in France; Ludwig Hohlwein in Germany; Gino Boccasile in Italy; and E. McKnight-Kauffer, Norman Rockwell, and Ben Shahn in the United States.

BRITAIN

Abram Games (b. 1914) is considered by many to be Britain's most talented graphic designer. His technical virtuosity is evident in *Join the ATS*, where Games employs a masterful combination of airbrush and "Braggadocio" type. The image was much criticized in Parliamentary debate as being too glamorous and it attracted much notice in the press where it was nicknamed the "Blond Bombshell." After an avalanche of publicity, the poster was withdrawn and replaced by a photographic image of a dowdy ATS private. Since the poster was officially and unofficially condemned, all copies were automatically destroyed, as paper had to be recycled for other purposes. The only known copy signed by both artist and model recently achieved a record price for a British World War II poster when it was purchased at auction in London by Poster America, a New York City Gallery. The post of "Official War Office Poster Designer" was specially created for Games during the war.

Pat Keely (d. 1970) was one of the most gifted designers active in Britain and had achieved pre-war fame for a series of posters for London Transport and Southern Railways. His *Wireless War* is typical of his advanced artistic style. Keely delineates the crucial yet little-known role of the British scientists, early masters of the new field of electronics, by using a delightfully dizzy form of abstract geometry. The ingeniousness of Keely's designs, the subtlety of his palette, and the playfulness of his images combine to make him one of the finest poster artists of the war years.

FRANCE

Jean Carlu (b. 1900) was a leading French designer when he came to the United States at the time of the 1939 World's Fair to organize an exhibition around the theme of "France at War." After France was overrun, Carlu stayed in the United States and was employed in the graphic section of the Office of War Information. He believed passionately that the United States' manufacturing capacity would turn the tide of the war. His poster *America's Answer—Production* won a medal from the Art Directors' Club of New York as the best poster of the year. The clean economical design with its clever integration of image and typography is characteristic of Carlu's superb style.

Paul Colin (1892–1985) was famed for his theater, dance, and cabaret posters. His pared-down graphic manner is evident in *Silence*, issued in 1940 just before the fall of France. The seemingly harmless chat of an ordinary-looking man and soldier is literally overshadowed by the spy. Color is used expressionistically; the pure white of innocence is contrasted with the ominous black of the spy; the dramatic spotlighting denotes drama afoot.

ITALY

Gino Boccasile (1901–1952), trained in Milan, was a diehard Mussolini propagandist whose powerful Fascist posters continue to shock the viewer almost fifty years later. His poster of an American GI produced in 1942 is so graphic it needs no title. A black American sergeant, with his arm around a priceless stolen Roman statue which bears a $2 price tag, leers at the viewer. This vicious racial caricature is meant to convey America's low regard for the high culture of ancient Rome to which Fascist Italy felt itself heir.

Italian World War II posters are extremely rare. Most were destroyed by the Italians themselves rather than risk reprisals that would most likely result from being caught with such an image after the Allied invasion in 1943. Boccasile pursued a successful career as a commercial artist both before and after the war. A fine selection of his posters was recently included in the major exhibition "Italian Posters" at the Palazzo Permanente in Milan.

UNITED STATES

E. McKnight-Kauffer (18990–1979) was trained in San Francisco and Chicago. McKnight-Kauffer moved to London in 1914 where he remained until returning to New York in 1940. While in England, McKnight-Kauffer produced a series of exceptional posters for Underground Railways and British Petroleum. His poster *You Can Set Their Spirit Free* typifies his "moderne" style. The outstanding design contrasts sharp barbed wire with the smooth, black classical figure of the Allied prisoner. The poster suggests that war prisoners' aid will provide a glint of hope in the bleak existence of the wary captive. McKnight-Kauffer was honored with one-man exhibitions at the Museum of Modern Art in 1937 and The Victoria and Albert Museum in London in 1955.

The reputation of Norman Rockwell (1894–1978), always solid in the United States, has achieved new luster since his death. The beloved and idealistic purveyor of traditional American values has recently been reappraised in museum exhibitions as one of the first "magic realists." His poster *Let's Give Him Enough and On Time* addressed the fact that America was ill-prepared for the global war it faced. Isolationist sentiment, the Great Depression of the 1930s, world-wide Fascist military buildup, and the Japanese sneak attacks on American bases in the Pacific all contributed to this dilemma, a small but poignant part of which is depicted in the poster. Hunched over his outdated machine gun, his fatigues in tatters, a lone GI fights on. Intent on his perilous task, he is oblivious of his dwindling ammo supply, but the viewer is not. Displayed in munitions factories, this striking Rockwell graphic demonstrated the importance of their task to munitions workers so distant from the front's deadly dangers.

Ben Shahn (1898–1969) emigrated from his native Lithuania to New York as a boy and made his reputation in the United States as the foremost artist of social issues. In his celebrated *This is Nazi Brutality*, Shahn portrays the painful scene of a handcuffed and hooded victim about to be shot. A telegram reports the arbitrary reprisals taken against men of Lidice after British commandos assassinated Nazi secret police chief Heydrich in Prague. The victim is compressed into tight airless space, a Surrealist technique for producing feelings of dislocation and shock.

FORECAST FOR FUTURE COLLECTING AND MARKET TRENDS

With prices for Toulouse-Lautrec posters now pushing the quarter-of-a-million-dollar mark, new attention has been focused on military posters, a still affordable market that is arguably still in the "ground floor" stages of expansion. Museum acquisitions make it a certainty that first-rate posters will be harder to find in the future. Museums also perform an important role in educating and informing the tastes of the public, which also broadens the market, thus increasing the competition for posters still in circulation.

Spanish Civil War posters are one of the areas we would target for future growth. Maurice Rickards has written that Spanish Civil War posters are among the finest poster images ever produced. The most accomplished graphic artists in Spain banded together to form syndicates that produced superb posters. Since these posters were produced in the war zone itself many of the posters were lost. In addition, a prominent library with the best collection of Spanish Civil War posters microfilmed the images and destroyed the originals on the grounds that they were too troublesome to store. Spanish Civil War posters have never been seen in great quantities and therefore are not as well known as either World War I or World War II posters. There is no prominent museum that displays these posters as of yet. For sheer aesthetic power, these posters are bound to be the "discoveries" of the future.

A handful of significant Italian posters of World War II appeared on the market for the first time in 1989, more than forty years after

Italy shifted its allegiance to the Allied cause. Whereas comparable German posters surfaced about ten years earlier, despite the Potsdam agreement mandating their destruction, posters of the Mussolini epoch are still virtually impossible to find.

It has long been thought that most Italian posters were destroyed by the Fascists themselves in the aftermath of Mussolini's surrender. War correspondents covering the Allied advance in Italy wrote dispatches mentioning the strange appearance of clean rectangular patches on walls and buildings where posters had obviously just been ripped down. Whether or not the appearance of the trickle of posters emanating from Italy will coax forth other unknown posters remains to be seen. Likewise, it is still unclear whether glasnost will reveal a similar cache of Russian posters, which, until now, have been virtual rarities in the military poster market.

WHERE TO GO TO SEE WAR POSTERS

Because of their great historical value, many outstanding collections of war posters have been given to and created by military museums around the world.

Notable museum collections outside of the United States include the War Memorial Museum in Canberra and the Maritime Museum in Sydney, Australia; the Imperial War Museum in London; the Musée de l'Armee in Paris; the Canadian War Museum in Ottawa; and the Herresgeschitchte Museum in Vienna.

In the United States, often local historical societies or military museums will have poster collections. In addition, important collections can be seen at the University of Texas, Austin; the War Memorial Museum, Newport News, Virginia; the Robinson Collection of the U.S. Naval Academy, Annapolis, Maryland; the Hoover Institution Archives at Stanford University, California; the U.S. Military Academy Museum at West Point, New York; and several others. (See Resource Guide for detailed information on U.S. museums.)

REFERENCE WORKS

Several talented writers have devoted their energies to creating reference works on war posters. Two notable writers are Joseph Darracott and Maurice Rickards, both of whom have published several titles in the field. Other writers and books include: *Wake Up America!* by

Walton H. Rawls; *What Did You Do in the War, Daddy?* by Peter Stanley; and *Art and Propaganda in World War II* by Zbynek Zeman. (See Bibliography for complete references on the above and other works.)

PRICE LISTINGS

Note: *See the Chapter "Important Notes on the Price Listings" for more information on the prices given. Also note that most World War I posters are lithographic, and most World War II posters are offset printed. Also note that some artists produced posters for both wars.*

WORLD WAR I

ANONYMOUS

Ber! Keres-kedok! Iparosok!, ca. 1917. Hungarian War Loan poster shows a river of gold flowing from a wealthy residence into an armaments plant; in background a steel worker and an angel. Very good condition, linen-mounted, 38" × 50". $300–$350

Bring Him Home. Triumphant Canadian veteran waits on sea wall with his pack for funds to put him on troop ship home; fine full color and strong painterly style. Fine condition, linen-mounted, 25" × 36". $350–$400

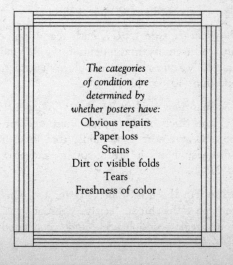

*The categories
of condition are
determined by
whether posters have:*
Obvious repairs
Paper loss
Stains
Dirt or visible folds
Tears
Freshness of color

Britain Needs You at Once. In this famous classic, St. George rears on his white horse to smote wicked green dragon; in full color with fiery background. Rare, very good condition, linen-mounted, 20″ × 30″.
$400–$500

British Women!—The R.A.F. Needs Your Help. Unusual recruiting poster depicts smartly uniformed belle on grassy strip near RE5; in sunny full color. Fine condition, 20″ × 40″. $225–$250

The Call to Duty/Join the Army, 1917. Early recruiting poster features bugler sounding call to arms from mountain top, behind him a huge flag curving gracefully against the sunrise glow; in attractive full color. Very good condition, 30″ × 40″. $200–$250

Canada War Savings Stamps Help Pay for the War, 1919. Wounded warrior seen in the thick of the action illustrated on the $5 War Savings Stamp acts as a stirring reminder that investing in stamps saves Canadian lives; chiefly in green, russets, and brown. Fine condition, 21″ × 27″. $75–$100

Crush the Prussian. For the third Liberty Loan, a victims' eye-view of devastating new tanks that broke decisively through the stalemate in the trenches; in fireglow and blacks. Very good condition, linen-mounted, 28″ × 40″. $250–$300

Courtesy of Meehan Military Posters

Doing My Bit—Four Years. Beaming Canadian soldier in kilt undaunted by prospect of long enlistment; sunny color. Very good condition, 24″ × 36″. $245–$285

Empruant National, stamped March 20, 1920, on image. Good condition, linen-mounted, 31″ × 47½″. $100 (Auction)

Executives and Workers Contribute to the War Loan. Hungarian, surreal image of armed soldiers awash in a sea of gigantic golden coins; intense colors. Scarce, very good condition, linen-mounted, 38″ × 49″. $325–$400

Exhibition for Prisoners of War, 1917. German prisoner dreams of home in a dark Siberian cell, with vicious-looking guard glaring through a tiny window; in red, gold, green, and charcoal. Very rare, fine condition, 24″ × 37″. $675–$775

Forward! To Victory with the 245 Grenadier Guards. Fearless charge by elite unit raised in Montreal; in full color with large red numeral. Mint condition, linen-mounted, 28″ × 41″. $185–$220

The Heroes of St. Julian and Festubert. Recruiting poster in French capped with a poem about front-line carnage; depicts soldier in full field kit shouldering arms in front of Canadian flag and twin maple leaves. Very good condition, 24″ × 37″. $125–$150

My Daddy Bought Me a Government Bond. Cute little blonde sporting a bright red bow hugs her Liberty Bond; naturalistic color. Fine condition, 20″ × 30″. $175–$200

National Service. Quote from Neville Chamberlain advising Germany be dealt "a blow straight between the eyes" is illustrated with two boxers; in black on yellow gold with red border. Fine condition, linen-mounted, 20″ × 30″. $250–$300

Polish Victims Relief Fund. Survivors seek solace from glowing image of beloved "Black Madonna"; charred ground softened by pastel mirage. Very good condition, linen-mounted, 20″ × 30″. $250–$300

Remember Belgium. Recruiting poster of stalwart Tommy pledged to avenge destruction shown—refugee column fleeing a smoldering village. Very good condition, 30″ × 42″. $125–$150

Remember Your First Thrill of American Liberty, 1917. New immigrants reminded of their first view of Statue of Liberty are asked to help those left behind; subtle red, white, blue, and stone gray. Fine condition, linen-mounted, 20″ × 30″. $185–$215

Save Seed for Victory. Subtitle "Good Seed Wins" demonstrates how war metaphors permeated economy. Scarce, very good colors, 21″ × 31″. $195–$225

Soldaten, 1918. Austrian poster shows member of the elite mountain troops in full battle gear with grenades, gas mask, etc. Very good condition, 25″ × 37″. $600 (Auction)

Something Doing Boys! Uncle Sam's on the Bridge. Enlist, 1916. This early Navy recruiting poster is one of the rarest of the genre. Behind Uncle Sam, rolling up one sleeve as he holds his binoculars, is a sailor raising Old Glory. 27″ × 41″. $900 (Auction)

Strike Now!, 1918. Probably by an official war artist, shows a Yank aiming bayonet at a cowering Hun in a trench; in black and white. Typical of reportage Pershing requested as a record of American bravery. Fine condition, 20″ × 30″. $135–$160

U-Boat Kills in the Mediterranean. German poster showing devastating effect of submarine warfare on Allied shipping; in red, yellow, sea blue, and black. Very good condition, horizontal 34″ × 26″.
                                                                               $595–$695

U.S. Marines. Service on Land and Sea. The original World War I
version of the famous poster of the Marine sergeant with rifle on
shoulder. Good condition, linen-mounted, 28″ × 39″.

$150 (Auction)

We're Both Needed to Serve the Guns, 1915. British poster from The
Parliamentary Recruiting Committee. Soldier and a worker shake
hands against a background of a battlefield and factory. Very good
condition, linen-mounted, horizontal 50″ × 39″. $200–$225

When the Enemy Strikes Stand Fast. Very unusual Chinese scroll poster
with strong image of Nationalist soldier placed above inspirational
message; in red, white, and blue. Uncommon, fine condition, 10″ ×
31″. $125–$150

YOU Buy a Liberty Bond Lest I Perish!, 1917. Statue of Liberty springs
to life to demand help in the wartime crisis; in sprightly color. Now
hard to find, fine condition, 20″ × 30″. $185–$215

ANTON

The Pen and the Sword. Elegant Morocco-bound book *(Mein Kampf?)*
with raised bands and gold embossing rests before large iron cross and
covered with golden sword; in rich beiges, golds, yellow, and green
on teal. Fine condition, linen-mounted, 23″ × 33″. $575–$650

AXSTER-HEUDTLASS

National Competition, 1938. Emblem of the Storm Troops is superimposed on a blood-red map of pre-war Germany; in red, brown, and
gold. Fine condition, 23″ × 33″. $450–$550

BARCHI

La Banca Commerciale Italiana, ca. 1917. Italian Loan poster depicts
a long column of winter troops in the snowy mountains all in shades
of blue. Minor soiling, on old linen, 38″ × 54″. $200–$225

WLADYSLAW T. BENDA (1873–1948)

Give or We Perish. Lovely dark-haired young girl pulls a shawl around
her head in poster appealing for relief for Armenia, Greece, Syria,
and Persia; in rich blacks on buff. Scarce, fine condition, linen-
mounted, 20″ × 30″. $350–$425

You Can Help. Beautifully drawn young woman knits warm woolen socks to be distributed by the Red Cross to men in the trenches; sepia charcoal with red logo in corner. Uncommon, mint condition, 20″ × 30″. $350–$425

BENEKER

Sure! We'll Finish the Job, 1918. Beaming farmer antes up for Victory Loan, used to repatriate American heroes; rousing color on sunny yellow. Fine condition, 26″ × 38″. $65–$80

LUCIAN BERNHARD (1883–1972)

Last Chance to Subscribe to the War Loan. Strong design by master calligrapher; black letters with red borders. Fine condition, 18″ × 27″. $135–$160

Subscribe to the War Loan. German U-boat captain and a soldier watch as an Allied ship sinks, silhouetted against blazing sky; in dramatic charcoals and orange. Very good condition, linen-mounted, 11″ × 16″. $135–$160

This is the Way to Peace—War Loan. Well-integrated design of armor-plated fist and traditional German lettering; in black and red. Very good condition, linen-mounted, 19″ × 26″. $350–$425

BESNARD

Emprunt de la Défense Nationale, 1917. The archangel Michael defends Madonna and Child symbolizing the French people. Very good condition, linen-mounted, horizontal 47″ × 31″. $125 (Auction)

BIEDERMANN

Hands Off! Every Dud is Dangerous. With a city in flames in the background, an adult warns a child that even a dud can be dangerous; in full color with red letters. Mint condition, 17″ × 24″.

$285–$335

BIRKLE

Halt!—Volunteers Needed, 1919. German troops on the eastern front, who fought successfully against the Russians, had an erroneous impression that the war was lost by treachery at the top rather than a failure of German arms. *Halt!* calls for volunteers to join a new right-wing private army to battle the left then gathering strength in eastern Germany. Hitler, himself a disgruntled veteran, later co-opted these armies. In black, gray, and red. Fine condition, linen-mounted, 28″ × 38″.   *$325–$400*

EDWIN H. BLASHFIELD (1848–1936)

Carry On! Buy Bonds to Your Utmost, 1918. Colorful rendering of Columbia charging forward with the flag alongside the troops on the battlefield. Very rare, linen-mounted, 41″ × 82″.   *$550 (Auction)*

Red Cross Christmas Roll Call, 1918. Full figures of Columbia and the Red Cross nurse. Very good condition, linen-mounted, 56″ × 83″.
                                                          $325 (Auction)

FRANK BRANGWYN (1867–1956)

Courtesy of Meehan Military Posters

At Neuve Chapelle, 1918. Rubric "Be a Man" illustrated by scout and artillery observer in heavy action; dramatic density of the charcoals suggests nightfall. Rare, privately issued by *Daily Chronicle*, mint condition, linen-mounted, 20″ × 30″.   *$345–$395*

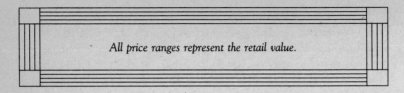

All price ranges represent the retail value.

Belgian and Allies Aid League. Dramatic scene of homeless and starving war refugees streaming toward viewer; rich charcoals. Fine condition, 30″ × 40″. $275–$325

Orphelinat des Armées, 1914. War orphans at a dreary table; dark, somber, and foreboding. On old linen, 39″ × 60″. $125 (Auction)

Orphelinat des Armées, 1914. Companion piece to the above, shows women carrying children past a cemetery, lilies in the foreground. On old linen, 39″ × 60″. $125 (Auction)

L. N. BRITTON

Eat More Corn, Oats and Rye, 1917. Exceptionally fine Deco conservation image in dramatic full color; for the U.S. Food Administration. Mint condition, linen-mounted, 21″ × 29″. $375–$450

Ten Million New Members by Christmas. Red Cross service flag seen through snowy window glowing in candlelight, with Christmas tree adding to festive scene; in warm colors with dark border. Very good condition, 20″ × 30″. $65–$80

BROEKMAN

The Indies Shall be Freed. Japanese occupation troops in Indonesia get the boot in this rare Dutch poster which was probably printed in England; in rich full color. Very good condition, linen-mounted, 24″ × 35″. $300–$350

CHARLES LIVINGSTON BULL (1874–1932)

Courtesy of Meehan Military Posters

Keep Him Free, 1918. Commanding eagle, by America's foremost naturalist painter of the time, guards squadron of Curtiss Jenny bi-planes trying out their wings; fine naturalistic color on deep blue sky. Mint condition, 20″ × 30″. $325–$400

Join the Army Air Service, ca. 1917. Printed by Alpha Litho Co. American eagle battles dark eagle in dramatic composition, with war planes in a smoke-filled sky and an explosion of red beneath. Good condition, 21″ × 27″. $3,000–$3,500

Save the Products of the Land. Cleverly subtitled "Eat More Fish—They Feed Themselves," depicts bass drifting through the seaweed; in limpid color. Mint condition, 20″ × 30″. $245–$285

LEONETTO CAPPIELLO (1875–1942)

Untitled Red Cross Poster, 1918. A rare Cappiello for the French war effort. Angel of Mercy leading a woman to the Red Cross house. Very good condition, linen-mounted, horizontal 46″ × 31″.

$225 (Auction)

B. CHAVANNAZ

Emprunt de la Paix, 1919. For the Peace Loan, a young woman holds a cornucopia out of which flows grains, coins, bills, and other bounty. Scarce, very good condition, linen-mounted, 30″ × 45″.

$125 (Auction)

Emprunt National, 1918. French poster depicts tank crew with rifles. Very good condition, linen-backed, horizontal 47″ × 31″.

$300–$350

HOWARD CHANDLER CHRISTY (*1873–1952*)

Christy accompanied Teddy Roosevelt and his Rough Riders to Cuba as an artist-correspondent, and was forevermore imbued with a martial spirit that he injected into his famed World War I posters.

Americans All, 1918. Columbia hangs laurel wreath over multi-ethnic list of war heroes, with huge American flag completing tableau; lushly painted in full color. Very good condition, linen-mounted, 28″ × 40″.

$250–$300

Clear the Way, 1918. Alluring maiden backed by rippling flag hovers over naval gun crew; in fresh luminous color. Fine condition, 20″ × 30″.

$245–$285

Fight or Buy Bonds, 1917. Spirited beauty waves Old Glory over vast column of American volunteers; in luminous full color. Mint condition, 20″ × 30″.

$295–$345

Same as above. Fine condition, linen-mounted, 30″ × 40″.

$375–$425

GEE!! I Wish I Were a Man, 1918. Naval recruiting at its most enticing, Christy girl tries on middy blouse for size; in naturalistic colors on buff background. Scarce classic, now rare, fine condition, linen-mounted, 27″ × 41″.

$1,150–$1,300

I Want You for the Navy, 1917. Windblown beauty tries on Navy blouse for size; full color on warm yellow. Fine condition, linen-mounted, 28″ × 40″.

$895–$1,100

If You Want to Fight, Join the Marines, 1915. Earliest, rarest, and finest of the renowned Christy recruiting series. Beautiful saucy sergeant waves bayonet as she urges massed troops forward; in shimmering naturalistic color. Very rare, mint condition, 30″ × 40″.

$1,250–$1,500

The Spirit of America, 1919. One of Christy's prettiest images, a fetching nymphet with flag; in glowing full color. Uncommon, very good condition, linen-mounted, 20″ × 28″. $250–$300

CLARK

Join the Tanks—See Service Soon—Treat 'em Rough! Early tank recruiting poster highlights desire to bash the Boche, with Tank Corps mascot "Black Tom" poised for excitement; in black and white. Fine condition, 25″ × 38″. $225–$275

CLAUSS

Armée Das Deutsche Blanke, World War I. German poster for seventh War Loan, a warrior attempting to chop off the heads of a serpent, wearing helmets of the various Allies. Good condition, old folds restored, linen-mounted, 23″ × 35″. $225 (Auction)

Armée Ein Deutscher Ware, ca. 1918. German poster shows silhouettes of naked soldier thrusting a spike at the foaming mouth of a capitalist serpent clutching bags of money. Good condition, old folds show, linen-mounted, 22″ × 36″. $200 (Auction)

HASKELL COFFIN

Help Us Help Our Boys. A young woman pastes a war poster on a wall (the reason World War I posters are scarce today!); in soft full color. Fine condition, 21″ × 28″. $75–$100

Courtesy of Meehan
Military Posters

Joan of Arc, 1918. Inspirational image of a radiant Joan, replete with upraised sword and shining armor, aimed at involving women in war savings; full color on cobalt. Mint condition, 20″ × 30″.

$225–$250

CONSTANT-DUVAL

Credit Nationale, 1920. Shows the ruins of a great building. Loan was for campaign to repair war damages. Fine condition, linen-mounted, 31″ × 45″. $250–$300

Bank of China, 1920. Deco delight by well-known travel poster artist shows exotically garbed figure beating the drum for war recovery loans; mostly silky purple and whites on patterned golds. Fine condition, linen-mounted, 31″ × 47″. $245–$285

FREDERICK GEORGE COOPER

Courtesy of Meehan Military Posters

America's Tribute to Britain. Based on a woodcut, depicts American eagle swooping down to crown majestic British lion with laurel wreath of victory; in slate blue on peach. Quite hard to find, mint condition, 20″ × 30″. $325–$400

COX

The Sword is Drawn—The Navy Upholds It! Fabulous image of Columbia, wreathed in laurel and wearing a red cloak with American eagle fastening, holding scroll reading "We can do no otherwise." Fine condition, linen-mounted, 28″ × 42″. $450–$550

CRALLOPANA

Banco di Roma, 1917. Lithographed by A. Barabino, Genova. Tall poster depicts a youth in sailor suit offering his piggy bank to a soldier in full battle array. Very good condition, linen-mounted, 27″ × 77″.
                                                        $200 (Auction)

DE LAND

Before Sunset Buy a U.S. Government Bond, 1917. Imaginative view of Miss Liberty at dusk, with sunset doubling as the American flag; in full color with shimmering reflections. Fine condition, linen-mounted, 20″ × 30″. $225–$250

DE MARIS

Have You Room in Your Heart for Us? Appeal for homeless French children abandoned in the midst of incredible ruins, with halo-like battle clouds swirling over the tots' heads; in lush color. Fine condition, 20″ × 30″. $175–$200

DEWEY

Our Daddy is Fighting at the Front for You, 1917. For the second Liberty Loan, irresistible children in patriotic outfits. Fine condition, 20″ × 30″. $75–$100

GEORGES DORIVAL

After the Battle, 1919. Fully laden Yank trudges back to his barracks across rainy windswept plain; in deep colors. Fine condition, linen-mounted, 30″ × 46″. $285–$325

JEAN DROIT

Emprunt Nationale, 1919. Marianne figure steers a golden wheel, embraced in a golden frame of wheat and the tricolor. Rare, very good condition, linen-mounted, 31″ × 46″. $150–$175

ELLGAARD

The Police—Your Friend, Your Helper, 1938. One of a series of posters honoring German police. Here policeman helps woman and child cross street, bus in background has Adolph Hitler Plaza as its destination; in full color. Fine condition, 23″ × 33″. $295–$345

The Police—Your Friend, Your Helper, 1918. Same series. Here policeman rescues child from a burning building. Full color, red lettering. Fine condition, 23″ × 33″. $275–$325

FRITZ ERLER (1868–1940)

Der 9te Pfeil Zeichnet Kriegsanleihe (Ninth War Loan), 1918. Nude bowman aiming arrow for the last shot, surrounded by dramatic flames; grays, burnt oranges, and yellow, blue letters. Fine condition, linen-mounted, 18″ × 27″. $350–$400

Helft Uns Siegen! (Help Us Win), 1918. Steel-helmeted soldier staring from barbed wire fortress at Verdun. Also issued as a field postcard. Somber naturalistic colors. Near mint, 16″ × 22″. $350–$400

EVERETT

Must Children Die and Mothers Plead in Vain?, 1918. Desperate mother clutches baby and toddler in dramatic appeal for assistance; naturalistic color offset by lemon yellow field. Very good condition, linen-mounted, 30″ × 40″. $195–$225

ABEL FAIVRE (1867–1945)

Credit Lyonnais, 1918. Dynamic design depicts life-and-death struggle of French poilu and Prussion eagle; in full color. Mint condition, linen-mounted, 31″ × 48″. $345–$395

We'll Get 'Em! (On les aura!), 1916. Widely imitated recruiting poster enthusiastically urging the troops forward; title from famous order of Petain of April 1916. Fine color, mint condition, linen-mounted, 32″ × 47″. $350–$425

CHARLES BUCKLES FALLS

E-E-E-Yah-Yip. Marine with bayonet also used as recruiting poster, overprinted with third Liberty Loan appeal; in black and white on orange. Fine condition, 19″ × 27″. $100–$125

Put the Pennant Beside the Flag, 1918. U.S. Shipping Board pennant fluttering alongside Old Glory. Very good condition, linen-mounted, horizontal 56″ × 40″. $300–$350

Ten Million Members by Christmas. Gleaming Christmas candle in front of Red Cross and glistening stars; bright full color. Very good condition, 20″ × 30″. $65–$80

This Device on Hat or Helmet Means U.S. Marines, 1918. Marine Corps insignia against a deep green background. Very good condition, linen-mounted, 28″ × 42″. $225–$250

Yanks in Germany Want More Books, 1918. A doughboy leaning against his backpack reading a book. 29″ × 33″. $350–$425

HARRISON FISHER (1875–1934)

Have You Answered the Red Cross Christmas Roll Call? Rosy-cheeked nurse reaches out to viewer on behalf of American troops marching on the horizon; naturalistic full color on soft green. Very good condition, 30″ × 36″. $95–$125

I Summon You to Comradeship in the Red Cross, 1918. Nurse wrapped in the American flag, the Capitol in the distance. Very good condition, linen-mounted, 28″ × 42″.   *$500 (Auction)*

JAMES MONTGOMERY FLAGG (*1877–1960*)

Be a U.S. Marine, 1918. Marine captain with .45 drawn against background of the Stars and Stripes. Very rare, near mint, 28″ × 40″.
                                                        $450–$500

Boys and Girls!, 1918. Uncle Sam encourages a girl and her brother to help win the war by contributing quarters; in color. Uncommon, mint condition, 20″ × 30″.   *$375–$425*

Courtesy of Meehan Military Posters

I Am Telling You, 1918. Uncle Sam encourages the purchase of War Savings Stamps; naturalistic color. Despite their modest cost, the stamps eventually raised over a billion dollars for the war effort. Mint condition, 20″ × 30″.   *$150–$175*

I Want You, 1917. *The* original classic; artist's self-portrait in 19th-century garb of his own devising that has become the standard image of Uncle Sam; primarily red, white, and blue. The famous pose was adapted from a British recruiting poster of Lord Kitchener. Rare, mint condition, linen-mounted, 30″ × 40″. $1,800–$2,200

The Navy Needs You! Don't READ American History—MAKE It! With fleet waiting in the distance, a sailor reminds a natty civilian of his duty as Miss Liberty appears overhead brandishing a sword and the flag. Becoming hard to find, slight restoration, linen-mounted, 28″ × 42″. $450–$550

Tell That to the Marines. Civilian, enraged by headline reporting German atrocities in Belgium, rolls up sleeves to join the colors. This image inspired the poem *The Appeal of a Poster,* published in the *New York Herald* and quoted in full in Rawls' *Wake Up America!* Another Marine classic, in naturalistic colors. Hard to find, mint condition, 30″ × 40″. $300–$350

Together We Win, ca. 1918. Exuberant trio strides to the docks as ships take shape in the background; sparkling palette. Fine condition, linen-mounted, 29″ × 39″. $275–$325

Wake Up, America! Civilization Calls Every Man, Woman and Child,
1917. Lovely innocent Columbia slumbers while world beyond erupts
in smoke and flames. Patriotic groups such as New York's Mayor's
Committee undertook to combat isolationism by issuing posters of
which this is a particularly beautiful and rare example. Mint condition, linen-mounted, 28″ × 40″. $2,500–$3,000

FORINGER

The Greatest Mother in the World. A young nurse cradles a wounded
Yank on stretcher in front of large Red Cross; in charcoals and red
on buff. Poster so effective it was reused in World War II. Fine condition, linen-mounted, 30″ × 40″. $75–$100

CHARLES FOUQUERAY

*Day in Honor of the African Army (Journee de l'Armée Afrique et des
Troupes Coloniales),* 1917. Image of whirling dervishes in action, ro-
mantically splendid presentation à la Delacroix in bright painterly
color. Fine condition, linen-mounted, 31″ × 48″. $650–$725

Day in Honor of the Serbs (Journée Serbe), 1916. Scene of epic Serbian
retreat over the mountains; in rich charcoals and deep wintry colors.
General Putnik, in his 70s and ill, stands with a nearly blind King
Peter, who rode in an ox cart to remain with his people. Fine condition, linen-mounted, 31″ × 45″. $275–$325

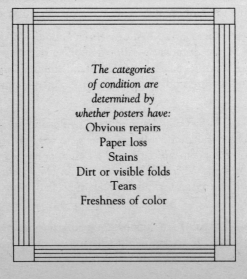

The categories
of condition are
determined by
whether posters have:
Obvious repairs
Paper loss
Stains
Dirt or visible folds
Tears
Freshness of color

MALCOLM GIBSON

Courtesy of Marc Choko

Rien à Faire sans l'Emprunt de la Victoire, ca. 1916. Depicts snow-covered factories sitting idle. A very special atmosphere in a very original World War I poster. Mint condition, 24″ × 36¼.″

$500–$600

B. H.

Teufel Hunden (Devil Dogs). Ferocious Marine mascot has dachshund on the run in this humorous recruiting poster ("devil dogs" was the German nickname for the Marines); black and white on orange field. Fine condition, 19″ × 27″. $100–$125

HALSTED AND ADERENTE

Columbia Calls, 1916. Classic early recruiting poster featuring Columbia with drawn sword planting flag of liberty atop the globe; full color on robin's-egg blue. Issued by preparedness advocates alarmed by Wilson's isolationist policies. Fine condition, 30″ × 40″. $325–$400

HARRIS

Good Bye, Dad, I'm Off to Fight for Old Glory. Capturing idealistic spirit of volunteers, doughboy bids dad and farmland adieu; attractive full palette. Fine condition, 20″ × 30″. $95–$125

LLOYD HARRISON

Foods from Corn. Depicts display of mostly desserts that use corn syrup sweetener; color on blue and gold ground. To encourage Americans to switch from sugar needed by our Allies to relatively plentiful corn syrup. Fine condition, 20″ × 30″.   *$150–$175*

HAZAN

Emprunt Nationale, 1920. Eos, the Goddess of the Dawn, raises her arms to a renewed countryside as she stands in the ruins of the war. In the sky is the word "Renaitre" (rebirth). Quite rare, good condition, linen-backed, 31″ × 47″.   *$125 (Auction)*

HERMLE

Kampft Mit!, ca. 1917. German War Loan poster shows silhouette of spike-helmeted soldier against burning ruins. Good condition, restored, linen-mounted, 23″ × 32″.   *$325 (Auction)*

HIDER

Canadiens-Français Enrolez-Vous, ca. 1917. French-Canadian recruiting poster shows soldiers going off to help their French brethren in the European battle. Good condition with some paper loss, 28″ × 40″. $100–$125

HOFFMANN

Yes! Hitler We Follow You! Photomontage poster (advanced technique for the early 1930s) with red lettering by Hitler's official photographer shows an arrogant Führer in trench coat and military uniform, backed by an enthusiastic throng of supporters. Very good condition, linen-mounted, 24″ × 34″. $575–$650

Yes!, 1933. Photomontage in black, white, and sepias. Shouldering shovels, an army of depression-era workers is on the march as Hitler purports to dig in. Rare, mint condition, linen-mounted, 23″ × 34″. $750–$900

LUDWIG HOHLWEIN (1874–1949)

Come With Me, 1930. Exceptional poster by Germany's best war and non-wartime poster artist. Shows soldier standing above the cheering throng; in full color. Rare, mint condition, 24″ × 33″. $875–$1,000

Luddendorf-Spende, 1918. Compelling image of seriously wounded vet staring intently at the tools he will need to master to find work; in subtle full color. The innovative mottled style is a Hohlwein trademark. Fine condition, linen-mounted, horizontal 37″ × 27″. $895–$1,100

Youth Labor Competition, 1934. Smiling youth grips hammer as he gets ready for vocational competition in this Nazi-sponsored event; in beiges, browns, black, and red. Very scarce, fine condition, linen-mounted, 24″ × 33″. $465–$550

ARGIET HUTAF

Treat 'Em Rough!, ca. 1918. Powerful Tanks Corps recruiting poster depicts a black tomcat, yellow eyes aglow, pouncing on enemy tanks; brilliant color. Very scarce, fine condition, linen-mounted, 26″ × 36″. $975–$1,200

ILLIAN

Keep It Coming—"We Must Not Only Feed Our Soldiers . . . ." Printed by W. F. Powers, New York. Parade of food trucks winds through the snow. Fine condition, 21″ × 29″. $95–$125

JANESCH

Combat Artists Exhibition at Royal Academy of Art, 1917. Moving depiction of soldier throwing potato masher as cover as he pulls wounded comrade to safety, with elegant calligraphy in stark contrast to harrowing image; in sepias. Very good condition, horizontal 34″ × 25″.
                                                                 $425–$500

LUCIEN JONAS

Credit Commercial de France, 1918. Three soldiers in foreground in trench, one hurling grenade; background an allegorical Marianne and massed troops. Very good condition, linen-mounted, 31″ × 47″.
                                                                 $225–$250

Day in Honor of Algerian Troops, 1917. Exotic scene depicts colonial enlistee bidding adieu to his family, his wife in full Berber jewels, his son toting a toy cannon; in full warm color. Very good condition, linen-mounted, 31″ × 47″. $285–$350

Day in Honor of the African Army, 1917. North American troops crash through barbed wire in fearless charge, cherry blossoms vibrating incongruously in sunlight; naturalistic color. Very good condition, linen-mounted, 31″ × 47″. $285–$335

Emprunt Français 5%, 1920. Nations coming to the aid of France; Uncle Sam offers a bag of money to Marianne. Very good condition, linen-mounted, horizontal 47″ × 31″. $400–$450

The Equitable Trust Company of New York, 1920. One of many posters sponsored by banks in Paris to rebuild France. Shows Yanks helping a grateful French family rebuild the war-torn homestead. Very good condition, linen-mounted, 31″ × 47″. $225–$275

Four Years in the Fight/The Women of France. For the United War Work Campaign, women carry molten shells to and from blast furnace; in muted colors with soft backlighting. Becoming hard to find, very good condition, 28″ × 42″. $125–$150

HELENE JONES

The Motor Corp of America, 1917. Two female ambulance drivers, their vehicle in background, a stretcher and medical bag at their side, one woman holding Old Glory. Very rare, 30″ × 40″.
$1,000–$1,200

MAURICE KAVAS

Exposition d'Art Décoratif, 1917. For the benefit of the soldiers in the trenches, a decorative arts show on the Champs Elysees. Very good condition, linen-mounted, 32″ × 47″. $300 (Auction)

KEALY

Women of Britain Say—"GO!" Famous recruiting poster of women stoically watching troops parade away in late afternoon light; in exceptional full color. Fine condition, linen-mounted and framed, 20″ × 30″. $375–$450

KING

Lest They Perish. Issued by American Committee for Relief in the
Near East, solemn mother with downcast eyes stands with baby in
midst of annihilated town; beautiful soft palette. Mint condition,
13″ × 18″.   *$150–$175*

ROLAND KRAFTER

War Album, 1917. Combat soldiers of the Tyrolean Kaiserjaeger, some
wounded, many with camouflage still stuck in their helmets, march
off for Christmas leave; in charcoals with delicate touches of red. Very
good condition, 25″ × 37″.   *$285–$325*

JOSEPH CHRISTIAN LEYENDECKER (1874–1951)

Courtesy of Meehan Military Posters

America Calls—Enlist in the Navy. Recruiting poster with Statue of
Liberty clasping hand of sailor; unusual round image shape, in color
on rich blue field. Extremely rare, fine condition, linen-mounted,
30″ × 40″.   *$850–$1,000*

Order Coal Now, 1918. Superb, famous image of Clydesdales waiting
patiently under leafy tree on hot summer's day; issued to remind home-
front to order their coal out-of-season so that supplies would be available for the front during the winter. Color illustration in Rawls' *Wake
Up America!* (see Bibliography). Mint condition, 20″ × 30″.
                                                            $575–$650

U.S.A. Bonds, 1918. Honoring Boy Scouts, the first organized group to distribute War Bond posters. Scout hands Miss Liberty sword inscribed with motto "Be Prepared." Very good condition, linen-mounted, 20″ × 30″. $275–$325

JONAS LIE

On the Job for Victory, 1918. Large-format drydock scene for the U.S. Shipping Board. Good condition, folds apparent, folded, horizontal 55″ × 39″. $750–$800

LO

U-Boat Calendar. John Bull is cut down to size by German subs during the course of 1917; soft full color on buff. Mint condition, horizontal 25″ × 20″. $500–$600

LONERGAN

Follow the Flag of the 5th Missouri Infantry. Recruiting poster of handsome color guard issued in a small edition urging recruits to join the "Joffre Regiment"; naturalistic color on butter yellow. Fine condition, linen-mounted, 24″ × 38″. $450–$550

LURIA-FOWLER

Save Sugar. Sugar and syrup balance perfectly on brass scales, while massed troops parade by on the horizon; naturalistic colors against black field. Fine condition, 20″ × 30″. $135–$160

WILLIAM MALHERBE

Banque Française, 1918. For the French Liberation War Loan, poilu grasps Marianne who in turn holds aloft the tricolor. Very good condition, linen-mounted, 31″ × 47″. $100 (Auction)

MATHESON

Know Him by This Sign, 1919. Smiling army medic identified by caduceus. Full color on apple green. Very good condition, linen-mounted, 20″ × 29″. $150–$175

All price ranges represent the retail value.

MCMEIN

Courtesy of Meehan Military Posters

Y.W.C.A. in Service for the Girls of the World, 1919. Sensitively drawn young volunteer gazes thoughtfully alongside Y blue triangle logo; in soft full color. Rare, mint condition, 20″ × 30″. $275–$325

MUELLER

Adventure and Action, 1919. The caissons go rolling along in unusual Field Artillery recruiting poster; full color against vivid orange and yellow sunset. Mint condition, 19″ × 25″. $125–$150

MAURICE NEUMONT (1868–1930)

Day in Honor of Raemaekers, 1916. Poster for exhibition of Raemaekers, Dutch artist who was hotly pursued by the Germans, depicts an elegantly dressed artist stepping out of a huge inkwell to skewer savagely drawn German Brunhilde with point of pen. Fine condition, linen-mounted. $250–$300

Galerie Brunners, 1918. War exposition in storefront window taped against bomb blasts. Full color, mint condition, linen-mounted, 23″ × 31″. $200–$225

On Ne Passe Pas (They shall Not Pass), 1918. Classic poster painted after sketches at Verdun. Ravaged poliu blocks the way to the fort after Petain's orders to hold every centimeter. Fiery color. Full-page color illustration in Rawls' *Wake Up America!* (see Bibliography). Fine condition, linen-mounted, 31″ × 47″. $450–$500

JOHN WARNER NORTON

Keep These Off the U.S.A., 1918. Famous image of the bloody boots against black background. Very good condition, some restoration, linen-mounted, 29″ × 38″. $375–$425

HERBERT PAUS

Help Deliver the Goods. Swabbie proudly hoists shells "to be delivered rush" regardless of the risks; in full color. Very good condition, linen-mounted, 28″ × 40″. $225–$250

Save for Your Child's Liberty, 1918. Famous image of naked boy and the Statue of Liberty's arm, but with a title change, printed by the Scottish War Savings Committee, Edinburgh. Very good condition, old folds show, linen-mounted, 30″ × 40″. $250–$300

EDWARD PENFIELD (1866–1925)

One of the most famous turn-of-the-century artists, Penfield was recently featured in a major poster exhibition at the Metropolitan Museum of Art in New York.

Enlist Now, Join the U.S. School Garden Army. Printed by American Lithographic Co., New York. Good condition, framed, 19¹³/₁₆″ × 29⅛″. $800–$1,000

Every Girl Pulling for Victory, 1918. For the United War Work Campaign, a pretty girl in middy blouse rows a boat named *Victory*; in soft naturalistic color on buff. Becoming scarce, mint condition, 20″ × 30″. $245–$285

JOSEPH PENNELL (1857–1926)

That Liberty Shall Not Perish from the Earth, 1918. Lower Manhattan, a towering inferno, in apocalyptic vision of bombing raid that decapitates Statue of Liberty; in sepias. Poster so sensational that Pennell wrote a book (now very rare) about its evolution. Mint condition, linen-mounted, 20″ × 30″. $225–$250

FRANCISQUE POULBOT (1879–1946)

Emprunt de la Défense Nationale, 1915. Mother and children saying goodbye to daddy as he leaves for the front with a column of troops; soft pastels against a white field. Very good condition, linen-mounted, 31″ × 47″. $300–$350

The Poilu's Day . . . Let My Daddy Come Home on Leave!, 1915. Engaging image of siblings dressed as poilu and nurse awaiting dad's return; mostly red, white, blue, and sepia on buff. Very good condition, linen-mounted, 32″ × 47″. $375–$425

LOUIS RAEMAEKERS (1869–1956)

Louis Raemaekers was an expatriate Dutchman whose artistry was such an effective propaganda tool that the Germans put a price on his head.

In Belgium Help, 1916. German expropriation of all produce and live-stock from occupied Belgium caused mass starvation. Gaunt mother and baby appeal for desperately needed aid; full deep color against sunset sky. Very good condition, 24″ × 39″. $225–$250

Will You be Ready Tomorrow to Make Munitions for Germany?, 1917. Subtitled "If Not, Invest in Liberty Bonds Today," depicts cold-blooded Hun aiming point-blank at helpless elderly man; in black and white. Fine condition, 12″ × 19″. $195–$225

RALEIGH

Courtesy of Meehan Military Posters

Blood or Bread. Sacrifices on battlefield demand sacrifices at home; full color on blue field. Fine condition, 20″ × 30″. $75–$100

Halt the Hun, 1918. Doughboy steps up to rout despicable Hun menacing defenseless children; strong charcoal design on blazing red oranges and hot pinks. Fine condition, linen-mounted, 20″ × 30″.
$125–$150

Hun or Home?, 1918. Hun, equated with subhuman ape, crawls on his hands to capture defenseless girl and baby; in graphic charcoals offset by delicate pinks, beiges, and orange. Fine condition, 20″ × 30″.
$125–$150

RICE

See Him Through. Knight of Columbus, pledged to support American volunteers overseas, points proudly to doughboy off to battle; naturalistic color. Fine condition, 20″ × 30″.
$75–$100

SIDNEY RIESENBERG

Civilians, 1918. Doughboy stops in mid-battle to appeal to viewer to support Jewish Welfare Board's campaign to aid soldiers; rich browns, blue Star of David on buff. Fine condition, linen-mounted, 20″ × 30″.
$175–$200

Over the Top, 1918. Triumphant doughboy hoists billowing flag; in bright painterly colors. Inspired by Sgt. Arthur Guy Emprey's best-selling book of the same title, made into a movie in 1917. Mint condition, 20″ × 30″.
$150–$175

Rally 'Round the Flag. Valiant "Soldiers of the Sea" storm serene tropical beach, with offshore fleet waving palms and sunlit sea seen behind assault party. Rare, very good condition, linen-mounted, 30″ × 40″.
$225–$250

A. ROBARTI

2me Emprunt de la Défense Nationale, 1916. Patriotic citizens stand at the foot of a statue of Marianne, each bringing her the money needed to carry on the war effort. Very good condition, linen-mounted, 31″ × 47″.
$325–$400

NORMAN ROCKWELL (1894–1978)

. . . *the Fighting Fourth*, 1918. Rockwell at 23 already showing the meticulous style that made him famous. Youngster shows off war savings buttons/merit badges; in full color. Rare, mint condition, linen-mounted, 10″ × 14″. $225–$250

A. ROUBILLE

Credit du Nord, 1918. French War Loan poster showing farm maiden carrying cornucopia and leading her bull. Very good condition, linen-mounted, 44″ × 31″. $275 (Auction)

SARKA

Lend Him a Hand, 1918. Helping hand, symbolizing home-front support, lifts Yank out of deep trench; naturalistic color, vigorous brushwork. Adaptation of *Leslie's Weekly* cover. Fine condition, linen-mounted, 12″ × 19″. $75–$100

SEM (AKA SERGE GOURSAT, 1863–1934)

A renowned artist, Sem was once commissioned to paint the murals in Maxims in Paris.

For the Last Quarter of an Hour, 1918. Weary poilus slog across barren no-man's land as elderly officer studies map on hillock; great attention to detail, in warm sunset colors. Fine condition, horizontal 47″ × 32″. $450–$550

For the Liberty of the World (Pour la Liberte du Monde), 1918. Beautiful image of colossal Statue of Liberty lifting torch over the shimmering ocean; in glorious golds modulating to deepest sea green. Fine condition, linen-mounted, 31″ × 46″. $925–$1,000

For the Triumph, 1918. Poilus streaming from heaven to parade through the Arch of Triumph in Paris; charcoals on buff. Rare, fine condition, linen-mounted, 32″ × 45″. $345–$395

SHERIDAN

Hey Fellows!, 1918. Soldier holds up books shipped from home, while another sits reading; in khakis, white, and gray on orange background. Very good condition, linen-mounted, 20″ × 30″.   *$135–$160*

SINDELAR

Uncle Sam Needs That Extra Shovelful, 1918. For the U.S. Fuel Administration (to conserve coal), depicts striker lit by the fire from the open boiler, Uncle Sam behind him. Tiny border chip, otherwise mint condition, 20″ × 28″.   *$200 (Auction)*

JESSE WILCOX SMITH *(1863-1935)*

Courtesy of Meehan Military Posters

Have YOU a Red Cross Service Flag?, 1918. Poster by well-known children's book illustrator shows beautiful child carefully placing a Red Cross flag below the Christmas wreath; in pastels. Fine condition, 22″ × 28″. $225-$250

We'll Help You to Win the War, Dad. Sensitively rendered, young Scout holds War Savings Stamp book as he says goodbye to his soldier dad; khakis on beige. Fine condition, 18″ × 28″. $175-$200

SPEAR

Workers Lend Your Strength, 1918. Symbiosis of worker and doughboy emphasized in image showing each working in parallel; full color, especially stone gray, blue, and red. Very good condition, 20″ × 30″.
$75-$100

STAHR

Be Patriotic. Columbia appeals to the viewer to sign the pledge to save food for our troops, Allies, and starving civilians caught in the crossfire; in color with lots of red, white, and blue. Very good condition, linen-mounted, 20″ × 30″. $125-$150

THEOPHILE-ALEXANDRE STEINLEN (1859–1923)

Journée des Reqions Liberées, 1919. Printed by I. Lapina, Paris. Shows a robin alone on a fencepost as the new dawn rises. Good condition, some paper loss and restorations, linen-backed, framed, 31⅞″ × 47⅜″.　　　　　　　　　　　　　　　　　　$650 (Auction)

Journée du Poilu, 1915. Printed by Devambez, Paris. Showing weary soldiers marching from the front. Good condition, some small tears, linen-backed, framed, 31½″ × 47″.　　　　　　　$450 (Auction)

Courtesy of Butterfield & Butterfield

Journée Serbe, 1916. Printed by I. Lapina, published in *La Guerre,* Paris. Good condition, several small tears and creases, linen-backed, framed, 30½″ × 47″.　　　　　　　　　　　　　$950 (Auction)

Save Serbia, 1918. Same image as *Journée Serbe,* above, but printed in English for distribution in the United States to solicit funds for the Serbian Relief Committee of America; in charcoals and delicate color. Fine condition, linen-mounted, 24″ × 36″.　　　　　$350–$450

Office de Renseiqnements Pour les Familles Dispersées, 1915. To aid families made homeless by the war; image of a man with two young children, right side of poster filled with lettering. Very good condition, linen-mounted, 25″ × 37″.　　　　　　　$600 (Auction)

ALBERT STERNER (1863–1946)

America's Tribute to France, 1920. Golden rays shine on French children planting white lily symbolizing the resurrection of France, with shattered cathedral backdrop reminding viewer that rebuilding is still urgent. Scarce, fine condition, 20″ × 30″. $185–$215

STROTHMAN

Beat Back the Hun, 1918. Hun with bloodstained fingers and knife leans across the ocean to fix startling green eyes on potential stateside victims; bright color with sophisticated intense resonances. Mint condition, 18″ × 27″. $225–$250

ADOLPH TREIDLER (1886–1981)

Beat Germany . . . Eat Less of the Food Fighters Need. Flags of the Allies remind viewer food is a vital weapon for the war effort; bright colors on gray. Very good condition, 20″ × 30″. $75–$100

Have You Bought Your Bond?, 1917. Historically important document: the first poster rushed into print for the Liberty Loan campaign; bronze statue beckons from a lovely blue sky. Fine condition, framed, 20″ × 30″. $195–$225

Help Stop This, 1918. "Keep Him Out of America"—Hun with bloody dagger stomps around pulverized village looking for fresh victims; full color. Fine condition, 20″ × 30″. $150–$175

Make Every Minute Count. Issued by the Emergency Fleet Corporation, a riveter concentrates on hull as desperately needed ships take shape in the yard; sunny colors. Fine condition, 20″ × 30″.

$95–$125

THOMAS TRYON

Surgical Dressings for War Relief, 1918. Shows a nurse and massed flags with illustrations around border of things to be made: bed sock, bandages, elbow rest, etc. Very good condition, linen-mounted, 28″ × 42″. $425 (Auction)

VARMANSKI

Russian War Loan, 1916. Russian cavalry officers charging over a plain, German infantry retreating in the distance. Rare, fine condition, linen-mounted, 27″ × 39″. $500–$600

Russian War Loan, 1916. Supply convoy on the way to the front. Rare, fine condition, linen-mounted, 27″ × 39″. $500–$600

Russian War Loan, 1916. Tsar's munitions factory aglow in the middle of the night as boxes are piled into a tiny truck for run to the front, with sample product looming at left; in deep nocturnal color. Fine condition, linen-mounted, 26″ × 39″. $325–$400

VERREES

Join the Air Service and Serve in France, 1917. Rare, richly textured image of diving Jenny and air spotters. Thousands volunteered for the Air Service, though only 1,200 pilots actually got to France. Mint condition, 25″ × 37″. $1,500–$1,800

VLADIMIR

Subscribe to War Loan and Help Valiant Soldiers to Victory, 1916. Russian cavalrymen armed with lances charge fleeing Huns in beautifully rendered battle scene; delicate natural color on buff. Rare, very good condition, linen-mounted, 27″ × 39″. $425–$500

War Loan, 1916. Russian caissons go rolling along, past abandoned German detritus and into the teeth of the gathering storm. Very good condition, linen-mounted, 27″ × 39″. $425–$500

VOLK

They Shall Not Perish, 1918. Determined Columbia, draped in swirling flag, raises sword protectively over head of frightened young girl; full color against inky black abyss. Very good condition, 30″ × 40″.
$175–$200

C. HOWARD WALKER

For United America, Division for Foreign-Born Women, 1918. Colorful Columbia with escutcheons of flags of many different countries which had sent immigrants to the United States. Very good condition, 28″ × 40″. $300–$350

WARDLE

The Empire Needs Men. Recruiting poster features young lion cubs helping old lion, representing Britain, defend itself; dark colors on gold. Mint condition, 20″ × 30″. $225–$250

WHELAN

Men Wanted for the Army, 1908. Cavalry recruiting poster featuring mounted bugler in dress blues sounding reveille in the western desert; glowing naturalistic style and color. One of the most romantic and beautiful recruiting posters ever issued and rarest of the three pre-war recruiting posters by this artist. Fine condition, linen-mounted, 30″ × 40″. $950–$1,100

ADOLPHE LEON WILLETTE (1857–1926)

Day in Honor of the Poilu, 1915. Lighthearted poster depicts poilu's first leave, after 11 months of battle, greeted by gleeful wife and excited pooch; charcoals on buff. Scarce, fine condition, linen-mounted, 32″ × 47″. $250–$300

Valmy (Banque de l'Union Parisienne), 1918. A glowering General Dumouriez protects wide-eyed teen; in charcoals with red touches. Poster compares the 1918 German retreat to the miraculous battle of Valmy in 1792 when the Prussians suddenly abandoned their attack on Paris. Image in mint condition, with tiny restoration on margin, linen-mounted, 32″ × 47″. $285–$335

WOBBEKING

War Booty Exhibition, Posen, 1917. Cavalry poster features "Death's Head Hussar" with lance. Rare, very good condition, framed, 34″ × 49″. $800 (Auction)

ELLSWORTH YOUNG

Remember Belgium, 1918. Famous poster of defenseless girl carried off by gun-toting Hun while her village burns; black silhouettes, flame colors, deep green field. Mint condition, 20″ × 30″. $135–$160

WORLD WAR II

ANONYMOUS

Adolf Hitler, ca. 1935. Larger-than-life black and white photo portrait of der Führer. Mint condition, 33″ × 40″. $600–$700

Allies in the Shipyards. Norwegians, Frenchman, Pole, Czech, and Belgian pictured bending to the joint task in the same British shipyard; photos and full-color flags. Fine condition, 15″ × 18″. $50–$75

American Labor . . . Producing for Attack. Spotlighted image of bronze figure of American laborer rolling up sleeves for wartime push; in bronze on blue. Figure was the work of Max Kalish, who also sculpted members of wartime cabinet at request of FDR. Very good condition, linen-mounted, 28″ × 40″. $95–$125

Anotoly Krohalov, 1941. Honoring exploits of Russian air ace Krohalov, pictures operational success on land, sea, and air over inspirational poem; in naturalistic color, mostly red, white, and blue. Fine condition, 18″ × 28″. $750–$900

Back 'Em Up!, 1944. Photo of four-star General Eisenhower saluting smartly before diagonal red and white stripes of Old Glory; photo, red, white, and blue. Fine condition, 20″ × 28″. $65–$80

Become a Nurse—Your Country Needs You. Uncle Sam demonstrates the importance of nursing by capping an attractive young nurse himself; in patriotic Kodacolor. Fine condition, 20″ × 28″. $75–$100

Better Dead Than a Slave, 1945. German poster showing remnants of the German armies, armed with 9 mm MP 40 Schmeisser (machine pistol) and a Panzerfaust (bazooka), uniting in a last-ditch attempt to defend the shrinking Reich. Hand-drawn, text in north German dialect, in pencil with red letters. Extremely rare, very good condition, linen-mounted, 23″ × 33″. $475–$600

Collect Books for the Army. German, soldier in steel helmet and greatcoat is engrossed in his reading; color photo on gray with orange letters. Fine condition, 12″ × 16″. $250–$300

Das Kann er Seiner Grossmama Erzahlen!!!, 1940. Caricatures of Jews are shown as responsible for all the ills of war by their manipulation of the media and support of social programs. Very good condition, linen-mounted, horizontal 47″ × 33″. $500–$600

Dein Kamerad, Dein Mann, 1940. Shows determined platoon of German infantry about to charge from a trench. Very good condition, linen-mounted, horizontal 47″ × 33″. $400–$450

Der Jude Kaufman, 1942. Propaganda aimed at the publisher of the Buenos Aires *Herald*, the "notorious Jew" Kaufman, shown here at his typewriter. Very good condition, linen-mounted, horizontal 47″ × 33″. $500–$600

The Downfall of the Dictators is Assured. One of a series of British posters highlighting successes against the Axis. Bristol Beaufighters banking over Rommel's fleeing columns in North Africa; mostly beiges, gunmetal, and yellows. Fine condition, 20″ × 30″.

$175–$200

The Downfall of the Dictators is Assured. Vast Allied armada steams past Rock of Gibraltar enroute to the invasion of North Africa; mostly beiges and sea blue. Fine condition, 20″ × 30″. $125–$150

Earn and Learn with the Indian Air Force, ca. 1939. Very rare Indian recruiting poster shows mechanics checking Vickers Wellington MK1 bomber; full color on yellow and brown. Very good condition, linen-mounted, 26″ × 40″. $295–$345

Ein Volk, Ein Reich, Ein Führer, ca. 1936. Large photographic portrait of Hitler in a military-style uniform. Ubiquitous in pre-war Germany, but most copies were destroyed in the de-Nazification program after the war. Mint condition, 33″ × 47″. $1,200–$1,400

Every Mother's Son is Counting on You!, 1944. Sailor mans anti-aircraft gun on landing craft above photos of cheerful aviators and ship's personnel; full-color invasion scene and photos. Fine condition, 30″ × 40″. $135–$160

Feind Hort Mit!, 1944. German "Don't Talk" poster shows hausfrau hushing her husband who is about to divulge troop movements. Very good condition, linen-mounted, 33″ × 46″. $450–$550

For God's Sake Send Planes!, 1942. Embattled GI, still wearing World War I-style tin helmet, cranks up field telephone in desperate appeal. Hard-to-find poster issued by Oldsmobile Division of GM; in full bright color on yellow. Fine condition, linen-mounted, 30″ × 40″.

$150–$175

Fly Hard and Often—Fly with the Marines, 1942. Great Marine victory depicts Grumman "Wildcat" downing Japanese Ki-43 as bomber plummets right in the vicinity of Mt. Fuji; in rich color. Very good condition, linen-mounted, 28″ × 40″. $225–$250

German Subs Off New York. Germans attempt to impress French by boasting of U-boat kills. Drawing of sub inspecting the result of its attack on a convoy, with the Statue of Liberty in the distance. Nine photos surround drawing illustrate sub's routine; duotone photos and drawing, red letters. Extremely rare, very good condition, horizontal 34″ × 25″. $500–$600

If You Must Talk . . . Tell It to the MARINES, 1942. Recruiting poster at its most direct; bold red, white, and blue graphic. Fine condition, linen-mounted, 30″ × 40″. $95–$125

Incendiary Bombs. With all of Germany's available manpower away at the front, women and children are left to face the horrors of allied bombing raids; in full color. Mint condition, 12″ × 17″.

$295–$345

Je Crois (I Believe). Striking design presents glowing cross rising from swastika, affirming that justice will prevail; in black and gray with red cross and starry deep blue sky. Quite scarce, very good condition, 20″ × 30″. $250–$300

Junior Army Officer. Handsome profile of young Landwehr officer, promoting enlistments of from 4½ to 12 years; naturalistic color against warm yellow glow. Fine condition, 17″ × 23″. $375–$425

Katyn, Forest of Death. Nazi propaganda trumpets the grizzly discovery of Soviet perfidy in the only atrocity yet unearthed that they themselves had not committed; telling photos and text set in red. Mint condition, horizontal 23″ × 33″. $500–$600

Keep Us Flying!, 1943. Rare poster featuring Major Robert Diez, hero of the Tuskeegee Squadron, in full flight harness; naturalistic color on sky blue. Fine condition, 20″ × 28″. $350–$425

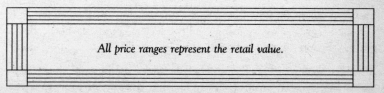

All price ranges represent the retail value.

La Crociata Europea (The European Crusade). Embattled Italy shown as a knight wielding mighty sword to shatter the chain binding Europe to Bolshevism, with flags of Germany, Italy, Hungary, Rumania, and Latvia waving in support; in full color. Mint condition, linen-mounted, 14″ × 19″. $500–$650

Let's Get 'Em!. Initialed "S.A." Lithographic poster showing crew of Nazi sub surrendering; in deep navy, red, and green-gold. Very good condition, 28″ × 42″. $125–$150

Let Us Go Forward Together. Photomontage poster showing a strong and confident Churchill with bevy of tanks and planes; photo set against blue field, elegant "Varsity" script. Mint condition, 20″ × 30″. $375–$450

Lightning Strikes the Axis, 1943. A "salute to a great plane," the P-38 Lightning. The plane is drawn in macro-detail. Folded, horizontal 42″ × 31″. $250 (Auction)

Lock Up These Papers, 1943. Red arrows point to documents with various security classifications; yellow letters, ominous black background. Scarce, very good condition, 14″ × 20″. $95–$125

More Production, 1942. Bomb labeled "More Production" blasts Japanese flag; a prize-winning design in the Museum of Modern Art's "Artists for Victory" contest. Fine condition, linen-mounted, 28″ × 40″. $150–$175

The More WOMEN at Work the Sooner We WIN!, 1943. Comely aircraft perfectionist in red smock adjusts plastic bomber bubble; full color. Hard to find, fine condition, linen-mounted, 14″ × 22″.

$75–$100

Murdering Jap, 1944. Horrifying illustration of newspaper insert that reads "5200 Yank Prisoners Killed by Jap Torture in Philippines." Japanese soldier slams defenseless American prisoner with rifle butt; in black and white on yellow and red. Fine condition, 17″ × 23″.

$135–$160

National Lottery, 1935. Perched on a swastika, the German eagle is pressed into service in this ad for the national Nazi lottery; in brown and red. Fine condition, 23″ × 33″.

$450–$550

National Service Wants You! Photomontage printed by Fosh & Cross, Ltd., London. Huge hand points finger at viewer; blue background. Fine condition, 20″ × 30″.

$65–$80

A Nazi is Smart. Poster depicts sinister-looking Nazi using his ingenuity to aid Reich production; in full color. Fine condition, 19″ × 25″.

$95–$125

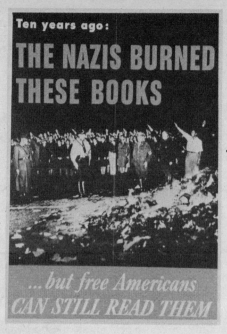

The Nazis Burned These Books, 1943. Photo of notorious book burning in Berlin organized by the Storm Troopers the year Hitler became chancellor of Germany; documentary photo, red border and letters. Hard to find, fine condition, 20″ × 28″. $175–$200

Never Was So Much Owed by So Many to So Few, 1940. Churchill quote to the valor of the RAF in the Battle of Britain, issued in tribute to their role in turning back better-equipped Luftwaffe; pilots beaming under fluffy clouds. Duotone, blue sky. Scarce, mint condition, 20″ × 30″. $475–$550

The 98k Carbine. German infantry training poster detailing mechanism of principal weapon, with cutaways and ammo specs included; each part a separate color for easy identification. Very good condition, linen-mounted, horizontal 51″ × 40″. $475–$575

Rumors Cost Lives. A shifty character is blamed for a U-boat captain's war crimes; in black, red, and olive. Very good condition, 20″ × 26″. $125–$150

She's Ready, Too. Blonde strides out from under the shadow of the American Cincinnatus, famous statue on Massachusetts' Lexington Common, to do her part by buying war bonds; in blonde, red, pale blue. Mint condition, 11″ × 14″. $45–$60

Sixteenth Congress of the Communist Party, 1930. Russian poster directly targeting Nazis as threat to the Communist system; in red, yellow, and black on buff. Fine condition, linen-mounted, horizontal 29″ × 21″. $195–$225

The Storm Troops Call. A film strip illustrates life in the Storm Troops of the early 1930s: rifle training, learning signals, physical training, etc. Photos with red letters. Very good condition, linen-mounted, 21″ × 33″. $325–$400

This is the Soviet Paradise, 1944. German poster using grim photos of dubious authenticity to make Occupied France fear Stalin more than Hitler; grim photos on red. Very good condition, linen-mounted, 45″ × 60″. $450–$550

This is What Awaits You, ca. 1937. French poster, issued by the Popular Front showing huge formation of Nazi bombers hitting Paris, urging France to gear up lest it meet the same fate as Madrid; in conte crayon, fires, letters on buff. Very rare, fine condition, linen-mounted, 32″ × 47″. $295–$350

This Man is Your FRIEND—He Fights for FREEDOM, 1942. Smiling Australian ANZAC trooper; with blue letters. (One of a series: Canadian, Chinese, Dutch, English, Ethiopian, Russian, etc.) Fine condition, 15″ × 20″. $35–$50

Untitled, Russian, 1943. With air support and a phalanx of red banners pointing the way to victory, massed Soviet armor advances along a broad front, with Lenin and Stalin adding the party stamp of approval to the panoply of battle; in full color. Mint condition, 23″ × 46″.
$1,200–$1,500

U.S. Marines Want You. Sometimes attributed to James Montgomery Flagg, this poster was probably produced just before U.S. entry into the war; in full color, mostly red, white, blue, and gold. Very good condition, linen-mounted, 20″ × 30″. $125–$150

V . . . Free Czechoslavakia. Morse code grafitti appeals for help in strong succinct graphic. Fine condition, 18″ × 24″. $75–$100

We Have Just Begun to Fight!, 1943. GI charges ahead buoyed up by string of legendary victories from Pearl Harbor to North Africa listed at his right; in silvery charcoals with red letters. Fine condition, 22″ × 28″. $95–$125

We're Helping Strike 'Em Out. Hard-to-find poster issued by Union Pacific depicts GI, backed up by munitions train, hurling grenade; in full color. Fine condition, 16″ × 23″. $65–$80

Who Stole Our North Africa? Roosevelt. Who Put Him Up to It? The Jew (French text), 1942. Vichy anti-Semitic poster shows Roosevelt being whispered to by Fiorello La Guardia. Extremely rare, in fine condition with minor staining, 47″ × 63″. $2,500 (Auction)

Why Pick Your Own Pocket?—Keep Your Victory Bonds and Certificates. Canadian lithographic poster depicting a workman in overalls pulling victory bonds from his pocket. Fine condition, 24″ × 36″.
$125–$150

You Keep Them Now; They'll Keep You Later. Hold on to Your Victory Bonds and Certificates. Canadian lithographic poster of man waving goodbye to anthropomorphic victory bonds; in lower image, the war bonds wave goodbye to the man in front of his house. Fine condition, 24″ × 36″. $125–$150

Your Boast, His Toast. Nazi in uniform of high-peaked cap, swastika, monocle, and iron cross, gleefully waves newspaper announcing sinking of an Allied troop transport; in dark colors, with red and black letters. Very good condition, horizontal 22″ × 17″.   *$195–$225*

ALBRECHT

Won't You Give a Bit More for the Front-Line Soldiers? Image of soldier looms large as civilians give to the war effort; in sepias and black. Fine condition, linen-mounted, 17″ × 24″.   *$250–$300*

ALDWINCKLE

Canada's New Army—Men Like You. Dispatch rider on pre-war motorcycle seen as modern parallel to luminous knight on a white charger filling the sky; in splendid glowing color. Fine condition, 24″ × 36″.
$135–$160

It's Our War. Muscular worker wields sledgehammer like a war club; in full color with shimmering aura, clever use of red, white, and blue. Very good condition, 21″ × 31″.   *$95–$125*

Whatever Your Job May Be, Fight. Steadfast worker and warrior are united in their vision of final victory; in full color with clever use of red, white, and blue. Fine condition, 21″ × 31″.   *$95–$125*

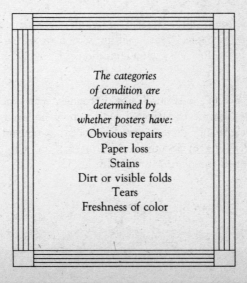

The categories
of condition are
determined by
whether posters have:
Obvious repairs
Paper loss
Stains
Dirt or visible folds
Tears
Freshness of color

ALEXANDER

Squash the Serpent, 1941. Russian poster in Ukranian folk art-style depicts Hitler as hapless reptile falling victim to soldier's boot and bayonet; in full color. Very good condition, 21″ × 29″. $675–$775

ANTON

Take Your Place in the Flying Corps. Extremely scarce poster for SS Air Corps Division never activated depicts young uniformed man with "SS" in background; great color. SS hoped to rejuvenate sagging Luftwaffe by adding an SS unit but shortages of trained men and war material doomed the plan. Mint condition, 32″ × 33″.

$2,500–$3,000

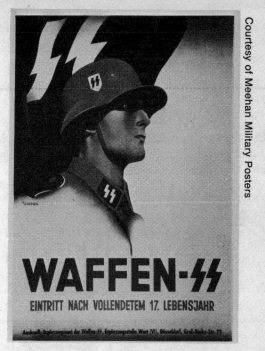

Waffen SS, 1941. Recruiting poster aimed at 17-year-olds. Backed by Waffen SS banner, recruit with features chiseled by a fanatical faith in Hitler looks ahead; fine color on glowing yellow. Rare, mint condition, linen-mounted, 22″ × 33″. $2,250–$2,500

JOHN ATHERTON (*1900–1952*)
A Careless Word . . . Another Cross, 1943. Ammo belt and helmet hang from a simple white cross in barren field; vividly rendered in full color. Fine condition, 22″ × 28″. $75–$100

Same as above. Fine condition, 28″ × 40″. $95–$125

For Freedom's Sake, 1943. Bronze figure of Cincinnatus from Lexington Common reminds viewers of their obligations; in full color. Fine condition, linen-mounted, 22″ × 28″. $90–$125

CECIL CALVERT BEALL (B. 1892)

And if Our Lines Should Form. Pinned down by enemy fire, a grimacing Leatherneck takes the time to plead for more supplies in rhyme; in rich jungle colors. Mint condition, 30″ × 40″. $150–$175

In the Strength of the Lord, 1945. Family shares bright beam radiating from figure of FDR speaking from heaven on behalf of victory bonds; in full color. Fine condition, 19″ × 26″. $95–$125

Keep 'Em Flying!, 1941. Pre-war poster resembling a puzzle picture with hidden objects, e.g., Uncle Sam's beard a sheaf of wheat; full color. Fine condition, 20″ × 28″. $95–$125

Courtesy of Meehan Military Posters

Loose Talk Can Cost Lives, 1942. Subtitled "Don't Be a Dope and Spread Inside Dope." A smirking Hitler eavesdrops on two workers' barroom conversation; in naturalistic style and color. Fine condition, 14″ × 20″. $75–$100

Now . . . All Together, 1945. Immortal image of Iwo Jima flag-raising based on famous AP photo; in naturalistic full color. Mint condition, 9″ × 13″. $45–$60

   Same as above. Mint condition, 20″ × 28″. $100–$150

WLADYSLAW T. BENDA (1873–1948)

Polish War Relief. Luminous portrayal of beautiful young mother protecting baby while older child peers fearfully over her shoulder; in black, white, and gray. Scarce, fine condition, linen-mounted, 30″ × 43″. $550–$600

BENTLEY

USCG *Setting the Course to Victory,* 1942. Captain and trusty helmsman have the situation well in hand; painterly colors against a dramatic sky. Very good condition, 30″ × 40″. $135–$160

BENTON

Play Safe, 1943. Common sense, safety equipment, and teamwork are touted as the only way to go in this shipyard; full color. Fine condition, 28″ × 42″. $50–$75

JOSEPH BINDER (1898–1972)

Courtesy of Meehan Military Posters

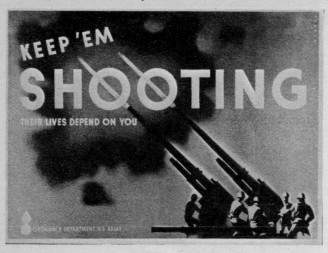

Keep 'Em Shooting—Their Lives Depend on You, 1942. Great design by leading American Art Deco posterist integrating legend and image: guns fire into the sky through the two o's in "Shooting"; in rich blue punctured by fiery colors. Fine condition, horizontal 40″ × 28″.

$195–$225

GINO BOCCASILE (1901–1952)

Fratricidio! (Fratricide!). Tommy and black GI jeer as a badly wounded yet valiant Italian soldier resists to the bloody end; in full color. Mint condition, linen-mounted, 26″ × 37″. (See color center section.)

$2,500–$3,000

La Germania e Veramente Vostra Amica (The Germans are Really Your Friends). A smiling German infantryman offers his hand in friendship while his other hand covers his heart, demonstrating sincerity; in full color. Mint condition, linen-mounted, 28″ × 40″. $3,000–$3,500

Sottoscrivete (They are Surrendering). Three bedraggled, dejected Allied POWs convey the propagandist's message: the Soviet soldier's brutality, the Tommy's timidity, and the black GI's inferiority (he alone is shoeless); in full color. Mint condition, linen-mounted, 28″ × 40″. $3,000–$3,500

Vostro Amico? (Your Friend?). A grisly skeleton wearing a British helmet grips a ruined wall as it advances through the rubble; in lurid full color. Mint condition, linen-mounted, 28″ × 40″.

$3,500–$4,000

BOOK

To Have and to Hold—Victory Bonds. Canadian lithographic poster of soldier hugging a little girl; green background. Fine condition, 24″ × 36″. $125–$150

BOTHAS

Bei Flakfeuer Gegen Splitterwirkung Sofort Deckung Sucher!, ca. 1944. German anti-aircraft fire in both day and night settings. Very good condition, on Japan paper, 23″ × 33″. $325–$400

ALEXEV BRODOVITCH (1898–1971)

Freedom from Want (Libres de Miseria), 1942. Illustration for one of FDR's Four Freedoms printed for distribution in Latin America; Nativity scene fills white hand while death and destruction are held by Nazi manacled hand; in bright color on modulated deep blue. Fine condition, linen-mounted, 14″ × 20″. $150–$175

BUSSE

NSFK (Nazi Flying Corps), 1941. Beaming Hermann Goering, looking younger and leaner than reality dictated, points to Fleigercorps emblem; naturalistic color on sky blue. Poster issued without letters and with recruiting message. Very good condition, linen-mounted, 24″ × 33″. $500–$600

JEAN CARLU (B. 1900)

America's Answer! Production, 1942. Outstanding design of gloved hand on wrench by famed French refugee artist, who was convinced that American production would determine the outcome of the war; in black, red, white, and blue. Rare, fine condition, linen-mounted, horizontal 40″ × 30″. $1,000–$1,200

Between the Hammer and the Anvil. Swastika smashed between Allied and French might; in full color on glowing yellow. Rare, fine condition, 15″ × 20″. $350–$425

Day Honoring French-British Alliance, 1939. United, Tommy and Frere Jacques travel the road to victory; full color. Scarce, very good condition, linen-mounted, horizontal 47″ × 32″. $725–$800

Give 'Em Both Barrels, 1941. Neat rhythmic Deco design of soldier firing Browning .30 machine gun echoed by worker firing rivet gun; in black, red, and yellow. Mint condition, horizontal 20″ × 15″.
                                                                        $200–$225

The New Bastille. French Marianne looks sadly from behind bars in metaphor for German occupation; in red, white, and blue. Fine condition, horizontal 20″ × 15″. $225–$250

Pacific 45 After Berlin . . . Tokyo!, 1945. Extremely rare poster only issued in Paris for a one-day event just before A-bomb was dropped; image of doomed Japanese plane in red, white, blue, and yellow. Very good condition, linen-mounted, 40″ × 61″. $975–$1,200

PAUL COLIN (1892–1985)

Silence, ca. 1940. Silhouette of sinister figure looming as it eavesdrops on the conversation of two friends. The scarce smaller format, pinholes in corners, linen-mounted, 15″ × 23″. $700–$900

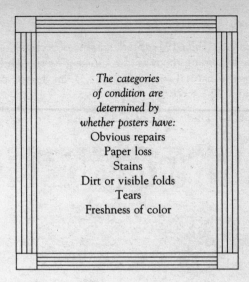

The categories
of condition are
determined by
whether posters have:
Obvious repairs
Paper loss
Stains
Dirt or visible folds
Tears
Freshness of color

They are Dying. Sporting an American helmet and firing a 1942 Thompson M1 machine gun, this Free French infantryman has his sights set on victory; in full color, especially blues and greens. Extremely rare (less than a handful are thought to exist), fine condition, linen-mounted, 15″ × 23″. $750–$900

BRADSHAW CRANDELL (1896–1966)

Are You a Girl with a Star-Spangled Heart?, 1943. Poetic title illustrated by glamorous WAC looking spiffy in front of waving flag; in sparkling patriotic color. Fine condition, 25″ × 39″. $150–$175

DENI

The Subjugation of the World (Moscow), 1943. An arrogant Führer, who dreamed of world subjugation, is cut down to size by Red Army might; in beiges, gold, white on black. Very good condition, horizontal 28″ × 23″. $550–$600

WALT DISNEY

You Can't Breakfast Like a Bird and Work Like a Horse, 1943. For the Food and Nutrition Committee of the California War Council, shows Donald Duck and Hortense laboring in a factory. Rare, very good condition, 12″ × 19″. $275 (Auction)

STEVAN DOHANOS (B. 1907)

Award for Careless Talk, 1944. Stark graphic of a claw-like hand with swastika ring extending the reward for someone's thoughtlessness . . . the iron cross; in natural colors, almost 3-D, on intense orange field. Fine condition, 20″ × 28″. $125–$150

Same as above. Fine condition, 28″ × 40″. $175–$200

Bits of Careless Talk, 1943. Heedless gossip enables Nazi to fit last piece of puzzle into place dooming convoy set to sail to England; in naturalistic color. Fine condition, 20″ × 28″. $150–$175

Same as above. Fine condition, 28″ × 40″. $175–$200

DORNE

Less Dangerous Than Careless Talk, 1944. A rattler in attack position drips blood from hideous fangs; in sinister actual color. Very good condition, 28″ × 40″. $125–$150

Somebody Blabbed, 1942. A pleading hand reaches from a watery grave while a floating sailor's cap nearby reminds the viewer of careless talk's high price; real color on rich blues. Fine condition, 14″ × 20″.
                                                    $75–$100

DUCO

New Zealand—Ally Down Under. ANZAC troops move out in setting that looks like a Pacific beach; in hot tropical colors. Unusual poster issued by New Zealand legation in Washington. Mint condition, linen-mounted, 24″ × 32″.   *$125–$150*

STAN EKMAN

Courtesy of Posters Plus

United . . . All America is on the March!, ca. 1943. Heroic soldier and worker gazing off confidently to the future. Good condition, linen-mounted, 28″ × 42″.   *$300–$400*

ENLEIGH

Let's Go . . . CANADA! Handsome young soldier sounds the call to arms before rippling Canadian flag; in full color. Mint condition, 12″ × 18″.   *$75–$100*

EXCOTTON

SANS MARINE!
PAS D'EMPIRE!

SOIS MARIN
SECRETARIAT D'ETAT A LA MARINE

Courtesy of Meehan Military Posters

Sans Marine—Pas D'Empire (No Navy—No Empire!). French sailor hails
a distant port of call which shimmers in the distance like a mirage;
mostly red, white, and blue. Fine condition, linen-mounted, 26″ ×
39″. $295–$325

FALTER

Remember Last December!, 1942. Memory of Pearl Harbor still fresh,
a grim-faced sailor stands at attention, determined to avenge December 7th; in full color. Very good condition, linen-mounted, 28″ ×
40″. $175–$200

War Puts Your Package on the Spot, 1943. Swabbie and his mates lug
ammo to the troops under the broiling sun, with plea to "Pack it
Right—Reach the Fight"; in full color. Fine condition, linen-mounted,
horizontal 40″ × 30″. $225–$250

The World Cannot Exist Half Slave Half Free—Work for Freedom!, 1942.
Clergyman and young family caught in the ominous shadow of bully
brandishing leather whip; reddish colors. Hard to find, fine condition,
linen-mounted, 28″ × 40″. $250–$300

FERENEZ

French Relief Fund. Marianne issues call to arms with flags of France, the United States, and Britain, and vast armada of ships and planes fills the background; in red, white, blue, and bronze. Fine condition, 28″ × 42″. $225–$250

ERNEST FIENE (1894–1965)

If You Can't Go Across . . . Come Across. Smiling young sailor flashes Victory sign with slogan "Buy War Bonds"; in happy full color. Fine condition, 11″ × 16″. $50–$75

JAMES MONTGOMERY FLAGG (1877–1960)

The Marines Have Landed, 1942. Shock troops keep their powder dry as they lead the charge in dynamic and colorful invasion scene. Late Flagg, extremely hard to find, mint condition, 30″ × 40″.

$325–$400

Want Action?—Join U.S. Marine Corps!, 1942. World War I image reissued early in the war, this poster still shows vet in pre-war kit; warm naturalistic color. Fine condition, linen-mounted, 30″ × 40″.

$325–$400

ABRAM GAMES (B. 1914)

Radio Location. England's most famous poster artist shows enemy plane intercepted on radar grid; mysterious atmosphere in red, blue, yellow, and grays. British radar was a major factor in winning the Battle of Britain. Mint condition, 20″ × 30″. $275–$325

GARDNER

Back 'Em Up! Daylight Bombing of Knapsack. British RAF members make perfect strike on power station; in naturalistic colors. Very good condition, 20″ × 30″. $175–$200

GAYDOS

China Fights On. Nationalist pilot scans the skies filled with Chinese aircraft; naturalistic color on deepening sky blue. Fine condition, 27″ × 41″. $150–$175

GOFF

Stop Loose Talk to Strangers—Enemy Ears are Alert. Graphic reminder to guard secrets; in red, blue, white, and black. One of the hardest to find of series privately printed by Seagrams. Very good condition, 20″ × 28″. $150–$175

GRAVES

I'm in This War Too!, 1944. WAC points to her service flag reminding viewers that distaff contribution is vital to victory; full color. Mint condition, linen-mounted, 13″ × 19″. $95–$125

Keep 'Em Flying, 1943. Recruiting poster for Air Cadet training program, young cadet flashes grin and Churchill's famous victory symbol; full color, mostly red, white, and blue. Fine condition, 25″ × 38″.
$135–$160

Right is Might, 1942. Uncommon early recruiting poster (the draft ended the need for army recruiting posters) features a phalanx of tanks moving forward with guns blazing; in full color. Fine condition, 25″ × 38″. $185–$215

GLENN GROHE (1912–?)

Courtesy of Meehan Military Posters

He's Watching You, 1942. Haunting specter of German spy peering over wall to learn Allied secrets; chilling graphic in black and deep blue on gold. Very good condition, 10″ × 14″. $275–$325

Same as above. Fine condition, linen-mounted, 28″ × 40″.
$950–$1,100

WILLIAM GROPPER (1897–1977)

Courtesy of Meehan Military Posters

Wipe That Grin Off!, 1943. Poster by well-known fine artist and cari-
caturist. Grinning Japanese soldier wipes blood off bayonet in sinister
admonition to buy bonds; privately issued by Abbott Labs, in full
color. Scarce, mint condition, linen-mounted, 9″ × 12″. $50–$75

HELWIG-STREHL

Auch Ich Helfe dem Führer, 1940. For the scrap metal drive for the
war effort, an elderly woman parts with her treasured brass samovar.
Very good condition, 23″ × 33″. $300–$350

HIRSCH

Carry Your Share. Poster by combat artist who saw action in the Pacific; signature inscribed on duffel bag, which one soldier is helping
another shoulder; in naturalistic sunny color. Fine condition, 11″ ×
16″. $50–$75

Speed the Day, ca. 1943. Soldier's fantasy of Victory parade, with
hometown band carrying hero on shoulder while confetti swirls around
his head; in full sunny color. Mint condition, 11″ × 16″. $50–$75

E. McKNIGHT-KAUFFER (1890–1979)

El Nuevo Orden (The New Order), 1942. Fantastic graphic of slobber-
ing Mussolini; one of the most memorable and rarest images of the
war. Fine condition, 14″ × 20″. $925–$1,200

For the Conquered, Steel! Not Bread. Vivid graphic of spotlight falling on Nazi dagger piercing hand of conquered in dramatic allusion to the Crucifixion; in bold color. Extremely hard to find, fine condition, 9″ × 12″. $95–$125

Norway Fights On, 1943. Majestic Norwegian flag lights up storm-darkened sea, although the homeland is occupied by Nazis; in red, white, blue, and black. Mint condition, 16″ × 23″. $175–$200

KOERNER

Fish is a Fighting Food—We Need More, 1943. Abundant catch tumbles from barrels, encouraging fishing industry to increase their efforts and civilians to eat fish so meat can be sent overseas. Seldom seen, fine condition, 20″ × 28″. $195–$225

If It'll Save a Second, It's a Great Idea. In an attempt to shorten the war, war workers play "beat the clock" alongside a giant watch; in naturalistic color, with glistening silvers on red-beige background. Fine condition, 28″ × 40″. $75–$100

THE KUKRYNISKY

In Moscow. Fires Obliterating Vile Fascists Entertain the Populace, 1941. Anthropomorphic Nazi plane falling to pieces over Moscow skyline, with human bodies caught in searchlights as they too break apart in mid-air; bright colors on blue. Extremely rare, very good condition, 23″ × 35″. $1,250–$1,500

LORENZ

Nazi Flying Corps, ca. 1937. Hitler youth salute Focke-Wulf FW 56's banking in formation at sunset; in bright sunny day color. The pseudo-sporting Flying Corps, which evolved into the Luftwaffe, was used by the Nazis to flaunt the Versailles Treaty. Extremely rare, fine condition, 17″ × 23″. $495–$650

MARKS

This is the Enemy, 1943. Winner in Museum of Modern Art's "Artists for Victory" contest portrays Nazi dagger impaling the Bible, with the text marker slipping out like a bright stream of blood; in full color on red. Fine condition, 20″ × 28″. $150–$175

Same as above. Fine condition, 28″ × 40″. $175–$200

MARTIN

Above and Beyond the Call of Duty, 1943. Portrait of Dorie Miller, recipient of the Navy Cross at Pearl Harbor for risking his life by manning deck gun he had never been trained to fire. Very rare, fine condition, linen-mounted, 20″ × 28″. $500–$600

SASCHAL MAURER

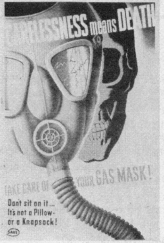

Courtesy of Meehan Military Posters

Carelessness Means Death—Take Care of Your Gas Mask, 1943. Partially obscured by a gas mask with a cracked eyepiece, a grinning skull reminds troops of the dire consequences of negligence; green, gray, red on butter yellow field. Fine condition, 24″ × 36″. $150–$175

MEYER-LAHUSEN

North Sea Hitler Youth, 1937. Uniformed Hitler youth stands proudly before medieval statue symbolizing Hitler's claim that the Nazis continued German tradition; mostly browns, red, and black. Mint condition, 23″ × 35″. $500–$600

MILLER

Every Cent the Government Spends Comes Out of Somebody's Pocket— in Taxes, 1946. Coins spill out of a coin purse; coppery shades on modulated blue. Fine condition, 20″ × 27″. $75–$100

To America's Honored War Dead, 1943. Soldier plays taps as Old Glory ripples in background; in red, white, blue, purple, black, and silver. Legend reminds viewers that "they died protecting individual liberty and opportunity . . . Let's live for that same principle." Mint condition, 20″ × 27″. $95–$125

Your Right to Vote is Your Opportunity to Protect . . . the Freedoms . . . Americans Fight Over There, 1943. Hand presses the free enterprise lever; red, white, blue, flesh tones, and black. Mint condition, 20″ × 27″. $75–$100

MJOLNIR

Home Army Fights for Freedom and Life, 1945. German poster by Hitler's favorite artist shows overage volunteer and infantryman (374th Battalion) standing shoulder-to-shoulder in a desperate attempt to defend the crumbling Reich; in full color with red lettering. Fine condition, linen-mounted, 24″ × 33″. $850–$1,000

Our Flags to Victory. Golden German eagle soars above phalanx of Nazi banners. Rare, in black, white, red, and bronze. Mint condition, linen-mounted, 23″ × 33″. $950–$1,100

Waffen SS. Decorated SS trooper stands at attention in front of Nazi battle standard designed by Hitler himself; in full color. Very good condition, linen-mounted, 20″ × 30″. $650–$750

MOORE

Buy That Invasion Bond, 1944. Invaders charge up active Normandy beachhead; early dawn color. Mint condition, horizontal 28″ × 20″.
                                                    $75–$100

MYERS

Don't Get Hurt, 1943. Combat infantryman looks up from submachine gun to address viewer; intense image in naturalistic jungle color. Fine condition, 30″ × 40″. $185–$215

NATHAN

Les Droits de l'Homme (The Rights of Man), ca. 1939. In the style of Cassandre, the artist's vision of the rights of man. Quite rare, very good condition, linen-mounted, 23″ × 28″. $200–$225

NUNNEY

The Downfall of the Dictators is Assured. Oblivious of enemy shells bursting around them, a British howitzer crew battles on in North Africa; vivid naturalistic style and color. Fine condition, 20″ × 30″.
$250–$300

ORIN

Enlist! Against a background of the world in flames, this Mexican soldier with rifle and shield is ready to protect his country; in blue, orange, gray, and black. Very good condition, linen-mounted, 27″ × 37″. $185–$215

PEEL

The Dutch Fight on to Victory, 1942. Using the national colors, a daring Dutch sailor signals the fleet with formation of planes and a battleship in the background; in red, white, blue, and orange. Fine condition, 24″ × 32″. $75–$100

PICKEN

Bonds Build Ships!, 1942. Depicts war bond money at work—majestic hull rises in busy shipyard; in full color. Privately printed by Abbott Labs, mint condition, 11″ × 16″. $45–$60

All price ranges represent the retail value.

JULIO PRIETO

Courtesy of Meehan Military Posters

Presente! Mexico's youth encouraged to support the war effort on home front; saluting student with small photos showing class work, sewing, calisthenics, and gardening. Very good condition, linen-mounted, 27" × 37".   *$150–$175*

RASKIN

Carry On! Badly wounded GI dictates letter by lantern light; in full color. Scarce Abbott Labs poster, mint condition, 11" × 15".   *$50–$75*

RICHARDS

They've Got More Important Places to Go Than You!, 1942. Subtitled "Save Rubber," a quartet of GIs literally flies along in their jeep; full sunny color. Fine condition, 28" × 40".   *$150–$175*

RIESENBERG

U.S. Marines, 1940. Pre-war reissue of classic World War I poster showing Marine in dress blues guarding the docks; in handsome vivid color. Now very hard to find, very good condition, linen-mounted, 28" × 42".   *$225–$250*

NORMAN ROCKWELL (1894–1978)

One of the century's most popular illustrators, Rockwell was a chronicler of everyday life in small-town America. Rockwell rarely used professional models as he found their expressions too artificial, but wandered the street until he found people who symbolized his ideal of the innate goodness of country people. He took many photos of his subjects to spare both artist and model the ordeal of posing.

Hasten the Homecoming, 1945. Meticulous detail and color in classic scene of ecstatic welcome for Willie Gillis by mama, siblings, shy girl peeking around corner, dog, neighbors, even Rockwell in doorway. Rare, fine condition, 20″ × 30″.   *$345–$395*

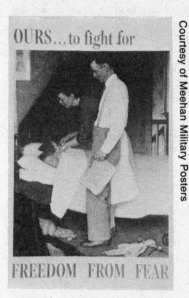

OURS...to fight for

FREEDOM FROM FEAR

OURS...to fight for

FREEDOM FROM WANT

Courtesy of Meehan Military Posters

Courtesy of Meehan Military Posters

OURS . . . to Fight For—Freedom from Fear, 1943. *Freedom from Want,* 1943. *Freedom of Speech,* 1943. *Freedom of Worship,* 1943. Individual posters illustrating the traditional values the United States was fighting for. The original oil paintings were exhibited by the Treasury Department in 16 cities as part of a massive bond drive where they were seen by more than a million people and raised $132 million. Fine condition, 20″ × 28″.   *$125–$150 each*

Same as above. Fine condition, 28″ × 40″.   *$150–$175 each*

Ours to Fight For . . . , 1943. FDR's "Four Freedoms," with all images on a single poster; in full naturalistic color and meticulous detail. Now very hard to find, fine condition, linen-mounted, 30″ × 40″.

$225–$250

ROMAY

They Can Take Only Our Bodies. A young Dutch resistance fighter, blindfolded against a brick wall, faces his execution bravely; in ironic sunny color. Fine condition, 14″ × 22″. $95–$125

SAALBURG

This was Once Good Earth!, 1944. Starving rooster and little dog with ribs you can count are all that is left of farmland, now a battlefield; total devastation underscored by stark moonlight palette. Fine condition, 20″ × 27″. $125–$150

Your War Bonds are a Stake in the Future, 1942. Design features title as inscription carved into wall plaque, Old Glory above; full color. Fine condition, 28″ × 40″. $125–$150

MARTHA SAWYERS

China—First to Fight!, ca. 1943. China first to be invaded by Japanese; exigencies of conflict evident in this determined family group. Very good condition, 27″ × 41″. $150–$175

YOU Can't Afford to Miss EITHER!—Buy Bonds Every Payday, 1944. Cool and competent aerial gunner grips handles of machine gun as Luftwaffe fighter plummets to earth; bravura brushwork in full color on sky blue. Mint condition, 10″ × 14″. $45–$60

WALTER SCHANKENBERG (1880–1961)

Help Him Get Through! Uncommon poster privately issued by Abbott Labs shows GI maneuvering through dense jungle; in full sun-dappled color. Fine condition, 11″ × 15″. $65–$80

JES WILLIAM SCHLAIKJER (B. 1897)

Make Haste Safely, 1942. US Army cautions production workers— output was vital to war effort; dramatically lit injured head in vivid color on rich green background. Fine condition, 28″ × 40″.

$95–$125

The M-1 Does My Talking with Your Cartridges, 1945. Soldier with rifle, cartridges in palm of his hand. Rare, fine condition, 14″ × 20″.

$350–$425

We Clear the Way, 1942. Tribute to the Corps of Engineers depicts engineer shouldering sledgehammer and rifle in his dual role as bridge and road builder and fighter; naturalistic color. Now scarce, fine condition, linen-mounted, 19″ × 25″.

$450–$550

HANS SCHMIDT

Courtesy of Meehan Military Posters

The Nazi Flying Corps. An eagle, potent symbol of German Nationalism, soars with a glider; full color. Mint condition, 17″ × 23″.

$485–$550

SCHREIBER

Fire Away!, 1944. Surfaced sub signals as wary lookout keeps watch from conning tower; blazing searchlights and sub's wake illuminate the scene; in full moonlight colors. Fine condition, 22″ × 28″.

$75–$100

Keep Him Flying!, 1943. One of the best U.S. Air Corps images, a handsome fighter pilot with six Japanese kills visible scans the sky as he buckles up for takeoff; naturalistic color, gorgeous sunrise. Fine condition, 22″ × 28″.

$150–$175

Same as above. Fine condition, 28″ × 40″.

$195–$225

BEN SHAHN (1898–1969)

This is Nazi Brutality, 1942. Gripping poster by renowned WPA artist shows haunting image of hooded and manacled victim up against the wall as reprisal for successful commando attack on Heydrich's head-quarters in Prague. Fine condition, 28″ × 40″. $450–$550

We French Workers Warn You . . . , 1942. Illustrates Nazi Vichy roundup of French workers deported to slave labor camps; in full color. Fine condition, horizontal 40″ × 28″. $350–$400

FRED SIEBEL

Someone Talked!, 1942. His fate the result of someone's thoughtless prattle, a drowning sailor's outstretched hand reaches in vain for res-cue; spotlit figure with midnight blue water. Fine condition, 28″ × 40″. $250–$300

SLOAN

Doing All You Can, Brother?, 1943. Searching gaze of wounded combat soldier confronts viewer; realistic close-up set against stormy desolate battlefield. Fine condition, 22″ × 28″. $75–$100

  Same as above. Very good condition, 28″ × 40″. $95–$125

DAN SMITH

Keep 'Em Flying, 1942. Recruiting poster with unfurled American flag against a sky filled with U.S. Army Air Corps bombers. Very good condition, linen-mounted, 30″ × 40″. $250–$350

SPELLENS

Give More Books, 1943. Victory Book Campaign poster features GI as a book illustration; in red, white, and blue. Mint condition, 14″ × 22″. $50–$75

SPEZIO

Be an Aviation Mechanic, 1940. Ground crew preps a Douglas B-18 bomber. Tape marks at corners, otherwise very good condition, linen-mounted, 25″ × 37″. $225–$250

STURBELLE

Belgium Fights On. Issued to harden the determination of Allied fighters and pilots, depicts Nazi firing squad about to mow down trussed-up hostages; great Deco design, pale colors offset by bright red letters. Very good condition, 19″ × 25″. $75–$100

SUNDBLOM

Ready, Join U.S. Marines, 1942. Marine drill instructor in dress blues braces for a new wave of recruits; snappy color and attitude. Very good condition, 28″ × 40″. $135–$160

ADOLPH TREIDLER (1886–1981)

CARE is Costly, 1945. Wounded sergeant slumps against wall awaiting medical aid; in full color. Fine condition, 19″ × 26″. $75–$100

My Girl's a WOW. Smiling GI proudly displays photo of his beautiful girl in her Rosie-the-Riveter garb; in bright naturalistic palette. This particular example is from Treidler's personal collection and is signed in pencil by artist at lower right. Fine condition, 28″ × 40″. $250–$300

HEINZ WEVER

Luftschutz ist Selbschutz (Air Defense is Self Defense), ca. 1944. Stylized archer aims his arrow at bombers flying overhead. Rare, very good condition, linen-mounted, 23″ × 33″. $450–$550

WHITCOMB

Be a Cadet Nurse, 1944. Premier illustrator depicts ravishing nurse in dress and hospital uniforms; in naturalistic color. Fine condition, 20″ × 28″. $75–$100

Join the Navy Nurse Corps. Pretty uniformed nurse beckons recruits winsomely; realistic color on warm pink background. Hard-to-find image, fine condition, 20″ × 28″. $125–$150

JUPP WIERTZ (1881–1939)

Nazi Flying Corps, 1937. Arado Ar68 El fighter, the last bi-plane used by the Luftwaffe, barrel rolls over bucolic German countryside, including new autobahn; in high-noon color. Scarce, mint condition, 12″ × 17″. $450–$500

NORMAN WILKINSON (1882–?)

You Buy 'Em, We'll Fly 'Em!, 1942. Pilot in open cockpit, fighters in the sky all around him. Very scarce in this large format, minor restoration, linen-mounted, 40″ × 60″. $750–$900

ADOLPHE LEON WILLETTE (1857–1926)

Candidat Anti-Semitic, 1943. Issued in France by occupying Nazis, reprint of 1889 poster printed when Willette ran for the Paris City Council as the "official anti-Semitic candidate"; to remind the French citizenry of its historic anti-Semitic roots. Very good condition, linen-mounted, 47″ × 63″. $325 (Auction)

WILLIAMS

American Field Service, 1942. Uniformed driver racing to rescue the wounded at bomb-rocked front; earth tones on orange with red letters. Very scarce, mint condition, 20″ × 28″. $325–$400

WOOTON

Help Britain Finish the Job! In exciting naval and aviation action, Spitfires down Nazi bomber whose target was the British carrier below; in full color. Fine condition, 20″ × 30″. $300–$350

WYETH

Buy War Bonds, 1942. Enraged Uncle Sam, majestically framed by billowing Old Glory, commands the viewer on behalf of both attacking GIs and planes of the Air Corps; dramatic, in full naturalistic color. Mint condition, 10″ × 14″. $50–$75

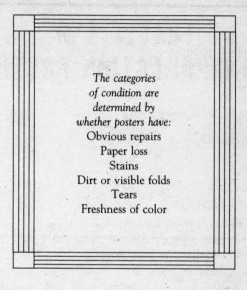

The categories
of condition are
determined by
whether posters have:
Obvious repairs
Paper loss
Stains
Dirt or visible folds
Tears
Freshness of color

TRAVEL AND
TRANSPORTATION POSTERS

Exotic ports of call, great cities of the world, skiing in the Alps, adventurous journeys to new destinations—travel and transportation posters are a major poster collecting field with global impact and numerous specializations. In this chapter we have included bicycle posters, steamship and ocean liner posters, train posters, and the multitude of posters for resorts, sports, fairs, and other destinations produced by numerous countries and thousands of artists.

Well-designed lithographic and even some offset travel and transportation posters are rapidly gaining in the market. While those created by notable artists have already established record prices, many are still affordable and within the reach of beginning collectors.

Bicycle posters are among the most popular early transportation posters. Happily, the bicycle craze of the late 1800s coincided with the Art Nouveau period poster craze, producing a wide range of stunning, colorful, and sometimes comical posters.

There was sharp competition among bicycle companies such as George Richard, Stella, Cycles Clément, Cycles Perfecta, and others. Companies commissioned some of the finest poster artists of the day to create bicycle posters, including Alphonse Mucha (1860–1939), Pal (aka Jean de Paléologue, 1860–1942), and Edward Penfield (1866–1925), plus a host of talented but lesser-known graphic artists.

Today, many collectors specialize in bicycle posters. This, coupled with the increasing popularity of bicycles both as a sport and as a means of urban transportation, has added to price increases in recent years.

"Travel posters of the 1920s and 1930s are still the most popular," comments Nancy Steinbock, a dealer from Albany, New York, who specializes in travel posters. "But even posters from the 1940s are becoming more collectible."

One popular area of travel posters from the 1920s and 1930s is ocean liners. The growth of the urban middle class and the opening of faraway countries after World War I led to a rapid increase in travel, and the 1920s saw a dramatic increase in travel via ocean liner. Many of the great ocean liners were deluxe floating palaces of Art Deco design, and the liner companies appealed to a sophisticated clientele with their advertising, also often executed in the sleek modern Art Deco style.

Among the ocean liner companies to look for are American Line; Compagnie Generale Transatlantique (most often abbreviated Cie. Gle. Transatlantique); Cunard; Hamburg America; Red Star Line; Holland-America Line; and Rotterdam-Lloyd Lines.

These companies often turned to well-known artists, many of whom also created posters for the rail lines: A. M. Cassandre (1901–1968); Paul Colin (1892–1985); Frank Newbould (1887–1950); Norman Wilkinson; the Dutch poster artist Wim Ten Broek (b. 1905); and others.

Even more popular today than the ocean liner posters are those for railroad lines from the same and earlier periods. These include British Rail posters, French Chemin de Fer posters, and posters for American and Canadian Rail companies.

"Among the most popular travel posters are the British Rail posters," Steinbock states. "They are very colorful and often have scenes of beaches, tourist destinations, and ships."

Steinbock cites numerous British Rail artists as those to watch for: Tom Purvis (1888–1959), who is known for his outstanding Art Deco designs using flat colors and simplified lines, and who also executed posters for Canadian Rail lines; Frank Newbould (1887–1950), a master of landscapes who was also a fine lithographer, working directly on the stones himself; Fred Taylor (1875–1963), who is perhaps best known for his architectural posters of cathedrals and cities; Jean Droit (1884–1961); Austin Cooper (1890–1964); Norman Wilkinson; and Charles Pears (1873–1958).

E. McKnight-Kauffer (1890–1954), who is famous for his posters for the London Underground, also designed posters for the British Rail companies. Lesser-known artists to look for are W. Smithson Broadhead, Claude Buckle, Norman Hepple, Littlejohns, and John Mace.

Travel by train peaked in the late 1920s and early 1930s, and the British Rail companies were among the biggest patrons of the poster in that country. There were four major rail lines in England at the time: the LNER (London and North Eastern Railway); the LMS (London Midland and Scottish Railway); Great Western Railways; and Southern Railways. Not many of these posters actually depict the trains themselves. Rather, many depict beach resorts, landscapes, and other colorful scenes.

Other poster patrons who commissioned numerous leading artists in England were the London Underground and the Shell Oil Company (see the price listings for English Posters for more on these in the chapter entitled "English, German, and Italian Posters").

Almost all British Rail posters were produced in two standard sizes, a vertical one-sheet 25″ wide × 40″ high (sometimes called a "double royal") and a large horizontal format 50″ wide × 40″ high (sometimes called a "quad royal").

This larger size is by far the most popular on the collecting market today. As little as five years ago most of these posters sold for under $1,000. Today many have reached the $2,000 to $3,000 range, and some go as high as $5,000 at auction. The market for these posters is expanding rapidly and future price increases are to be expected.

The French State Railways, or Chemin de Fer (literally: road of iron), also commissioned numerous outstanding artists to design posters. The earliest Chemin de Fer artist of note is Misti (aka Ferdinand Mifliez, 1865–1923), who executed posters in an Art Nouveau style at the turn of the century.

The most widely recognized Chemin de Fer artist, whose work truly stands head and shoulders above the rest, is A. M. Cassandre (1901–1968). (See also the chapter entitled "French Posters" for more about Cassandre.) Cassandre's train posters for the Etoile du Nord (1927), Nord Express (1927), L'Oiseau Bleu (1929), and Chemin de Fer du Nord (1929) are masterpieces of avant-garde design and sell in the thousands of dollars. He is recognized as the originator of a style in advertising that would influence many generations of graphic artists to follow.

Second to Cassandre in popularity for executing Chemin de Fer posters in an Art Deco style is Roger Broders (1883–1953). Broders' style uses the bold colors and simplified forms of Art Deco styling, and his posters for Monte Carlo and other resorts are highly sought after.

Another important Chemin de Fer artist whose work is beginning to receive more attention is Constant-Duval. Constant-Duval is today hard to find in poster reference books, but he was a prolific artist in the 1920s and 1930s. His most stunning works are a series he created for the Chemin de Fer de Paris à Orléans, featuring the many chateaux of the Loire River Valley. Constant-Duval had his own "atelier" or workshop and designed in a painterly style that set the tone for numerous other posterists. Constant-Duval used some of the best-known lithographers to execute his work, including Chéret's publisher Chaix, Lucien Serré, and Mucha's printer Champenois. The two latter printers produced numerous posters for the Chemin de Fer in the 1920s and 1930s.

Other outstanding Chemin de Fer artists to look for are George Dorival, known also for his World War I posters; E. Paul Champseix; Louis Houpin; Andre Milaire; Roger Soubie; and F. Schultz-Wettel who produced posters for the Chemin de Fer d'Alsace et de Lorraine, a branch of the French State Railways whose commissions are among the best French Rail posters. (See color center section.)

Posters for the Canadian Pacific Railways have enjoyed new visibility in recent years, due mainly to the publication of a book that chronicles their history and illustrates dozens in full color: *Canadian Pacific Posters 1883–1953*, by Marc H. Choko and David L. Jones (see Bibliography).

The Canadian Pacific Railway was incorporated in 1881 with the mandate to build and operate a rail line from eastern Canada to the Pacific Ocean. From the beginning, the promotion of colonization and immigration along the company's lines was an integral part of the CPR's strategy. The company also eventually expanded into steamships and air travel.

The earliest posters encouraged "settlement," but by the 1920s and 1930s the CPR posters were appealing to tourists and travelers. Many of the posters were produced anonymously by staff artists, but noted artists to look for include Tom Purvis, Roger Couillard, Peter Ewart, Norman Fraser, Alfred C. Leighton, Kenneth Denton Shoesmith, and others.

In the United States, travel by car quickly became a more popular means of transportation than the railroad. This, coupled with the fact that the railroads were not state-run and state-promoted, meant that less American train posters were created.

"American train travel posters from the 1920s and 1930s are hard to find," comments Nancy Steinbock. "Some of the best are posters for the New York Central Railroad, the New Haven Railroad, and the Boston-Maine Railroad. Northern Pacific Railways also produced many good posters, notably by artist Gustav Krollman."

Steinbock also notes American poster artists Dorothy Waugh; Leslie Ragan, who created posters for the New York Central Line as well as other companies; Sascha Maurer, whose ski posters for the New Haven Railroad are strong and appealing; and others who are gaining recognition.

American aviation and airline posters are also good collectibles. According to Steinbock, from the 1940s the best are those for Pan Am. In the late 1940s, American Airlines commissioned E. McKnight-Kauffer (1891–1951), who produced a series of notable posters for both American and European destinations. Earlier aviation posters are difficult to find and are highly prized by collectors of aviation memorabilia.

"Beyond 1955, much of the interest in travel posters died out," Steinbock explains. "I think it is primarily because after that date most posters are photographic and they simply look too contemporary, like something you would see in a travel agency today. The only exceptions would be those with a strong design element."

Sports-related travel posters are enjoying great popularity today, especially those for golf, skiing, racing, and tennis. Poster artists as early as Chéret were commissioned to produce posters for horse races, and others we've already noted such as Cassandre, Broders, and Sacha Maurer produced train posters which promoted sports destinations. Outstanding German sports posterists to look for include Ludwig Hohlwein (1874–1949) and Jupp Wiertz (1881–1939). One Austrian-American, Joseph Binder (1898–1972), also produced outstanding sports-related travel posters such as his famous ski poster for Austria (see color center section). Binder, who holds the reputation as America's foremost Art Deco poster artist, was commissioned to produce the official poster for the 1939 New York World's Fair.

World's Fairs, festivals, and other special events are among the most popular "destination" travel posters, including the 1933 Chicago Century of Progress, which had posters designed by at least three artists including Weimar Pursell.

"Other American travel posters which are doing well on the market include the Lake Placid Olympics of 1932, National Park posters, and anything related to New York City," adds Steinbock.

Many artists named above, such as British Rail artists, Hohlwein, and Cassandre produced resort destination posters. Other outstanding artists of resort posters include Sem (aka Serge Goursat, 1863–1934); Henri Gray (aka Henri Boulanger, 1858–1924); Belgian Art Nouveau artist Privat Livemont (1861–1936); and Adolph Treidler, who worked in the Art Deco style. Swiss artists who have received acclaim for their travel posters include Otto Baumberger (1889–1961); Emile Cardinaux (1877–1936); and Herbert Matter (1907–1984), who was a pioneer of the photomontage poster.

As with the other travel poster fields above, the best destination posters to collect are those from before World War II, most of which were lithographically printed. There are hundreds and hundreds of fine destination poster designs available on the market. Due to the fact that many were produced anonymously or by lesser-known artists, and in large quantities both for posting and distribution to travel agencies, prices can still be in the low range of $200 to $400.

The growing popularity of early travel posters also means that new research will be done to uncover more about the artists who created them. These stunning images and fine decorative works help us recall places we have been or dream of places we would like to see.

REFERENCE WORKS

In addition to the book on Canadian Pacific posters noted above, several good reference books on travel posters are: *Cent Ans d'Affiches de Chemin de Fer* by Pierre Belvès; *Travel Posters* by Bevis Hillier; and *The Golden Age of the Railway Poster* by J. T. Shackleton. Several other references are also available. (See the special Travel and Transportation section in the Bibliography.)

PRICE LISTINGS

CYCLE POSTERS

> **NOTE:** *See the chapter "Important Notes on the Price Listings" for more information on the prices given.*

ANONYMOUS

Courtesy of Poster Mail Auction Company

Buffalo! Cycles Americains. French Art Nouveau design lithograph depicting a woman thumbing her nose at rabbits who can't keep up with her. Good condition, linen-mounted, 36″ × 49″.

$600 (Auction)

Cycles Clément, ca. 1905. Man in green suit holds aloft the company banner as he leads a countryside parade of cyclists. Good condition, linen-mounted, 46″ × 62″. $700–$900

Cycles G. Richard, ca. 1900. Lithograph printed by G. Bataille, Paris. Depicts a woman in blousy pants riding her cycle towards Paris. Good condition, linen-mounted, 34″ × 48″. $250 (Auction)

Cycles George Richard, ca. 1898. Art Nouveau design in muted tones of red, tan, brown, and green on a mottled brown background, with the four-leaf clover Richard logo. Very good condition, linen-mounted, 39″ × 54″. $325 (Auction)

Cycles Soleil, ca. 1896. Pierrot and lady with cycle. Good condition, linen-mounted, 38″ × 50″. $550 (Auction)

Cycles Stella, ca. 1900. Lithographic poster of a witch pedaling across the sky on her Stella bicycle; in yellow, green, and blue. Good condition, linen-mounted, 23″ × 31″. $400–$500

Cycles "Triumph"—Usine à Coventry, ca. 1886. Lithograph printed by F. Appel. Shows one man cycling, one standing beside his bicycle. Mint condition, 39″ × 54″. $2,000–$3,000

Gran Premi de Barcelona, 1933. Rare and outstanding design for the first Barcelona International Motorcycle Racing Championship; in orange, gray-green, brown, and tan. Very good condition, linen-mounted, 19″ × 27″. $500–$600

Le Trefle à Quatre Feuilles, ca. 1910. For Cycles George Richard; a young woman astride her bicycle, the backdrop a giant four-leaf clover. Very good condition, linen-mounted 41″ × 55″.

$125 (Auction)

The New York Sunday Journal, 1896. Advertising the May 10 special bicycle issue of this tabloid, showing a woman on her bicycle. Good condition, shrink-wrapped, 15½″ × 22″. $75–$100

CECIL ALDIN (1901–1935)

Rudge-Whitworth/Britain's Best Bicycle, 1900. John Bull and Britannia pedal through the countryside; in yellow, red, green, and black. Rare, very good condition, horizontal 25″ × 20″. $350–$400

FABIANO

Michelin. Enveloppe Velo, ca. 1912. Bibendum with his cigar behind young woman holding the bending tires, green background. Very good condition, linen-mounted, 30″ × 46″. $250 (Auction)

FERNEL

George Richard Cycles, ca. 1910. Muted color design of young woman on her bicycle. Four-leaf clover, trademark of the company, in the pattern of her dress and as logo. Good condition, linen-mounted, 39″ × 54″. $350–$450

FRITAYRE

Cycles et Motos Ravat, ca. 1930. Motorcyclist speeds across a wooden bridge, the supports for which are the letters spelling RAVAT. Very good condition, linen-mounted, 21″ × 29″. $225–$275

GEO HAM (AKA GEORGES HAMEL, 1900–1972)

Untitled, ca. 1930. Lone motorcyclist speeds across the poster from left to right. Good condition, horizontal 25″ × 18″. $300–$400

PAOLO HENRI

Cycles P. Bernard, ca. 1905. Lithographic poster showing ladies in delightful garb. Very good condition, linen-mounted, 35″ × 49″.

$325 (Auction)

F. J. MARTIN

Styl'Son. La Moto de Grand Style, ca. 1930. Speeding stylish motorcycle and rider, curvature of the earth beneath, with French, British, and American flag designs across top. Very good condition, linen-mounted, 31″ × 46″. $225 (Auction)

L. MATTHEY

Favor, ca. 1932. Lithographic poster for bicycle, moped, and motorcycle, all shown here to be "right on target"; in yellows, blues, reds. Very good condition, linen-mounted, 46″ × 62″. $350–$400

MICH

Pneu Velo Hutchinson, 1930s. Clown rides bicycle with tire on his back, dog in the basket; yellow background. Very good condition, linen-mounted, 47″ × 63″. $300–$350

MISTI (AKA FERDINAND MIFLIEZ, 1865–1923)

Cycles Clément, ca. 1900. Lithographic poster showing lady cyclist pointing skyward at a Japanese lantern. Very good condition, linen-mounted, 34″ × 100″. $650–$700

ALPHONSE MUCHA (1860–1939)

Cycles Perfecta, ca. 1897. Lithograph printed by Champenois, signed in the stone. Woman with flowing hair leans over the handlebars of her bicycle. Mint condition, a fine example of both the artist and bicycle posters, linen-mounted, approx. 41½" × 59".

$12,000–$15,000

PAL (AKA JEAN DE PALÉOLOGUE, 1860–1942)

Cleveland Cycles, ca. 1900. An Indian in feathers and leggings astride his new Cleveland bicycle. Good condition, linen-mounted, framed, 43" × 58". $400–$500

Cycles Liberator, 1899. Famous Pal image of bare-breasted Germanic mythological figure with enormous sword standing next to her Liberator cycle; in red, black, green, brown against a yellow background. Very good condition, linen-mounted, 43" × 59". $500 (Auction)

ROGER PEROT

Cycles Peugeot, 1931. Lithograph printed by Hachard & Cie, Paris. Good impression, linen-mounted, 31⅜" × 47⅛". $750–$800

ABEL PETIT

Leon Vanderstuyft, 1928. Shows the world champion on his motorcycle beating out a bicyclist and a speeding train (named "Rapide"). Very good condition, linen-mounted, 47" × 63". $200–$300

FRANCISCO TAMAGNO (1851–?)

Cycles Automoto, ca. 1902. Wood nymph in yellow robe plucking a shamrock with a bicycle propped against a tree; at bottom, a rendering of the auto plant in St. Etienne. Good condition, linen-mounted, 46″ × 62″. $600–$800

E. THELEU

Peugeot, ca. 1910. Typical country postman with pipe and moustache delivering the mail to the farm on his new Peugeot motorcycle. Very good condition, linen-mounted, 43″ × 57″. $225 (Auction)

WALTER THOR (1870–1929)

The Beeston Humber, ca. 1910. A young woman and her lapdog enjoy a spin on their Humber bicycle at quayside; in strong primary colors. Good condition, linen-mounted, 37″ × 52″. $150 (Auction)

CHARLES TICHON

Cycles l'Etoile, 1895. Soft sepia poster shows a dapper cyclist flashing his new headlamp at a friend, also a cyclist. Very good condition, linen-mounted, 35″ × 50″. $400–$600

OCEAN LINER POSTERS

Note: *See the chapter "Important Notes on the Price Listings" for more information on the prices given.*

ANONYMOUS

American Line, ca. 1900. Lithograph printed by American Litho. Colorful steamship poster with small fishing vessel passing before large passenger liner. Good condition, a very good example of the style, framed, 36″ × 40″. $900–$1,500

Chesapeake Steamship Company, ca. 1910. Lithograph printed by A. Horn & Co., Baltimore. Central image of steamship with destinations printed at bottom; in greens and golds. Fine condition, 30″ × 38″. $500–$750

Cie. Gle. Trans-Atlantique. Algerie Tunisie Via Marseille, ca. 1935. Steamship *Ville d'Alger* at sea in a diamond of blue against red field. Very good condition, linen-mounted, 24″ × 39″. $300–$350

Cunard—Boston to Europe, ca. 1930. Lithograph in purples, yellows, and white for Cunard's "New Steamers (20,000 tons)," with a large ship moving toward the viewer and off the page. One of a number of posters Cunard produced in the 1920s and 1930s. Mint condition and an excellent example of Cunard poster design, linen-mounted, 25″ × 40″.   *$1,200–$1,500*

Cunard Line, 1950s. Offset-printed poster depicting the entire Cunard fleet at sea. Good condition, framed, horizontal 44″ × 32″.

$450 (Auction)

Empress of Britain. Lithograph printed by Sanders, Phillips & Co., The Bagnard Press. Good condition, folds apparent, horizontal 40″ × 25″.   *$500–$600*

Fabre Line, Mediterranean/New York, ca. 1950. Striking image of a steamer in brilliant yellow field, bordered by French and American flags forming a huge arrow towards its destination. Deep blue field. Mint condition, 24″ × 40″.   *$200 (Auction)*

Hamburg-America Line. Two Grand Cruises Around the World, 1904. Printed by Ketterlinus, Philadelphia. Within the ship's wheel is a globe showing the routes of the cruises; surrounding the wheel are people and places of different ports along the way. Very good condition, linen-mounted, 30″ × 40″.   *$600–$700*

London and Edinburgh Shipping Company, London and Scotland, ca. 1889. Lithographic poster showing one-stack steamer sailing "3 times weekly from London, from Leith." Mint condition, very collectible, linen-mounted, horizontal 40″ × 30″. $2,500–$3,500

M/S Scandinavia, 1982. Offset-printed poster depicting a stylized, elongated liner sailing toward the viewer; in white, greens, violets. Fine condition, 23″ × 39″. $225–$275

M/S Stella Polaris, ca. 1948. Colored photograph of the luxury yacht at the mouth of a fjord with the midnight sun low on the horizon. Unusual Swedish poster, in very good condition, linen-mounted, 23″ × 34″. $300–$350

Red Star Line, Antwerpen/New York/Canada, ca. 1950. Ocean liner in close-up steams across the background of a huge red star. Fine condition, 20″ × 26″. $200 *(Auction)*

OTTO ANTON

Hamburg-Amerika Line, ca. 1930. For the voyage to the Mediterranean; three North African women preparing a dish on a sunny Moorish porch, the ship seen in the harbor through the portals. Very good condition, linen-mounted, 24″ × 38″. $300–$350

Nach Amerika. White Star Line American Line, ca. 1930. For sailings from Hamburg to New York. Nice lettering beneath the ship reflected in the water. Very good condition, linen-mounted, 17″ × 25″. $400–$500

CENNI

Italian Line. For Your Voyages by Sea, 1925. For trips on the *Italia,
Cossulich,* and *Lloyd Triestino.* Stylized policeman points at inset of
photographic representation of liner at dockside. Very good condition, 28″ × 41″. $500–$700

ROGER CHAPALET

Cie. Gle. Transatlantique, Linea Francesca, 1930s. Lithograph printed
by JAD, Rue St. Lazare, Paris, signed in the stone. An ocean liner
deck, poolside, with elegant people around the pool; blank space at
bottom for sailing information. Fine condition, a good example of the
Art Deco style, linen-mounted, 24½″ × 39¼″. $275–$350

PAUL COLIN (1892–1985)

Cie. Gle. Transatlantique French Line, ca. 1950. A stylized elongated
liner sails on a tri-color background; in white, red, blue, and black.
Very good condition, linen-mounted, 24″ × 39½″. $650–$700

EDOUARD COLLIN

Courtesy of Poster Mail Auction Company

Cie. Gle. Transatlantique/Paris-Bordeaux-Casablanca. Lithographic poster depicting a train and an ocean liner in red, salmon, and black on
a light blue field. Good condition, linen-mounted, 25″ × 39″.
                                                        $400–$450

TOM CURR

Atlantic Summer Holidays by Cunard, ca. 1920. Charming and colorful shipboard image of flapper flirting with Cunard deckhand. Very good condition, linen-mounted, 25″ × 39″. $325 (Auction)
$600–$700

JEAN DESALEUX

Messageries Maritimes, ca. 1950. Colorful 1950s design shows a family enjoying their holiday on the cruise ship. Very good condition, linen-mounted, 25″ × 40″. $200–$250

D.R.O.

Red Star Line (Antwerpen–New York), ca. 1925. Lithograph with monogram in the stone. Fine condition, linen-mounted, 26″ × 42″.
$850–$900

ALPHONS DULLAART

Holland-America Line, 1949. A peasant girl gazes out at the newly launched *New Amsterdam*. Very good condition, linen-mounted, 24″ × 38″. $300–$400

ALBERT FUSS

Nach New York. Hamburg Amerika Line, ca. 1929. Excellent "Deco" styling of the four looming Hamburg-America prows: the *Hamburg*, the *Deutschland*, the *New York*, and the *Hansa*. Very good condition, linen-mounted, 24″ × 34″. $225 (Auction)

Hamburg-Amerika Line, ca. 1930. For Mediterranean cruises, a North African coastal town with the Hamburg-Amerika liner in the distance. Fine condition, with some creases in paper, linen-mounted, 25″ × 39″. $300–$400

Nordlandfahrten, ca. 1929. For Hamburg-Amerika Line. The midnight sun over glaciers, steamship, two Lapps in costume in foreground. Very good condition, 24″ × 33″. $350–$400

GABBLARD

Batavier Lijn/Rotterdam-Londen, 1930. A steamship sails under the Tower Bridge in London; in blue, red, white, and black. Very good condition, 25″ × 39½″. $800–$900

GAILLARD

Holland-Afrika Lijn, ca. 1935. Looming stylized prow of liner with globe showing the route from Holland through the Mediterranean, the Canal, and around the Horn of Africa, back to Holland. Very good condition, linen-mounted, 25" × 39". $400–$450

TOM GILFILLON

To the Hebrides, ca. 1929. Scottish design shows the sun setting on a loch, passengers on a luxury cruise ship in foreground. Very good condition, linen-mounted, 25" × 40". $475 *(Auction)*

GILBERT HALLAND

Cie. Havraise Peninsulaire, ca. 1935. For travel to Madagascar, Reunion, East Coast of Africa, Algeria, and Tunisia; one-stacker under steam. Very good condition, linen-mounted, 28" × 40".

$400–$500

SANDY HOOK

En Mediterranée Par Les Messageries Maritimes, ca. 1920. Lithographic poster showing the Sphinx looming behind the cruise ship *Champollion.* Very good condition, linen-mounted, 28" × 40". $800–$900

Indochine Par Les Chargeurs Reunis, ca. 1925. The steamship *Quichen* at sea, a junk alongside, both reflected in the water. Fair condition, linen-mounted, 29" × 39". $600–$700

Messageries Maritimes Anvers-Extreme-Orient-Dunkirk-Indo Chine, ca. 1920. Colorful port scene, loading the steamer with cargo, passengers to follow. One of the rare Messageries Maritimes series by Hook. Very good condition, linen-mounted, 29" × 41". $600–$800

Messageries Maritimes Font le Tour du Monde, ca. 1920. The cruise ship *Paul Lecat* steaming at sea, high in the water. Good condition, some restoration, linen-mounted, 27" × 39". $600–$800

FRANK NEWBOULD (1887–1950)

Orient Line—West Indies Cruise, ca. 1935. Lithograph. Fair condition, linen-mounted, 25" × 40". $650–$750

MAX PONTY

Cie. de Navigation Paquet, 1920. Lithograph printed by Hachard & Co., signed in the stone. Strong stylized image of two-stack steamer in black, reflection in blue. Mint condition, linen-mounted, 26″ × 40″. $1,500–$1,700

MAURICE RANDALL

Blue Star Line. Mediterranean Cruises, ca. 1930. English poster showing the Casbah through a magnificent portal, the ship anchored in the distant harbor. Scarce, very good condition, linen-mounted, 25″ × 39″. $400–$500

HARRY HUDSON RODMELL

Mashimi Maru, 1928. Shows the great vessel steaming, tug pulling away; with Japanese lettering. Rare, very good condition, linen-mounted, horizontal 41″ × 32″. $800 (Auction)

ODIN ROSENVINGE

Cunard to Europe, ca. 1920. Lithograph printed by Turner and Dunnett, signed in the stone. Dramatic *SS Berengaria* looms up with orange and blue sky behind. Very good condition, mounted to cardboard and framed, 24″ × 39″. $475–$500

JOSEPH ROVERS

Rotterdam-Lloyd Royal Mail Line, ca. 1927. Lithograph by Emrik and Bingher, Haarlem, Holland. For travel to Egypt, Ceylon, Sumatra, Singapore, Java; native in foreground, ship dominating the horizon. Very good condition, 19″ × 28″. $300–$400

GEORGES RUMSEY

American Export Lines, ca. 1948. French; for travel to the Mediterranean and USA on the *S.S. Constitution* and *S.S. Independence,* the "sun liners" which are "air conditioned." Very good condition, linen-mounted, 25″ × 39″. $500–$600

ALBERT SEBILLE (1874–1953)

Cie. Gle. Transatlantique "France," ca. 1912. Lithograph printed by Champenois showing the great four-stacker approaching the Statue of Liberty. Good condition, some restoration, linen-mounted, horizontal 42″ × 29″. $800–$900

G. SOULI

Messageries Maritimes La Marseillaise, 1949. Clean design of cruise ship on a placid sea with emblems of the French royal house. Very good condition, linen-mounted, 24″ × 39″. $300–$400

KEES VAN DER LAAN

Maatschappij Zeeland Nieuwe Dagbooten, 1930. Close-up of a liner's smokestack and nearby deck; in blue, red, and white. Very good condition, 24½″ × 39″. $800–$900

G. VAN DUFFELEN

Holland Amerika Lyn, 1922. A seagull fills the frame above the ocean, with an ocean liner in the distance; in blues, orange, and creams. Very good condition, 27″ × 36″. $600–$700

HOAL Holland, 1922. For the HOAL shipping line; depicts ocean liner in the distance; in blues, oranges, and creams. Very good condition, 27″ × 36″. $600–$700

VIANO

Compagnie de Navigation Paquet "Senegal," ca. 1930. Striking portrait of Senegalese gentleman. Very good condition, linen-mounted, 24″ × 39″. $400–$500

WAGSTAFF

Round Voyages by P & O, ca. 1929. Colorful image of junks in a Far Eastern harbor; for trips to Australia, Japan, and China. Very good condition, linen-mounted, 25″ × 40″. $400–$500

All price ranges represent the retail value.

NORMAN WILKINSON (1882-?)

LMS—Tilbury for the Continent, ca. 1935. Lithograph signed in the stone. Nighttime view of ship leaving port for the Continent. Wilkinson had an extensively long career doing travel posters, including ships, from at least 1906 to the early 1940s. Mint condition, a fine example, linen-mounted, horizontal 50" × 40".   *$1,150–$1,350*

TRAIN POSTERS

Note: *See the chapter "Important Notes on the Price Listings" for more information on the prices given.*

ANONYMOUS

Durham, ca. 1935. Lithograph for the LNER. View of the bridge and castle. Very good Condition, 25" × 40".   *$175–$225*

Exposicion Conmemorative del Primer Centenario del Ferrocarril en España, 1948. Mid-1800s traveling family watches a passenger train arrive; in tones of brown, green, etc. Fine condition, linen-mounted, 12″ × 19″.   *$150–$200*

Michigan Central Train at Niagara Falls, ca. 1890. Lithographic poster of train discharging passengers at the Falls. Good condition and a fine example of American vintage train posters, original frame and mat, horizontal 36″ × 26″.   *$1,500–$1,600*

Norwich, ca. 1935. Lithograph for the LNER. Painterly design with earth tones. Very good condition, 25″ × 40″. $200–$250

Peterborough, ca. 1930. For the LNER; depicts Cardinal Wolsey's 1530 Easter visit to the great Benedictine abbey founded in 655; black with muted tones of tan, orange, yellow, green, gray, and bright splashes of red. Fine condition, linen-mounted, horizontal 50″ × 40″.

     $1,100–$1,200

Travel While Sleeping, 1930s. For the Chemin de Fer for use in Britain; depicts steamship, route from London to Paris, sleeping compartment on train. Very good condition, linen-mounted, 24″ × 39″.

     $400–$450

York, ca. 1935. Lithograph for the LNER. View of a street in the village and women gathered to talk. Very good condition, plain paper, 25″ × 40″. $200–$250

J. HUGO D'ALESI

Chemin de Fer P.L.M./Excursions au Mont-Blanc, 1893. Scenes of Mont-Blanc, with banner reading "Excursions . . ." diagonally across the middle. Good condition, 30″ × 41½″. $450–$500

L. BLUMEN

Strasbourg, ca. 1930. Chemin de Fer d'Alsace de Lorraine lithographic poster printed by the Imprimerie Alsacienne in Strasbourg, depicting the canals and half-timbered houses of this regional capital. Impressionistic style, very colorful, good condition, linen-mounted, 30″ × 40″. $350–$400

A. BRENET

Speed, Punctuality, Comfort, 1950. A train speeds toward the viewer; in white, green, and brown. Very good condition, 24″ × 39½″.
$275–$325

BRENET AND BOUVRY

Locomotive Diesel Electrique, ca. 1948. Unusual poster showing a speeding diesel (by Brenet) and a cutaway of same (by Bouvry). Very good condition, linen-mounted, horizontal 47″ × 31″. $275–$325

BRIEN

Scotland, ca. 1935. For the LMS and the LNER; a salmon swimming upstream, stylized and colorful. Very good condition, linen-mounted, horizontal 50″ × 40″. $2,000–$2,500

W. SMITHSON BROADHEAD

Clacton-on-Sea, ca. 1935. For the LNER, elegantly dressed woman in foreground, the promenade and sea seen in the distance. Very good condition, linen-mounted, horizontal 50″ × 40″.   *$1,900 (Auction)*

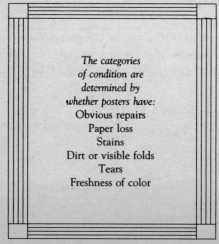

*The categories
of condition are
determined by
whether posters have:*
Obvious repairs
Paper loss
Stains
Dirt or visible folds
Tears
Freshness of color

ROGER BRODERS (1883–1953)

From the author's collection (Photo by Robert Four)

Le Rhin, ca. 1930. Alsace and Lorraine Railways lithographic poster printed by Lucien Serré with text in English for use outside of France, showing an expansive view of the river, with small figures of a farmer and his family and a horse-drawn hay wagon. Broders is known as a fine Art Deco travel poster artist. Fine condition, 24½″ × 39″.

$700–$900

Sur La Côte d'Azur, ca. 1928. For the PLM Railway, the quintessential Art Deco travel poster. Woman in swimsuit on the beach, arms upraised to the sun; stylized sunlight, palm trees, etc. Very good condition, linen-mounted, 25″ × 39″. $2,000 (Auction)

CLAUDE BUCKLE

Beauty Abide, Nor Suffers Mortal Change, ca. 1935. A Scottish landscape for the LMS with representations from the Romans through the 1930s tourists who have visited the site. Good condition, linen-mounted, horizontal 48″ × 39″. $350–$450

Ross-on-Wye, ca. 1935. For Britain's Great Western Railway; an idyllic look at the town. Very good condition, linen-mounted, 24″ × 39″. $300–$350

ADOLPHE MOURON CASSANDRE (1901–1968)

Nord Express, 1927. The locomotive and power lines disappear to the horizon. Very good condition, one of Cassandre's finest designs, 30″ × 41″. (See color center section.) $7,000–$9,000

E. PAUL CHAMPSEIX

From the author's collection
(Photo by Robert Four)

Carcassonne, ca. 1930. Chemin de Fer lithographic poster printed by Lucien Serré depicting the walled fortress in the south of France. Very colorful, with use of metallic gold ink on the sky and on decorations around coats of arms. Very good condition, rare, linen-mounted, 24″ × 39″. $600–$700

CLEMENT CLEMSON

Pays de Galles, ca. 1890. Early chromolithographic poster by Courmont Frères. For the LNER and Chemin de Fer de l'Est for tours to Ireland and Great Britain. Very good condition, linen-mounted, 28″ × 41″. $350–$450

V. L. DANVERS

Sunny Rhyl, 1940s. Lithograph signed in the stone, printed by Charles and Reed, Ltd., London, for the LNER. Shows a busy beach scene from a distance, including pool, bathhouse, and outdoor theater. Fine condition, a good example of the style, linen-mounted, 24¾″ × 40″. $300–$400

GEORGE DORIVAL

La Mare de Circqueboeuf, ca. 1930. Chemin de Fer lithographic poster printed by Lucien Serré depicting a forest scene near Trouville-Deauville with a grove of stunning white birches, executed in the painterly travel poster style made popular by Constant-Duval. Good condition, linen-mounted, 24″ × 39″. $400–$450

CONSTANT-DUVAL

Azay le Rideau, 1925. Chemin de Fer lithographic poster printed by Champenois showing a painterly aspect of the Loire Valley chateau. One of a series of posters of famous French chateaux designed by Constant-Duval. Good condition, linen-mounted, 31″ × 42″.

$400–$450

From the author's collection (Photo by Robert Four)

Chateau of Amboise, 1922. Chemin de Fer lithographic poster printed by Champenois with English text for distribution outside of France. Fine condition, a very good example of the artist's style, linen-mounted, 27″ × 40″. $400–$450

Chateau de Blois, ca. 1927. Chemin de Fer lithographic poster printed by Champenois showing the interior courtyard of the Loire Valley chateau, with its Louis XII wing and its famous exterior stairway built by Francois I. Good condition, linen-mounted, 28½″ × 40″.

$350–$400

Chateau de Langeais, ca. 1925. Chemin de Fer lithographic poster printed by Lucien Serré showing a view of the tiny village and the fortress chateau. Good condition, linen-mounted, 29″ × 41″.

$325–$375

Chenonceaux, 1926. Chemin de Fer lithographic poster printed by Chaix for the "circuits automobiles"—car tours of the Loire valley. Very good condition, an excellent example of Constant-Duval's chateau posters, linen-mounted, 29″ × 41″. $550–$600

Le Mont St. Michel, ca. 1925. Chemin de Fer lithographic poster printed by Champenois. An evening view of the rugged monastery before roadways were built out to the tidal island. Very good condition, an excellent example of the artist's style, linen-mounted, 30″ × 40″. $650–$700

Le Puy Girou (1694m), 1930. Chemin de Fer lithographic poster printed by Lucien Serré. A beautiful view of the valley with a tiny village and a goat herder. Good condition, linen-mounted, 24″ × 39″. $350–$400

Orleans, 1925. Chemin de Fer lithographic poster printed by Chaix. Subtitled "La Loire et La Cathédrale" and showing a view of Orleans from the opposite side of the river. Very good condition, linen-mounted, 30″ × 40″. $450–$500

FAURE

Chemin de Fer d'Orleans, 1929. Unusual stylized design to promote the auto train shows a man with his car tucked under his arm, stretched out in a speeding train. Very good condition, linen-mounted, 24″ × 38″. $400–$500

LOUIS FERNEZ

Tougourt, 1925. For Algerian Railways; depicts a group of stylized Berbers in foreground, walled city behind. Printed in France. Good condition, linen-mounted, 28″ × 41″. $350–$400

BRYAN DE GRINEAU

The Royal Scot, ca. 1935. Lithograph signed in the stone. Nice design by an artist who specialized in posters of Scotland and Ireland. Two bright red trains speed past each other. Mint condition, very collectible, linen-mounted, horizontal 50″ × 40″.   *$1,150–$1,350*

HILL

Cornwall, ca. 1935. For Great Western Railway; Polperro Harbour in all its serenity. Very good condition, linen-mounted, horizontal 50″ × 40″. $600–$800

LOUIS HOUPIN

La Bretagne/Ses Granites, 1930. Chemin de Fer lithographic poster for the coast of Brittany, printed by Daude Freres. Stunning blues and reds with a painterly style. Mint condition, 25″ × 39½″.

$400–$450

HUMBAIRE

Corse, 1938. For the Chemin de Fer; outline of Corsica, with ruins of a walled city, a ship. Fine condition, with slight paper discoloration, linen-mounted, 24″ × 39″. $400–$600

JULIEN LACAZE

Grottes de Han, ca. 1910. Belgian, for Northern Railway; the "most beautiful trip" to the caves at Han, in sunset colors. Very good condition, linen-mounted, 29″ × 40″. $300–$350

Bains de Mer de la Manche et de l'Océan, 1911. For the Chemin de Fer; the rockbound coast is featured for reduced price trips. Good condition, linen-mounted, 29″ × 41″. $200–$300

ROBERT E. LEE

Railway Express Agency, 1929. REA agent with package, his truck behind him; wonderful colors in a style reminiscent of Ludwig Hohlwein. Very good condition, an outstanding example of the artist's style, linen-mounted, horizontal 56″ × 36″. $1,100 (Auction)

LITTLEJOHNS

Courtesy of Nancy Steinbock Fine Posters and Prints

Whitley Bay, ca. 1935. Lithograph signed in the stone. Art Deco style by this artist who worked for LNER in the 1920s and 1930s. Swimmers in alcove with sunlight shimmering on people and the water. Mint condition, very good example of the style, linen-mounted, horizontal 50″ × 40″. $2,250–$2,750

JOHN MACE

The English Lakes, ca. 1935. Poster for the LMS depicting an intricately colored landscape. Very good condition, linen-mounted, horizontal 50″ × 40″. $600–$750

MARC

Algeria, 1931. To take the train from Quai d'Orsay Station for the shortest route to Algeria via Port-Vendres; depicts a walled city at the edge of the Sahara, in primary colors. Text in English. Very good condition, linen-mounted, 25″ × 40″. $250–$300

A. MARTIN

Regie des Chemin de Fer de l'A.O.F., ca. 1938. Electric train coming out of jungle with map of African train routes. Colorful. Very good condition, linen-mounted, 24″ × 39″. $250–$350

FRANK MASON

Aberdeen, ca. 1935. For the LNER; shows the beach at the resort, deep blues and greens predominate. Very good condition, linen-mounted, horizontal 50″ × 40″. $1,200–$1,400

Harwich for the Continent, 1934. For the LNER; night scene of two ships, lighted from their interiors, passing. Very good condition, horizontal 50″ × 40″. $2,000 *(Auction)*

LEO MAXY

Royan, ca. 1895. For the Chemin de Fer; shows the entire beach and casino at the famed resort. Some restoration at folds, linen-mounted, horizontal 49″ × 38″. $225 *(Auction)*

MICHAEL

Whitley Bay, ca. 1935. For the LNER; an old sea dog pointing out to a young lad the way things used to be, in the background a beach crowded with cabanas. Very good condition, linen-mounted, horizontal 50″ × 40″. $1,000 *(Auction)*

ANDRE MILAIRE

Le Mont St. Michel, 1922. Lithograph for the Chemin de Fer printed by Joseph Charles, Paris, signed in the stone. Sunset view of Mont St. Michel with rich orange sky predominating. Very good condition, 29¼″ × 41¼″. $250–$300

MISTI (AKA FERDINAND MIFLIEZ, 1865–1923)

Courtesy of Poster Mail Auction Company

Vicinaux/Haute Saone, 1903. For the Chemin de Fer. Two turn-of-the-century ladies in elegant traveling clothes rest in the French country-side; in soft muted tones of green, blue, brown, and red. Very good condition, linen-mounted, 23″ × 32″. $240 (Auction)
$500–$700

HARRY N.

Warnemunde-Gedser/Expressroute to the North, 1935. Four white geese fly north over a map of Germany to Norway; in white, blue, and green. Fine condition, 24″ × 39″. $550–$600

ARSENE NANLEZ

Paris-Londres, ca. 1899. For the Chemin de Fer de l'Ouest; young lady quayside on the Thames with Westminster in background. Fine condition, with minor foxing, linen-mounted, 26″ x 38″. $300–$350

ROCCO NAVIGATO

Chicago Temple by the Chicago Rapid Transit. Lithograph of a famous Chicago structure. With the land deeded in perpetuity for a church, a clever developer built an office building with the church and steeple 20 stories above grade. Good condition, linen-mounted, 41″ × 76″.
$1,200–$1,800

NEU

Lisbonne Son Soleil, ca. 1925. For the Portuguese Railways; pictures two native women at dockside with platters balanced on their heads, passing a fisherman at his boats. Very good condition, linen-mounted, 24″ × 39″. $200–$300

FRANK NEWBOULD (1887–1950)

North Berwick, ca. 1935. Lithograph, signed in the stone. Beautiful, bright beach scene in Art Deco style—a man with golf clubs and two women, one in a bathing suit, seated for a picnic. One of England's top poster artists of the 1920s–1930s, Newbould used contrast with light, dark, and color to great effect. Mint condition, fine example of Newbould's work, linen-mounted, horizontal 50″ × 40″.

$2,250–$2,750

ATELIER PHI

Le Portel, ca. 1905. For the Chemin de Fer du Nord; shows the beach at Boulogne and a traditionally dressed peasant woman. Very good condition, linen-mounted, 26″ × 40″. $300–$400

PICKING

Norfolk Coast, ca. 1935. For the LMS; figures of sunbathers against red-and-white cabanas, bright yellow predominates. Old folds evident, linen-mounted, horizontal 50″ × 40″. $600 *(Auction)*

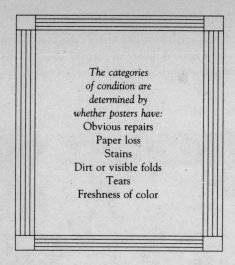

The categories
of condition are
determined by
whether posters have:
Obvious repairs
Paper loss
Stains
Dirt or visible folds
Tears
Freshness of color

W. V. D. POLL

UW Vervoersweg, 1935. A railway switching station with the tracks receding in strong lines toward the distance; in browns, cream, and purple. Fine condition, 23½" × 39". $700–$800

R. G. PRAILL

Scotland by L.M.S., 1935. A scene of a lake with a few trees in the foreground and mountains in the background; in cream, violets, and blue. Very good condition; 24½" × 40". $450–$550

RICHARD PRIESS

Mit dem Rheingold, ca. 1930. Lithograph signed in the stone. A train speeding toward the viewer, with the train's route from Luzern to London in the lower left. Mint condition, linen-mounted, 40" × 60". $750–$950

PUPPO

Sorrento, 1954. For the Italian State Railways. Highly stylized, colorful young peasant couple dancing with the sea in the background. Very good condition, linen-mounted, 25" × 39". $250–$300

TOM PURVIS (1888–1959)

Getting Ready on the East Coast, ca. 1935. Old salt sits on a box of kippers as his mate watches him paint the new name on the bow of his dory. The name is a play on words—Eleanor spelled ELENER for the LNER. Very good condition, linen-mounted, horizontal 50″ × 40″. $1,800 (Auction)

Courtesy of Marc Choko

Canadian Pacific/Happy Cruises, 1937. Lithograph printed by N. and A., London, signed in the stone. A woman, dressed for a cruise, perches smiling on the ship's railing. Tom Purvis designed a couple of posters for CPR; this one was reissued in silk-screen, but silk-screen versions are very rare. Fine condition, linen-mounted, 24″ × 36″.

$900–$1,200

LESLIE RAGAN

New York—The Upper Bay from Lower Manhattan, ca. 1935. Offset-printed poster. New York Central's view of lower Manhattan and Battery Park, with the Bay and the Statue of Liberty in the background. Ragan was the premier artist for New York Central Railroad posters, as well as others in the United States in the 1930s. Mint condition, a very good example of an American rail poster, linen-mounted, 25″ × 40″. $850–$1,000

See America, 1939. For the railroads of the United States, Mexico, and Canada, and the Pullman Company; shows Indian Chief with headdress, Mexican with sombrero and guitar, and an Eskimo woman. Exhortation in French to visit the railroad exhibition at the World's Fair. Good condition, linen-mounted, 27″ × 39″.

$1,300 (Auction)

ROBERTS

Dungeness, ca. 1930. For "the world's smallest railway"; a ship passing a lighthouse as the sun sets. Very good condition, linen-mounted, 25″ × 39″. $150 (Auction)

HENRI ROVEL

Bone Guelma et Prolongemants, ca. 1900. For the Chemin de Fer; excellent example of "photochromo-gravure" printing from Societe Lyonnaise. Early North African poster shows City of Tunis with large minaret, three other desert cities. Good condition, linen-mounted, 28″ × 41″. $400–$450

E. A. SCHEFER

Paris-Vichy 3 H. 49, 1935. Kinetic poster of speeding train in blue, black, and white. Very good condition, linen-mounted, 24″ × 39″.
$475 *(Auction)*

F. SCHULTZ-WETTEL

Riquewhir, ca. 1930. Chemin de Fer d'Alsace et de Lorraine lithographic poster printed by Imprimerie Alsacienne in Strasbourg, showing the fields outside of the town with its half-timbered houses. Mint condition, an excellent example of Alsacian rail posters, 24½″ × 39″. (See color center section.) $700–$750

ROGER SOUBIE (1898–?)

Le Haut-Barr, ca. 1930. Chemin de Fer d'Alsace et de Lorraine lithographic poster printed by Imprimerie Alsacienne in Strasbourg, showing a colorful natural scene with high cliffs. One of a few travel posters created by this well-known French posterist. Mint condition, 29½″ × 41″. $700–$900

ANDRE STRAUSS

La Corse, 1927. Chemin de Fer lithographic poster printed by Vaurigard advertising the "Pacqebots Fraissinet" which cross from France to Corsica. Painterly scene of a Corsican village in gorgeous dusty tones. Mint, 31″ × 42″. $400–$450

SURBEK

The Electric Brunig Line, 1935. Railroad tracks wind through the Swiss countryside; in pink, green, and brown. Fine condition, 25″ × 39″.
$350–$400

FRED TAYLOR (1875–1963)

Ipswich, ca. 1925. For the LNER; lithograph printed by the Danger-field Printing Co., signed in the stone. A scene from Dickens in browns and greens: Mr. Pickwick riding past "The Ancient House" in Ipswich. Fine condition, linen-mounted, horizontal 50″ × 40″.
$850–$1,000

Liverpool Cathedral, ca. 1935. For the LNER; detailed architectural image of the Cathedral with choirs massed in the sanctuary. Very good condition, linen-mounted, horizontal 50″ × 40″.
$1,200–$1,400

Norwich/L.N.E.R. An architecturally imposing design of the Cathedral founded in 1096 by the first bishop of Norwich. Fresh image in very good condition, linen-mounted, horizontal 50″ × 40″.
$1,600–$1,800

York, ca. 1935. Duotone, architectural poster of York Minister Cathedral for the LNER. Very good condition, linen-mounted, horizontal 50″ × 40″.
$1,300–$1,500

M. TONKES

Londen-Vlissingen-Harwich, 1935. Dutch; a very stylized train in blue, red, and white. Fine condition, 24″ × 39″.
$700–$800

TRAAP

50 Jahre Gotthard, 1935. A train, marked with the Swiss cross, nearly fills the entire poster; in black, red, yellow, blue. Very good condition, 25½″ × 39½″.
$800–$900

G. TROUSSAUD

Ribeauvillé, ca. 1930. Chemin de Fer d'Alsace et de Lorraine lithographic poster printed by Imprimerie Alsacienne in Strasbourg, showing the small town square and fountain with a maiden in traditional costume. Mint condition, 24½″ × 39″.
$600–$650

F. L. VAN NESS

St. Louis Limited . . . Chicago & Eastern Illinois R.R., 1907. Lithograph signed in the stone. Steam locomotive with passenger cars in a pastoral setting; the title is embossed in the wooden frame. Fine condition, very good example of American train poster, framed, horizontal 36″ × 26″.
$1,500–$1,750

NORMAN WILKINSON (1882–?)

Ireland for the Holidays, ca. 1925. For the LNER; lithograph printed by David Allen & Sons, London, signed in the stone. Scene of Kingston Harbor in muted colors. Very good condition, linen-mounted and framed, horizontal 49″ × 39″. $800–$900

Isle of Man, ca. 1938. For LMS Railway; a galleon offshore. Good condition, horizontal 50″ × 40″. $1,400–$1,600

DORIS ZINKEISEN

Durham, ca. 1935. For the LNER; the highly regarded British designer gives us a stylized scene of pilgrims going to the resting place of St. Cuthbert. Very good condition, linen-mounted, horizontal 50″ × 40″. $1,100–$1,300

AVIATION POSTERS

Note: *See the chapter "Important Notes on the Price Listings" for more information on the prices given.*

ANONYMOUS

Courtesy of Nancy Steinbock Fine Posters and Prints

Avia, 1937. An Art Deco airplane ad in maroon and gray showing a close-up of a plane, two propellers in motion. Good condition, linen-mounted, 22″ × 28″. $700–$900

B.O.A.C. Across the World, 1940. An African tribesman, shading his eyes, looks up into the sky; in blues, purples, and cream. Fine condition, 20″ × 30″. $350–$500

L'Afrique du Sud par Clipper, 1951. Pan Am Clipper at top flies over scenes of Southern Africa: a village; a herd of gazelles; a beach scene; and a lion surveying the savannah. Very good condition, linen-mounted, 24″ × 40″. $200–$250

Moscow Aeroflot Airlines, 1950. A stylized woman in folk costume and boots dances, with a Moscow building in the background; in red, greens, blue, and yellow. Very good condition, 27″ × 39″.

$350–$400

BUTTGEN

Lufthansa . . . Your Velvet Carpet to the World, ca. 1960. Offset, signed in the matrix. A propeller plane landing on a purple carpet. Fine condition, linen-mounted, 24″ × 35″. $100–$200

L. E.

Fly Imperial Airways, England/Africa, 1932. Bold and colorful graphics symbolizing speed and flight. Yellow, red, black, and gray. Good condition, plain paper, 19″ × 29″. $300–$325

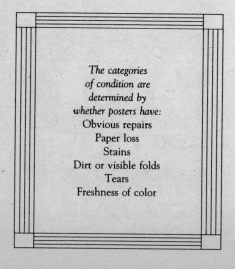

*The categories
of condition are
determined by
whether posters have:*
Obvious repairs
Paper loss
Stains
Dirt or visible folds
Tears
Freshness of color

FALCUCCI

Europe/Air France, 1950. A collage of European scenes, including the Eiffel Tower and a windmill; in reds, white, and blues. Fine condition, 24″ × 39″. $375–$425

CHARLES FOUQUERAY

Courtesy of Nancy Steinbock Fine Posters and Prints

VIE Exposition International de Locomotion Aérienne, 1919. Lithograph by this artist who was well known for World War I posters. A large Curtiss-Jenny flies above Marianne blowing her horn, other planes and blimps from the air show in the background; subdued colors. Mint condition, and a great example of early aviation posters, linen-mounted, 30″ × 46″. $800–$1,000

GAMY

Coupe Gordon Bennett, 1909. Very early open aircraft in the Gordon Bennett race. Matted and framed, horizontal 38″ × 22″.

$200 (Auction)

Coupe de Berlin, 1909. Panoramic vista of two very early aircraft flying over a field in the Berlin Air Race, blues and violets predominate. Good condition, horizontal 35″ × 18″. $350–$450

ANDRE GOFFIN

Brussel Eeuwfeest Stadion, 1948. For an air show in Brussels; a stylized design of planes and a helicopter. Very good condition, linen-mounted, 24″ × 34″. $200–$300

HOLLAND

See Europe by Imperial Airways, the British Airline, 1930s. Lithograph printed by Stuarts, Kingsway House, London, signed in the block. Air-view of cathedral and surrounding houses in sketchy realistic style. Fine condition, 19″ × 29½″. $150–$200

E. MCKNIGHT-KAUFFER (AKA EDWARD KAUFFER, 1891–1951)

Courtesy of Poster Mail Auction Company

American Airlines/All Europe, 1948. Crisp design of the globe with a banner having stripes on one side, stars on the other; in red, tones of blue, black, brown, tan on a white field. One of a series of very good designs by this well-known artist. Fine condition, 30″ × 40″.
$275–$300

American Airlines/England, ca. 1948. Bold image of a British castle in orange, gray-green, black, and white set against a strong red background. Very good condition, linen-mounted, 30″ × 40″.
$200–$250

American Airlines/Mexico, 1949. Stylized rendering of straw-hatted Mexican carrying large birdcage; in the background hangs a blue "Over the World" poster with AA's logo; in ochre, tones of tan, blue, and black. Fine condition, 30″ × 40″. $200–$250

American Airlines/Paris, 1948. Winged victory boldly superimposed on a field of white with colorful lettering. Very good condition, linen-mounted, 30″ × 40″. $250–$275

Courtesy of Poster Mail Auction Company

American Airlines/To New York, ca. 1948. Impressive stylized image of towering city skyline against a sky blue background; in blue, red, gray, black on white. Very good condition, linen-mounted, 30″ × 40″.
$300–$350

REGIS MANSET

Paris/Air France, 1950. A plane flies over a scene of Paris, with the Eiffel Tower prominent; in white, blue, and red. Very good condition, 24″ × 39″. $375–$400

EDMOND MAURUS

Europe/Air France, ca. 1950. A plane flies across the monuments of Europe; in bright pink and orange. Fine condition, 12″ × 19½″.
$175–$200

WEIMAR PURSELL

American Airlines to New York, ca. 1955. Colorful, stylized modernist skyline of the city. Very good condition, linen-mounted, 30″ × 39″.

$400–$450

VASSERELLI

Courtesy of Nancy Steinbock Fine Posters and Prints

Air France—Amérique du Sud, 1948. Offset in soft colors, primarily purples and yellows, by this well-known French posterist of the 1940s. A four-engine plane goes towards a misty Rio with a row of lights on sugarbowl. Mint condition and highly collectible, 25″ × 40″.

$500–$650

VINCI

Air France, 1937. Pre-war design for world-wide travel via the French National Air Line. Very good condition, linen-mounted, 24″ × 39″.

$300–$350

All price ranges represent the retail value.

SPORTS POSTERS

Note: See the chapter "Important Notes on the Price Listings" for more information on the prices given.

ANONYMOUS

Greyhound Racing, 1920s. Colorful stock British poster shows the dogs going over a hurdle at the track. Good condition, linen-mounted, 40″ × 60″.   *$350 (Auction)*

Gstaad, ca. 1930. Skiers standing up in bed of 1930s truck making its way through the snow, Matterhorn in background. Very good condition, linen-mounted, 25″ × 39″.   *$225 (Auction)*

Guy Laroche de Squash, 1984. For the Second International Squash Championships in Paris sponsored by Guy Laroche; squash player on court, almost like chalk on blackboard. Very good condition, linen-mounted, 47″ × 68″.   *$300–$400*

Play Golf in Czechoslovakia, 1930s. For the courses at Carlsbad, Pistyan, Prague, and Marienbad. Male golfer, wrists cocked, begins his downswing; hotel is beyond the fairway and green. Very good condition, 24″ × 37″.   *$550 (Auction)*

This Summer Sun Valley, 1941. Female figure skater in a leap, the lodge behind her. Good condition, 26″ × 38″.   *$750 (Auction)*

CARIGIET ALOIS

Arosa, 1931. Famous design of woman skier against pure white field. Fair condition, 36″ × 50″.   *$100 (Auction)*

GEORGES AROU

Sports d'Hiver, 1931. For the Chemin de Fer; ski poster of blue-clad downhiller, scarf flying, poles stretched back. Rare, very good condition, 24″ × 39″.   *$500–$600*

JOSEPH BINDER (1898–1972)

Autriche. Stunning ski poster by the leading Austrian-American Art Deco poster artist. Binder's bold graphics won him the commission to do the New York World's Fair poster of 1939. This poster was printed with the word "Austria" in several languages. Mint condition, 24½″ × 37½″. (See color center section.)   *$800–$1,000*

ROGER BRODERS (1883–1953)

Courtesy of Nancy Steinbock Fine Posters and Prints

Chamonix Mt. Blanc—Tous les Sports d'Hiver, ca 1930. Lithograph signed in the stone. Rarely seen hockey game with bright contrasting colors. Broders' name is synonymous with outstanding travel and sports posters. Mint condition, an excellent example of the artist's style, linen-mounted, 25″ × 40″. $800–$1,100

ADOLPHE MOURON CASSANDRE (1901–1968)

Italia, ca. 1930. Lithograph signed in the stone. A montage of objects representing various sports—skiing, tennis, golf, yachting, and mountain climbing—over a background of Italian countryside. One of top poster artists of the 20th century, Cassandre is known for his classic strong Art Deco designs. Mint condition, very collectible, linen-mounted, 25″ × 42″. $1,200–$1,800

FARIA

Sports d'Hiver à Chamonix, ca. 1920. Winter scene of the Cachat Majestic Hotel; skiers, skaters in foreground, snow covering eaves of hotel. Very good condition, linen-mounted, horizontal 64″ × 47″.

$1,200 *(Auction)*

GORDE

Jeux Mondiaux F.I.S., 1936. For the World Ski Championships at Chamonix Mont Blanc; three of the five Olympic rings shown in the French tri-color. Very good condition, linen-mounted, 24″ × 39″.

$300–$350

HANS HANDSCHIN (*1899–1948*)

Wintersport Glarner-land Schweiz, ca. 1930. Stylized skier in profile on his downhill run. Very good condition, shrink-wrapped, 27″ × 39″.

$200–$300

HECHENBERGER

New Hampshire, 1941. Lady carrying skis on her shoulder, silhouetted against brilliant blue sky. Very good condition, 24″ × 36″.

$250–$300

E. HERMES

Winter in Switzerland, ca. 1930. Lithograph signed in the stone, by one of the top Swiss poster artists who worked with winter sports. A well-balanced design of a skier fixing his boot; in greens, white, off-whites, and browns. Mint condition, linen-mounted, 25″ × 40″.

$600–$800

HOFFMANN

Grand Concours Interregional de Gymnastique, 1928. A young gymnast bugler calls athletes to Vienna for the competition, a variety of flags fluttering in the background. Very good condition, linen-mounted, 46″ × 63″.

$400–$500

LUDWIG HOHLWEIN (*1874–1949*)

Golf in Deutschland, ca. 1930. Lithographic poster depicting a female golfer at the end of her follow-through. Very good condition, 25″ × 40″.

$1,400 (Auction)

HUNTER

New Hampshire, ca. 1938. Man on skis against stylized snowflake all superimposed over a silver map of the state of New Hampshire. Unusual, very good condition, 22″ × 34″.

$350–$450

JIM

Gstaad, ca. 1935. Swiss, printed by Muller; a group of skiers in a gondola-type ski tow going up the slope. Very good condition, linen-backed, 25″ × 40″. $1,000–$1,200

MATTER, HEININGER, STEINER

Grindelwald, ca. 1935. Swiss photomontage jointly produced by these three pioneering designer/photographers. Color photo of man's face, black and white photo of skiers, mountains in rear. Very good condition, 40″ × 25″. $1,300–$1,500

SASCHA MAURER

Courtesy of Poster Mail Auction Company

Ski/The New Haven R.R., ca. 1940. Striking image of a smiling man with skis thrown over his shoulder. Printed in blue, green, red, orange, and brown. Very good condition, linen-mounted, 28″ × 42″.
$650–$700

Ski/The New Haven R.R., 1940. A man on skis lunges toward the viewer over the large word 'Ski''; in blue, white, yellow, and red. Very good condition, linen-mounted, 28″ × 41″. $675–$725

Winter Sports/New England, 1940. Close-up of a woman skier with a big smile in front of a snow-covered slope; in blue, white, red, and flesh. Fine condition, linen-mounted, 27″ × 42″. $650–$700

PLETSCHER

Winter Sports/Fly There by SwissAir, 1950. A family of three on skis is met by a large dog; in blues, yellow, and red. Very good condition, 25″ × 40″. $250–$300

J. REVS

Plaza de Toros, Madrid, 1945. Lithograph printed by Ortega, Valencia, signed in the stone. The classic bullfighting poster; the greatest bullfighter of all time, Manolete, was featured on this day. Fine condition, a very good example of bullfighting posters, 21″ × 41″. $250–$350

MAURICE RICAND

VII Jeux Universitaires Internationaux, 1937. For the collegiate track and field international games held in conjunction with the 1937 Paris World's Fair. Very good condition, linen-mounted, 24″ × 39″.

$300–$400

LESTER RUBIN

McGregor Winter Sportswear, ca. 1950. Three men dressed in various types of winter sportswear on a snow-covered slope. Very good condition, 21½″ × 37″. $450–$500

RUPRECHT

Eidg. Turnfest, 1947. For the gymnastics festival in Bern; a Swiss athlete wrapped in flag leads the opening ceremonies. Very good condition, linen-mounted, 36″ × 50″. $150 (Auction)

JUPP WIERTZ (1881–1939)

Sun and Snow in Germany, ca. 1930. Ski and poles in snow casting long shadows, skiers coming down a hill in the distance. Good condition, linen-mounted, 25″ × 39″. $300–$350

DESTINATION POSTERS

Note: *See the chapter "Important Notes on the Price Listings" for more information on the prices given.*

Courtesy of Poster Mail Auction Company

Boulogne-Sur-Mer, 1952. Nicely designed poster for the International Exposition of Fishing and Related Industries. Foreign flags form the border, and the sun appears above the scene as a woman's face in a golden glow. Very good condition, linen-mounted, 24″ × 39″.

$275-$325

Brides Les Bains, ca. 1890. In the style of Hugo d'Alesi, an early scenic travel poster with vignettes for the Savoie region. Good condition, linen-mounted, 30″ × 40″. $300-$350

Exposicion Internacional Barcelona, 1929. Lithograph printed by Rieusset, S. A., Barcelona. Fountains illuminated by lights, figures approaching the exposition hall; in browns, blues, pinks, greens. Very good condition, linen-mounted, 26″ × 21″. $275 -$350

Grundelwald, ca. 1930. Swiss bucolic landscape of greensward, the Alps, glacier. Very good condition, linen-mounted, 25″ × 39″.

$300-$350

Kurort Gorz, ca. 1895. Swiss lithographic poster from Graz for the Sudbahn Hotel owned by the renowned hotelier Theodore Gunkel. Slight restoration at old folds, linen-mounted, 28″ × 39″.

$300-$350

Lugano, 1937. Shows the people of Lugano in their resort town; in cream, red, and oranges. Very good condition, 26″ × 32½″.

$200–$250

Passugg, ca. 1925. Swiss; showing the resort hotel as seen from across a valley, the small town within. Very good condition, linen-mounted, 36″ × 50″. $475 (Auction)

Praha, ca. 1930. Unusual travel poster for the Czech "Ancient City of Art." Very good condition, linen-mounted, 24″ × 37″.

$200–$250

PVV: Prager Internationale Mustermesse, 20-27 Marz, 1927. Lithograph printed by Unie, Prague, signed unclearly in the stone. An elegant Deco woman speaks on the telephone. Fine condition, linen-mounted, 24½″ × 37″. $250–$350

Sintra, ca. 1930. Advertising the city in Portugal as the "8th Wonder of the World"; shows people on the broad steps of a museum. Very good condition, linen-mounted, 32″ × 45″. $200–$250

Visitez La Yugoslavie, 1950. A sunbather on the beach is offered a bowl of food by a young boy; in creams, white, and yellow. Fine condition, 27¾″ × 40. $350–$400

ALLERUP

Le Danemark, 1937. Girl bather in white one-piece suit seen from the back as she dashes into the surf, arms upraised. Very good condition, linen-mounted, 28″ × 39″. $200 (Auction)

JAN AUVIGNE

Algérie Tunisie Maroc, 1934. Red Casbah at edge of desert, deep blue night sky. Very good condition, linen-mounted, 25″ × 39″.

$300–$350

OTTO BAUMBERGER (1889–1961)

Lake of Thun, ca. 1934. Sailboats on the lake, mountains behind. Very good condition, 25″ × 40″. $500–$600

Zurichsee, ca. 1935. Steamer ferry crossing the lake, Swiss flag on prow of vessel. Very good condition, 28″ × 39″. $400–$450

EDWARD BITLE

Sion (Valais). Suisse, ca. 1910. Shows the Swiss town nestled in the Alps, an older gent walking along leading a burro with a local lady riding sidesaddle. Good condition, linen-mounted, horizontal 40″ × 29″.   *$300–$350*

MONTAGUE B. BLACK

Colwn Bay/North Wales, 1935. Looking out over the countryside to the Bay; in oranges, blues, and yellows. Fine condition, linen-mounted, 24″ × 39″.   *$400–$450*

L. BLASETT

Italia Viterbo, ca. 1912. Shows part of the ancient Roman city, a medieval arcade on top of a Roman aqueduct, at dusk, with lights peeking from windows. Good condition, with restoration across top area, linen-mounted, horizontal 44″ × 30″.   *$400–$450*

BEN BLOSSUM

Norway/Summer Season, 1950. A summer countryside scene with mountains in the background; in blues, white, green, and red. Fine condition, 24¾″ × 39″.   *$375–$425*

ALEXANDRE BORTNYIK

9th–18th May 1931, Budapest International Fair, 1931. Lithograph printed by Athenaeum, signed in the stone. Bright red arrow locates Budapest on outline map of Europe—a striking graphic design in black, white, and red. Very good condition, 25″ × 37¼″.   *$200–$275*

ROGER BRODERS (1883–1953)

Gorges de la Diosaz, 1930s. In the Vallee de Chamonix, stylized man crosses a footbridge through the gorge. One fold in linen, 24″ × 39″.
$700 (Auction)

CLAUDE BUCKLE

Bangor, 1935. A scene from the Irish seaside town; in browns, blues, and greens. Fine condition, 25″ × 39¾″.   *$375–$400*

Buxton, 1949. For the Derbyshire spa of blue waters; an overhead view of the luxurious facilities offered to tourists. Good condition, linen-mounted, horizontal 50″ × 40″.   *$300–$325*

BULDRICH

Besucht Spanien, 1929. View from the river of a stone bridge in the foreground, the city of Toledo in the background; in blues, greens, and yellows. Fine condition, 24″ × 39″. $700–$800

DAN BUZZI

Locarno Suisse Riviera, 1944. From above, looking down on the town's buildings; in blue, green, and reds. Fine condition, 25½″ × 38½″. $550–$650

CALLOT

Chennevieres s/Marne, ca. 1910. "On the banks of the Marne," a woman in bathing costume sits in the prow of a rowboat dipping her toes in the water. Rare subject matter, very good condition, linen-mounted, 39″ × 58″. $450–$500

EMILE CARDINAUX (1877–1936)

Winter in Switzerland, 1921. Lithograph printed by Wolfsberg, signed in the stone. Shows numerous people skiing and sleigh riding in white snow with mauve shadows. Fine condition, linen-mounted, framed, 28″ × 42″. $1,150–$1,300

ADOLPHE MOURON CASSANDRE (1901–1968)

Italia, 1936. Lithograph printed by Craf. Coen & C., Milano/Enit, monogram in the stone. A geometric border contains Roman columns and an outline of the Madonna and Child; in red, green, white, blues, pink, orange, and black. Fine condition, linen-mounted, 25″ × 40″. $1,100–$1,300

CELLO

Chambéry-Dolan, ca. 1930. French poster showing a lake with a sailboat, fir trees, mountains. Very good condition, linen-mounted, horizontal 63″ × 47″. $500 (Auction)

MANIFESTO CODOGNATO

Puglie Castel del Monte, 1935. A castle sits on a hill overlooking a valley; in oranges and greens. Fine condition, linen-mounted, 24″ × 29″. $450–$500

PIERRE COMMARMOND

Argeles-Gazost, ca. 1930. For the French resort in the Pyrenees; stylized, with a mountain goat overlooking the town and the mountains in the distance. Very good condition, linen-mounted, 25" × 39".

$300–$350

CONTEL

Lisieux, 1923. A painterly scene of La Rue aux Revres makes it look medieval. Mint condition, 24" × 39". $300–$350

DABO

La Syrie et Le Liban, 1927. Shows the "Environs of Damascus" in brilliant colors, most unusual for its time. Very good condition, linen-mounted, 30" × 40". $450–$500

La Syrie et Le Liban, 1927. Shows The Temple of Ba'alsamin at Palmyre, Queen of the Desert. Wonderful colors, as above. Very good condition, linen-mounted, 30" × 40". $500–$600

HIPOLITO DE CAVLEDES

Leon/Poème de Lumière et de Pierre, 1930. An aerial view of a cathedral—"Tombeau de Rois/Visitez L'Espagne"; in cream, brown, and orange. Fine condition, 24" × 39". $350–$450

DESHAYES

Le Sud Algérien Temacine-Touggourt, 1925. Colorful scene of a casbah as seen from the desert, a Berber family with a single camel heading into the Sahara. Very good condition, linen-mounted, 28" × 41". $300–$350

RENE DEVALERIO

Saint-Nectaire, ca. 1927. Stylized Art Deco design of fashionable women in foreground, the resort in the distance. Very good condition, linen-mounted, 24" × 39". $500–$600

FNOUKOVA

Visit Prague, 1935. Looking up through the supports of a bridge to a cathedral in the background. Fine condition, 24¾" × 35". $375–$425

HENRI FOLART

Voyages en Algérie et Tunisie, 1910. Lithographed by Daudé Frères; pictures an Arab on a camel peering out over sands of the Sahara. Very good condition, linen-mounted, 28″ × 41″.   *$275 (Auction)*

MOLINA GALLENT

Valencia, 1923. For the Festival, a stylized landscape with figures of entertainers scattered about; mainly in reds and blacks. Good condition, linen-mounted, 44″ × 63″.   *$150 (Auction)*

GAULIDES

Leert Tropisch Nederland, 1941. "See Tropical Netherlands at the Colonial Museum in Amsterdam"; in cream, brown, and orange. Very good condition, 25″ × 39″.   *$450–$475*

GEBHARDT

Fêtes du Nouvième Centenaire de St. Emeric, 1930. Hungarian, for the Festival in Budapest; shows the medieval saint in regal attire coming down the river preceded by three doves. Very good condition, linen-mounted, 24″ × 37″.   *$300–$350*

PHOTO GEIGER

Flims, Switzerland, 1940. Evergreen trees surround a lake; in grays and white. Very good condition, 24″ × 39″.   *$200–$250*

H. GRAY (AKA HENRI BOULANGER, *1858–1924*)

Le Treport-Mers, 1897. Bathing beauty at the beach three hours from Paris. Very good condition, linen-mounted, 31″ × 42″.

$500–$700

Trouville, ca. 1899. A bathing beauty suspended on a rope over the bay which has "the purest waters of France." Very good condition, linen-mounted, 49″ × 71″.   *$450–$600*

IVAR GULL

Norway/The Land of the Midnight Sun, 1939. Puffins sit on a rock in the foreground, while in the background fish leap out of the water and the sun shines through the mountains. Fine condition, 24½″ × 39″.   *$550–$650*

Norway/The Land of the Midnight Sun, 1939. A Viking-style building in front of a fjord; in browns, purples, and blues. Fine condition, 24″ × 39″. $550–$600

HALLMAN

Suede, 1924. For the Land of the Midnight Sun; depicts train crossing trestle in forest at base of mountain. Very good condition, linen-mounted, 29″ × 41″. $450 –$500

CH. HALLO

Voyages en Espagne, 1930. A peasant stands in front of an archway through which is seen a stone bridge leading to a city; in yellow, browns, and grays. Fine condition, 29″ × 41″. $450–$500

HANS HANDSCHIN (1899–1948)

Flims, ca. 1933. Lithograph signed in the stone. An Art Deco woman in bathing suit enters the water; in blues, off blues, and white. Handschin did many posters for the Swiss during the 1920s and 1930s. Mint condition, linen-mounted, 28″ × 42″. $600–$800

HANICOTTE

En Hollande-Pecheur, ca. 1900. A country fisherman in wooden shoes at the wharf, carrying a yoke over his shoulders, a heavy basket dangling from each end. Very good condition, 30″ × 33″. $200–$250

HECTEN

Prager Messe, 12–21 Marz, 1948. Strong design of Prague buildings and skyline; in beige, red, black, and blue. Very good condition, 24″ × 37½″. $350–$400

HENDEN

Trondheim, Norge, Vinterleker, 1939. Lithograph printed by Norsk Lith Offkin, Oslo, Norway. Good condition, 39″ × 24¼″. $250–$300

WALTER HERDEG (1908–)

St. Mortiz, ca. 1935. Photomontage of child in snowsuit atop clouds, caricature yellow sun looking on. Very good condition, 25″ × 40″.
$250–$300

LUDWIG HOHLWEIN (1874–1949)

Germany for Holidays, 1940. A fashionably dressed young woman holds an umbrella to shield her from the sun; in white, red, blue, and beige. Fine condition, 24″ × 39″. $1,100–$1,300

Winter in Bayern, ca. 1911. A woman sits on a sled on a snow-covered hillside; in white, blues, grays, yellow. Very good condition, 26½″ × 36″. $1,700–$2,000

ROLF JUNA

75 Jaar Gotthardspoorweg, ca. 1935. Palm trees in the foreground mask railroad tracks and a city scene in the background; in greens, blues, and yellows. Fine condition, 24″ × 39″. $450–$550

KARPELLUS

Kaiser Jubilaums, 1908. Lithograph printed by Kunstanstalt Sperl, Vienna, signed in the stone. A winged statue with arm upraised in the foreground; in the background the city of Vienna. Very good condition, 24″ × 40″. $700–$800

KARR-BELL

Enghien-Les-Bains, 1898. Art Noveau poster for the resort shows allegorical lady against the water. Good condition, horizontal 36″ × 29″. $300–$400

JULIEN LACAZE

Route des Pyrenees, ca. 1920. Colorful landscape with open touring bus filled with people in foreground. For the "Grands Services d'Auto-Cars from Biarritz to the Mediterranean." Very good condition, linen-mounted, 29″ × 41″. $500–$600

W. LINDE

Latvia Invites You, 1930s. Lithograph signed in the stone. In very colorful, naturalistic style, depicts a man and woman in native dress waving to a distant passing train. Fine condition, 24¼″ × 42″.
                                                          $150–$175

EMIL LOMAUX

Thuin, ca. 1895. Belgian Art Nouveau travel poster, beautiful woman and small vignettes of the town. Very good condition, linen-mounted, 38″ × 53″. $275 (Auction)

MARTON

La Provence Romaine, 1935. Fine, Cassandre-like design against deep blue field of Roman ruins, statuary, cyprus trees. Very good condition, linen-mounted, 24″ × 40″. $400–$500

Roman & Mediaeval France, 1935. A collage of Roman ruins, with two columns and the head of a statue in the foreground; in blue, white, and green. Very good condition, 24″ × 39″. $325–$375

FRANK H. MASON

Edinburgh, ca. 1930. A path leads through a park of flowers, trees, and monuments; in white, gray, and black. Fine condition, 24″ × 39″. $450–$500

HERBERT MATTER (1907–1984)

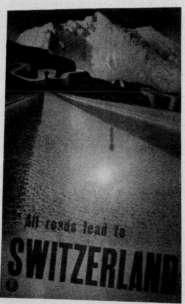

All Roads Lead to Switzerland, ca. 1935. Photomontage. Roads in foreground lead to snow-covered mountains with blue sky in background; in gray, white, and blue. Matter was a pioneer Swiss artist in the field of photomontage. Mint condition, a very good example of the artist's style, linen-mounted, 25″ × 40″. $1,200–$1,400

Courtesy of Bernice Jackson

Engelberg Trübsee, 1935. Photomontage. A woman holds up a gloved hand to cover half her face (glove has a snowflake motif); in grays, white, and blues. Fine condition, 25½ ″ × 40 ″. $1,300–$1,500

Pontresina/Engadin, 1935. Photomontage. A mountain climber's hat with goggles and edelweiss on the band, in front of a backdrop of remote mountains; in grays, blues, greens. Very good condition, 25 ″ × 40 ″. $1,300–$1,500

MELAI

Ireland Invites You. Springtime Festival, 1955. Basque-like figure in white wool sweater and red beret seated at the seaside as he weaves a multicolored sash. Good condition, linen-mounted, 24 ″ × 40 ″.
$200–$250

MIESSEN

Ostend-Dover, ca. 1950. Neptune with his trident rises out of the sea, reaching out his arms to connect the two ports; in white, green, and yellow. Fine condition, 24 ″ × 39 ″. $300–$350

MIRACOVICI

Valcov Roumanie, Bouches du Danube, 1930s. Lithograph signed in the stone. Gondolas pole upstream on a waterway overhung with beautiful willow trees. Fine condition, 26½ ″ × 38 ″. $225–$250

MONC

Espagne Canaries, 1950. A woman in folk costume of long striped skirt, apron, and vest climbs a stair. Fine condition, 24″ × 39″.

$300–$350

FRANK NEWBOULD (1887–1950)

Redcar, ca. 1930. Lithograph printed by S. C. Allen & Company, signed in the stone. An old fisherman in an orange slicker watches a child fishing; both are sitting in a green rowboat. Fine condition, a very good example of Newbould's style, linen-mounted and framed, horizontal 50″ × 40″. $1,750–$2,000

MARTIN PEIKERT (1901–1975)

Pontresina Engadin, 1940. Flowers grow out of a trellis covering a window; in blues, red, green, and cream. Fine condition, 25″ × 39″.

$375–$400

St. Moritz, ca. 1935. Giant red tiger lily against the deep blue lake. Very good condition, linen-mounted, 24″ × 38″. $350–$400

WEIMAR PURSELL

Chicago World's Fair, 1933. Lithograph printed by Neely Printing Co., signed in the stone. Art Deco design of building of the Fair; in deep blue and orange against a yellow background. Very good condition, 28″ × 42″. $800–$1,200

LEONARD RICHMOND

Ramsgate, ca. 1935. The home of "bracing breezes and summer sunshine." High perspective of the resort's many attractions, including swimming pool, beach, and promenade. Very good condition, linen-mounted, horizontal 50″ × 40″. $500–$600

RENE ROUSSEL

Le Moulin à Orgéval Restaurant Hotel, ca. 1925. A bucolic scene with the hotel in background, guests canoeing, fishing. Very good condition, linen-mounted, 29″ × 40″. $200–$250

JOSEPH ROVERS

Visit the Seaside Resorts in Holland, ca. 1920. Ladies in swimsuits and cloche hats at the North Sea beach. Very good condition, linen-mounted, 25″ × 39″. $300–$350

VICTOR RUTZ

Arosa, 1935. Swiss, for the town of Arosa; a woman swimmer against deep blue water. Good condition, 36″ × 50″. $400–$450

SANDOR

Courtesy of Poster Plus

See . . . Hear . . . Play . . . World's Fair . . . A Century of Progress, 1934. Lithograph printed by Goes Litho, signed in the stone. Tower radiating waves, with female fair guide; small sheet attached in upper left says "Gone Forever October 31"; in blues, oranges, and greens. Very good condition, a very good example of a World's Fair poster, acetate envelope, 26″ × 40″. $600–$1,000

SEGER

Autriche, ca. 1935. For the various Austrian baths and resorts, copy in French for use in France. Goddess atop pedestal, trees, mountains. Very good condition, linen-mounted, 25″ × 40″. $250–$300

SELLHEIM

Australia Surf Club, ca. 1935. Sensational stylized design of women on beach holding a lifeline to their friend in the surf. Very good condition, 25″ × 40″. $850 (*Auction*)

SEM (AKA SERGÈ GOURSAT, 1863–1934)

Cannes, ca. 1925. Lithographic poster depicting fruits and flowers superimposed over a view of the Mediterranean. Fine condition, linen-mounted, horizontal 46″ × 31″. $400–$500

Monte Carlo Beach, Le Paradis Retrouvé (Paradise Refound). Amusing poster of Adam and Eve on a skiboard with a sea serpent swimming alongside and Monte Carlo in the distance. Very good condition, horizontal 47″ × 31″. $400–$500

SHEFFER

Courtesy of Poster Plus

World's Fair . . . Chicago . . . A Century of Progress, 1933. Lithograph printed by B. E. Co., signed in the stone. Woman standing on globe surrounded by Fair buildings and skyscrapers; in greens, golds, blues, and pinks. Mint condition and a highly sought-after image. Linen-mounted, 28″ × 42″. $700–$900

SOLEGAONKAT

See India, 1934. Vivid design of dancers at the Ajanta Frescoes in the Cave Temples. Very good condition, 26″ × 40″.   *$225 (Auction)*

L. R. SQUIRRELL

Northumberland, 1930. Rolling hills, stone walls, and sheep; in browns and greens. Very good condition, 25″ × 40″. $275–$325

KENNETH STEEL

Royal Deeside, 1935. Through the evergreen trees in the foreground the town can be seen in the distance; in blues, yellows, and browns. Very good condition, 24″ × 39″. $275–$325

ANDRE SUREBA

Les Gorges du Tarn, ca. 1920. Dark and brooding image of boat being poled through the great gorge. Unusual, very good condition, linen-mounted, 29″ × 43″. $300–$350

JAMES THIRIAR

Bruxelles Exposition, 1935. A line of drummers in 18th-century costume parade in the foreground. Fine condition, 24″ × 39″.

$450–$500

ALFREDO TIENDA

San Sebastian, 1955. Two mermaids frolicking with an open clam shell, the symbol of welcome in the Basque country. Very good condition, linen-mounted, 25″ × 39″. $300–$350

TONELLI

Pourquoi pas l'Irlande?, 1950s. By the Irish Tourist Board for use in France; a 1950s man, half in business suit, half in bathing gear. Rare, good condition, linen-mounted, 24″ × 38″. $250–$350

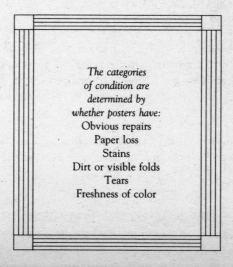

*The categories
of condition are
determined by
whether posters have:*
Obvious repairs
Paper loss
Stains
Dirt or visible folds
Tears
Freshness of color

ADOLPH TREIDLER (1886–1921)

Courtesy of Nancy Steinbock Fine Posters and Prints

Bermuda, ca. 1947. Lithograph signed in the stone. Art Deco design in pastel colors, a formally dressed couple dances at night with full moon and an ocean liner in the background. Treidler had a long career as an illustrator and poster artist, staring with World War I through 1950. Mint condition, a very good example of the artist's style, linen-mounted, 30″ × 40″. $750–$900

FRITZ UHLICH

Park Hotel Alpenhof, ca. 1935. Stylized design of dancers at the hotel ballroom. A rare German poster printed on two sheets, but here backed together. Very good condition, linen-mounted, 29″ × 40″.
$1,000–$1,200

JOHN VICKERY

Outposts of Empire/Ceylon. A native man in a light suit walks in front of palm trees and a building; in blues, greens, and tans. Very good condition, 20″ × 24¾″. $300–$350

WERTTACH

Spend Summer Days in Vienna, ca. 1930. Stylized lady in white brimmed hat and dress gazing at Vienna's grandeur. Very good condition, 25″ × 36″. $400–$500

WHER

Ungarn, 1940. Hungarian, a stylized man and woman court; in black, white, and blue. Fine condition, 24½″ × 37″. $400–$450

JUPP WIERTZ (*1881–1939*)

Bayreuth. La Ville de Richard Wagner, ca. 1935. Painterly design shows the famed fountain and, behind it, the Opera House. Very good condition, linen-mounted, 24″ × 40″. $300–$350

In a German Forest, ca. 1935. A small herd of deer graze peacefully in a forest glade. Shades of green predominate. Mint condition, 25″ × 40″. $250–$300

Romantic Germany, ca. 1935. A castle peeks above a green forest as an example of "Old World Charms of Medieval Towns." Mint condition, 25″ × 40″. $350–$400

NORMAN WILKINSON (*1882–?*)

Berkshamsted School, 1940. A view of the inside of the church; in cream, orange, and yellow. Fine condition, 24½″ × 40″.

$450–$500

YOSHI

Visit Japan/N.Y.K. Line, ca. 1935. A Japanese bridge in the foreground, in the background a house on a hillside; in orange, reds, and grays. Fine condition, 21″ × 30½″. $600–$650

MAGIC POSTERS

Abracadabra! Magic posters are as weird and dramatic as the legendary magicians they promoted. The posters were intended to be as baffling and intriguing as the magic acts themselves and the best are outstanding colorful examples of fine lithography as well as being both historical and curiosity pieces.

Magic collectors usually don't specialize in posters. Rather, they collect everything from handcuffs to magic apparatus, to autographs and books on conjuring. Magic collectors have their own collecting circles, performing societies, and even exclusive private clubs.

International competition for the best magic memorabilia is fierce. So much so that the earliest and best posters from legends such as Robert Houdin (1805–1871), Harry Kellar (1869–1922), Chung Ling Soo (1861–1918), Howard Thurston (1869–1936), and Harry Houdini (1874–1926) have almost disappeared entirely from the active market.

For those who may be surprised not to see Harry Houdini's name at the top of this chronological list, you can at least rest assured that his posters are the most valuable of all. Houdini was not only a master showman, but also a master publicist, and one who took full advantage of the Golden Age of Lithography in this country to commission stunning and immediately eye-catching designs to promote his appearances.

Prior to Houdini's time, posters for magic performances were much like posters for any other entertainment. Today, these are referred to by most collectors as "broadsides" rather than "posters." Generally speaking, before the advent of color lithography and the illustrated advertising poster, broadsides devoted more room to information than to illustration. Broadsides were usually produced as woodcuts or wood engravings, much like the illustrations of Civil War battles in *Harper's Weekly*.

Broadside for Robert Houdini.
Photo by Robert Four, from a private collection

Robert Houdin, from whom Houdini "borrowed" his name, was one of the world's first great and well-known magic performers. His broadsides illustrate the kind of announcement used to attract audiences in the mid-1800s (see photo).

The famous Houdini "Water Torture Cell" trick.
Photo by Robert Four, from a private collection

Much more impressive and awesome is Houdini's 1917 poster printed by Strobridge Litho of Cincinnati, Ohio, depicting his famous

"Water Torture Cell" trick. This poster, should it ever come to the market, could easily sell for $8,000 to $10,000 (see photo).

Both Strobridge and Otis Litho of Cleveland were well known for their fine-quality lithographic magic and circus posters, sometimes printed in as many as eight to ten colors. In terms of American posters, these two companies are often cited as the best printers to look for.

Other early magicians to watch for are Kar-Mi; Chang, a Panamanian magician; and the Fak Hongs, a turn-of-the-century company who were better known in Europe than in this country. For some European engagements, the Fak Hongs commissioned the great German lithographer Adolph Friedländer, who was known as the "King of Lithographers for Performers."

Friedländer and his sons produced perhaps as many as 10,000 images from 1872 to 1938. Best known for posters for the Max Schumann, Hagenbeck, and Busch circuses, the Friedländers also created posters for a wide variety of magic and vaudeville entertainers. Unfortunately, many thousands of his posters were destroyed when the printing company was forced to close its doors under Nazi persecution. His posters, printed in relatively small quantities, can bring hundreds of dollars more than posters by other printers of the same era.

The magic collecting and magic poster collecting field began to heat up in the late 1970s, some say because of the resurgence of interest in American history after the 1976 Bicentennial.

The auction firm Swann Galleries in New York has long been the venue of choice for sellers and buyers of magicana. In 1981, Swann hosted the sale of a large part of the collection of magician Melbourne Chistopher, which he had built and held for many years. That auction, filled with important posters and memorabilia, caught the magic collecting world off-guard with the prices it realized.

The following year, Swann's President George Lowry announced that one of the world's most important magic collections, the John Mullholland (1898–1970) Collection, would be sold as a single lot. Housed in the Player's Club in New York since the final years of Mullholland's life, the collection is now at the Mullholland Library of Conjuring and Allied Arts in Los Angeles, where it is open to serious scholars by application only. As both a magician, magic scholar, and writer, Mullholland collected nearly 4,000 books including scarce early titles, four hundred Houdini typescripts of magic feats,

2,000 photographs, over two hundred posters, and much, much more.

In 1989, Swann auctions continued to include magic posters and featured two hard-to-find posters of Chung Ling Soo. Promoted as "The Marvelous Chinese Conjurer," Chung Ling Soo's real name was William Robinson. A native New Yorker, Robinson entered the magic business as an illusion builder for the great Harry Kellar.

Photo by Robert Four, from a private collection

Kellar, whose career roughly corresponded with that of Houdini, although he started earlier, was not as promotion-oriented as Houdini and is thus less known today. His "Levitation of Princess Karnac" act, depicted in a 1904 Strobidge poster, made him a popular favorite (see photo).

The levitation act, and the devils whispering in his ear, would be passed on to his successor Howard Thurston. In one rare poster, Thurston illustrates his levitation act with his assistant Fernanda Myro, who was the mother of well-known actress Imogene Coca.

Thurston in turn introduced other magicians to the public, including Tampa, billed as "England's Court Magician," and Harry Alvin Jansen (1882–1955), who he hired as his assistant in 1923.

Houdini passed on his magic secrets as well, willing his illusions and apparatus to his brother Hardeen, who had a successful career. Hardeen passed on his own and his brother's tricks and memorabilia to his protégé Sid Radner of Holyoke, Massachusetts, who loaned many of the items for permanent display to the Houdini Museum in Niagara Falls.

Other well-known magicians whose posters are more accessible and more easily found in the market today include Claude Alexander

Coulin (1880–1954), who went by the name of "Alexander," and Charles Carter (1874–1936), who was known as "Carter the Great." Both of these magicians were popular during the late 1920s and early 1930s when vaudeville began to eclipse magic as a popular form of entertainment.

Alexander rode with the times, promoting himself as a psychic and seer, headlining in vaudeville and writing a successful newspaper column. Carter's posters, printed mostly by Otis Litho, are stunning examples of magic poster art and a good place for a beginning collector to start while they are still available on the active market. Carter, who had eight successful world tours, opened the first permanent magic theater on Broadway. It was a financial disaster and marked the end of a certain era in magic performance.

Today's magic performers, who appear as often on television as they do on stage, have also created some collectible posters, which, although offset rather than lithographic, will always have a value to magicana buffs. Among those to look for are Doug Henning, David Copperfield, and Le Grand David, who produces a weekly stage show of great old-time magic in Beverly, Massachusetts.

WHERE TO GO TO SEE MAGIC POSTERS

Several museums in the country have fine collections of magic posters (and many of the same museums also have circus, theater, and other entertainment poster collections). Three notable collections are in New York City at The Museum of the City of New York, The New York Historical Society, and The Billy Rose Theater Collection at the New York Public Library. (See Resource Guide for additional information.)

PRICE LISTINGS

Note: *See the chapter "Important Notes on the Price Listings" for more information on prices given. Entries are arranged alphabetically by name of magician or act.*

ANONYMOUS

Untitled, 1899. Exquisite lithographically printed image of mustached magician in white tie and tails with rabbit, hat, peonies, plant, fishbowl, doves, skillet. Printed by Strobridge Litho, a superb example of 19th-century American lithography. Very good condition, framed, 17″ × 25″. $500 (*Auction*)

ALEXANDER (AKA CLAUDE ALEXANDER COULIN, 1880–1954)

Photo by Robert Four, from a private collection

Alexander/The Man Who Knows, ca. 1920. Large litho crayon portrait of turbaned vaudeville mystic on bright red background; his piercingly penetrating gaze follows the viewer's every move. Very good condition, very collectible, 28″ × 42″. $125 (*Auction*)

Ask Alexander, ca. 1920. The mindreader's turban forms a question mark around his face; in yellow, red, tan, and green against a jet black background. Fine condition, a few tiny holes at top, 27″ × 41″.
$125–$150

CARTER (AKA CHARLES CARTER, 1874–1936)

Carter Beats the Devil, ca. 1920. Lithograph printed by Otis Litho. A turbaned Carter shows a poker hand of aces which beats the Devil at his own game. Very good condition, 14″ × 22″. $100–$150

Carter the Great/Condemned to Death for Witchcraft Cheats the Gallows, ca. 1920. Lithograph printed by Otis Litho. Depicts angry Chinese with raised fists as Carter ascends from hanged hooded figure. Printed on four panels, one panel with small creases and a break at one fold; otherwise very good condition, 80″ × 104″. $650 *(Auction)*

Carter the Great/Marvels that Obfuscate the Will, Charm the Imagination, Confound Intelligence!, ca. 1920. Lithograph printed by Otis Litho. Carter holds the world in his hand as he is watched over by Cagliostro, Herrmann, Robert Houdin, Chung Ling Soo, and Kellar. Very good condition, printed on eight panels, horizontal 160″ × 104″.

$700 *(Auction)*

Courtesy of Poster Mail Auction Company

Carter the Great Sweeps the Secrets of the Sphinx and Marvels of the Tomb of Old King Tut to the Modern World, ca. 1920. Lithograph printed by Otis Litho in several colors. Carter on a camel with red devil and sphinx in background, witch and imps chasing an Arab in foreground. Mint condition, a fine example of the artist and of color lithography, 27″ × 41″. $600 *(Auction)*

Carter the Great/The Elongated Maiden, ca. 1920. Lithograph printed by Otis Litho. Carter in a Chinese costume with scenes from his famous "Stretching a Lady" illusion; deep blue background. Chinese assistants, devils, goblins, and owls add to the bizarrely mysterious image. Very good condition, on three panels, 27″ × 41″.

$600 (Auction)
$250–$350

Same as above. Very good condition, on three panels, 41″ × 77″.

$300 (Auction)

Carter the Great/The Modern Priestess of Delphi, ca. 1915. Lithograph printed by Otis Litho. A beautiful brunette sits amid cacaphony of swirling color, screaming banshees, and Carter's serene face floating in the background. Fine condition, linen-mounted, 41″ × 77″.

$300–$350

Carter the Great/The Vanishing Sacred Elephant, ca. 1920. Lithograph printed by Otis Litho. Features enormous elephant, Carter portrait, red devils—"The acme of human achievement, the summit of human effort." Very good condition, linen-mounted, 80″ × 104″.

$700–$900

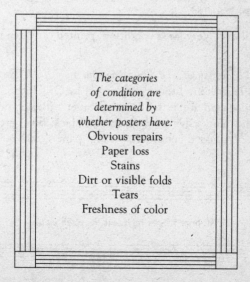

The categories
of condition are
determined by
whether posters have:
Obvious repairs
Paper loss
Stains
Dirt or visible folds
Tears
Freshness of color

Carter the Great, The World's Weird Wonderful Wizard, ca. 1920. Lithograph, printed by Otis Litho. Carter in colorful garb looking into a crystal ball out of which are flying devils, cards, and bats. This poster was printed in various sizes, some up to eight sheets! Mint condition, 14″ × 26″.   *$150–$200*

   Same as above. Very good condition, printed on three panels, 41″ × 77″.   *$300 (Auction)*

Do the Dead Materialize? The Absorbing Question of All Time/Carter the Great, ca. 1920. Stone lithograph printed by Otis Litho. Carter performs the magician Kellar's "Spirit Cabinet" illusion with winged devils, goblins, and a flying witch; in red, black, blue, green, yellow, and orange. Very good condition, on four panels, 80″ × 106″.
$350 (Auction)
$400–$450

All price ranges represent the retail value.

CHANG AND FAK-HONG (SEE ALSO FAK HONGS)

Chang and Fak-Hong's United Magicians Presents: A Night in Tokyo, ca. 1925. Oriental magician in red robes stands over a fiercely blazing cauldron as a serpent circles around them; in the smoke of the blaze are vignettes of the illusions featured in the show. Fine condition, horizontal 43″ × 30″. $150 (Auction)
$350–$400

Chang and Fak-Hong's United Magicians Presents: Elle, ca. 1925. Mysterious female figure stands atop a dais enveloped in the fumes of a smoking urn; rabbits, cards, ducks, and flowers are strewn at her feet. Fine condition, 17″ × 25″. $300–$350

Chang and Fak-Hong's United Magicians Presents: The Bhuda, ca. 1925. Chinese wizard conjures up serpents, devils, ducks, and skeletons against a blue-green background. Very good condition, 17″ × 25″. $150–$200

The Great Chang and Fak-Hong's United Magicians Presents: The Noe Ark, ca. 1925. Animal-filled image for Panamanian magician who successfully toured the world many times, here teamed up with Fak-Hong for a combined circus and magic tent show. Fine condition, horizontal 43″ × 30″. $150 (Auction)

CHUNG LING SOO (AKA WILLIAM ROBINSON, 1861–1918)

Chung Ling Soo, ca. 1910. Lithograph printed by Horrocks & Co., London. The magician in a full frontal portrait against a dark background. Very good condition, linen-mounted, 20″ × 29¾″.

$400 *(Auction)*

Marvellous Chinese Conjurer, ca. 1910. Lithograph printed by James Upton Birmingham. The magician holds a bowl of rice in one hand and festooning ribbons in the other, with additional figures breathing fire, swallowing candles, etc. Very good condition, some restorations, very sought after, linen-mounted, 20″ × 29¾″. $1,100 *(Auction)*

Courtesy of Swann Galleries

The Marvellous Chinese Conjurer, ca. 1910. Lithograph, printed by Horrocks & Co., London. A bust portrait of the magician surrounded by Oriental fans and flowers. Good condition, 19¼″ × 29¼″.

$700 *(Auction)*

FAK HONGS

The Fak Hongs, ca. 1910. Lithographic poster designed by Adolph Friedländer. Black hooded mystic is seen against a fiery red background as he studies his book of ancient incantations. Very good condition, with folio folds, 28″ × 37″. $300 (Auction)

Numero d'Illusion—Le Plus Grand du Monde, ca. 1915. Lithographic poster printed by E. Mirabet, Valencia. Medallion portraits of the Hongs at the top, numerous devils and magicians performing a variety of magical stunts beneath. Linen-mounted, two sheets, 49″ × 75¼″.
$600–$900

All price ranges represent the retail value.

Courtesy of Poster Plus

George—The Supreme Master of Magic, ca. 1929. Lithograph printed by Otis Litho. Swirling imagery of George, cards, devils, Buddha against a blue background. Very good condition, linen-mounted, 20″ × 27″. $250–$300

Same as above. Fine condition, Chartex-backed, 20″ × 26″. $110 (Auction)

Same as above. Fine condition, Chartex-backed, 27″ × 41″. $135 (Auction)

Same as above. Mounted to a board with white tape covering borders, folds show, framed, 23″ × 29″. $80 (Auction)

George the Supreme Master of Magic on His Triumphal American Tour, 1920s. Lithographic poster printed by Otis Litho, a fantastic 20-sheet billboard mounted on a single piece of linen backing. $2,500 (Auction)

George/Triumphant American Tour, ca. 1929. Lithographic poster printed by Otis Litho. An owl whispers secrets of darkness into George's ear. Fine condition, 27″ × 41″. $200 (Auction)

Same as above. Fine condition, Chartex-backed, 27″ × 41″. $85 (Auction)

GERMAIN

The Master of Magic, ca. 1915. Lithographic poster depicting a bust portrait of the magician in profile with two winged devils. Mounted to stiff paper, trimmed to image with original margins lacking, 23½″ × 37½″. $50 (Auction)

The Wizard (Witch's Cauldron), ca. 1915. Lithographic poster printed by Schmitz-Horning Co., Cleveland. In shades of black and orange, showing the magician conjuring a female spirit from the smoke of a fire, while a witch concocts a brew and a black cat arches its back. Linen-mounted, three sheets, 41¾″ × 79¼″. $700 (Auction)

DOUG HENNING

The Sensational Houdini Water Torture Escape, ca. 1971. Offset color poster shows Mr. Henning submerged in a water cabinet. Good condition, 29¾″ × 45¾″. $60 (Auction)

HENRY

Henry and His Own Company, ca. 1915. Lithograph printed by the Scioto Sign Co., Kenton, Ohio. Bust portrait of Henry and insets of him doing various tricks. Fair condition, linen-mounted, 23¾″ × 36″. $100–$125

HARRY HOUDINI (1874–1926)

Harry Houdini, King of Cards, ca. 1900. Lithograph printed by National Pr. & Eng. Co. Portrait of the young magician, with a close-up of the master's hands moving decks of cards. While this is not the most exciting of Houdini's posters, any poster of him is hard to find on the market. Fine condition, 21″ × 28″. $2,000–$2,500

MONSIEUR DE JEN

The Great Magician, ca. 1920. Lithographic poster portrait of the magician printed by Jontzen, Cleveland. Good condition, with a few small chips at edges, 28¼″ × 42″. $150–$250

KAR-MI

Kar-Mi Performing the Most Startling Mystery of All India, 1914. Dramatic image of a magician with lightning emanating from his fingers before a group of frightened viewers; colorful on a midnight blue field. Fine condition, horizontal 41″ × 28″. $400–$450

Kar-Mi Swallows a Loaded Gun Barrel and Shoots a Cracker from a Man's Head, 1914. Artist: Joseph B. Hallworth. Lithograph depicting this trick; wonderfully bright and gaudy color. Fine condition, horizontal 41″ × 28″.   *$200 (Auction)*

LEON

Les Magique Leons/The Whirlwind Illusionists in the "Palace of Mystery," ca. 1920. Lithographic poster for The Great Leon, a vaudeville head-liner for over 20 years; after 1919 he embarked on several interna-tional tours. Fine condition, 20″ × 30″. $160 (Auction)

NICOLA

Courtesy of Swann Galleries

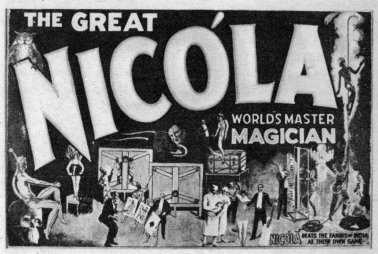

The Great Nicóla—World's Master Magician. Lithographic poster show-ing various magic tricks including the Indian rope trick, the cutting of bodies, etc. Good condition, 8¾″ × 13½″. $400 (Auction)

SELVAGGIO

Selvaggio, ca. 1920. Lithograph duotone in blue and white. A full portrait of the magician with a devil standing behind him and a num-ber of magic apparatuses. Good condition, 23″ × 31½″. $150–$250

SMITH

Mysterious Smith/America's Greatest Transformist, ca. 1910. Litho-graphic poster printed by American Poster Corp. Smith was a large-scale magician of the time. Very good condition, relatively rare, linen-mounted, 22″ × 28″. $500 (Auction)

SOLANIS

Solanis—Le Magicien Moderne, 1945. Artist: Conde. Against a black background, all the paraphernalia of "the modern magician," including top hat, red-white-and-blue doves, cards, flowers. Also small flags of United States, USSR, France, Britain—a magic act celebrating the victory of the Allies. Very good condition, linen-mounted, 25″ × 37″. $200–$250

SORCAR

Sorcar . . . Presents the Magnificent Magic Show Ind-Dra-Jal—Magic of India, ca. 1940. Lithographic poster printed by Shivran, Bombay. Bust portrait of the magician with raised hands, wearing a bejewelled green turban. Good condition, small marginal tears, 39¼″ × 78¾″.
$250–$350

THURSTON (AKA HOWARD THURSTON, 1869–1936)

Chicago American Says "Go See" THURSTON, ca. 1905. Black and white lithographic poster printed by Strobridge Litho, showing sketches made at the McVickers Theater by the cartoonist French. Good condition, horizontal 41″ × 28″.   *$1,000 (Auction)*

Thurston. Original gouache design for 24-sheet poster for Thurston's great touring magic/illusion show; from the archives of the Enquirer Job Printing Co., Cincinnati. Green face of magician at left with midnight blue name in a shaft of yellow running the full width of the poster. Painted on heavy card stock, very good condition, horizontal 25″ × 14″.   *$175 (Auction)*
$300–$400

VICTORINA TROUPE

The Great Victorina Troupe, ca. 1914. Lithographic poster for the performer Kar-Mi appearing under another name. Colorful, with several magic vignettes. Very good condition, 27″ × 41″.   *$300 (Auction)*

CIRCUS POSTERS

Inventive, colorful, and most of all fun with their depictions of wild beasts, clowns, elephants, and death-defying acts, circus posters are a special area of poster collecting unto themselves. Luckily, because there were and still are so many circuses in this country and abroad, and because many of the fine posters were printed in the tens of thousands to publicize circus road shows, many great images can still be bought—you guessed it—for peanuts.

That's not to say that all circus posters are inexpensive or easily obtained. Certainly some of the earliest and best, from Forepaugh, Sells, Barnum & Bailey, Ringling Brothers, Buffalo Bill's Wild West, and others now command big-top prices. Specialized collectors compete in the auction arena whenever a rare or early circus poster goes "on the block."

The circus was an early form of entertainment, dating back to the days of Rome. Advertising and publicity professionals trace the roots of their field back to the "front man" who came to town to publicize the arrival of the circus, plastering posters to every available wall before the arrival of the circus parade. It should therefore come as no surprise that the earliest illustrated poster in the poster collection of The Library of Congress is a circus poster: an 1856 colored woodcut poster, measuring 11 feet in width and advertising "Five Celebrated Clowns Attached to Sands, Nathan Co.'s Circus"; it was used to advertise a traveling company.

Circus posters were designed to emphasize the spectacular feats, great performers, and amazing clowns audiences would see in the ring. In many cases, they stretched the imagination—and the truth. But as

P. T. Barnum is famed to have said, "There's a sucker born every minute," and circus fans wanted to believe what they saw advertised.

Virtually all of the early American circus posters, like many magic posters, were printed by the great lithography company of Strobridge in Ohio, even for American circus tours in Europe. Their masterful work meant vivid colors, exciting imagery, and startling effects. After about 1910, other printers also specialized in circus and entertainment posters: Erie Litho, Illinois Litho, Morgan Litho in Cleveland (which became famous for cinema posters), and several others, almost all in the Midwest. Unfortunately, the individual designers who created the circus posters for these companies almost never signed the posters.

European circuses, too, had their favorite printers, but head and shoulders above the rest is the German firm of Adolph Friedländer (1851–1904), who until recently was practically unknown and uncollected in this country. From the years 1872 to 1938, Friedländer and his sons designed and printed nearly 10,000 different exciting posters for the Carl Hagenbeck Circus, the Max Schumann Circus, the Circus Busch, and other legendary European companies.

Over 9,000 posters of this great printer were destroyed when the Nazis forced the closing of the printing firm in the late 1930s. This rarity, coupled with their fantastic designs, means Friedländer posters in most instances command much higher prices than other circus posters.

Another factor which contributes to their scarcity is that Friedländer often issued posters in small editions, with a minimum order of twenty-five to a maximum of probably no more than 3,000. Strobridge littered cities and towns across the United States, sometimes with as many as 30,000 copies of a given poster.

Early circuses in this country included Adam Forepaugh Circus, which operated from 1867 to 1894, and Adam Forepaugh & Sells Bros. Circus, owned by James A. Bailey (of Barnum & Bailey), which operated from 1896 to 1907.

Rivalry between circuses was common, and P. T. Barnum of Bridgeport, Connecticut, who had made his fame and fortune as a promoter for Tom Thumb and opera star Jenny Lind, created his own circus in 1872, later to merge with Bailey's to create the Barnum & Bailey Circus in 1888. This circus, called "The Greatest Show on Earth," reigned supreme until it was challenged by a new venture started by a family of brothers from Baraboo, Wisconsin: The Ringlings.

The Ringling Brothers Circus, which operated from 1884 to 1918, eventually came to buy the Barnum & Bailey show, but did not merge their names until 1916. Posters from The Ringling Brothers Circus before it combined with Barnum & Bailey are especially prized by collectors.

In the active market in the United States today collectors are more likely to find posters for Ringling Brothers and Barnum & Bailey (RBB & B) combined shows than any of those mentioned above. Of these, the pre–World War II lithographic posters will always be the most valuable, but RBB & B posters from the 1940s and 1950s are often well executed and are surfacing more and more on the market.

Other earlier American circuses to watch for are: the Sells-Floto Circus, which operated independently from about 1906 to 1929 when John Ringling bought it out, merging it completely with his own company in 1932; the Christy Bros. Circus, from 1920 to 1930; the Cole Bros. Circus, which toured from about 1935 to 1950 when it merged with another to become the Clyde Beatty and Cole Bros. Circus; the Downie Bros. Circus, which traveled primarily on the East Coast from 1926 to 1939; and the Hagenbeck-Wallace Circus from 1906 to 1938.

Post–World War II circuses to watch for are the Cristiani Bros. Circus; the Kelly-Morris and Kelly and Miller Bros. Circuses; and the Wallace Bros. Circus. Contemporary smaller one-ring circuses which emphasize the artistry of circus acts are today's circus collectibles, such as The Big Apple Circus in New York, and the French Cirque de Soleil and Cirque de Demain. In addition, one can often find exciting vintage and modern circus posters from many short-lived and lesser-known circuses. In starting out, you might want to focus on a particular circus or on a particular theme, such as animals, clowns, or high-wire acts.

The circus poster market has not experienced the steep climbs and rapid changes of many other poster fields in the last ten years. Generally speaking, circus poster collectors are not necessarily looking for an "investment" in the poster market but rather have a love of the circus and are looking to invest their time in a rewarding hobby. This means that even a beginning collector can look to acquiring truly outstanding examples of circus poster art for under $500.

WHERE TO GO TO SEE CIRCUS POSTERS

In addition to the museums that were mentioned in the chapter on "Magic Posters," another place to see circus posters is the Bridgeport Public Library in Bridgeport, Connecticut, home of P. T. Barnum. The Barnum Museum, also in Bridgeport, doesn't specialize in posters but you can have fun seeing memorabilia, specially designed carriages that carried Tom Thumb, costumes, cannons, and more. The Ringling Museum in Sarasota, Florida, also has some posters, but not as many as you might expect because the museum's main attraction is really the Venetian palace home of John and Mable Ringling and their extensive art collection housed in a separate art museum. (See Resource Guide for museum listings.)

REFERENCE WORKS

There are numerous good references on circus posters (not to mention on circuses themselves). One author, Charles Philip Fox, has two large pictorial works on circus posters, and one of the early auctions of posters at Phillips auction house in New York focused entirely on circus posters. (See Bibliography.)

PRICE LISTINGS

Note: See the chapter "Important Notes on the Price Listings" for more information on prices given. Entries are listed alphabetically by name of circus or act.

BARNUM & BAILEY
(SEE ALSO RINGLING BROTHERS AND BARNUM & BAILEY)

Barnum & Bailey Greatest Show on Earth, ca. 1895. Printed by Strobridge Litho. Portraits of Barnum and Bailey with antelopes surrounding a single giraffe as the main image. Good condition, repairs, linen-mounted, horizontal 41″ × 27″. $400–$500

Barnum & Bailey Greatest Show on Earth, ca. 1897. Printed by Strobridge Litho, in French for a French tour, with horses and clowns in an outdoor portrait. Horizontal 41″ × 27″. $500–$700

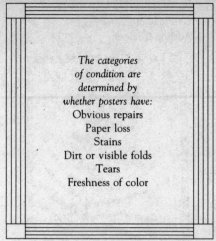

The categories
of condition are
determined by
whether posters have:
Obvious repairs
Paper loss
Stains
Dirt or visible folds
Tears
Freshness of color

The Berzacs, 1910. Barnum & Bailey poster printed by Strobridge Litho, for the animal trainers Cliff Berzac and Madame Berzac. Single folio fold evident, framed, horizontal 41″ × 27″.   *$300 (Auction)*

Felix and 99 Other Famous Clowns, ca. 1933. Barnum & Bailey poster printed by Central Printing and Illinois Litho. Charming clown portrait against deep blue background. Very good condition, 27″ × 41″.
$60 (Auction)

Les Météors Volants, 1900. Barnum & Bailey poster printed by Strobridge Litho, in French for a French tour. Depicts a two-man trapeze act in action. Good condition, horizontal 41″ × 27″. $600–$800

BUFFALO BILL

Buffalo Bill's Wild West Bucking Mustangs, ca. 1900. Lithograph printed by Hoen & Co., Baltimore. Three cowboys on buckers. Repaired border tears not affecting image, on Japan paper, horizontal 40″ × 29″.
$450–$600

Col. W. F. Cody "Buffalo Bill," 1908. Lithograph by Strobridge Litho showing Buffalo Bill posed on horseback. Excellent condition, mounted on Japan paper, 43″ × 62″. $2,500–$2,750

CIRQUE DES CIRQUES

Le Cirque des Cirques, ca. 1925. Lithograph. A conductor directs a line of horses walking on their hind legs. Fine condition, good collectible, horizontal 15½″ × 11½″. $50–$65

CIRQUE DANIELLIS

Courtesy of Poster Mail
Auction Company

La Femme Araignée, ca. 1910. French circus sideshow poster; a woman whose body is that of a spider. Colorful and weird. Fine condition, 31″ × 47″. $125 *(Auction)*

CIRQUE DE DEMAIN

Cirque de Demain, 1987. By Raymond Savignac. Offset-printed poster designed for the 10th Circus Festival and depicting a clown who has tied himself in a knot. Mint condition, linen-mounted, 46″ × 63″.
$150–$250

CIRQUE D'HIVER

Cirque d'Hiver, ca. 1910. By Charles Levy. Lithograph printed by Affiches Americaines. Russian bears engaging in a variety of playful antics. Minor restoration, linen-mounted, 33″ × 47″. $400–$500

CIRQUE PINDER

Cirque Pinder, ca. 1910. Lithographic poster depicting enormous smiling clown face beautifully drawn and printed. Very good condition, linen-mounted, 53″ × 83″. $500 *(Auction)*

CLYDE BEATTY—COLE BROS.

The Greatest Circus on Earth. By Roland Butler. Great image of a tiger attacking, almost leaping off the poster. Notice the slight difference in the slogan from "The Greatest Show on Earth," a Ringling Brothers copyrighted trademark to this day. Mint, horizontal 28″ × 21″.
$150–$175

CRISTIANI BROS. CIRCUS

Cristiani Bros. 3 Ring-Wild Animal Circus. Fiercely growling tiger and lion; in orange, brown, black, blue-green, yellow, and dark blue. Very good condition, 28″ × 41″.
$50–$75

Cristiani Bros.—Big Wild Animal Circus. Great design with giraffe, lion, hippo, rhino, polar bear, and tiger. Printed in red, green, yellow, and blue. Very good condition, horizontal 30″ × 20″.
$100–$125

All price ranges represent the retail value.

Cristiani Bros.—World's Largest Circus. Two women balance on horse-back while clown riding with them takes a tumble. With Johnstown date tag affixed to bottom; in red, green, yellow, and blue. Fine condition, 28″ × 49″.   *$75–$100*

DAYTON

Better See the Dayton Show—It's Worth It, ca. 1920. Lithographic poster printed by Great Western Printing Co., St. Louis. Shows a balding clown with a tin can on his head. Edges with scattered chipping, linen-mounted on slightly larger sheet, approx. 42¼″ × 28″.

$150–$250

DOWNIE BROS.

Downie Bros. Big 3 Ring Circus, ca. 1925. Lithographic poster printed by Erie Litho. Smiling clown in center, surrounded by other scenes including one where he is being chased by a skeleton. Very good condition, 27″ × 41″.   *$200–$225*

Downie Bros. Big 3 Ring Circus, ca. 1934. Lithographic poster printed by Erie Litho. A montage of equestrian feats performed by girl jockeys, with a rearing black stallion in the center. Very good condition, horizontal 41″ × 28″.   *$175–$200*

Downie Bros. Big 3 Ring Circus, ca. 1934. Lithographic poster printed by Erie Litho. Clown's face peeks through a circle on a field of stars and triangles of bright colors. Very good condition, linen-mounted, horizontal 41″ × 28″.   *$150–$175*

HAGENBECK-WALLACE CIRCUS

An Exciting Fox Hunt, ca. 1930. Lithographic poster shows a hunt scene with horses and dogs. Very good condition, linen-mounted, horizontal 41″ × 27″.   *$400–$500*

Carl Hagenbeck-Wallace Circus, 1929. Lithographic poster printed by Erie Litho. Smiling clown face on an orange background. Very good condition, 26″ × 40″.   *$200–$250*

Hagenbeck-Wallace Circus/Cristiani Troupe, ca. 1935. Lithographic poster shows six performers—men and women—atop a striding white horse within the ring. Fine condition, minor repairs, linen-mounted, 28″ × 41″.   *$200–$350*

Hagenbeck-Wallace Wild Animal Circus, ca. 1930. Famous circus performer and circus owner Clyde Beatty in the ring with an entire menagerie of animals. Very good condition, linen-mounted, 27″ × 41″.   *$500–$550*

KELLY AND MILLER BROS.

Al G. Kelly and Miller Brothers Circus. Terrifying scene shows a native being gored by a rhino. Mint condition, 20″ × 30″.   *$100–$150*

KELLY-MORRIS CIRCUS

Anthropoid Apes. Color silk-screen of snarling ape bending the bars of his cage. Yellow, blue-green, red, and black. Good condition, 20″ × 28″. $60–$75

Kelly-Morris Circus. Silk-screen image of seals in the ring, playing on horns, and with the traditional ball. Good condition, 21″ × 28″.

$50–$60

KING BROS. & CRISTIANI COMBINED CIRCUS

King Bros. & Cristiani Combined Circus. Performing bears in red, brown, yellow, blue, and black. Remnants of torn date tag for Pottstown, Pennsylvania, still affixed; should be removed. Good condition, with brown paper tape reinforcing edges at back, 28″ × 48″.

$20 *(Auction)*

LEMEN BROTHERS

Courtesy of The Antique Poster Collection

Lemen Brothers' World's Best Shows, ca. 1885. Black and white intaglio printed by United States Ptg. Co., Cincinnati, Ohio. Features a boxing kangaroo and a lion, bear, and baboon riding horseback, but stars "Rajah, the largest elephant that walks the earth—2 inches taller than Jumbo." In 1881 when Barnum became partners with Bailey in the Barnum & London Circus, they introduced the famous elephant Jumbo and started a war with several other circuses over who had the largest elephant. Rare, very good condition with exception of clipped corner, very good example of the genre, framed, 13″ × 17″.

$500–$600

RINGLING BROTHERS AND BARNUM & BAILEY

Child Wonder of the World/Don't Miss Mister Martin, Jr., ca. late 1940s. RBB & B poster. Colorfully realistic portrait of a child prodigy performer. Good condition, taped edges, horizontal 41″ × 36″.

$75–$100

Durbar of Delhi, 1934. RBB & B lithographic poster printed by Central Printing & Illinois Litho. Great colorful image showing 13 elephants and Indian riders. Very good condition, linen-mounted, horizontal 28″ × 21″.

$200–$300

Francis Brunn/Greatest Juggler the World Has Ever Known. RBB & B poster. Full-length portrait display of amazing juggling and balancing skills; in red, yellow, pink, and black against a strong blue background. Very good condition, 21″ × 27″.

$150–$200

Great Alzanas. RBB & B poster. Four high-wire daredevils; in yellow, green, blue, black, and flesh tones against a bright red background. Very good condition, horizontal 27″ × 20″.

$75–$100

Holidays, 1940s. RBB & B poster. A bright-faced clown with red nose promotes the great American circus; orange, red, green, yellow, blue against a deep mottled brown background. Mint condition, horizontal 28″ × 19″.

$350 (Auction)

The Incomparable Alfred Court, Master Trainer, ca. 1941. RBB & B poster. Portrait of the great animal trainer in the ring, with wild cats on their perches and a leopard on his shoulder. Good condition, horizontal 41″ × 27″.

$250–$350

Incredible Unus/The Talk of the Universe. RBB & B poster. Man in top hat balances on one finger on a ball; in yellow, light green, blue, black, and pink. Very good condition, 20″ × 27″.

$150–$200

Jenny Rooney and Her Beautiful Aerial Gymnastic Ballet, 1935. RBB & B lithographic poster printed by Erie Litho, showing 14 images of the performers gracefully climbing ladders and swinging from the trapeze. Very good condition, horizontal, 42″ × 28″.

$200–$225

Old King Cole and Mother Goose, ca. 1943. RBB & B poster, signed G. H. For the Norman Bell Geddes spectacular, the only circus presentation ever created by the great American industrial designer. A richly colored design of clowns in delightful 17th-century costumes. Very good condition, linen-mounted, horizontal 41″ × 28″.

$350–$400

Ringling Brothers and Barnum & Bailey, 1940s. Spotlight shines on two dancing elephants "in an original ballet/composed by Igor Stravinsky/ staged by George Balanchine!" In tones of blue with yellow, brown, pink, red, black. Rare, fine condition, linen-mounted, horizontal 28″ × 19″.   *$350 (Auction)*

RBB & B (No Other Title). Maxwell Caplan color image of laughing red-nosed clown against a brilliant blue field. Very good condition, 21″ × 28″.   *$75 (Auction)*

RBB & B (No Other Title). Bill Bailey design with four giraffes feeding in a field of tall grass; in orange, brown, yellow, green, red, and blue. Good condition, 21″ × 28″.   *$50–$100*

RBB & B (No Other Title). Yawning hippo surfaces from a jungle lake; in brown, red, blue, and black with yellow background. Good condition, 21″ × 28″. $50–$100

RBB & B (No Other Title). Roaring lion emerges from the right against a blue background. Good condition, with brown tape at back reinforcing edges, horizontal 28″ × 21″. $50–$60

RBB & B (No Other Title), ca. 1935. Well-known RBB & B image of the great clown seated, holding a parasol. Deep blue field, colorful impression. Very good condition, linen-mounted, 27″ × 41″.
$850 *(Auction)*

RBB & B (No Other Title), ca. 1935. Colorful stock poster printed by Erie Litho shows four clowns, mule, and duck. Very good condition, 27″ × 41″. $60 *(Auction)*

RBB & B (No Other Title), 1943. Poster by Lawson Wood, a prominent circus poster illustrator, of a family of monkeys entering the big top as they pay "Admission 2 Nuts" to an elephant; in red, yellow, blue, green, brown, and black. Good condition, horizontal 28″ × 21″. $100–$125

RBB & B (No Other Title), ca. 1950s. Image of attacking tiger and lion; in red, blue, black, brown, and orange on a bright yellow field. Very good condition, with very minor water stain at top, 28″ × 44″.
$85 *(Auction)*

Miss Rose Rieffenach, 1933. RBB & B lithographic poster printed by Illinois Litho Co., for the "Hungarian Queen of Equestrianism," shown posing with her white horse. Very good condition, linen-mounted, 27″ × 41″. $250–$300

World's Biggest Menagerie. RBB & B poster designed by Bill Bailey. Charging rhino emerges from a yellow-green jungle landscape. Very good condition, with small repaired tear, horizontal 28″ × 20″.

$40 *(Auction)*

SELLS-FLOTO CIRCUS

Rose Millette, 1932. Lithographic poster printed by Illinois Litho. A cameo portrait of the equestrienne along with a shot of her in the ring receiving flowers from a clown. Similar poses were used by other bareback riders as early as 1910 in Barnum & Bailey posters. Fine condition, horizontal 42″ × 28″. $300–$350

WALLACE BROS. CIRCUS

Courtesy of Poster Mail Auction Company

Wallace Bros./World's Largest Circus. Three elephants with their trunks raised and a clown; in red, yellow, blue, brown, and green. Fine condition, with Bill Posters & Billers union stamp, 28″ × 41″.

$40 *(Auction)*

Wallace Bros. Circus. The word "CIRCUS" in giant letters on and around which dozens of performers are leaping, dancing, and lion-taming. Good condition, horizontal 41″ × 28″. $75–$100

Wallace Bros./World's Largest Circus. Four trapeze artists and a tight-rope walker all in mid-air. Very good condition, horizontal 41″ × 28″. $80–$120

Note: *The following entries are listed alphabetically by artist name.*

ANONYMOUS

Untitled, ca. 1880s. Lithographic in reds, greens, yellow, pink, blue, violet, and flesh tones. Twelve acrobats in action, filling scene; square stone wall on left, circle of interior scene on right. Fine condition, very good example of color lithography for the circus, linen-mounted, horizontal 38″ × 27½″. $500–$700

I. DOLA

Princesse de Cirque, ca. 1930. Brightly printed Art Deco-era poster of striking woman in red dress, feathered hat, being pursued by masked hero on horseback. Very good condition, linen-mounted, 32″ × 46″. $300–$400

ADOLPH FRIEDLÄNDER

Untitled. Lithograph printed by Friedländer Litho, Germany. Depicts a troupe of 13 performing polar bears of all ages; great wit, great color. Mint condition, linen-mounted, horizontal 74″ × 54″. $1,000 (Auction)

LUCIEN LEFEVRE

Kangourou Boxeur, 1893. Delightful image of bare-chested mustached gent engaged in pugilistics with gloved 'roo. Fine condition, with some restoration at old folds, linen-mounted, 33″ × 47″. $375 (Auction)

HERBERT LEUPIN

Knie, ca. 1956. For the circus that year in Switzerland, a colorful jack-in-the-box clown with the letters K-N-I-E balanced on his knee. Mint condition, 36″ × 50″. $550 (Auction)

VAUDEVILLE AND
THEATER POSTERS

When one thinks of cabaret posters, one might immediately think of French posters for the Moulin Rouge, Josephine Baker, and Mistinguett. Executed by some of the best artists of the Art Nouveau and Art Deco periods in France and other countries, many of these have passed into the realm of "artists' posters." (You can find many of them listed under specific artists in the chapters of this guide dealing with posters of European countries.) Theater posters, too, have a noble artistic heritage, such as Mucha's elaborate designs for Sara Bernhardt.

However, there is a whole arena of English and American theater and vaudeville posters from the turn of the century, which today is still a good place to start for the beginning collector. Prices in this area have remained somewhat reasonable, even though in many cases these posters are quite rare. In addition, numerous highly collectible American theater and Broadway posters have been created over the past six decades, although one should avoid the "souvenir" poster editions, printed in the thousands, for most of today's Broadway musicals such as *Annie* and *A Chorus Line*. In the latter case, there have even been posters issued that were never used to promote either the Broadway or touring company performances of *A Chorus Line*.

Numerous influences resulted in the very American art form that is the Broadway musical. Traditions from the dramatic stage, opera and operetta, the cabaret, vaudeville, and follies all contributed to its development.

While the dramatic stage was also flourishing, at the turn of the century the circus was by far the most popular form of entertainment. Large circuses attracted record crowds who followed their parades through the streets of hometown America (see also the chapter on "Circus Posters"). In Europe, as the cabarets grew into larger-scale theaters on the Champs Elysées, the evening's entertainment soon featured circus-type acts by jugglers, acrobats, and even trapeze artists. A new form of entertainment, called follies, which most often featured a chorus line, would also become popular. Vaudeville or variety theater was being created.

Opera and operetta were among the most highly regarded forms of musical entertainment (see also the special section on French Opera Posters), and in England, no form of operetta was more popular than Gilbert and Sullivan. Called the most enduring of all Victorian entertainments, Gilbert and Sullivan operettas are performed more frequently than any other theatrical works with the possible exception of Shakespeare.

In 1990, the Morgan Pierpoint Library in New York City launched an outstanding exhibition of Gilbert and Sullivan memorabilia that included several posters from their large permanent collection of over 75,000 items. While no other Gilbert and Sullivan troupe will ever be as sought after as the D'Oyly Carte Opera Company, it is still possible to collect fine examples of Gilbert and Sullivan posters, especially those from touring British stock theater companies.

Between 1870 and 1900, the American theater developed at a phenomenal pace. New means of advertising attracted new audiences from this country's rapidly expanding population. The Library of Congress reports that by 1900 there were more than five hundred touring attractions and thousands of theaters and "opera houses" across the country as the West was opened up by the expansion of railroad travel.

By the turn of the century, many vaudeville performers and theater troupes had stock posters printed to which a "date strip" could be added to announce local performances. Harder to find are those posters which were designed specifically for a certain engagement, as they were distributed in very small quantities, usually only within the vicinity of the theater itself.

The same holds true of most early American vaudeville, theatrical, and musical performances, as well as most Broadway shows up until the mid-1950s, when posters for performances began having a much broader distribution throughout metropolitan and suburban areas. For example, with the exception of a musical benefit concert for World War I veterans in 1921, Gino Francesconi, archivist for Carnegie

Hall, reports an extremely difficult time locating original posters for performances and musical presentations that took place there.

The identity of most of the artists who created early theater and vaudeville posters has been lost, although there are some notable exceptions. Collectors should look for well-designed and printed examples by famous lithographers. Many of the same printing companies which produced these posters were known for their work with circus, magic, and other forms of entertainment, such as Friedländer in Germany and Strobridge and Erie Litho in the United States. Another printing company to watch for is National Printing and Engraving, which created stunning posters for numerous theatrical productions in New York City before World War I.

Certain theater posters from as recently as the 1970s are also sought after. For example, works by Paul Davis for New York theaters and for the Lincoln Center are highly prized, although still affordable. (See also the chapter entitled "Contemporary Poster Publishers and Patrons" for more on Lincoln Center posters.)

WHERE TO GO TO SEE THEATER POSTERS

Many of the same museums which have large collections of circus, magic, and other forms of entertainment posters also have vaudeville and theater posters. Already mentioned in those chapters are The Museum of the City of New York, The Billy Rose Theater Collection at the New York Public Library, and the New York Historical Society. In addition, Harvard University and The Library of Congress have extremely large and impressive collections of theater posters. (See Resource Guide for museum listings.)

PRICE LISTINGS

VAUDEVILLE POSTERS

Note: *See the chapter "Important Notes on the Price Listings" for more information on prices given. Many vaudeville posters were created anonymously, and they are listed below in alphabetical order by the name of the vaudeville act.*

AVOLO MIDGETS

Ambassadeurs, ca. 1910. Lithograph printed by Ch. Levy, Paris, for the Champs Elysées appearance of this novelty act. Good condition, linen-mounted, 23‴ × 32″. $130 (Auction)

LARRY BENNER'S FANTASIES OF 1929

Larry Benner's Fantasies of 1929. Poster printed by Donaldson Litho of a lovely chorus girl with pink stocking and an elaborate headdress; in pink, yellow, blue, green, and red. Excellent condition, 20″ × 28″. $100 (Auction)
                    $250–$300

LES CHARLESKY

Les Charlesky, ca. 1905. Artist: Latscha. Lithographic poster printed by Affiches Latscha, Paris, for the "celebrated singers and fantasy comedians." A woman in Edwardian dress, carrying a parasol, catches the eye of a gentleman as she strolls through the park. Very good condition, 32″ × 47″. $450–$500

CHARL'XM

"*Le Pierrot Chanteur*, ca. 1905. Artist: A. Dupuis. Lithographic poster designed by the printer for the "Singing Clown." The face of Pierrot looks out from a circle. Fair condition, 32″ × 47″. $400–$450

MR. AND MRS. STUART DARROW

Funny Shadows, ca. 1915. Red and black poster, possibly produced by stencil or silk-screen, printed by Donaldson Litho Co., Newport, Kentucky. The Darrows on each side of a screen on which are projected fabulous shadow figures. Linen-mounted, good condition, approx. 27¾″ × 22¼″. $300–$350

THE AL. G. FIELD BIG MINSTRELS

The Cornallas, Lady & Gentlemen Acrobats in a Marvelous Exhibition of Athletic Agility, Engaged at a Weekly Salary of $1,000, ca. 1910. Lithograph printed by Donaldson Litho., Cincinnati. A number of acrobats, all in white, perched upon each other's shoulders or flying through the air. Linen-mounted, approx. 27¾″ × 41¾″.

$300–$350

LES FRÈRES CELMARS

Les Frères Celmars, ca. 1910. Lithographic poster for this balancing act called "Unique en leur Genre." Black and white design with red lettering. Good condition, 31″ × 47″. $110 (Auction)

THE LAURETTIS

Originals Gentlemen Acrobates, ca. 1910. Lithograph printed by E. Delanchy, Paris. Vignettes of the two Laurettis in various acrobatic positions. Linen-mounted, approx. 41¼″ × 29¼″. $300–$325

PICKMAN

Pickman, ca. 1888. Lithographic poster featuring Pickman, a famous mind-reader, known for solving crimes through telepathy. Good condition, some restoration, 37″ × 50″. $200–$250

PLESSIS

The Man with 36 Heads. French lithographic portrait on thin orange paper of impersonator with inset drawings as Napoleon and Nelson. Good condition, 24″ × 33″. $75–$95

PROF. HARRY DE ROSA

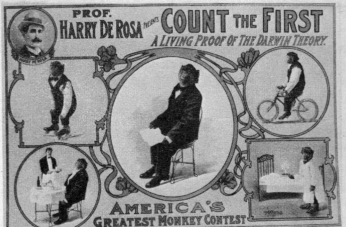

Courtesy of Poster Mail Auction Company

Count the First/A Living Proof of the Darwin Theory. Scarce Donaldson Litho poster with vignettes of a monkey act mimicking human activities, with nice Art Nouveau embellishments. Fine condition, linen-mounted, horizontal 41″ × 28″. $200 (Auction)

ROBERTYS

Robertys Equilibriste de Force, ca. 1900. Belgian poster for unusual balancing act shows large bust with smaller drawings of various tricks. Very good condition, folio folds, 33″ × 43″. $300–$350

ROBSON AND CRANE

The Knaves of Shakespeare, ca. 1890. Black and white lithograph printed by Forbes Co., Boston. A popular comedy duo of the late 1800s. Fair condition, linen-mounted, 23″ × 28¼″. $250–$450

RONCO

The Phenomenal Ronco, ca. 1910. Muscular performer in his "Grande specialty act" at "The Meddlessex Opital of London—modele of Casino de Paris"; American flag dominates and surrounds him. Very good condition, linen-mounted, 23″ × 34″. $800 (Auction)

Les Waltons, ca. 1925. Artist: Finot. For the marionette troupe, shows Josephine Baker, Chevalier, Harold Lloyd, Chaplin, others, all as marionettes. Very good condition, linen-mounted, 45″ × 61″.

$350 (Auction)

THEATER POSTERS

> *Note:* See the chapter "Important Information on the Price Listings" for more information on prices given. Theater and cabaret posters can also be found listed under many specific artists in the price listings following chapters on European countries.

ANONYMOUS

From the author's collection (Photo by Robert Four)

Believe Me, Xantippe, by Frederick Ballard, ca. 1915. Lithographic poster printed by National Printing & Engraving Co., New York. Depicts a scene from the play in bold, expressionist graphics and bright colors. Mint condition, 28″ × 42″. $400–$450

Ben-Hur, 1906. Lithographic poster printed by Strobridge Litho, featuring a vignette from the fourth act of the play, for the Klaw and Erlanger "Stupendous Production." Very good condition, linen-mounted, 22″ × 28″. $350–$400

Bronson Howard's Greater Shenendoah, ca. 1890s. Lithograph in blue, red, yellow, brown, flesh tones. Soldiers in every sheet, details and colors are crisp. Rare, fine condition, an excellent example of early American theater posters, shrink-wrapped, 77″ × 109½″.

$15,000–$20,000

A *Daughter of Cuba*, by Jean Mawson, ca. 1910. Lithographic poster printed by Erie Litho Co. A young Red Cross woman in a trench holding an American flag, surrounded by dead Spanish soldiers and victorious American soldiers. Very good condition, linen-mounted, approx. 28″ × 42″.

$350–$400

Davy Crockett, ca. 1870, starring Edwin F. Mayo. Lithographic poster printed by Courier Litho Co., Buffalo. Detailed and colorful depiction of Crockett and woman on his horse; in yellow, white, flesh tones, blue, brown, green, pink. Good condition, a very collectible poster, linen-mounted, horizontal 27¾″ × 20″.

$400–$550

Garrett O'Magh, 1901. Lithographic poster printed by Strobridge Litho and featuring actor Chauncey Olcott in a play aimed at the Irish immigrant community; shows the star with five little children as he sings "Paddy's Cat." Very good condition, linen-mounted, 27″ × 41″.

$300–$400

The Gondoliers, ca. 1915. British, stock, theatrical lithographic poster for Gilbert and Sullivan operetta shows a smiling older dandy with cane; in green, black, yellow, and red. Mint condition, a very good example of theatrical stock posters, 20″ × 30″.

$150–$175

How Hopper Was Side-Tracked, 1906. Lithographic poster printed by National Printing & Engraving Co., New York. A drawing room scene with men fighting and women swooning. Good condition, linen-mounted, 28″ × 42″.

$300–$350

Hoyt's—A Bunch of Keys—Polished Up to Date, ca. 1895. Lithographic poster printed by Forbes Co., Boston. A busy hotel lobby scene with people rushing up stairs and through the door. Fine condition, a good example of early theater advertising, framed, 26″ × 41″.

$450–$500

Humanity, by Sutton Vane, ca. 1890s. Lithographic poster printed by Springer & Welty Co. Two swordsmen on horses battle, while a third sits terrified behind one of them. Excellent technique, dynamic movement, sharp images, fine detail. Good condition, linen-mounted, 26½″ × 40″. $700–$900

Iolanthe, ca. 1930. British, stock, theatrical lithographic poster for touring Gilbert and Sullivan troupe pictures young girl; in blue, red, yellow, green, and black. Fine condition, Chartex-backed, 20″ × 30″. $100–$150

Julia Arthur. Lithographic poster printed by J. Ottmann Litho Co., Puck Bldg., New York. Close-up portrait of the beautiful actress with jewels around neck; in green, reds, orange, yellow, flesh tones, blues, with gold background. Painterly technique, delicate and precise. Very good condition, framed, 19″ × 23½″. $1,200–$1,500

Courtesy of Stephen Ganeles

The Mikado, ca. 1915. British, stock, theatrical lithographic poster for the Gilbert and Sullivan musical play features a close-up of a very Western-looking actress in Japanese dress and hairdo with a snow-capped mountain in the distance. Mint condition, a very good example of Gilbert and Sullivan stock posters, 20″ × 30″.

$125–$150

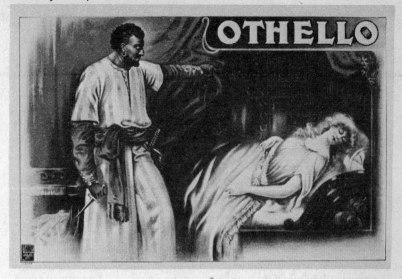

Othello, ca. 1915. British, stock, theatrical lithographic poster of Othello, dagger in hand, pulling aside the bed curtain to gaze at the sleeping Desdemona. Mint condition, horizontal 30″ × 20″.

$175–$200

The Stronger Sex, 1907. Lithographic poster featuring a scene from the drama, "direct from the Apollo Theater London." Good condition with border damage, linen-mounted, 27″ × 41″.   *$125 (Auction)*

Who is She?, ca. 1900. Lithographic poster printed by Stafford & Co. of Great Britain. Mustached masked executioner attired in Mephistophelean red rests his ax upon the block, awaiting his next victim. The smoke from his cigarette forms ghostly images of anguished victims; in red, blue, black, yellow, brown. Fine condition, 20″ × 30″.

$150–$200

H. BRODSKY

Monna Vanna, by Maeterlinck, ca. 1910. Stock lithographic poster with powerful design of two men walking together through a curtain, effectively suggesting the symbolist imagery inherent in this 1902 play; in red, green, black on white paper. Very good condition, 20″ × 30″. $175–$200

C. BRUNET

Courtesy of Butterfield & Butterfield

Aurigemma Teatro Novedades, ca. 1900. Lithographic poster printed by Henrich, Barcelona. Good condition, linen-mounted, shrink-wrapped, 27½″ × 40″.   *$225 (Auction)*

PAUL DAVIS

The Cherry Orchard, 1978. A Paul Davis classic portrait design for the Lincoln Center production of the Chekhov play. Very good condition, linen-mounted, 41″ × 81″. $300–$400

For Colored Girls Who Have Considered Suicide When the Rainbow is Enuf, 1977. Portrait poster using a subway-tile background for graffiti lettering. Very good condition, linen-mounted, 41″ × 81″.
                                         $400–$450

All price ranges represent the retail value.

Courtesy of Poster Mail Auction Company

Henry V, 1976. Features Paul Rudd in the title role in the Delacorte Theater production given as part of the 20th anniversary of free Shakespeare performances in New York's Central Park. Very good condition, 30″ × 40″. $200–$250

Courtesy of Poster Mail Auction Company

Three Penny Opera, 1976. Haunting portrait of Raul Julia; one of the true classics of American theatrical poster design for the performances at the Vivian Beaumont Theater at Lincoln Center. Very good condition, linen-mounted, three-sheet, 41″ × 81″. $400–$450

DUDLEY HARDY

The Geisha, ca. 1900. Lithographic poster showing an actress in Japanese costume for the production at Daly's Theater by Mr. George Edwards' Company. Good condition, linen-mounted, 19" × 29".

$200 (Auction)

GEORGE MCMANUS

Bringing Up Father, ca. 1925. Rare poster for the musical done as a cartoon of four men in evening dress getting hot dogs from a street vendor as they sit at a curb. Very good condition, linen-mounted, 20" × 28".

$225 (Auction)
$500–$600

LUCIEN METIUET

Cyrano de Bérgerac, 1898. Lithograph printed by Verneau, Paris, signed in the block. Full profile of Cyrano in battle. Very good condition, linen-mounted, 30¾" × 90".

$1,500–$2,000

GUY VENTOUILLAC

Courtesy of Stephen Ganeles

Bobino, 1973. Offset poster featuring Ventouillac's photograph of Josephine Baker in her final comeback performances, arms upraised, in a lace/net costume and huge plumed headdress. Very good condition, 32" × 47".

$100–$150

MARCEL VERTES

Courtesy of Stephen Ganeles

Simone Frévalles dans "La Malibran," ca. 1925. Lithographic poster depicting the actress in a flapper dress, with long necklaces and wrist bangles. Fine condition, a very good example of theater personality poster, 32″ × 47″. $600–$700

CINEMA POSTERS

By Katherine A. Harper

Katherine Harper is a writer and editor from Cleveland, Ohio. She has been collecting motion picture posters for many years, specializing in newspaper and/or crime material with an emphasis on lobby cards from 1925–1946. She has a special interest in players Charles Bickford, Dan Duryea, and many lesser character actors. Write: 2885 Pease Drive # 226, Rocky River, OH 44116.

In early 1989, a movie poster dealer purchased three "Our Gang" rerelease one-sheets at a memorabilia store. These aren't especially rare; ordinarily, he wouldn't have paid them much attention, but the $5 price tag was more than he could resist. He was able to resell one of them the same afternoon, at a $25 profit. The purchaser, in turn, resold the $5 poster a few days later . . . for $75.

Such skyrocketing prices are not uncommon. This, plus the public's growing awareness of motion picture paper's variety and beauty, has made it *the* poster collectible of the era. Both movie buffs and investors are taking notice.

POSTER STYLES

Cinema posters were first produced in Europe in the late 1800s to advertise the nickelodeon wonders of Georg Melies and the Lumiere Brothers. The earliest issues were letterpress lists of titles, sometimes called broadsides. Those with illustrations usually pictured the delighted reactions of audiences rather than the films themselves.

Shortly after the turn of the century, American lithographers began a trade in this unique advertising item. Cleveland, Ohio, became the unchallenged "Movie Poster Capital of the World": a dozen top-class poster printing firms flourished there through the 1960s, including the Otis, Continental, ABC, and Morgan Lithograph Companies. (Of these "Golden Age" plants, only Continental continues to produce movie posters.) Other well-known printers of cinema posters are the Tooker Lithograph Company and the H. C. Miner Company of New York.

As with other advertising items, movie posters were produced in a variety of standard sizes. The most popular was and is the *one-sheet*, a single piece measuring $27'' \times 41''$. Other common sizes are the $14'' \times 36''$ *insert*, sometimes erroneously called an *insert card*; the $22'' \times 28''$ *half-sheet*, and others whose names show their size relative to a one-sheet: *three-sheet* ($41'' \times 81''$, printed in two sections), *six-sheet* ($81'' \times 81''$, three sections), and *twelve-, twenty-four-, and ninety-six-sheets* (billboard sizes). These main posters may come in as many as four versions each, identified by the letters "A," "B," "C," or "D" in the lower margin.

A *caveat to the collector:* when purchasing posters sight unseen, be sure to ask the seller the style letter. It may be worth your while. A good example of the potential difference is the one-sheet for John Huston's 1950 caper classic *The Asphalt Jungle.* Style B pictures the entire cast, including two shots of Marilyn Monroe. Style A, however, shows only a brick wall!

Lobby cards, $11'' \times 14''$, were usually printed in sets of one *title card* and seven *scene cards*. The title card is generally the most attractive of a set and includes a list of the major cast members, director, and technicians. In many cases, it is a reduction of the half-sheet poster. Scene cards contain photos from the movie and often handsome border art derived from the title card. Some lobby sets, notably those printed after World War II and/or issued by RKO or Paramount, have no title card and contain eight scene cards. Others may be in sets of nine or ten (e.g., Disney) or, as in the case of Lon Chaney's *The Phantom of the Opera*, eighteen. Silent era cards are in sepia or black and white; those from the major studios may be hand-colored or heliotyped in shades of blue, yellow, and brown. *Jumbo lobby cards*

(14″ × 17″) have no white border and are printed in vibrant colors.

Lobby cards bear their studio's hallmarks. Those from early Goldwyn pictures can be baffling to the collector, as the name of the film was omitted from all but the title card. Fox and a number of independent studios released lobby cards measuring 7″ × 9″, 8″ × 10″, and other odd sizes until the late 1920s. Silent era cards may contain dialogue or descriptive captions, a practice continued by MGM well into the 1940s.

These captions were often unintentionally hilarious, as in the 1919 drama *Thunderbolt:* "He had denied motherhood to her—the roaring heavens outside had returned his hereditary storm rage which made his mind a blank—*now* was her chance!"

Warner Brothers/First National produced "lobbies" on both mat stock and linen-textured paper during its "Golden Age." The latter, though easily damaged, are considered the more collectible.

Lobbies picturing cattle stampedes, players' backs, very long shots, etc., are referred to by collectors as *dead cards*. These can usually be purchased for very little. Don't dismiss them as trash! I recently paid $10 sight unseen for a dead card from *The Secret Six* (1931), described in a catalog as "lab scene, unknown men." One of the "unknowns," kneeling to examine a dead body, is Clark Gable. This small detail increases the card's value by almost 3,000%.

Window cards (average 14″ × 22″), *jumbo window cards* (22″ × 28″), and *mini window cards* (8″ × 14″) were, as their names imply, exhibited in shop windows. These posters have an area of white space above the design on which theaters imprinted their name and screening dates. This was often trimmed in order to fit the card into a standard frame. On occasion, e.g., *Dirigible* (1930), window cards were produced in eye-catching jigsaw shapes.

The above sizes are representative of American posters only. Foreign releases come in a myriad of styles, shapes, and sizes. Each country has its own standards. For a complete description of the varieties among European, Asian, and Central and South American paper, see Gregory J. Edwards' *The International Film Poster* (see Bibliography).

Beware the "OC" or "Other Company" poster! From cinema's earliest days, "pirate" printers produced their own, less expensive paper for major releases. Though often attractive, Other Company material is worth only a fraction of that produced by the studio. OC posters and lobbies do not feature the name of the studio or production company. Larger pieces may have a minuscule disclaimer in a box at lower right. These are not to be confused with *stock posters*, which have an all-purpose design of a cartoon character, cowboy star, etc., and were used for every release, only the title being changed.

Posters available for any single title are pictured in its four- to eighty-page "pressbook" or "campaign book," an informative—and sometimes lavish—catalog sent to theater owners. The pressbook can be a handy research aid to the collector or film student as it contains not only depictions of available paper and clip-out newspaper ads, but also potential exploitation ideas, commercial product tie-ins, and notes on the players and the making of the film. Though technically not poster material, pressbooks are themselves collectible items.

The Margaret Herrick Library of the Academy of Motion Picture Arts and Sciences in Hollywood recently confirmed the originality of a *Hell's Angels* three-sheet through a microfilmed 1930 pressbook. The poster had been sold as a rerelease item because, though the signed Hap Hadley art was similar to that on originals, there was no indication of distribution by United Artists. The AMPAS pressbook pictures two styles of three-sheet—one of which was the item in question. This confirmation more than tripled the poster's value.

The last two digits of a cinema poster's year of release are printed in its lower right-hand corner. The letter "R" before the date indicates a reissue, as do the statements "A 20th-Century Fox Encore Presentation," "An MGM Family Classic," or "A Realart Film Release" (Sound Era only). Duo-tone posters, photographic pieces printed in one color, are nearly always rereleases. Don't let their dissimilarity to the originals discourage you from buying; a 1950s *Little Caesar* duo-tone one-sheet, though unattractive, is worth over $150.

ARTISTIC DESIGN

The vast majority of movie posters were designed by studio artists, whose identities are unknown today. In many cases, human figures were painted by one person, backgrounds by another, and the lettering by still another. Photographs of a New York lithograph company ca. 1935 show workers using the same cut-out, pre-painted hands and faces on poster after poster.

Known contributors to the art of the movie poster are generally better recognized for their popular work. John Held, Jr.'s flapper and college-boy caricatures appear on a number of "flaming youth" posters of the Jazz Age. Alberto Varga and Hap Hadley's cheesecake poses of popular starlets graced the paper of the 1930s and 1940s. Norman Rockwell was responsible for strong American portraits on the posters for such films as *Along Came Jones* (1945) and *The Magnificent Ambersons* (1941). The grotesque geometric figures of Saul Bass gave a distinctive look to paper of the 1950s and 1960s, including that for *Vertigo, Saint Joan,* and *The Man With the Golden Arm.*

Canadian posters for U.S. titles were usually printed by American houses simultaneously with those for domestic release. The only real differences between a Canadian and a U.S. poster are the former's title—which reflects that of the British release—and the censor's stamp that invariably appears in the center of the main image. If the movie did not meet the censor's approval, a large white sticker is affixed directly to the poster.

STARTING YOUR OWN COLLECTION

Because of the vast amount of available material, collectors of cinema posters tend to limit themselves to a particular topic, player, director, genre, or even studio. For example, I specialize in lobbies from silent era–1940s newspaper and gangster pictures, plus a number of talented, but little-known actors such as Russell Hopton and Noel Madison.

Some collectors are *completists* whose goal is to obtain every possible item in their chosen field. They may narrow their scope to one or two major players (Barbara Stanwyck, Richard Dix, Clara Bow) or character actors (Barton MacLane, Thelma Todd, Warner Richmond). Their choice of directors ranges from the legendary John Ford and Billy Wilder to cult favorites Edgar G. Ulmer and John Waters. Topics run the gamut from steam locomotives to ventriloquist's dummies to men in women's clothing. It's easy to see that in the motion picture poster business, collecting is purely a matter of taste.

Over the past decade, many people have found their poster collections evolving from a weekend hobby into a full-time business. Morris Everett, Jr., a fund-raising consultant, is the owner of The Last Moving Picture Company, a poster shop in Cleveland, Ohio. He proudly states that his private collection of cinema posters is the largest outside a museum in the United States. This is due not only to his dedication and hard work, but to his atypical goal: to own one good piece from every movie ever made—*every* movie, from classics like *The 39 Steps* and *Morocco* to the low-budget *Sidelong Glances of a Pigeon Kicker*.

His collection, which overflows its warehouse, contains over 1,500,000 still photographs, lobby cards, and posters of every size. His favorite pieces are the title card from *Showboat* (1932) and the original half-sheet from Walt Disney's *Pinocchio*. Why? "The colors are super, so super," he murmurs, clearly in love.

In his twenty-nine years of collecting, Everett has become expert in predicting trends and providing advice to the novice. "Today's market is soft," he comments. "It won't stay that way, but for now, it's soft. An actor is suddenly in demand—like James Cagney a few years ago—and everybody drags out all their Cagney material. The Cagney collectors buy up all the pieces they need, and suddenly nobody wants Cagney anymore. Not at a high price, anyway. There's a glut of material. Even John Wayne's prices are a little soft right now."

Everett predicts that an upcoming trend will be paper from the initial films in a successful series, e.g., *Nightmare on Elm Street* or *Star Trek*. He adds, "Those posters always sell better when the latest in the series comes out. Trouble is, what happens when they stop making those movies?" Players to watch include James Stewart and Douglas Fairbanks, Jr. "Over the past few years, Stewart's become one of the family," he explains. "He's somebody to grow old with. I think he's going to be very, very big."

The recent upsurge in prices shouldn't discourage the beginning collector. New material will always be inexpensive, and no matter how high the market goes, the collector can find occasional treasure troves in flea markets and people's attics. A beginner shouldn't expect to get a bargain on pieces greatly in demand, especially from shops dealing specifically in movie memorabilia. Cinema posters are big business and, in that setting, should be treated as such.

The 1990s have brought about a number of new trends. Shop owners, once deluged with requests for "cult" actors such as John Wayne, Shirley Temple, Marilyn Monroe, and James Dean, now report a steady trade in materials featuring less prominent stars: Donald O'Connor, Ida Lupino, Walter Brennan. Ten years ago, it was nearly impossible to find buyers for larger posters; today, three-sheets and six-sheets command hefty prices in auctions and dealer catalogs. Other current vogues are the "bad girl," motorcycle, and juvenile delinquent movies of the 1950s and 1960s, science fiction, and the film noir, a moody, angst-ridden style of post-war crime film.

The preceding paragraphs apply almost exclusively to items from the "Golden Era" of motion pictures—and movie paper. Posters of later years are, for the most part, photographic offsets. There are no more mini window cards or jumbo lobbies, no stone lithographs. Posters are put together quickly and cheaply—and look it. Today's graphics are often computer-generated and lack the warmth of an artist's touch. Although lobby cards are still printed, title cards are a thing of the past. Little or no effort is expended on side art.

This is not to say that there is no longer any motion picture art of merit. The one-sheet for *Tucker: A Man and His Dream* (1988) features a strong chalk portrait that captures the flavor of post-war America. An artist named Amsel has attracted notice for his work on, among others, the posters for the 1978 version of *The Big Sleep* and *Raiders of the Lost Ark*. You should note, however, that all of these movies take place in the 1930s and 1940s; in each case, the artist was deliberately trying to invoke the style of the period. A few other recent pieces are pretty in their own way, but no poster of the past two decades can hold a candle to the early issues—not one.

A final word of caution to the collector: movie posters are a lovely and unique form of art. Unfortunately, where there is art, forgers follow. In recent years, a number of clever copy posters have been passed off as originals, the most well-known among dealers being a set of lobby cards from *A Hard Day's Night*. An unknown "entrepreneur" has produced several sets on 20-year-old stock that not only look but feel like the real thing. His only mistake was not noticing that the originals had at one time been put up with thumbtacks. The holes show up clearly in the reproductions but, when the cards are held up, no light shines through. As always, *caveat emptor*.

Collecting movie paper is absorbing and fun, whether for a hobby or for investment purposes. Posters are waiting in cellars and old theaters, flea markets and tag sales, antique shops, and attics. Hundreds, perhaps thousands of items are available on any given topic.

All you have to do is go out and find them.

WHERE TO GO TO SEE CINEMA POSTERS

Several museums have outstanding collections of cinema posters, including The Library of Congress and the Margaret Herrick Library at the Academy of Motion Picture Arts and Sciences in Beverly Hills. In New York, The Billy Rose Theater Collection at the New York Public Library has a huge collection, featuring not only cinema but also stage and other popular entertainment posters.

Luckily for collectors of cinema posters, there are several major shows and conventions every year where you can see posters firsthand, which is always the best way to get to know a field of collecting.

The events are *not* specifically for poster collectors but for lovers of old films. Each has at least one exhibition room set aside for buyers and sellers of poster material. The major events are *Cinecon*, a convention for members of the National Society for Cinephiles; *Cinevent*, held over the Memorial Day weekend in Columbus, Ohio; and *Cinefest*, held in March in Syracuse, New York, under the aegis of the Syracuse Cinephile Society. Dozens of smaller conventions—some for fans of westerns, silents, etc.—are held across the United States on weekends, generally during the spring and summer months. (See Resource Guide for details of these museums, events, and societies.)

REFERENCE WORKS

In addition to *The International Film Poster* by Gregory J. Edwards already mentioned, another important reference work on cinema posters is *Reel Art: Great Movie Posters from The Golden Age of the Silver Screen* by Stephen Rebello and Richard Allen. Two excellent reference books on lobby cards are *Lobby Cards, The Classic Films* and *Lobby Cards, The Classic Comedies,* both by Kathryn Leigh Scott illustrating the outstanding Michael Hawks Collection. In addition, cinema collectors have the advantage of having several specialized newspapers and publications, including *Big Reel* and *Classic Images.* (See the special section in the Bibliography for complete references on these and other books.)

Special Focus: What's Hot?

Note: *It sometimes seems as though everything in the cinema poster field is hot. Today, just a few of the most sought-after classic movie titles and stars are:*

BY TITLE

Adventures of Sherlock Holmes, 1939

Black Cat, 1934

Black Friday, 1940

Bride of Frankenstein, 1935

Broadway Melody, 1929

Casablanca, 1942

Citizen Kane, 1941

Dracula, 1930

42nd Street, 1942

Frankenstein, 1931

Gone With the Wind, 1939

The Hound of the Baskervilles, 1939

Hunchback of Notre Dame, 1923

Invisible Man, 1933

Invisible Ray, 1935

The Jazz Singer, 1927

King Kong, 1933

Little Caesar, 1930

The Mummy, 1932

Murders in the Rue Morgue, 1931

The Raven, 1935

Wizard of Oz, 1939

BY STAR OR PRODUCER AND YEARS OF THE FILMS MOST SOUGHT AFTER

Fred Astaire/Ginger Rogers (1930s)

Humphrey Bogart (1930s to early 1940s)

James Cagney (1930s)

Frank Capra films (late 1920s to late 1940s)

Lon Chaney (early silent films to 1930)

Charlie Chaplin (early silent films to 1940)

Bette Davis (1930s)

Marlene Deitrich (1920s and 1930s)

Walt Disney films (1920s to 1950)

W. C. Fields (early silent films to 1940)

Erroll Flynn (late 1930s and early 1940s)

Clark Gable (1930s)

Greta Garbo (1920s and 1930s)

Betty Grable (1930s)

D. W. Griffith films (from as early as 1908 to 1930)

Jean Harlow (late 1920s to mid-1930s)

Alfred Hitchcock films (1925 to 1960)

Al Jolson (late 1920s to late 1930s)

Buster Keaton (1920s)
Laurel and Hardy (1920s to 1940)
Marx Brothers (1930s to 1950)
Tyrone Power (1930s)
Tarzan films (late 1920s to mid-1940s)
Shirley Temple (early 1930s)
Rudolph Valentino (early silent films to 1920s)
Eric Von Stroheim films (1920s)
John Wayne (late 1920s to late 1940s)
Mae West (1930s)

When you come across a classic poster, it's best to have a Hollywood film history guide to help determine the release date of films from the above producers and stars. Three useful reference works we've found are books on the movies, rather than books on posters: *The Great Movie Stars: The Golden Years* and *The Great Movie Stars: The International Years*, both by David Shipman, and *Rating the Movies* by the editors of *Consumer Guide*. This latter is an oversize paperback with capsule reviews and is designed to be used for selecting video-tapes or viewing TV movies, but we find it a good, quick, alphabetical reference tool for titles, dates, and stars. (See Bibliography.)

PRICE LISTINGS

Note: *See the chapter "Important Notes on the Price Listings" for more information on prices given. For an explanation of sizes (half-sheet, one-sheet, window card, etc.) and for certain terms used in the listings, see Katherine Harper's chapter on "Cinema Posters." Also note that of all the fields of poster collecting, cinema posters are changing most rapidly in terms of price. Check with a reputable dealer for the latest price on the posters which interest you the most.*

IN ALPHABETICAL ORDER BY FILM TITLE

Abbott & Costello Meet Frankenstein, 1948. Style A half-sheet poster from the comedy/horror crossover film marking the end of Universal's monster-movie cycle begun in the 1930s. Scarce, very good condition, linen-mounted, horizontal 28″ × 22″. $700 (Auction)

Abbott & Costello Meet the Keystone Cops, 1955. Half-sheet poster of Bud Abbott and Lou Costello in a very popular entry in the series. Good condition. $50–$75

Abbott & Costello Meet the Killers, 1955. Belgian poster from the movie in which Boris Karloff rules the comedy duo. Very good condition, linen-mounted, 14″ × 18″. $50 *(Auction)*

Across the Pacific, 1942. Insert depicts Humphrey Bogart wrestling a gun away from a Japanese naval officer. Very good condition, a good example of a Bogart poster. $350–$450

Adam's Rib, 1923. Title card for silent Cecil B. DeMille film with Milton Sills and Anna Q. Nilson. Rare, good condition. $75–$100

Adventures of Robin Hood (Les Aventures de Robin des Bois), French rerelease 1948. Stone lithograph presents Flynn in striking Technicolor. Very good condition, linen-mounted, 47″ × 62″. $600 *(Auction)*

The Adventures of Sherlock Holmes, 1939. One-sheet offset poster with excellent images of the girl (Ida Lupino), Watson, and Holmes in deerstalker cap. Both poster and lobby cards on this title are very scarce. Fine condition, a highly sought-after title, linen-mounted. $4,400 *(Auction)*

Same as above. Insert of Basil Rathbone and Nigel Bruce standing between Moriarty and the Crown Jewels. Rare. $4,500 *(Auction)*

Courtesy of Camden House Auctioneers

Same as above. Half-sheet poster, style A; fine colorful cameo of Basil Rathbone and Ida Lupino, similar to title lobby card. Good condition, horizontal 28″ × 22″. $3,500 *(Auction)*

Affair in Trinidad, 1952. Belgian poster featuring a sassy Rita Hayworth from the movie, also starring Glenn Ford. Linen-mounted,
14″ × 19″.   *$50 (Auction)*

African Queen, 1952. One-sheet poster with bright composite artwork
for director John Huston's splendid blend of character and adventure,
starring Humphrey Bogart and Katharine Hepburn.

                                             $600 (Auction)

After the Thin Man, 1936. Half-sheet poster of William Powell and
Myrna Loy in the second film in the series, also starring Jimmy Stewart. Colorful design features head shots of Powell, Loy, and Asta,
along with vignettes from the film. Very rare, good condition but with
some water staining and wear at creases.   *$1,500–$2,000*

Alexander Graham Bell, 1936. Title lobby card for Fox's film with
Loretta Young, Don Ameche, and Henry Fonda. Good condition.

                                             $125–$150

  Same as above. Scene card with close shot of Young and Ameche.

                                             $65–$85

Alibi, 1942. English window card with James Mason and Margaret
Lockwood. Mint condition.   *$25–$50*

All About Eve, 1950. Insert poster featuring the urbane George Sanders and the tough Bette Davis, along with young and lovely Marilyn Monroe. Very good condition, 14″ × 36″. $225 (Auction)

Same as above. 27″ × 41″. $375 (Auction)

All This and Heaven Too, 1940. French, stone lithographic poster; Bette Davis and Charles Boyer star in this sensual romance by Anatole Litvak. Linen-mounted, 47″ × 63″. $400 (Auction)

All Through the Night, 1942. Warner Brothers title card with Humphrey Bogart and Peter Lorre, with nice shot of Bogart with gun. Good condition, but with border wear and repairs. $125–$150

Same as above. Scene card with Bogart holding gun on others. Good condition. $100–$125

An American in Paris, 1951. One-sheet poster captures carefree essence of Gershwin-scored classic, winner of Best Picture Oscar, starring Gene Kelly and a young Leslie Caron. Fine condition, linen-mounted. $400 (Auction)

Same as above. Window card with beautiful colors and design, uncut and unfolded. $125–$150

Same as above. Lobby card with great close-up of Kelly and Leslie Caron. Good condition. $50–$75

Angels Over Broadway, 1940. One-sheet poster of a young Rita Hayworth appears with Douglas Fairbanks in this Gotham melodrama. $200 (Auction)

All price ranges represent the retail value.

Courtesy of Camden House Auctioneers

Angels with Dirty Faces, 1938. One-sheet poster with dazzling portraits of gangster Cagney, priest O'Brien, a sinister Bogart, and the Dead End Kids, from the classic Warner Brothers film chronicling the divergent career paths of two playmates. $4,500 *(Auction)*

Anna Christie, 1930. Lobby card for first sound film of Greta Garbo; nice colors and border design on this scene card with great close-up of Garbo and Marie Dressler. Rare, good condition with some border repair. $750–$900

Courtesy of Camden House Auctioneers

Anna Karenine, 1935. Original Belgian release poster from the film of Tolstoy's romantic tragedy starring Greta Garbo. Linen-mounted, 24″ × 33″. $1,100 *(Auction)*

Anthony Adverse, 1936. Half-sheet headlining Fredric March and Olivia de Havilland. Horizontal 28″ × 22″. $70 (Auction)

The Apartment, 1960. One-sheet with Jack Lemmon, Shirley Mac-Laine, and Fred MacMurray. Billy Wilder classic and Best Picture of 1960. Good condition. $35–$50

Arrowsmith, reissue 1944. Insert with Ronald Colman, Helen Hayes, and Myrna Loy. Pretty reissue in full color. $45–$60

Arsenic and Old Lace, 1944. Lobby card for Frank Capra classic with Cary Grant, picturing Grant tied up! Good condition. $50–$75

Same as above. One-sheet, good condition, 27″ × 41″.
$200 (Auction)

Same as above. Title card with big face of Grant. Good condition.
$175–$200

Assistant Wives, 1927. One-sheet, stone lithographic poster printed by Morgan pictures Charley Chase embroiled in kitchen warfare. Very good condition. $900 (Auction)

Atom Man vs. Superman, 1950. One-sheet poster of Kirk Alyn in one of the most famous and rarest of the serials. Beautiful comic-book artwork from chapter six—"Atom Man's Challenge." Fine condition.
$350–$450

Babes in Arms, 1939. Lobby scene card for classic puttin'-on-the-show film from MGM, depicting Judy Garland and Mickey Rooney in minstrel number. Good condition. $60–$75

Babes in Toyland, 1934. Beautiful lobby card from this rare early Laurel and Hardy feature film classic. Great colors and design with super shots of the comic stars. Fine condition. $1,350–$1,500

Babes on Broadway, 1941. One-sheet poster from the spirited Busby Berkeley-directed showcase for Judy Garland and Mickey Rooney, Hirschfeld caricature at bottom. Good condition. $425 (Auction)

Bad for Each Other, 1953. Insert poster from this film starring Charlton Heston. 14″ × 36″. $50 (Auction)

Bambi, 1948. Full set of eight lobby cards from the Disney masterpiece, billed "A Great Love Story." 14″ × 11″. $1,100 (Auction)

The Bank Dick, 1940. Lobby card from the film headlining W. C. Fields. $200 (Auction)

Barefoot Contessa, 1954. One-sheet poster with glamorous color depicting Bogart and Ava Gardner. $70 (Auction)

The Barkleys of Broadway, 1949. Three-sheet poster featuring Fred Astaire and Ginger Rogers dancing their way across the poster for this witty musical. Good condition. $550 (Auction)

Batman, 1966. One-sheet poster of Adam West in the famous feature-length film from the TV series, picturing the entire cast. Good condition, becoming harder to find. $75–$100

Beauty and the Beast, 1946. French, stone lithographic poster with delicate and expressive artwork illustrates Jean Cocteau's classic fairy tale. Linen-mounted, 48″ × 60″. $4,000–$5,000

Behold My Wife, 1920. Beautiful early Paramount half-sheet poster from this silent film features great Indian motif. Rare, good condition. $85–$110

Belle De Jour, 1967. French poster from Bunuel's sexy hit starring Catherine Deneuve. Framed, 23″ × 31″. $100 (Auction)

Belle of the Nineties, 1934. Half-sheet featuring a radiant Ms. West being toasted by a horde of well-dressed gentlemen. Paper-mounted. $600 (Auction)

Beyond the Rocks, 1922. Title lobby card for silent film with Gloria Swanson and Rudolph Valentino. Great shot of Swanson in gown and Valentino in tux. Very rare, fine condition. $650–$750

Bhowani Junction, 1955. One-sheet poster featuring a luscious full-length image of Ava Gardner. Good condition, framed. $225 (Auction)

The Big Sleep, 1946. Half-sheet poster featuring thrilling portraits of Bogart and Bacall facing off in Howard Hawks' classic Philip Marlowe film noir. Rare, good condition except for large tear, framed, 22″ × 28″. $450 (Auction)

Same as above. Scene card with shot of Bogart and Bacall with Jean Heydt. Good condition. $175–$200

The Birds, 1963. One-sheet poster for the Alfred Hitchcock classic. Hitchcock items are highly sought after by collectors, but many are still available at affordable prices. Good condition.   *$125–$150*

Same as above. Good condition, half-sheet.   *$100–$125*

Same as above. Good condition, insert.   *$100–$125*

Same as above. Good condition, lobby card set.   *$125–$150*

Birth of a Nation, rerelease 1927. Lithographic one-sheet poster from D. W. Griffith's classic feature, with stunning and explosive design. Rare, restored, linen-mounted.   *$4,000 (Auction)*

The Black Cat, 1941. Lobby card from the film headlining Basil Rathbone.   *$125 (Auction)*

The Black Swan, ca. 1940s. Fine stone lithographic one-sheet poster for international release of Tyrone Power's 1942 escapade as Morgan the Pirate, shows a variety of action scenes.   *$500 (Auction)*

Bluebeard, 1944. Insert for the film noir classic with John Carradine, directed by Edgar G. Ulmer. Hard to find, good condition. *$50–$75*

Boom Town, 1941. Lobby card with great close-up of Clark Gable and Claudette Colbert from this MGM classic. Good condition.
                                                          $125–$150

Boy Meets Girl, 1938. Beautiful linen lobby card from Warner Brothers with great shot of James Cagney, Pat O'Brien, and Frank McHugh. Good condition.   *$250–$300*

The Brain Eaters. One-sheet poster depicts woman's head with elongated teeth, empty yellow eyes, and an exposed brain—"crawling, slimy things terror-bent on destroying the world!" Very good condition, linen-mounted.   *$325–$375*

Break of Hearts, 1935. Half-sheet featuring fabulous close-ups of Hepburn and Boyer in luscious color. Horizontal 28″ × 22″.
                                                          $900 (Auction)

Breakfast at Tiffany's, 1961. One-sheet poster of Audrey Hepburn in the classic film from Blake Edwards. Good condition. *$250 (Auction)*

The Bride Wore Black, 1967. French poster featuring the ever-popular Jeanne Moreau from the film directed by Truffaut. Good condition, framed, 23″ × 30″. $100 (Auction)

The Bride Wore Red, 1937. Half-sheet poster featuring Joan Crawford, Robert Young, and Franchot Tone from MGM; great colors and design. Good condition. $250–$300

Brides of Dracula, 1960. One-sheet poster of Peter Cushing billed as the most evil blood-lusting Dracula of all! $100 (Auction)

The Bridge on the River Kwai, 1958. One-sheet poster for the David Leon classic with Alec Guinness, William Holden, and Jack Hawkins. Good condition. $100–$125

Same as above. Good condition, lobby card set. $100–$125

Bright Eyes, 1934. Half-sheet poster featuring a graphic and stylish portrait of Shirley Temple in her first star vehicle. Very good condition, heavy stock, very collectible. $900 (Auction)

Bright Eyes (Op Mot Skyene), ca. 1935. Scandinavian, stone lithographic poster presents a fetching Temple. 26″ × 38″.

$650 (Auction)

Bronze Venus, rerelease 1941. Three-sheet poster features a sultry full-length pose of the beautiful young Lena Horne. Rare, 41″ × 81″.

$300 (Auction)

The Bull-Dogger, 1924. Stunning stone lithographic one-sheet poster depicting Bill Pickett as The World's Colored Champion of the Mexican Bull Ring, from the silent era. $550 (Auction)

Same as above. Three-sheet poster, rare, linen-mounted.

$800 (Auction)

Bullets or Ballots, 1936. French, stone lithographic six-sheet poster with powerful imagery and dynamic colors from the gangster classic starring Edward G. Robinson and Humphrey Bogart. Good condition.

$650 (Auction)

The Burning Span, The Eleventh Episode of the Red Ace. Morgan three-sheet poster from this early film starring Maria Walcamp, produced by Jacques Jaccard. Fair condition, framed. $100 (Auction)

Bus Stop, 1956. One-sheet poster of Marilyn Monroe in one of her best and most famous roles. Great design of Don Murray holding Monroe around the waist as she leans over a sign containing the title and credits. Hard to find, good condition. $325 *(Auction)*

Same as above. Half-sheet, fair condition, horizontal 28″ × 22″. $150 *(Auction)*

Same as above. Lobby card with Marilyn Monroe in nightclub costume. Good condition. $60–$80

Courtesy of Camden House Auctioneers

Cabin in the Sky, 1943. Style C, legendary Hirschfeld one-sheet poster from Minelli's classic, all-black musical, stunning graphics. Very good condition, rare. $1,500 *(Auction)*

Caesar Film, Roma, ca. 1902. Artist: Ballester. Extremely early Italian film poster from the era when the movies being released had no titles. A naked girl at a Roman bath is leered at by two men in togas. Ballester continued doing film posters for another 50 years, becoming ultimately Italy's finest film poster artist. Mint condition, linen-mounted, 27″ × 39″. $300 *(Auction)*

Caine Mutiny, 1954. One-sheet poster starring Humphrey Bogart and Jose Ferrer. $175 *(Auction)*

Camelot, 1968. Six-sheet poster featuring Richard Harris and Vanessa Redgrave in the classic film. Good condition. $50–$75

Same as above. Beautiful special deluxe 12-card lobby card set measuring 12½″ × 16¼″. Very rare, good condition. $85–$110

Camille, 1936. MGM lobby card for the Greta Garbo classic, with nice shot of Garbo and Robert Taylor. Fine condition. $400–$500

Captain Kidd, 1945. Title card depicting swashbuckler Charles Laughton and Randolph Scott. Good condition. $35–$50

Captains of the Clouds, 1942. Lobby card set of eight cards featuring James Cagney on six of the eight in this Michael Curtiz Warner Brothers flying classic. Good condition. $450–$550

Careless Lady, 1932. Beautiful one-sheet, stone lithographic poster of Joan Bennett sitting pensively in a black chair, with John Boles' face in the blue hearts that float around her. Very good condition.

$250–$300

Carnal Knowledge, 1971. Foreign release poster from Mike Nichols' dark look at sexual relations in the 1970s, starring Jack Nicholson. 30″ × 40″. $75 (Auction)

Casablanca, 1943. Insert of Bogart in full color, with Bergman, Henreid, and supporting actors shown in duo-tone. Only one other size (41″ × 81″) on this title shows the same images; the standard 27″ × 41″ poster is unexciting. Offset, fine condition, one of the best collectibles of the era, 14″ × 36″. $7,700 (Auction)

Same as above. Lobby card, portrays Bogart and Bergman from one of the all-time greats, highly prized. $1,600–$2,000

Same as above, reissue 1949. Lobby card from the first reissue of this Humphrey Bogart classic, duo-tone with Bogart and Peter Lorre. Fine condition. $100–$125

Cat on a Hot Tin Roof, 1958. One-sheet poster from the Tennessee Williams classic starring Elizabeth Taylor and Paul Newman. Fantastic image of Taylor at her most beautiful. Good condition. $65–$90

The Charge of the Light Brigade, 1936. Half-sheet poster featuring illustration of "The Charge" plus romantic inset of Flynn/de Havilland. Only this size and the 14″ × 36″ on this title are in color; all other sizes/styles are duo-tone. Offset, very good condition, Japan paper, 28″ × 22″. $3,000–$5,000

Same as above. Famous portrait lobby card of Flynn and Olivia de Havilland. Linen card, very good condition. $1,000–$1,200

Same as above. Scene card shows Flynn with arm in sling. Very good condition. $850–$900

Same as above. Spanish, stone lithographic poster features a fiery action portrait of Errol Flynn, vibrant color. Linen-mounted, 27″ × 39″. $400 (Auction)

Charles Chan in Panama, 1940. Title lobby card with Sidney Toler as Charlie Chan. Good condition, except numerous tack holes in corners. $75–$100

The Chase, 1966. Six-sheet poster from the Sam Spiegel-produced film of sex and violence in the South starring Marlon Brando and Jane Fonda. $75 (Auction)

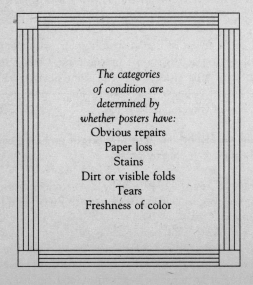

*The categories
of condition are
determined by
whether posters have:*
Obvious repairs
Paper loss
Stains
Dirt or visible folds
Tears
Freshness of color

Chicken Feed, 1927. One-sheet, Morgan, stone lithographic poster from Hal Roach's "Our Gang" pathecomedy. Extremely rare.

$2,250 (Auction)

Same as above. Three-sheet poster poses the kids lined up for a backyard magic show. Very rare and collectible. $2,250 (Auction)

China Seas, 1935. Title lobby card for MGM classic with Clark Gable, Jean Harlow, Wallace Beery, Lewis Stone, and Rosalind Russell. Beautiful colors and shots of the stars. Very rare, good condition.

$1,350–$1,500

Same as above. Scene card. Linen-mounted. $425 (Auction)

Chinatown, 1974. One-sheet poster from Roman Polanski's film noir classic with Jack Nicholson and Faye Dunaway. Very pretty artwork and design; probably the most sought-after poster from the 1970s. Hard to find, good condition. $100–$125

Citizen Kane, 1941. Title card from Welles' seminal masterpiece, explosive graphics against lush yellow background. Extremely desirable piece.   *$1,300 (Auction)*

City for Conquest, 1940. One-sheet poster features head shots of a passionate James Cagney and Ann Sheridan against a silhouetted city skyline. Very good condition, a very good Cagney poster, linen-mounted. (See color center section.)   *$1,250–$1,500*

   Same as above. Linen lobby card with great close shot of Cagney
   and Sheridan. Good condition.   *$150–$200*

City Lights, 1931. Lobby card from the Charlie Chaplin classic, with good shot of Chaplin visiting the blind girl (Virginia Cherrill). Nice colors and border design. Very rare, good condition.   *$500–$600*

Clash by Night, 1952. Half-sheet poster for the film starring Barbara Stanwyck. Horizontal 28″ × 22″.   *$200 (Auction)*

The Clock, 1945. Lobby card featuring a beautiful portrait of Judy Garland and Robert Walker. Good condition.   *$60–$90*

Conflict, 1945. Title lobby card shows Humphrey Bogart, Alexis Smith, and Sydney Greenstreet. Very good condition, a good Bogart collectible.   *$150–$200*

Conquest, 1937. Lobby card from the film featuring Greta Garbo and Charles Boyer.   *$200 (Auction)*

The Corn is Green, 1945. One-sheet poster from the film starring Bette Davis. Paper-mounted. $275 (Auction)

Corsair, 1931. Half-sheet poster from the film starring Chester Morris. Fair condition, horizontal 28″ × 22″. $90 (Auction)

Cover Girl, 1944. Half-sheet poster from the film featuring Rita Hayworth and Gene Kelly. $100 (Auction)

Courtesy of Camden House Auctioneers

The Covered Wagon, 1923. Style A, Morgan one-sheet poster for James Cruze's epic adventure. An important poster from the first big western. 27″ × 41″. $1,200 (Auction)

The Creature from the Black Lagoon, 1954. French, stone lithographic poster depicting Julia Adams' underwater seduction by the gill man. Linen-mounted, 24″ × 31″. $200 (Auction)

The Creature Walks Among Us, 1956. Half-sheet poster from the film featuring Jeff Morrow and Rex Reason. Horizontal 28″ × 22″.
                                                        $150 (Auction)

The Curse of Frankenstein, 1957. One-sheet poster featuring Christopher Lee and Peter Cushing in the first of the Hammer line of horror films, with image of Frankenstein's gruesome face. Rare, good condition. $65–$90

Cyrano de Bérgerac, 1951. Insert featuring Jose Ferrer in the role which won him the Best Actor Oscar; very pretty design and colors. Good condition. $75–$100

Same as above. Good condition, title lobby card. $30–$50

Dames, 1934. One-sheet poster from the Busby Berkeley musical, depicts two leggy dames holding the title up, also photo headshots of the cast including Ruby Keeler, Dick Powell, and Joan Blondell. Very good condition, a great collectible, linen-mounted. (See color center section.) $3,000–$4,000

The Damned, 1969. Italian release poster from Luchino Visconti's study of decadence in the Third Reich. 27″ × 37″. $25 (Auction)

Dancing Lady, 1933. Title lobby card from classic MGM film with Clark Gable, Joan Crawford, Fred Astaire (his first film), and the Three Stooges. Good condition. $975–$1,100

The Dark Command, 1940. Title lobby card from the film featuring Claire Trevor and John Wayne. $325 (Auction)

The Dark Corner, 1946. One-sheet, stone lithographic poster featuring Mark Stevens, Lucille Ball, and William Bendix in one of the best of the Fox films noir. Man peering mysteriously through Venetian blinds; Lucille Ball stands outside. Good condition. $300–$500

Same as above. Insert, good condition. $125–$150

Same as above. Lobby card with Stevens and Bendix, good condition. $25

Dark Passage, 1947. Three-sheet offset poster, and the only Bogart/ Bacall collaboration in which the American posters are in color. Only one other size for this film (14″ × 36″) shows this image of Bogart and Bacall with the San Francisco Bay Bridge in the background. Fine condition, a great example of Bogart/Bacall posters, linen-mounted, 41″ × 81″. $2,000 (Auction)

Same as above. Lobby card with close-up of Bogart. Good condition. $100–$125

Dark Victory, 1939. Lobby card from Warner's tear-jerking masterpiece shows Davis dying of a brain tumor. Very collectible, light Canadian censor stamp (does not impair image). $850 (Auction)

The Day the Earth Stood Still, 1951. One-sheet poster dominated by the indestructible Gort from Robert Wise's intelligent science-fiction masterpiece. Good condition, tape remains on back, coveted 1950s poster.   *$850 (Auction)*

Dead Reckoning, 1947. Style A, one-sheet with fine artwork of Bogart as ex-GI on the trail of a comrade's killer. Fair condition.

$200 (Auction)*

The Desk Set, 1957. Lobby card set featuring Spencer Tracy and Katharine Hepburn. Good condition.   *$85–$110*

Desperate Journey, 1942. Lobby card for wartime Warner Brothers action/adventure film with Errol Flynn and Ronald Reagan. Good condition.   *$150–$175*

The Devil's Brother (Frère Diable), 1935. Stone lithographic poster for French release. Whimsical Laurel and Hardy by artist Benari from their adaptation of the operetta "Fra Dia Volo." Linen-mounted, 47″ × 63″.   *$1,000 (Auction)*

Dial M for Murder, 1954. One-sheet poster with dynamic graphics from Hitchcock's Grace Kelly/Ray Milland classic shocker. Good condition, linen-mounted.   *$325 (Auction)*

Diamond Horseshoe, 1945. Title lobby card from the film featuring Betty Grable and Dick Haymes. 14″ × 11″.   *$100 (Auction)*

Dirty Harry, 1971. Half-sheet poster featuring Clint Eastwood in the first of the *Dirty Harry* films. Rare, good condition.   *$100–$125*

Disorderly Conduct, 1932. Rare one-sheet poster for early Fox film with Spencer Tracy, Sally Eilers, and Dickie Moore. Fine condition.
                                                                    $350–$400

Dive Bomber, 1941. Half-sheet poster featuring Errol Flynn and Fred MacMurray. Good condition, horizontal 28″ × 22″. *$200 (Auction)*

Dodge City, 1939. Belgian poster from the Michael Curtiz big-scale western inspired by the Wyatt Earp legend, starring Olivia de Havilland and Errol Flynn. Linen-mounted, 12″ × 14″.   *$300 (Auction)*

  Same as above. French, stone lithographic poster with art by Constantin Balinsky. Linen-mounted, 47″ × 63″.   *$275 (Auction)*

Don Juan, 1926. Lobby card with John Barrymore in sword fight from the Warner Brothers classic—the first film released with a music and sound effects soundtrack. Good condition.   *$250–$300*

Double Indemnity, 1944. Lobby card with Fred MacMurray and Edward G. Robinson in the Billy Wilder film noir classic. Good condition.   *$50–$75*

Courtesy of Camden House Auctioneers

Down Argentine Way, 1940. One-sheet, Tooker, stone lithographic poster in luscious Technicolor of Grable, Ameche, and the great Carmen Miranda. Very good condition.   *$1,600 (Auction)*

Dr. Jekyll and Mr. Hyde, 1941. Lobby card set with Spencer Tracy, Ingrid Bergman, and Lana Turner from the classic MGM horror film based on the Robert Louis Stevenson novel. Great design and colors, good condition. $675–$800

Same as above. Title lobby card. 14″ × 11″. $250 (Auction)

Dr. No, 1962. One-sheet featuring Sean Connery as James Bond in the first film in the long series. Becoming very hard to find, good condition. $250–$350

Same as above. Insert, good condition. $175–$200

Same as above. Lobby card set, good condition. $200–$250

Dr. Strangelove, 1963. Half-sheet poster from the Stanley Kubrick cold-war comedy classic with Peter Sellers, George C. Scott, and Sterling Hayden. Good condition. $100–$125

Same as above. One-sheet, good condition. $100–$125

Same as above. Insert, good condition. $85–$110

Same as above. Lobby card set, good condition. $75–$100

Dr. Zhivago, 1965. Half-sheet from the David Lean classic with Omar Sharif and Julie Christie. Good condition. $50–$75

Dragnet, 1954. Four lobby cards depicting Jack Webb as the unflinching Joe Friday, from the film that spawned the popular TV series. 14″ × 11″. $50 (Auction)

Drums, 1938. French, stone lithographic poster from this Korda adventure starring Sabu and Raymond Massey. Linen-mounted, 30″ × 46½″. $100 (Auction)

Duck Soup, 1933. Half-sheet offset poster with Art Deco-style illustration of the four Marx Brothers. Very good condition, a highly sought-after example of Marx Brothers posters, linen-mounted, 28″ × 22″. $8,000–$9,000

Duel in the Sun (Duel Au Soleil), rerelease 1963. French release poster from the film featuring Jennifer Jones and Gregory Peck. Linen-mounted, 47″ × 63″. $275 (Auction)

Dumbo, 1941. Three-sheet poster with interesting flag title treatment from a Disney classic. Rare, very collectible, fair condition.

$2,500 *(Auction)*

Each Dawn I Die, 1939. Jumbo window card presents Cagney and Raft in classic prison face-off. $500 *(Auction)*

The Eagle, 1925. Half-sheet with colorful Valentino love scene from entertaining Cossack adventure tale. Fair condition, heavily restored, still very desirable, horizontal 28″ × 22″. $1,100 *(Auction)*

East of Eden, 1955. Half-sheet poster featuring Julie Harris and James Dean. Good condition, horizontal 28″ × 22″.   *$225 (Auction)*

Same as above. One-sheet, very good condition.   *$325 (Auction)*

Same as above. One-sheet, fair condition.   *$125 (Auction)*

Easter Parade, 1948. Lobby card with Judy Garland, Fred Astaire, and Peter Lawford. Good condition.   *$50–$75*

Elmer Gantry, 1960. Half-sheet poster with Burt Lancaster and Shirley Jones. Good condition.   *$25–$50*

Same as above. Lobby card set, good condition.   *$35–$60*

The Exorcist, 1974. One-sheet poster for this modern classic horror film. Good condition.   *$20–$40*

Face in the Sky, 1933. Beautiful one-sheet, stone lithographic poster of Marian Nixon sitting on ledge above Spencer Tracy and Stuart Erwin; very rare early Tracy film for Fox. Very good condition.   *$425–$500*

Fahrenheit 451, 1967. One-sheet poster for classic sci-fi directed by Francois Truffaut from the Ray Bradbury novel. Good condition.   *$45–$70*

The Fall of Babylon, 1919. Half-sheet poster with detailed artwork of sleeping maidens. Extremely rare poster from the separate release of the Babylon sequence from Griffith's *Intolerance* (1916). Horizontal 28″ × 22″.   *$600 (Auction)*

Fantasia, 1940. British poster with a spectacular array of fine pastel colors for this Walt Disney classic. 30″ × 40″.   *$1,000 (Auction)*

Same as above. Rare lobby card. Good condition.   *$75–$100*

Fantastic Voyage, 1966. One-sheet poster featuring Raquel Welch in sci-fi classic. Good condition.   *$35–$60*

Same as above. Lobby card set, good condition.   *$45–$70*

Fatty's Garage, ca. 1920s. French, stone lithographic poster from a classic silent comedy starring Fatty Arbuckle, art by Roberty. Good condition, linen-mounted, 40″ × 63″.   *$900–$1,000*

Fellini's Satyricon, 1969. Exotic French poster for the exotic Fellini masterpiece. Framed, 23″ × 30″.   *$125 (Auction)*

Festival du Film Cannes, 1947. Artist: Jean Luc. Very rare early Cannes Film Festival poster shows a motion picture camera, an inset of the town, all against a deep blue night sky. Very good condition, linen-mounted, 24″ × 39″.   *$750 (Auction)*

Five Easy Pieces, 1970. One-sheet poster from Jack Nicholson's brilliant character study.   *$100 (Auction)*

Flaming Fathers, ca. late 1920s. Finely detailed, Morgan, stone lithographic three-sheet poster from Hal Roach's Max Davidson pathe-comedy, great comic graphics. Rare in this size.   *$300 (Auction)*

Same as above. Very rare one-sheet.   *$325 (Auction)*

Flying Elephants, ca. late 1920s. Vivid one-sheet, whimsical, Morgan, stone lithographic poster portrays Stan Laurel (pre-Hardy) and Jimmie Finlayson in furry cavemen garb. Very rare.   *$1,000 (Auction)*

Flying Tigers, 1942. Lobby card with nice close shot of John Wayne and Anna Lee. Good condition, but many border pin holes.
$50–$75

Follow the Fleet, 1936. Morgan one-sheet poster from Irving Berlin's super dreadnaught of musical shows featuring Astaire and Rogers at their patriotic best, lyrical and dreamy. Linen-mounted.
$2,950 (Auction)

Footlight Serenade, 1942. Style A, one-sheet, Tooker lithographic poster successfully sells Grable and her Million Dollar Legs.
$850 (Auction)

For Me and My Gal, 1942. Beautiful, stone lithographic one-sheet from the musical with Judy Garland, Gene Kelly, and George Murphy, directed by Busby Berkeley. Shows full figure of Garland in costume. Rare style, good condition.   *$250–$300*

Same as above. One-sheet, Tooker, stone lithographic poster depicting Garland in the hands of Busby Berkeley, subtle colors.
$675 (Auction)

All price ranges represent the retail value.

Forbidden Planet, 1956. One-sheet with Robby the Robot carrying a limp Anne Francis across the rugged terrain of MGM's seminal science-fiction masterpiece. One of the most beautiful posters from the 1950s. $850 (Auction)

Same as above. Good condition, six different lobby cards.
$100–$125

Forever Amber, 1947. Lobby card with Linda Darnell and Cornell Wilde. Beautiful, stone lithographic artwork, great colors. Good condition. $65–$90

Forever Darling, 1956. One-sheet poster headlining Lucille Ball, Desi Arnaz, and James Mason. $175 (Auction)

Fort Apache, 1948. Appealing John Wayne half-sheet poster delivers strong cavalry vs. Indians battle scene, style B. Horizontal 28″ × 22″. $275 (Auction)

Four's a Crowd, 1938. One-sheet poster from the film starring Errol Flynn and Olivia de Havilland. $350 (Auction)

A Free Soul, 1931. Starring Norma Shearer. 14″ × 22″.
$175 (Auction)

Friendly Persuasion, 1956. Half-sheet poster from the William Wyler classic starring Gary Cooper and Anthony Perkins. $200 (Auction)

The Fugitive Kind, 1960. One-sheet poster of Brando and Joanne Woodward from the Tennessee Williams' doom-laden melodrama.
$25 (Auction)

Fun in Acapulco, 1963. Fun one-sheet poster of Elvis Presley.
$175 (Auction)

Funny Face, 1957. Three-sheet with great Hepburn graphics from the Gershwin musical also starring Fred Astaire. Linen-mounted.
$150 (Auction)

Gaslight, 1944. One-sheet rare and classic poster presents a delicate Ingrid Bergman, a sinister Charles Boyer, and a stalwart Joseph Cotten in fabulous MGM melodramatic artwork. Framed.

$700 (Auction)

Same as above. One-sheet with fine pastel portraits of the stars.

$500 (Auction)

Same as above. Title lobby card. Fair condition. $200 (Auction)

Same as above. One-sheet. $850 (Auction)

Giant, 1956. One-sheet poster with Rock Hudson, Liz Taylor, and James Dean from George Stevens' epic of love and greed in the oil fields. $350 (Auction)

Same as above. Lobby card with famous shot of Dean in car. Good condition. $65–$90

Same as above. Half-sheet. $200 (Auction)

Same as above. One-sheet, linen-mounted. $275 (Auction)

Same as above. Lobby card with Dean and Hudson. Good condition. $55–$80

Same as above. Lobby card with Dean and Taylor. Good condition. $50–$75

Same as above. Lobby card with Taylor and Hudson. Fair condition. $20–$45

Same as above. Lobby card with Taylor and Sal Mineo. Good condition. $30–$55

Same as above. Rare, original, large French poster; better artwork than the American version. $200–$225

Same as above, rerelease 1963. One-sheet with Liz, Rock, and James Dean together. Framed. $225 (Auction)

Gilda, 1946. Style B one-sheet offset by Morgan of the definitive "femme fatale" (Rita Hayworth) in one of the most sought-after film noir posters. None of the other sizes of posters for this film show Rita in the slinky gown, smoking a cigarette, not giving a damn. Extremely rare, fine condition, very collectible, linen-mounted. (See color center section.) $3,000–$4,500

Same as above. Style B one-sheet. $4,250 (Auction)

The Girl Can't Help It, 1956. One-sheet featuring Tom Ewell and Jayne Mansfield. Paper-mounted. $325 (Auction)

The Girl of the Golden West, 1938. One-sheet poster from the film featuring Jeanette MacDonald and Nelson Eddy. $150 (Auction)

The Godfather, 1972. Half-sheet from the Marlon Brando Academy Award film. Good condition. $35–$60

  Same as above. Good condition, one-sheet. $45–$70

  Same as above. Good condition, three-sheet. $45–$70

  Same as above. Minor border repairs, half-sheet. $25–$50

The Gold Rush, rerelease. One-sheet with an entertaining caricature of Charlie Chaplin. Fair condition, framed. $200 (Auction)

Gone With the Wind, 1939. Poster reproduced from an oil portrait of Clark Gable and Vivien Leigh for Selznick's "Greatest Movie Ever Made." Missing bottom portion (additional credits), linen-mounted, 41″ × 60″. $3,000–$4,000

  Same as above, rerelease 1961. Beautiful lobby card in full color; close-up of Clark Gable and Vivien Leigh embracing. Good condition. $35–$60

  Same as above, rerelease. Italian photolithograph. Framed, 27″ × 40″. $275 (Auction)

Goodbye Girl, 1977. French release poster featuring Richard Dreyfuss and Marsha Mason from Neil Simon's super hit. 48″ × 60″. $50 (Auction)

Goodbye Mr. Chips, 1939. Robert Donat and Greer Garson portraits adorn this wonderful Tooker one-sheet poster. Donat won Academy Award for his sensitive performance in this great film. Linen-mounted. $400 (Auction)

  Same as above. Jumbo window card with expressive colors captures Donat's quintessential English schoolmaster. $200 (Auction)

The Graduate, 1967. Italian photolithographic from the 1960s' classic film starring Dustin Hoffman and Anne Bancroft. Framed, 18½″ × 26½″. $50 (Auction)

The Grand Illusion, 1937. French, stone lithographic poster from Jean Renoir's World War I classic starring Erich von Stroheim; moody blues and grays. Linen-mounted, 48″ × 60″.   *$3,000 (Auction)*

The Great Gatsby, 1949. One-sheet featuring Alan Ladd.

$225 (Auction)

The Great Lie, 1941. One-sheet from film starring Bette Davis.

$450 (Auction)

Green Goddess, 1930. Stunning one-sheet, stone lithographic poster from this early Warner Brothers Arliss film with George Arliss, H. B. Warner, and Alice Joyce. Rich colors and design. Very good condition.   *$200–$225*

Gunga Din, 1939. Lobby card from the adventure classic. Close shot of Cary Grant and Doug Fairbanks, Jr., with girls (one is Joan Fontaine). Rare, good condition.   *$450–$500*

A Hard Day's Night, 1964. The rare Pop Art poster from the Beatles' highly inventive, madcap first feature. Heavy stock, 40″ × 60″.

$700–$800

Same as above. Complete set of eight lobby cards in their original sleeve. Mint condition.   *$500 (Auction)*

Same as above. Horizontal 28″ × 22″.   *$200 (Auction)*

Harry Carey Portrait. French, stone lithographic poster with lively Roberty dramatic illustration of the first-rate American cowboy star. Linen-mounted, 47″ × 63″. $350 (Auction)

The Harvey Girls, 1945. Lively one-sheet poster from MGM's musical salute to waitresses out west, stars Judy Garland. $450 (Auction)

The Heat's On, 1943. Hard-to-find Mae West film. Two different lobby cards, each with nice close shot of West, good condition.

$65–$90 each

Heaven Can Wait, 1943. One-sheet featuring Gene Tierney and Don Ameche. $300 (Auction)

Heidi, 1937. Belgian electrotype poster from the Zanuck hit portraying a bright Shirley Temple beside Jean Hersholt in fairy tale colors. Linen-mounted, 24″ × 33″. $400 (Auction)

Held for Ransom, 1938. Full set of eight lobby cards, fine color, included in this lot are nine black and white still photographs from the movie. $35 (Auction)

Hell's Kitchen, 1939. Colorful, Continental one-sheet poster with Ronald Reagan and the Dead End Kids. $375 (Auction)

Help!, 1965. One-sheet featuring the Beatles from this classic 1960s' frenetic musical hit. Framed. $350 (Auction)

Same as above. Great lobby card with the Beatles performing. Good condition. $35–$60

High Noon, 1952. Half-sheet poster from this Gary Cooper and Grace Kelly classic directed by Fred Zinnemann which won an Oscar for Cooper. Great artwork of Cooper. Very rare, worn and some repairs.

$175–$200

Same as above. Powerful image of Cooper dominates this rare-sized poster, best artwork of any American paper. Mounted on masonite, 40″ × 60″. $375 (Auction)

Hondo, 1953. French poster portraying a potent John Wayne in this duo-tone beauty. Linen-mounted, 23″ × 31½″. $100 (Auction)

Same as above. One-sheet with great cowboy portrait of Wayne, intact 3-D logo. Some restoration. $350 (Auction)

Horsefeathers, 1932. Paramount lobby card with great shot of Harpo doing his "gooky" face to menacing Nat Pendleton and friend in this early Marx Brothers film. Card is also autographed by Groucho Marx (signed "Forever, Groucho Marx"). Extremely rare, good condition.

$850–$950

Courtesy of Camden House Auctioneers

Hound of the Baskervilles, 1939. Style A half-sheet with silhouette artwork from this Sherlock Holmes horror/adventure starring Basil Rathbone. Fine condition. $3,750 (Auction)

All price ranges represent the retail value.

Courtesy of Camden House Auctioneers

House of Dracula, 1945. One-sheet poster with dramatic Universal artwork features an intense John Carradine as Dracula commanding Frankenstein and the Wolfman. Very collectible, fine condition.

$1,600 (Auction)

Same as above. Beautifully colored full set of lobby cards pictures Dracula, Frankenstein, and the Wolfman. Very rare, fine condition with original envelope. $2,000 (Auction)

Courtesy of Camden House Auctioneers

House of Fear, 1944. Full set of eight lobby cards for the Sherlock Holmes classic starring Basil Rathbone and Nigel Bruce, with original shipping sleeve (numbered "44/380"). $1,100 (Auction)

House of Wax, 1953. Six-sheet (in two pieces) from the 3-D horror classic starring Vincent Price. $375 (Auction)

How Green Was My Valley, 1941. One-sheet Tooker poster with Walter Pidgeon, Maureen O'Hara, and Roddy McDowell from this John Ford Academy Award-winning Best Picture. $300 (Auction)

The Hucksters, 1947. One-sheet poster with Clark Gable, Deborah Kerr, and Ava Gardner from the MGM post-war ad game exposé. $150 (Auction)

Hudson's Bay, 1941. Three-sheet poster starring Paul Muni. Linen-backed. $100 (Auction)

Hush, Hush, Sweet Charlotte, 1965. One-sheet from this fun horror film with Bette Davis, Olivia de Havilland, and Mary Astor. Good condition. $45–$70

Same as above. Good condition, half-sheet. $45–$70

Same as above. Good condition, lobby card set. $60–$85

The Hustler, 1961. Half-sheet from very popular Paul Newman pool classic. Good condition. $65–$90

Same as above. Good condition, insert. $65–$90

Same as above. Mint condition (unused), six-sheet. $85–$110

I Met Him in Paris, 1937. Style A one-sheet with multicolored, stylish Deco design, starring Claudette Colbert and Melvyn Douglas. Linen-mounted. $350 (Auction)

In Old Chicago (L'Incendie Chicago), ca. 1938. Original release, French stone lithographic from the very expensive Chicago fire spectacle, stars Tyrone Power and Alice Faye. Some restoration, linen-mounted, 47″ × 63″. $550 (Auction)

Intermezzo, 1939. One-sheet poster of Ingrid Bergman and Leslie Howard in the first U.S. film by Bergman. Beautiful artwork and design on this classic; Howard and Bergman gaze into each other's eyes. Good condition. $750–$900

Same as above. Window card, good condition. $200–$225

The Invaders. One-sheet poster from the film starring Laurence Olivier, Leslie Howard, and Raymond Massey. Very good condition, linen-mounted. $550–$600

Invasion of the Body Snatchers, 1956. Explosive and terrifying three-sheet from Don Siegel's pods-from-space commie-scare classic. Linen-mounted. *$375 (Auction)*

Same as above. Horizontal 28″ × 22″. *$100 (Auction)*

It Came from Beneath the Sea, 1955. Fun one-sheet poster with Ray Harryhausen's giant animated octopus attacking San Francisco.
$125 (Auction)

It's a Wonderful Life, 1946. Lobby card set from one of the all-time classics from director Frank Capra, starring Jimmy Stewart and Donna Reed. Material on this title has become extremely hard to find and is probably the most requested title. Jimmy Stewart is pictured on every scene card of the set. Great colors and design with some super scenes. Good condition. $2,000–$2,200

Same as above. Single lobby card, #3, with Stewart and Reed dancing in high-school gym. Good condition. $275–$300

Same as above. Single lobby card, #8, with famous shot of Stewart and Reed after the dance in borrowed clothes singing "Buffalo Gals." Good condition. $225–$250

Jailhouse Rock, 1957. With Elvis Presley. Title card with great artwork portrait in beautiful bright colors. Good condition. $100–$125

Jezebel, 1938. One of the prettiest title cards ever produced with great portrait of Bette Davis. Davis won her second Oscar for this film. Extremely rare, good condition. $3,000–$3,200

Joe Kidd, 1972. Dynamic graphics of Clint Eastwood, signed Sidney Beckerman (producer). Framed, 40″ × 76″. *$200 (Auction)*

Journey to the Center of the Earth, 1959. One-sheet poster with James Mason in the sci-fi classic from Jules Verne. Hard to find, good condition. $50–$75

Julius Caesar, 1953. Three-sheet poster featuring a brooding Brando as Mark Anthony, bright colors. *$275 (Auction)*

Jungle Book, 1942. One-sheet poster from the Kipling jungle fantasy starring Sabu; poster represents film's magical Technicolor imagery. Linen-mounted.   *$600 (Auction)*

Just Around the Corner, 1938. Lobby card from the film headlining Shirley Temple.   *$275 (Auction)*

Key Largo, 1948. Great scene card (#5) from the John Huston classic with Humphrey Bogart, Lauren Bacall, and Edward G. Robinson. Close shot of Bogart and Robinson. Good condition.   *$100–$125*

   Same as above, 1949. Original Italian release (l'Isola Corallo), extraordinary artwork by Martinati is superior to all American paper on same title. Linen-mounted, 40″ × 60″.   *$175 (Auction)*

   Same as above, reissue 1953. Good condition, one-sheet (duo-tone).   *$50–$75*

The Killers, 1946. Belgian poster with breathtaking portrait of Burt Lancaster from the movie also starring a luscious Ava Gardner. Linen-backed, 14″ × 18″.   *$75 (Auction)*

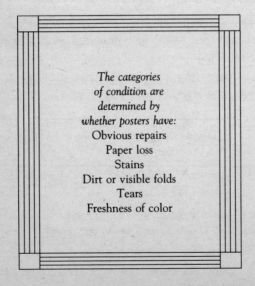

*The categories
of condition are
determined by
whether posters have:*
Obvious repairs
Paper loss
Stains
Dirt or visible folds
Tears
Freshness of color

Courtesy of Camden House Auctioneers

Courtesy of Camden House Auctioneers

King Kong, 1933. French, stone lithographic poster with spectacular Rene Peron art capturing the magic and myth of beauty and the beast atop the Empire State Building. Extremely rare, linen-mounted, 48″ × 60″. $12,000–$15,000

Same as above, rerelease 1942. Three-sheet with superb artwork reminiscent of original campaign but with World War II planes. Extremely rare, linen-mounted (see photo above, left).

$2,500 *(Auction)*

Same as above. Unforgettable artwork, striking and powerful colors, similar to original six-sheet portrays Kong on rampage in New York. Fine condition, 14″ × 22″ (see photo above, right).

$1,500 *(Auction)*

Same as above, rerelease 1947. One-sheet with classic artwork rendered in three colors. Any paper on this film is very rare and extremely collectible. Linen-mounted. $1,300 *(Auction)*

Same as above, rerelease 1952. Three-sheet poster shows towering Kong holding Fay Wray in his clutches; duo-tone. Fair condition, framed. $450 *(Auction)*

Same as above, rerelease 1956. One-sheet with nice full-color artwork. Fair to good condition. $185–$210

King of Kings, 1927. Beautiful one-sheet, Morgan, stone lithographic poster depicts "March of the Little Blind Girls" from DeMille's grand silent epic. $800 *(Auction)*

King's Row, 1941. One-sheet poster shows a red book with the movie title and sketches of several scenes. Stars include Ann Sheridan and Ronald Reagan. Very good condition, linen-mounted. $850–$950

L'Etrangère. Artist: Guy Gerard Noel. Dramatic image of blonde woman from the rear, naked except for translucent red shawl; black background. Old folds show, linen-mounted, 47″ × 63″.

$1,000 (Auction)

La Dolce Vita (La Douceur de Vivre), 1960. Original French release from Fellini's trendsetter features the explosive Anita Ekberg. 47″ × 63″. $275 (Auction)

La Donna De Fiume, 1955. Italian poster featuring full-length tortured portrait of a young Sophia Loren. Framed, 39″ × 55″.

$800–$1,000

La Ronde (Circle of Love), 1964. French poster with a fetching and seductive portrait of a very young Jane Fonda from the film directed by Roger Vadim. 22″ × 30″. $50 (Auction)

Same as above. 48″ × 60″. $125 (Auction)

Lady from Nowhere, 1936. One-sheet with great artwork of passionate couple ("Dangerous to Kiss!") for this Columbia picture starring Mary Astor. Good condition. $85–$110

Lady from Shanghai, 1947. Style A half-sheet poster from Orson Welles' cinema tour de force offers a classic Hayworth. Signed by Welles.

$600 (Auction)

Lady in the Lake, 1946. Insert poster with stylish imagery from Raymond Chandler's complex private-eye thriller. Linen-mounted.

$175 (Auction)

The Lady Vanishes, rerelease. Four Film Classic lobby cards from the Hitchcock shocker, starring Michael Redgrave and Paul Lukas; sepia photographic. $75 (Auction)

Larceny, Inc., 1942. Lobby card from Warner Brothers film with Edward G. Robinson and Broderick Crawford. Good condition.

$35–$60

The Last Command, 1928. French, stone lithographic poster with highly dramatic and expressive graphics from the movie starring the great Emil Jannings and directed by Josef Von Sternberg. Linen-mounted, 23″ × 31″. *$150 (Auction)*

The Last Gangster, 1937. Belgian electrotype poster with atmospheric powerful portraits of E. G. Robinson and James Stewart from this classic vengeance melodrama. 24″ × 30½″. *$250 (Auction)*

The Last of Mrs. Cheyney, 1937. Jumbo window card for Joan Crawford/William Powell vehicle about a con woman who falls in love. *$275 (Auction)*

The Last Tango in Paris, 1972. Foreign release poster featuring Brando from Bertolucci's sizzling sexual superhit. Framed, 27″ × 41″. *$50 (Auction)*

Laura, 1944. Title card from the film featuring Gene Tierney and Dana Andrews. *$250 (Auction)*

Lawrence of Arabia, 1963. One-sheet poster from the David Lean classic with Peter O'Toole and Alec Guinness. Very high demand, striking graphics. Good condition. *$125–$150*

Same as above. Lobby card set, good condition. *$125–$150*

Same as above, rerelease 1971. Lobby card set in full color, good condition. *$50–$75*

Lawyer Man, 1932. Beautiful one-sheet, stone lithographic poster with great full-face portrait of William Powell, with Joan Blondell in background; great colors and Art Deco design. Very rare, fine condition. *$450–$500*

Leave Her to Heaven, 1946. Beautiful one-sheet, Tooker, stone lithographic poster captures this classic film noir, starring Gene Tierney. *$900 (Auction)*

Let's Make Love, 1960. Three-sheet from the movie in which Marilyn Monroe seduces the immortal Yves Montand, directed by Cukor. Fair condition. *$175 (Auction)*

The Letter, 1940. Rare poster, one-sheet, from Wyler's magnificent production of the Somerset Maugham drama in which Davis delivers one of her most exciting performances. Features double portraits of Bette Davis. Linen-mounted.   *$1,100 (Auction)*

Life and Adventures of Buffalo Bill, ca. 1910. Lithograph printed by Riverside Printing, Milwaukee. Heads of four Indians at center with vignettes around them; in rich colors. Very good condition, very collectible, linen-mounted and framed, 28″ × 42″.   *$1,500–$2,000*

The Life of the Party, 1920. Lobby card from the film featuring Roscoe (Fatty) Arbuckle.   *$350 (Auction)*

Lifeboat, 1944. Original Spanish issue, stone lithographic poster of Hitchcock's pressure-cooker adventure on the high seas. Bankhead and Slezak featured, art by Soligo. Linen-mounted.   *$225 (Auction)*

Limelight, 1951. French release, stone lithographic poster presents spectacular color portrait of Chaplin as a down-and-out music hall comedian. Linen-mounted, 47″ × 63″.   *$375 (Auction)*

The Little Foxes, 1941. One-sheet offset poster of Bette Davis in costume in one of her best roles. After 1941, nearly all posters of Davis films were lackluster. Fine condition, an excellent example of a Davis poster, linen-mounted. $4,000–$6,000

Same as above. French, stone lithographic poster features Bernard Lancy art in a flowing, full-length pastel portrait of Bette Davis at her most dangerous. Linen-mounted, 47″ × 63″. $1,000–$1,500

The Little Princess, 1939. Style B one-sheet poster for Temple's lush Technicolor tale of a waif in Victorian London. $800 (Auction)

Lolita, 1962. Artist: Roger Soubie. The great image of Sue Lyon with the lollipop and sunglasses, for the original French release of the Stanley Kubrick classic. Mint condition, linen-mounted, 47″ × 63″.
$800 (Auction)

Same as above. Four different lobby cards, each with James Mason. Good condition. $15–$25 each

Lone Star, 1951. Luscious color one-sheet poster; Clark Gable straps on six-guns for Ava Gardner. Framed. $175 (Auction)

Lost in a Harem, 1944. Half-sheet poster starring Abbott and Costello. Matted, horizontal 28″ × 22″. $250 (Auction)

Love from a Stranger, 1937. Six lobby cards including title card with a handsome Basil Rathbone and Anne Harding, good color.
$75 (Auction)

Love Happy, 1949. Three-sheet, stone lithographic poster offers whimsical caricatures of the Marx Brothers for their last film. Very collectible. $400 (Auction)

Same as above. Full set of lobby cards, including the rare Marilyn and Groucho card, eagerly sought. Fine condition. $500 (Auction)

Love Me Tender, 1956. This early Presley poster, a one-sheet, features a full-sized Elvis with guitar. $225 (Auction)

Love on the Run, 1936. Lobby card; great shot of Clark Gable and Joan Crawford with pretty border design. Good condition.
$100–$125

Made for Each Other, rerelease. One-sheet Morgan poster with James Stewart and Carole Lombard. $100 (Auction)

Mademoiselle Charlot. French, stone lithographic poster with superb Chaplin action scene in soft, beautiful colors. Linen-mounted, 47″ × 63″. $1,500–$2,000

Magnificent Obsession, 1935. One-sheet poster from the classic Lloyd C. Douglas soap opera with Irene Dunne and Robert Taylor. Beautiful artwork on this first version; head shots of Dunne and Taylor, with a small stream of other figures from the movie. Good condition.
                                                                    $400–$450

The Maltese Falcon, 1931. Early Warner Brothers lobby card from the first version of the Dashiell Hammet classic. Scene of Bebe Daniels in bed holding gun on Ricardo Cortez as Sam Spade. Great colors and border design of statuette. Very rare, fine condition. $250–$300

The Maltese Falcon, 1941. Portrait lobby card with Humphrey Bogart and Mary Astor from the John Huston detective classic. Nice border design and colors. Good condition. $1,350–$1,500

Same as above. Linen-mounted, 47″ × 63″. $1,400 *(Auction)*

Same as above. Lobby card with close-up of Bogart and Gladys George in embrace. Some repairs and border restoration.
                                                                    $875–$1,000

Same as above. Lobby card of scene in Spade apartment—Ward Bond holds Bogart back from slugging Barton MacLane as Astor and Peter Lorre (with bloodied face) look on. Good condition.
                                                                    $1,100–$1,300

Man About Town, 1932. One-sheet poster from film with Warner Baxter, Karen Morley, and Conway Tearle. Great artwork and 1930s' design of couple in passionate embrace. Some border repair.
                                                                    $100–$125

The Man Who Knew Too Much, 1934. Offset half-sheet poster with a terrific image of scarred-face Peter Lorre plus a menacing scene on the rooftops of London. This poster is one of only a few known to exist on this early Hitchcock film. Very good condition, very collectible. $6,000–$8,000

The Man Who Shot Liberty Valence, 1962. Insert poster of John Wayne and Jimmy Stewart in the John Ford western classic. Good condition.
$65–$90

Same as above. Good condition, four different lobby cards, each with Wayne.
$15–$25 each

Same as above. Good condition, one lobby card with Stewart.
$10–$20

The Man in Possession, 1931. Beautiful Art Deco, one-sheet, stone lithographic poster for the MGM film with Robert Montgomery, Charlotte Greenwood, and C. Aubrey Smith. Depicts Robert Montgomery in tux; very colorful with gold and sky-blue background. Good condition.
$175–$200

The Manchurian Candidate, 1962. One-sheet poster from the classic political cold-war drama by John Frakenheimer with Frank Sinatra, Laurence Harvey, and Angela Lansbury. Withdrawn for over 25 years and only recently rereleased. Rare, good condition.
$65–$90

Same as above. Good condition, half-sheet.
$65–$90

Same as above. Good condition, lobby card set.
$75–$100

Same as above. Good condition, six-sheet.
$65–$90

Same as above. Good condition, three-sheet.
$65–$90

Marie Antoinette, 1938. Lobby card with super colors and design from MGM. Tyrone Power about to kiss Norma Shearer with caption "A queen . . . but, first of all . . . a woman in love!" Fine condition.
$350–$400

Marilyn Monroe Personality Posters, 1972. Pair of promotional posters entitled "The Legend and The Truth." 18″ × 24″. $175 (Auction)

Early Marilyn Monroe Publicity Poster. Full-length photo of a young Marilyn wearing a red and white striped bikini. Good condition, but some water stains, framed, 21″ × 62″. $225 (Auction)

Marilyn, 1963. One-sheet Monroe poster from the feature-documentary narrated by Rock Hudson. $150 (Auction)

The Mark of Zorro, 1920. Half-sheet from the silent classic with Douglas Fairbanks, Sr. and Noah Beery, probably Fairbanks' best film. Displays profile of Fairbanks and Marguerite De La Motte in tinted tones. Very rare, good condition. $850–$1,000

A Married Woman, 1965. French poster from the Jean-Luc Godard turgid, three-cornered romance film. 48″ × 60″. $75 (Auction)

Mary of Scotland, 1936. Beautiful RKO lobby card with Katharine Hepburn and Fredric March. Unusual border design. Good condition.
$200–$225

Courtesy of Camden House Auctioneers

The Mask of Fu Manchu, 1932. Lobby card, fabulous portrait of Karloff as the master Oriental criminal; great Art Deco styling and colors. Very rare. $1,700 (Auction)

The Masquerader, 1933. Stone, lithographic one-sheet poster with great 1930s artwork and design. Ronald Colman pictured twice and Elissa Landi in the background. Fine condition. $500–$600

Mata Hari, 1932. Original Belgian release of famous early talkie depicts Garbo as the World War I femme fatale in dancing girl garb. Very good condition, linen-mounted, 24″ × 33″. *$1,000 (Auction)*

Meet Me in St. Louis, 1944. Half-sheet poster for Judy Garland classic directed by Vincent Minnelli. Super colors and MGM design. Very rare, good condition. $500–$600

Merry Melodies, 1941. Continental stock one-sheet for Leon Schlesinger's Vitaphone short subjects. Hard to find. *$350 (Auction)*

Mickey and the Seal, ca. 1940s. Fantastic French poster shows Mickey, Goofy, Donald, and Minnie, in Technicolor. 24½″ × 31½″.
$200 (Auction)

Mildred Pierce, 1945. Pretty lobby card in full color (most other sizes on this film are duo-tone) with great shot of Joan Crawford, Zachary Scott, and Jack Carson. Crawford won her Oscar for the lead in this film noir classic. Good condition. $65–$90

Same as above. One-sheet with Oscar-winning Crawford as housewife-turned-success. Fine condition. *$475 (Auction)*

The Miracle Rider, 1930. Gorgeous Morgan Litho one-sheet poster from cowboy giant Tom Mix's only serial, prominently features Tony, Jr., the wonder horse. Framed. *$850 (Auction)*

Miracle on 34th Street, 1947. Great lobby card from this Christmas classic with Edmund Gwenn and John Payne. Good condition.

$50–$75

Miss Fatty Bathes, ca. 1920s. French, stone lithographic poster of Roberty art with a Nouveau influence featuring Fatty Arbuckle in drag. Linen-mounted, 47″ × 63″.

$1,000–$1,500

Miss Sadie Thompson, 1954. One-sheet poster from the film featuring Rita Hayworth and Jose Ferrer. Paper-mounted.

$175 (Auction)

Mississippi Gambler, 1953. Great Tyrone Power image commands the artwork for this poster from the Universal adventure film. 40″ × 76″.

$200 (Auction)

Monkey Business, 1952. One-sheet poster with Cary Grant and Ginger Rogers. Linen-mounted.

$250 (Auction)

Same as above. One-sheet poster with Marilyn Monroe and Cary Grant; rare Monroe poster with shots of all. Good condition.

$200–$225

Monsieur Beaucaire, 1924. Rare title card and one scene card from one of Valentino's most famous costume roles as the masquerading Duke in Booth Tarkington's colorful court drama. Very rare and collectible.

$600 (Auction)

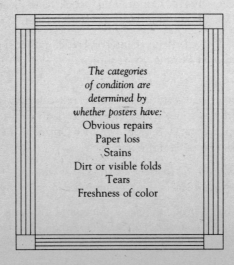

*The categories
of condition are
determined by
whether posters have:*
Obvious repairs
Paper loss
Stains
Dirt or visible folds
Tears
Freshness of color

Montana, 1950. French poster with sepia and green colors combining for a dramatic effect; from the Warner Brothers western starring Errol Flynn and Alexis Smith. Linen-mounted, 23½″ × 30½″.

$100 (Auction)

Courtesy of Camden House Auctioneers

Moon Over Miami, 1941. Style B, one-sheet, Tooker, stone lithographic poster emphasizes Grable's Million Dollar Legs. Avidly sought title. $1,600 (Auction)

Movie Crazy, reissue 1949. One-sheet poster from the nice reissue of the 1932 Harold Lloyd film. Good condition. $25–$50

Mr. Deeds Goes to Town, 1936. Title card shows large photo of Gary Cooper and Jean Arthur sitting on a park bench with their arms around each other, also a drawing of the couple kissing. Good condition, a good example of an early Cooper poster. $300–$350

Mr. Mouse Takes a Trip, rerelease 1953. Mickey Mouse one-sheet poster from this 25th anniversary animated film; duo-tone.

$200 (Auction)

Mr. Smith Goes to Washington, 1939. Lobby card from the Frank Capra classic. Great graphics: Jimmy Stewart about to get into a fight with Jack Carson as Thomas Mitchell tries to restrain him. Good condition. $150–$175

The Mummy's Curse, 1944. Six-sheet poster of a colossal Chaney in full monster make-up as the immortal Kharis. Rare Universal paper, good condition. $1,300 (Auction)

The Mummy's Tomb, rerelease. Realart one-sheet poster, a massive portrait of Lon Chaney, Jr., commands the poster for this classic mummy movie. Fair condition. $150 (Auction)

Music in the Air, 1934. Lobby card for rare Gloria Swanson film. Close-up shot of her with John Boles. Good condition. $100–$125

Same as above. Lobby card of Swanson and Boles singing.
$100–$125

Mutiny on the Bounty, 1935. Lobby card from the film starring Clark Gable and Charles Laughton. Fair condition, linen-mounted.
$250 (Auction)

My Favorite Wife, 1940. One-sheet poster from the Leo McCarey screwball comedy classic starring Cary Grant and Irene Dunne. RKO poster with beautiful artwork and colors shows Grant on phone in foreground, two women in background. Very rare, very good condition with some tape stains on border. $600–$700

Same as above. One lobby card with Grant and Randolph Scott, good condition. $50–$75

My Gal Sal, 1942. Preferred style B, one-sheet, Tooker, stone lithographic poster emphasizes a leggy Rita Hayworth. Good condition.
$450 (Auction)

My Little Chickadee, 1940. Lobby card from the film starring Mae West and W. C. Fields. $225 (Auction)

The Mysterious Island, 1929. Title card from this first version of the Jules Verne classic, a rare, early Technicolor film starring Lionel Barrymore. Great colors and design: a man and woman entangled in an octopus. Good condition. $150–$175

Nabonga, 1944. One-sheet poster from the film starring Buster Crabbe and introducing Julie London; classic schlock ("Nabonga" means gorilla!). $100 (Auction)

Naughty Marietta, 1944. Three-sheet poster featuring Jeanette Mac-Donald and Nelson Eddy. $400 (Auction)

Courtesy of Camden House Auctioneers

The Navigator, 1924. Fabulously rare title card and scene card from
Buster Keaton's biggest commercial success, directed by Donald Crisp
for Joseph Schenck at MGM. A gag-filled thrilling comedy set on a
schooner at sea. Rope title treatment, broad coloring, and humorous
subtitle for scene card, "You can depend on Buster in an emergency."
Museum-caliber material, white, mint condition.

$3,500 (Auction)

Same as above. Lobby card depicts Keaton down a deck tube, bright
red and green. Mint condition. $1,300 (Auction)

Same as above. Lobby card features exciting at-sea rescue against a
broad yellow backdrop. Mint condition. $1,000 (Auction)

Same as above. Lobby card of Keaton in his bath. Very rare, mint
condition. $1,200 (Auction)

Same as above. Lobby card shows Keaton wooing his maiden against
a vivid green background. Mint condition. $1,300 (Auction)

Same as above. Scene card of Keaton about to be sealed into diving
gear, beautiful yellow background, intricate detail. Exceptionally
rare, mint condition. $1,500 (Auction)

New Moon, 1940. Lobby card from the film headlining Jeanette Mac-Donald and Nelson Eddy.   *$75 (Auction)*

Niagara, 1953. One-sheet from the film starring Marilyn Monroe and Joseph Cotten.   *$425 (Auction)*

Same as above. One of Monroe's most alluring posters, a one-sheet, presents her as the faithless bride out to murder her husband. Very collectible, paper-mounted.   *$475 (Auction)*

A Night at the Opera, rerelease 1948. Three-sheet poster from this MGM great features wonderful caricatures of the Marx Brothers. Fair condition, linen-mounted.   *$375 (Auction)*

A Night in Casablanca, 1946. One-sheet poster from this film of the Marx Brothers vs. Nazis in North Africa; fine caricatures of Groucho, Chico, and Harpo. Fair condition.   *$350 (Auction)*

No Man of Her Own, 1932. French, stone lithographic poster with sinister portrait of Clark Gable, stark and highly dramatic. Linen-mounted, 25″ × 33″.   *$800 (Auction)*

No Marriage Ties, 1932. RKO one-sheet poster of Richard Dix and Elizabeth Allen, with great early 1930s style and colors. Fine condition.   *$375–$425*

North by Northwest, 1958. One-sheet poster featuring Cary Grant in the Alfred Hitchcock classic of suspense. Good condition.

$150–$175

Same as above. Lobby card set with Grant on all cards, good condition.   *$250–$300*

Same as above, reissue 1966. One-sheet in full color, good condition.   *$50–$75*

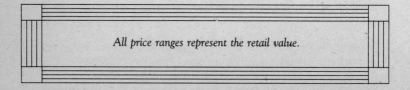

All price ranges represent the retail value.

Notorious, 1946. One-sheet poster shows Grant and Bergman embracing in the shadow of the deadly "cellar key." Very good condition.
$1,600 *(Auction)*

Same as above. Complete set of eight colorful lobby cards feature Bergman and Grant in action scenes. $1,300 *(Auction)*

Now I'll Tell One, ca. late 1920s. One-sheet, Morgan, stone lithographic poster from Hal Roach's silent pathecomedy featuring a young Stan Laurel. Depicts Charley Chase playing William Tell at home. Extremely rare, museum quality. $600 *(Auction)*

Now Voyager, 1942. One-sheet, Continental lithographic poster documents doomed love of spinster Bette Davis for suave Paul Henried. $800 *(Auction)*

Same as above. French, stone lithographic poster with Herve art immortalizing Davis' tragic search for love in the face of destiny. Linen-mounted, 47″ × 63″. $475 *(Auction)*

Old Acquaintance, 1943. Half-sheet poster from the film starring Bette Davis and Miriam Hopkins. $200 *(Auction)*

The Old Maid, 1939. One-sheet poster, a magnificent photolithographic portrait of Bette Davis in this post–Civil War tear-jerker.

$950 (Auction)

On the Avenue, 1937. One-sheet poster with Dick Powell and Madeleine Carroll highlighted against city skyline at night. Also shows Alice Faye and the Ritz Brothers. Rare, good condition. $375–$425

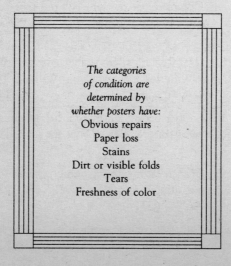

*The categories
of condition are
determined by
whether posters have:*
Obvious repairs
Paper loss
Stains
Dirt or visible folds
Tears
Freshness of color

On the Waterfront, 1954. One-sheet poster for Elia Kazan's modern masterpiece presents a moody Brando about to explode; also starring Lee J. Cobb, Karl Malden, and Eva Marie Saint. Framed, good condition. $250 (Auction)

Same as above. One-sheet. $425 (Auction)

Same as above. Framed, half-sheet. $300 (Auction)

Same as above. Framed, 19″ × 13″. $150–$200

Same as above. Original release Italian lobby card, features Brando and Eva Marie Saint; beautiful color. Framed, 19″ × 13″.
$50 (Auction)

One Exciting Night, 1922. Half-sheet poster for D. W. Griffith's creation of the first spooky house, horror/mystery film. Rare, good condition. $300 (Auction)

One Eyed Jacks, rerelease. Poster featuring a giant scowling Marlon Brando. Framed, 40″ × 76″. $1,000–$1,200

The Original Katzenjammer Kids. Rare poster, one-sheet, from this early cartoon comedy. $400 (Auction)

Our Gang, ca. 1930s. French, stone lithographic stock poster sports colorful art by Florit, featuring Spanky, Darla, and the gang. Linen-mounted, 47″ × 63″. $400 (Auction)

The Outlaw, 1943. One-sheet poster for the film starring Jane Russell.
$475 *(Auction)*

The Ox-Bow Incident, 1942. Explosive Tooker, stone lithographic one-sheet poster focuses on lynch mob from Wellman's brilliant western classic. $475 *(Auction)*

Pack Up Your Troubles, 1932. Beautiful lobby card from early feature film of Laurel and Hardy. Great shot of both the boys. Fine condition.
$350–$400

Pal Joey, 1957. Insert poster of Sinatra, Hayworth, and Novak. Framed, 14″ × 36″. $175–$225

Pals of the Saddle, 1938. Morgan three-sheet poster featuring the three Mesquiteers—John Wayne, Max Terhune, and Ray "Crash" Corrigan. Linen-mounted. $1,250 *(Auction)*

Pandora and the Flying Dutchman, 1951. Belgian poster with Ava Gardner and James Mason immersed in Technicolor sensuality. Linen-mounted, 14″ × 22″. $75 *(Auction)*

Paris Honeymoon, 1939. Morgan three-sheet poster, starring Bing Crosby; in shining colors. Linen-mounted. $325 *(Auction)*

Pat and Mike, 1952. Three-sheet poster from the Cukor-directed film features joyous photographic portraits of Tracy and Hepburn. Linen-mounted. $175 *(Auction)*

Patton, 1970. One-sheet poster for the film which won Best Picture and Best Actor Award (George C. Scott). Good condition. $35–$60

The Paul Street Boys. French poster with art by Paul Colin creating an unusually arresting image from the movie starring George Breakston. Linen-mounted, 12″ × 23″. $25 *(Auction)*

The Pearl of Death, 1944. One-sheet poster from this Basil Rathbone/Nigel Bruce Sherlock Holmes adventure, featuring Rondo "Creeper" Hatton. Rare, fair condition. $375 *(Auction)*

Persona, 1967. Insert poster from Ingmar Bergman's obsessive journey into madness starring Liv Ullmann and Bibi Andersson. Framed.
$50 *(Auction)*

Peter Pan, 1953. One-sheet poster for the animated classic from Walt Disney features Peter with small vignettes of other characters. Rare, fine condition. $150–$175

The Philadelphia Story, 1940. One-sheet for the George Cukor classic headlining Cary Grant, Katharine Hepburn, and James Stewart.
$500 (Auction)

Same as above. Beautiful lobby card with nice shot of Hepburn, Roland Young, and Virginia Weidler, good condition. $85–$110

Picnic, 1956. One-sheet poster from the film starring William Holden and Rosalind Russell; Holden wreaks sexual havoc in a small American town. Framed. $200 (Auction)

The Picture of Dorian Grey, 1945. Very nice MGM lobby card with Hurd Hatfield, good condition. $30–$50

Pinocchio, 1940. Lobby card from the classic Walt Disney animated feature. Framed. $375 (Auction)

Plainsman, rerelease. French, stone lithographic poster features Gary Cooper from the Paramount epic directed by DeMille, also starring Jean Arthur; vibrant colors. Linen-mounted, 23″ × 32″.
$200 (Auction)

Play Girl, 1932. One-sheet poster with a great Art Deco design of Loretta Young holding a small baby for this early Warner Brothers film. Good condition. $200–$225

Play It Again, Sam, 1972. One-sheet for this Woody Allen classic with Diane Keaton. Good condition. $25–$50

Pluto's Blue Note, 1947. Rare Walt Disney cartoon poster, one-sheet, fine pastel-colored Morgan Litho mounted on card stock.
$200 (Auction)

Pluto's Housewarming, 1946. One-sheet, Morgan, stone lithographic poster sports extraordinary full-frame image of Pluto in action. Rare and desirable. $900 (Auction)

Poor Little Rich Girl, 1936. Lobby card. Great Fox colors and design for this shot of Shirley Temple, Alice Faye, and Jack Haley. Good condition. $175–$200

Porgy and Bess, 1959. Half-sheet poster for this classic musical with Sidney Poitier, Dorothy Dandridge, Pearl Bailey, and Sammy Davis, Jr. Good condition. $35–$60

The Postman Always Rings Twice, 1946. John Garfield and Lana Turner appear in this one-sheet Tooker Litho poster seething with illicit desire. Framed. $700 *(Auction)*

Same as above. Garfield and Turner on this pretty lobby card from the film noir classic. Good condition. $100–$125

Courtesy of Camden House Auctioneers

Potemkin, 1925. Original Russian poster for export (1930s' reissues were photolithos of this) for Eisenstein's classic revolutionary documentary. Shows sailor (with title on hatband) in front of ship. A distinguished and historic collector's item, linen-mounted, 24″ × 36″. $2,000 *(Auction)*

The Presbyterian Church Wager, 1970–1971. Insert poster from the film starring Warren Beatty and Julie Christie before the film title was changed to "McCabe and Mrs. Miller." $150 *(Auction)*

The Pride and the Passion, 1957. Beautiful artwork on this Belgian poster for the film with Frank Sinatra, Cary Grant, and Sophia Loren. Good condition, 21¼″ × 24¼″. $25–$50

The Prisoner of Zenda, 1936. One-sheet poster headlining Ronald Coleman. $125 (Auction)

Private Lives of Elizabeth and Essex, 1939. French, stone lithographic poster with a playfully elegant carmine portrait of Errol Flynn; also starring Bette Davis and Olivia de Havilland. Linen-mounted, 47″ × 63″. $425 (Auction)

Psycho, rerelease 1966. One-sheet poster for the Hitchcock classic starring Anthony Perkins. One of the most requested titles on want lists; looks exactly like the original with only the addition of "It's Back." Good condition. $65–$90

Same as above. Good condition, half-sheet. $65–$90

Same as above. Great lobby card set, good condition. $85–$110

Same as above, rerelease 1969. Rolled half-sheet. $30–$55

Purple Noon, 1961. One-sheet from the film starring Elaine Delon. $50 (Auction)

Pursuit to Algiers, 1945. One-sheet poster for atmospheric Rathbone/Bruce Sherlock Holmes collaboration, features artwork of ship in the high seas. $475 (Auction)

Queimada! (Burn!), 1969. Italian poster from the film starring Marlon Brando. 26″ × 37″. $75 (Auction)

Quérelle, 1981. Artist: Andy Warhol. Unusual Warhol film poster for the original German release of the cult movie by Fassbinder starring Brad Davis. Done in several color combinations, this is the lime green version with the red tongue. Mint condition, 25″ × 38″. $250 (Auction)

Racket Busters, 1938. Continental Litho three-sheet poster features Bogart and George Brent, along with Warner Brothers' bombshell graphics; great crime poster. Linen-mounted. $600–$800

The Rains Came, 1939. French poster with impressive graphics from this high-class disaster epic set in India starring Tyrone Power, Myrna Loy, and George Brent. Linen-mounted, 15½″ × 23″. $50 (Auction)

The Razor's Edge, 1946. Insert poster from the Somerset Maugham classic starring Tyrone Power and Gene Tierney. Hard to find, good condition. $275–$325

Same as above. Lobby card of Tierney and Power in close-up. Good condition. $50–$75

Rebecca of Sunnybrook Farm, 1932. One-sheet, Fox, stone lithographic poster for the film with Ralph Bellamy and Marion Nixon; the first version of the popular book. Great colors and design. Fine condition.
                                                              $350–$400

Rebel Without a Cause, 1955. Four lobby cards all depicting James Dean; terrific cards from the super classic, also starring a young Natalie Wood. $400 (Auction)

Same as above. Japanese poster. Framed, 20″ × 30″.
                                                          $125 (Auction)

Riders of the Deadline, 1943. Magnificent Morgan Litho one-sheet poster with William Boyd as the heroic Hopalong Cassidy.
                                                          $200 (Auction)

Rio Grande, 1950. French, stone lithographic poster with dramatic action from John Ford's classic western starring John Wayne and Maureen O'Hara, graphics by Cartier Dargouge. Linen-mounted, 47″ × 63″. $300 (Auction)

River of No Return, 1954. Three lobby cards including title card—all feature early screen images of Marilyn Monroe. Good condition.

$50 (Auction)

Road to Morocco, 1942. One-sheet poster for Paramount's comedy classic with Hope, Crosby, Lamour, and the talking camel. Good condition. $250 (Auction)

Road to Singapore, 1940. Complete set of eight lobby cards for the first road picture, starring Bing Crosby, Dorothy Lamour, and Bob Hope.

$225 (Auction)

Same as above. One-sheet poster with full-length poses of stars, fine color. $600 (Auction)

The Roaring Twenties, 1939. Linen lobby card for the famous Warner Brothers gangster classic. Great shot of James Cagney, Humphrey Bogart, Gladys George, Rosemary Lane, Jeffrey Lynn, and Frank McHugh, all with raised glasses in toast. Good condition. $875–$1,000

Same as above. Lobby card showing posed shot of Cagney with Lane and George. Good condition. $700–$800

Roberta, 1935. Marvelous window card features the early Astaire/Rogers pairing that led them to stardom. Fine condition, framed.

$1,800 (Auction)

Rockabye, 1932. RKO one-sheet poster for film with Constance Bennett, Joel McCrea, Paul Lukas. Great portrait of Bennett. Good condition. $300–$350

Roman Holiday, 1953. One-sheet poster with Gregory Peck and Audrey Hepburn. $125 *(Auction)*

The Roman Spring of Mrs. Stone, 1961. Featuring the beautiful Vivien Leigh at the hands of young Warren Beatty. 40″ × 60″.

$50 *(Auction)*

Romeo and Juliet, 1968. British release poster from Franco Zeffirelli's hit starring Olivia Hussey. 20″ × 30″. $25 *(Auction)*

Room at the Top, 1959. One-sheet from the film starring Laurence Harvey and Simone Signoret (Academy Award). Good condition.

$25–$50

Sahara, 1943. Style B one-sheet poster shows great Bogey in the Tank Corps. Scarce. $275 *(Auction)*

Sailors Beware, 1927. Stunning Morgan, stone lithographic three-sheet poster from Hal Roach's pathecomedy headlining Stan Laurel before teaming with Hardy. Museum-caliber material. $1,400 *(Auction)*

Same as above. One-sheet, small piece missing from corner.

$4,000 *(Auction)*

Salomé, 1918. Artist: C. Bourdin. Very colorful French two-panel from original release of one of vamp Theda Bara's most famous costume roles. Extremely rare, linen-mounted, 60″ × 89″. $950 *(Auction)*

Salomé, 1953. One-sheet from the film starring Rita Hayworth and Stewart Granger. $125 *(Auction)*

San Antonio, 1945. Continental one-sheet poster of Errol Flynn and Alexis Smith from Warners' splashy Texas epic. $225 *(Auction)*

Same as above. One-sheet. $375 *(Auction)*

Sands of Iwo Jima, 1949. One-sheet poster features gun-wielding John Wayne charging the beach in his first Oscar-nominated performance.

$300 *(Auction)*

Santa Fe, 1959. Technicolor poster for this Randolph Scott grand-scale western. Framed, 40″ × 76″.   *$275 (Auction)*

The Scarlet Claw, 1944. One-sheet poster from this Rathbone/Bruce Sherlock Holmes film with horror graphics features a bright flaming claw. Scarce, fine condition.   *$700 (Auction)*

Scarlet Empress, 1934. Belgian release electrotype poster featuring Marlene Dietrich, finely detailed and lusciously colored. Linen-mounted, 24″ × 33½″.   *$1,500 (Auction)*

Scarlet Pimpernel, 1935. Lobby card with great close-up of Leslie Howard and Merle Oberon in this adventure classic. Fine condition.
$100–$125

Same as above. Another lobby card of Howard and Oberon. Good condition.   *$75–$100*

The Sea Hawk, 1940. Striking French, stone lithographic poster by Herve Morvan from the Errol Flynn/Michael Curtiz swashbuckling classic, exciting action and colors. Linen-mounted, 47″ × 63″.
$300 (Auction)

Search for Beauty, 1934. Beautiful Paramount one-sheet poster with "30th International Search for Beauty Contest Winners" shown in the background encircling a globe; featuring Buster Crabbe, Ida Lupino, and Robert Armstrong. Good condition.   *$150–$175*

The Searchers, 1956. Spanish poster with art by Jano, illustrating John Ford's adult western starring John Wayne and Natalie Wood. Linen-mounted, 27″ × 39″.   *$175 (Auction)*

Same as above. Belgian poster. Linen-mounted, 14″ × 19″.
$100 (Auction)

Second Fiddle, 1939. Beautiful Fox, stone lithographic one-sheet with portraits of stars Tyrone Power, Sonja Henie, and Rudy Vallee designed around a musical note. Fine condition.   *$250–$300*

Courtesy of Camden House Auctioneers

The Seven Year Itch, 1955. Three-sheet poster for this Marilyn Monroe and Tom Ewell classic, probably the most popular of the Monroe films. The famous image of Marilyn Monroe with her white dress being blown skyward from the wind coming up through a subway grate. Mint condition. $1,100 (Auction)

Same as above. One-sheet with great artwork of a saucy Monroe. Very rare, good condition. $375–$450

Same as above. Colorful lobby card (#5) with Monroe, Ewell, Sonny Tufts, and Robert Strauss. Fine condition. $65–$90

Same as above. Colorful lobby card with classic scene of Monroe in bathtub with her big toe stuck in faucet as Victor Moore tries to free her. Fine condition. $85–$110

Same as above. Title lobby card. $250 (Auction)

Same as above. Window card. 14″ × 22″. $275 (Auction)

The Shadow Strikes, 1937. One-sheet poster for the film with Rod LaRocque and Lynn Anders; based on the pulp and radio thriller. The shadow looms large in the background over the other characters. Very rare, good condition. $150–$175

Shall We Dance, 1937. Lobby card from the film headlining Fred Astaire and Ginger Rogers. $375 (Auction)

Shanghai Madness, 1933. One-sheet, stone lithographic poster from this rare, early Fox film. Great portrait artwork of Spencer Tracy and Fay Wray. Good condition. $400–$450

She Had to Say Yes, 1933. One-sheet poster for this early Warner Brothers film with Loretta Young and Lyle Talbot; directed by Busby Berkeley. Young and Talbot gaze into each other's eyes in this Art Deco design. Fine condition. $200–$225

She Wolf of London, 1946. Full lobby card set in original Universal wrapper, excellent color; starring young June Lockhart. Mint condition. *$125 (Auction)*

She Wore a Yellow Ribbon, 1949. Belgian poster, great artwork of John Wayne from the John Ford epic western adventure. Linen-mounted, 14″ × 19″. *$75 (Auction)*

The Sheik, 1921. French, stone lithographic poster from the original release, evoking all the majesty of the Silent Film era; starring Rudolph Valentino and Agnes Ayres. Extremely rare, linen-mounted, 48″ × 60″. *$12,000–$15,000*

Sherlock Holmes and the Voice of Terror, 1942. One-sheet poster with good color and imagery from this Basil Rathbone/Sherlock Holmes mystery. *$700 (Auction)*

Sherlock Holmes in Washington, 1942. One-sheet poster; the White House serves as backdrop to Rathbone's Holmes mystery. Good condition. *$425 (Auction)*

The Shocking Miss Pilgrim, 1946. A complete set of eight lobby cards in original sleeve for the film featuring Betty Grable and Dick Haymes. *$125 (Auction)*

Show Business, 1944. Half-sheet paper with Eddie Cantor, very pretty colors. Good condition. $45–$70

Sidewalks of New York, 1931. Lobby card for this early Buston Keaton sound film. Keaton being held at gunpoint by Cliff Edwards. Very rare, fine condition. $250–$300

Sing and Be Happy, 1937. One-sheet, Fox, stone lithographic poster with great colors and design for the film with Tony Martin, Joan Davis, and Allan Lane. Good condition. $65–$90

Singing in the Rain, 1952. One-sheet poster for this MGM musical classic. Famous shot of Gene Kelly, Debbie Reynolds, and Donald O'Connor all walking with umbrellas; great color and design. Very rare, good condition, linen-mounted. $450–$500

Same as above. Half-sheet poster featuring Gene Kelly, Donald O'Connor, and Debbie Reynolds. Framed. $300 (Auction)

Same as above. Linen-mounted three-sheet. $525 (Auction)

Same as above. Colorful title card of Kelly, Reynolds, and O'Connor. Good condition. $125–$150

Slave Ship, 1937. Tooker one-sheet poster with marvelous portraits of Warner Baxter, Wallace Beery, and Mickey Rooney. Mounted on rice paper. $400 (Auction)

Snow White and the Seven Dwarfs, 1937. Style A one-sheet poster with caricatures of all the dwarfs for Walt Disney's first full-length animated feature. Good condition, linen-mounted. $1,400 (Auction)

Same as above, rerelease 1943. Half-sheet. $250 (Auction)

Same as above, rerelease 1951. One-sheet, linen-mounted.
$300 (Auction)

Some Like It Hot, 1959. One-sheet poster for the Billy Wilder classic comedy starring Marilyn Monroe, Tony Curtis, and Jack Lemmon. Great shot of all three, Curtis and Lemmon dressed as women. Very rare, good condition. $350–$400

Same as above. Three-sheet. $375 (Auction)

Same as above. French release poster. 48″ × 60″. $225 (Auction)

Something to Sing About, 1936. Half-sheet poster starring James Cagney. Horizontal 28″ × 22″. $85 (Auction)

Son of Frankenstein, 1939. Belgian poster with luminous sinister graphics of Rathbone, Karloff, and Lugosi from one of the greatest of the Universal Frankenstein series. Linen-mounted, 14″ × 18″.
$275 (Auction)

Son of the Sheik, 1926. Half-sheet poster of Rudolph Valentino and Vilma Banky in classic embrace from Valentino's last film, a full-blooded, fast-paced masterpiece. Horizontal 28″ × 22″.
$950 (Auction)

The Song of Freedom, ca. 1936. One-sheet from the original U.S. release for English Paul Robeson fable of dockworker-cum-opera-star-cum-leader-of-his-African-tribe. Unusual and very rare.

$600 *(Auction)*

The Sound of Music, 1965. Seven different lobby cards from the Julie Andrews musical hit. Andrews on all but one. Good condition.

$45–$70 *for all*

Spartacus, 1961. One-sheet (Academy Award version) from Kirk Douglas' smash hit, winner of four Academy Awards. Good condition.

$35–$60

Same as above. Insert (Academy Award version), good condition.

$35–$60

Spellbound, 1945. One-sheet poster from the Hitchcock classic thriller. Striking image of Ingrid Bergman and Gregory Peck (with razor). Very good condition, a good example of a Hitchcock poster, linen-mounted.

$1,500–$1,700

Same as above. Lobby card with full-length shot of Bergman and Peck in skiing gear. Good condition.

$85–$110

Spider Woman, 1943. One-sheet poster from one of Sherlock Holmes' most interesting adventures, featuring Gale Sondergaard. Good color, rare.

$600 *(Auction)*

Same as above. Full set of lobby cards, including rare shot of Holmes in disguise. Very collectible, fine condition.

$1,200 *(Auction)*

Same as above. Half-sheet with spider web imagery, one of the best Holmes' posters. Horizontal 28″ × 22″.

$450 *(Auction)*

Sporting Blood, 1937. Half-sheet poster featuring Maureen O'Sullivan and Robert Young. Beautiful MGM design and colors. Good condition.

$35–$60

The St. Louis Kid, 1934. Great title card from the early James Cagney Warner Brothers classic with super shot of Cagney. Cagney material has become in great demand in the last few years. Very rare, slight border repair.

$950–$1,100

Stagecoach, 1939. Belgian poster with brilliant artwork by Wik from the movie starring John Wayne and directed by John Ford. Linen-mounted, 14″ × 18″.

$250 *(Auction)*

A Star is Born, 1954. A luminous Judy Garland dominates the art for this very rare and collectible one-sheet poster; director Cukor's first-rate film also stars James Mason. Framed.   *$850 (Auction)*

Same as above. Three-sheet poster. Good condition with slight loss at extreme bottom, linen-mounted.   *$550 (Auction)*

State Fair, 1933. Beautiful Fox, stone, lithographic one-sheet poster featuring Will Rogers, Janet Gaynor, and Lew Ayres in the 1930s' classic. Very rare, good condition.   *$400–$450*

Same as above. Title card.   *$75–$100*

Stella Dallas, 1937. Lobby card close-up of Barbara Stanwyck and John Boles from this Sam Goldwyn classic.   *$50–$75*

Same as above. One-sheet poster, good condition.   *$200 (Auction)*

Step Lively, 1944. Half-sheet poster with Frank Sinatra. Nice colors and design, early Sinatra. Rare, good condition.   *$45–$70*

The Story of Dr. Wassell, 1944. Stunning and complex Morgan one-sheet poster from the C. B. DeMille Technicolor hit, portrays Gary Cooper amid flaming jungle graphics.   *$175 (Auction)*

Strange People, 1932. Beautiful obscure, Chesterfield one-sheet poster with John Darrow and Gloria Shea; looks like a silent poster. Good condition.   *$65–$90*

The Stranger, 1946. Half-sheet poster from Welles' film noir classic with Orson Welles, Loretta Young, and Edward G. Robinson. Good condition.   *$65–$90*

Same as above. Lobby card with Welles and Young.   *$25–$50*

Strangers of the Evening, 1932. One-sheet, stone lithographic poster for a rare, early mystery film with Zazu Pitts and Lucien Littlefield. Great colors and Art Deco design. Fine condition.   *$100–$125*

The Strawberry Blonde, 1941. One-sheet poster with caricatures of James Cagney, Olivia de Havilland, and Rita Hayworth from this movie where a turn-of-the-century dentist wonders whether he married the right girl.   *$300 (Auction)*

A Streetcar Named Desire, 1951. One-sheet headlining Vivien Leigh and Marlon Brando. Fair condition.   *$250 (Auction)*

Strike Up the Band, 1940. Insert poster from the musical classic directed by Busby Berkeley with Judy Garland and Mickey Rooney. Super colors and MGM design. Rare, fine condition (rolled).

$275–$325

Suddenly Last Summer, 1960. Six-sheet poster featuring a shining full-length pose of Liz Taylor in a white bathing suit from the Tennessee Williams' classic film, also starring Monty Clift and Katharine Hepburn. $275 (Auction)

Same as above. Insert poster, framed. $150 (Auction)

Summer Stock, 1950. Three-sheet poster with Judy Garland and Gene Kelly. $300 (Auction)

Same as above. Half-sheet poster. $125 (Auction)

Summertime, 1955. One-sheet featuring Katharine Hepburn and Rossano Brazzi. Paper-mounted. $225 (Auction)

The Sun Also Rises, 1957. One-sheet poster from the film starring Tyrone Power, Ava Gardner, Mel Ferrer, Errol Flynn, and Eddie Albert. Paper-mounted. $175 (Auction)

Sunday, Bloody Sunday, 1971. One-sheet poster from this complex adult film, starring Glenda Jackson and Peter Finch. Framed.

$50 (Auction)

Sunset Boulevard, 1950. One-sheet poster from the Billy Wilder classic with Gloria Swanson, William Holden, and Erich Von Stroheim. Super artwork of Swanson; one of the most requested titles. Very hard to find, good condition. $500–$600

Superman and the Mole Men, 1951. One-sheet poster features great shots of the mole men and a spectacular George Reeves in this highly coveted poster from the first Superman feature. One of the top fantasy posters of the 1950s. $700 (Auction)

Superman the Movie, 1978. French poster featuring Christopher Reeve aloft in his first Man of Steel epic. 48″ × 60″. $125 (Auction)

Svengali, 1931. Lobby card from this rare, early sound Warner Brothers classic. Great scene of John Barrymore as Svengali menacing Marian Marsh as Trilby. Fine condition. $250–$300

Sweet Bird of Youth, 1962. One-sheet poster from this early Paul Newman film, also starring the talented Geraldine Page and Rip Torn.
$100 (*Auction*)

Swing Time, 1936. One-sheet offset poster by Morgan features Astaire and Rogers dancing with much "joie de vivre." This film ranks with *Top Hat* as one of the two best Fred/Ginger musicals; this poster compares well with *Top Hat* posters. Very good condition, an excellent example of the genre, linen-mounted. $5,000–$6,000

Tail Spin, 1939. Beautiful Fox, stone lithographic one-sheet poster from the film with Alice Faye, Constance Bennett, Nancy Kelly, and Jane Wyman. Features Faye, Bennett, and Kelly as pilots in upper corner, with planes zooming around the poster. Fine condition.
$175–$200

Tales That Witness Madness, 1968. Italian poster for the horror anthology starring Brigitte Bardot and Jane Fonda. 26½″ × 37½″.
$50 (*Auction*)

Tales of Manhattan, 1942. Preferred style B, Tooker, stone lithographic one-sheet poster presents dazzling skyscraper title treatment.
$550 (*Auction*)

The Tango Tangle, rerelease. One-sheet, stone lithographic poster with unusual Charlie Chaplin caricature. $250 (*Auction*)

Tarzan and the Huntress, 1947. Beautiful RKO title card with Johnny Weissmuller. Good condition. $65–$90

Tarzan Triumphs (*Le Triomphe de Tarzan*), 1943. French release poster from the film starring Johnny Weissmuller. Linen-mounted, 47″ × 63″. $225 (*Auction*)

Taxi, 1932. Great Belgian crime poster pairs a tough James Cagney with the tender Loretta Young. Linen-mounted, 24″ × 31″.
$500 (*Auction*)

Tea and Sympathy, 1956. The lovely Deborah Kerr is featured on this one-sheet poster from Vincent Minelli's sensitive love story. Framed.
$75 (*Auction*)

Terror by Night, 1946. Half-sheet poster with a fine graphic representative of the Rathbone/Bruce Sherlock Holmes' mystery/adventure series. Fine condition but once folded, horizontal 28″ × 22″.

$350 (Auction)

Tess of the Storm Country, 1932. Two one-sheet, Fox, stone lithographic posters. One of Janet Gaynor at the helm of a boat, with Charles Farrell by her side. Second shows Gaynor and Farrell head-to-head at the top with two men fighting below. Very rare title from the popular 1930s team. Fine condition. $225–$250 each

Courtesy of Camden House Auctioneers

The Testament of Orpheus (*Le Testament d'Orphée*), 1960. Original French release; Jean Cocteau designed this graphic for his poetic fantasy. A stunning collector's item, fine condition, linen-mounted, 47″ × 63″. $1,600 (Auction)

That Lady in Ermine, 1948. Three-sheet poster featuring a breathtaking Grable pin-up from this cheerful Lubitsch musical comedy. Linen-mounted. $325 (Auction)

That's the Way It Is, 1970. Elvis' portrait commands this three-sheet poster from the documentary production. $75 (Auction)

Same as above. Insert poster, framed. $125 (Auction)

There's No Business Like Show Business, 1954. Insert poster from the film headlining Ethel Merman, Donald O'Connor, and Marilyn Monroe.   *$175 (Auction)*

They Died with Their Boots On, 1941. Colorful Warner Brothers lobby card from the classic western with Errol Flynn. Nice shot of Flynn on horseback. Good condition.   *$250–$300*

They Shoot Horses, Don't They?, 1969. Insert poster from acclaimed Jane Fonda, Red Buttons 1930s' marathon dance tragedy. Framed, 14″ × 36″.   *$75–$125*

The Thirty-Nine Steps, rerelease. Exquisite one-sheet poster from the stylish Hitchcock masterpiece features subtle color portraits of Robert Donat and Madeleine. Framed.   *$600 (Auction)*

Courtesy of Camden House Auctioneers

This Gun for Hire, 1942. Insert poster from this film noir masterpiece that launched the careers of gunman Ladd and sultry Lake. Very rare and collectible, rolled.   *$1,100 (Auction)*

The Three Musketeers, 1935. Beautiful jumbo window card from the Dumas classic with Paul Lukas and Walter Abel. Good condition, 22″ × 28″. $45–$70

Same as above. Fair condition, horizontal 26″ × 22″. $75 (Auction)

The Three Musketeers, 1948. Insert poster featuring Lana Turner and Gene Kelly. $100 (Auction)

Thunderball, 1965. One-sheet poster from the film starring Sean Connery as James Bond. Nice art. Good condition. $100–$125

Thunderball/You Only Live Twice, reissue 1971. Combo lobby card set from nice Connery as Bond reissue. Good condition. $35–$60

Titanic, 1953. Beautiful title card from this classic film starring Barbara Stanwyck and Clifton Webb. Good condition. $25–$50

To Be or Not to Be, 1942. French, stone lithographic poster of Jack Benny and Carole Lombard from one of the greatest comedies of all time, features art of Duccio Marvasi. Linen-mounted, 47″ × 63″. $325 (Auction)

Same as above. Title card with head shots of Carole Lombard and Jack Benny. Very good condition. $300–$350

To Have and Have Not, 1944. Lobby card from the first film with Bogart and Bacall, the adaptation of the Ernest Hemingway novel. Classic scene of Bacall lighting Bogart's cigarette. Good condition. $150–$175

Same as above. One-sheet poster of Bogie and Bacall embrace. Very good condition, a good example of Bogart/Bacall posters, linen-mounted. $1,000–$1,200

Tom Jones, 1963. One-sheet from the Academy Award winner (Best Picture) starring Albert Finney. Framed. $50 (Auction)

Tom Hat, rerelease 1953. One-sheet poster headlining Fred Astaire and Ginger Rogers. $425 (Auction)

Torch Song, 1953. One-sheet from the film starring Joan Crawford. $200 (Auction)

Tower of London, 1939. Lobby card from the classic Universal horror film with Boris Karloff and Basil Rathbone. Good condition.

$250–$300

Same as above. Style A, brightly colored, one-sheet, Morgan stone lithographic poster of a maniacal Karloff. $550 *(Auction)*

Transatlantic Merry-Go-Round, 1934. Half-sheet poster with Jack Benny. Horizontal 22″ × 28″. $475 *(Auction)*

Treasure of the Sierra Madre, 1948. French, stone lithographic poster with gorgeous Rene Paron artwork capturing the magic of Huston's dark journey into the soul, starring Humphrey Bogart, Tim Holt, and a memorable Walter Huston. Linen-mounted, 47″ × 63″.

$400 *(Auction)*

Same as above. Half-sheet poster with great color and artwork, two portraits of Bogart. Horizontal 28″ × 22″. $600 *(Auction)*

Same as above, reissue 1953. One-sheet with nice art as used on first release. Fine condition, duo-tone. $50–$75

20,000 Leagues Under the Sea, 1954. Window card from the film starring Kirk Douglas and James Mason. 14″ × 22″. $90 *(Auction)*

2001: A Space Odyssey, reissue 1971. One-sheet poster, nice "Star-Child" version. Good condition. $15–$30

Two-Faced Woman, 1941. Lobby card with fantastic close shot of Garbo dancing, with caption reading "Garbo dances . . . in her gayest romance!" Good condition. $175–$200

Under Capricorn, 1949. Belgian poster from the movie featuring the unbeatable combination of Hitchcock, Joseph Cotten, and Ingrid Bergman. Linen-mounted, 14½″ × 19″. $25 *(Auction)*

Union Pacific, 1939. One-sheet poster with spectacular title treatment promotes DeMille's epic western. Linen-mounted. $450 *(Auction)*

The Unknown (*l'Inconnu*), 1927. French release, unusual design by artist Chenal from this Lon Chaney/Joan Crawford collaboration. Linen-mounted, 43″ × 58″. $700 *(Auction)*

The Vagabond (*Vagabonden*), ca. 1920s. Original Mutual poster from Scandinavian release of Chaplin's most important two-reeler. Good condition, linen-mounted, 24″ × 35″. $800 *(Auction)*

Veronica Lake Portrait, 1946. French, stone lithographic poster with art by Soubie, elegant and luscious. Highly prized, 22″ × 24″.

$450 (Auction)

Vertigo, 1958. One-sheet poster for this Hitchcock classic features Saul Bass' artwork creating one of the most compelling graphics in modern posters, with James Stewart and Kim Novak. $375 (Auction)

Same as above. Half-sheet. $200–$225

Same as above. One lobby card with Stewart and Barbara Bel Geddes. $25–$50

Same as above. Six different lobby cards (all show Stewart and Novak). $35–$60 each

Viva Maria, 1965. French poster featuring Brigitte Bardot and Jeanne Moreau. 48″ × 60″. $125 (Auction)

Viva Zapata!, 1952. Spanish release poster from the film starring Marlon Brando and Anthony Quinn. 28″ × 40″. $150 (Auction)

Wabash Avenue, 1950. Very rare, style B, one-sheet, stone lithographic poster features famous full-bodied pin-up of Grable doing the shimmy at the 1892 World's Fair. $550 (Auction)

Warrior's Rest, 1962. Three-sheet poster from the film starring Brigitte Bardot. $125 (Auction)

Watch on the Rhine, 1943. One-sheet poster featuring Bette Davis and Paul Lukas. Paper-mounted. $475 (Auction)

Waterloo Bridge, 1940. Title card from the romance classic. Great shots of Vivien Leigh and Robert Taylor. Fine condition.

$250–$300

We're Not Dressing, 1934. One-sheet Paramount poster features shipwrecked Crosby, Lombard, and Burns and Allen in the South Pacific. Mint condition, linen-mounted. $350 (Auction)

Weekend in Havana, 1941. One-sheet, Tooker, stone lithographic poster stars Alice Faye and features Carmen Miranda with trademark hat. Very collectible, linen-mounted. $400 (Auction)

West Side Story, 1962. One-sheet Natalie Wood classic. All posters are Academy Award version. Good condition. $35–$60

Same as above. Insert. $35–$60

Same as above. Lobby card set. $45–$70

Same as above, 1968 reissue. Half-sheet. $15–$30

Same as above, 1968 reissue. Six-sheet. $20–$45

West of Rainbows' End, 1938. One-sheet, stone lithographic poster with action portrait of cowboy legend Tim McCoy.   *$525 (Auction)*

When Strangers Marry, 1944. Beautiful Monogram, stone lithographic one-sheet poster for this hard-to-find film noir with Robert Mitchum and Kim Hunter. Good condition. $35–$60

Whirlwind, 1933. One-sheet, Morgan action poster portraying Tim McCoy. Linen-mounted.   *$125 (Auction)*

Whispering Smith, 1949. One-sheet poster from Alan Ladd's first Technicolor western. Framed.   *$150 (Auction)*

Whispering Wires. One-sheet poster shows an apprehensive young woman and her lady's maid, surrounded by mysterious scenes from the movie. Very good condition, linen-mounted. (See color center section.) $700–$800

White Christmas, 1954. Insert poster from the film starring Bing Crosby and Danny Kaye.   *$200 (Auction)*

White Woman, 1933. Paramount lobby card with great shot of Carole Lombard and Charles Laughton. Rare Lombard title. Good condition.
$250–$300

Whoopee, 1930. Insert with excellent Technicolor/Deco styling for Busby Berkeley's first Hollywood picture as choreographer, starring Cantor. Linen-mounted.   *$750 (Auction)*

Wild in the Country, 1961. Insert poster with Elvis Presley. Good condition. $75–$100

Same as above. Lobby card set. $85–$110

Courtesy of Camden House Auctioneers

The Wild One, 1953. Best poster on this classic, a three-sheet, shows fine portrait of Brando in leather with gang at bottom. Very desirable, linen-mounted. $1,100 (Auction)

Without Love, 1945. One-sheet poster headlining Spencer Tracy and Katharine Hepburn. Linen-mounted. $100 (Auction)

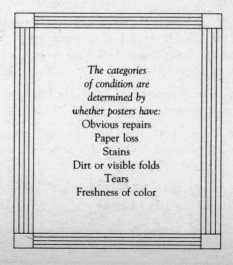

*The categories
of condition are
determined by
whether posters have:*
Obvious repairs
Paper loss
Stains
Dirt or visible folds
Tears
Freshness of color

Courtesy of Camden House Auctioneers

The Wizard of Oz, 1939. Lobby card, scene of Oz saying farewell, a finely detailed card from MGM's Technicolor triumph.

$2,700 (Auction)

Same as above. Offset title lobby card with very good images of Judy and each major actor/character plus caricatures of various scenes; illustrations on this title card do not appear in other sizes of posters from this film. Fine condition, very collectible.

$4,000–$6,000

Woman of the Year, 1942. Preferred style D, beautiful one-sheet, Tooker, stone lithographic poster from George Stevens' powerful pairing of Hepburn and Tracy (their first!). Very collectible.

$750 (Auction)

Women in Love, 1969. French poster depicts the celebrated Alan Bates/Oliver Reed nude wrestling match. Framed, 23″ × 30″. $300–$350

A Yank in the R.A.F., 1941. One-sheet, Tooker, stone lithographic poster promotes Grable and Power in this classic wartime flag-waver.

$650 (Auction)

Yankee Doodle Dandy, 1943. Lobby card from the film starring James Cagney, autographed by James Cagney. $550 (Auction)

Yolanda and the Thief, 1945. One-sheet poster from Astaire's surrealistic fantasy directed by Minelli. Very scarce. $275 (Auction)

You Belong to Me (Tu M'Appartiens), 1941. French release poster for the comedy film of a lady doctor who's wary of her male patients, starring Barbara Stanwyck and Henry Fonda. Linen-mounted, 47" × 64". $200 (Auction)

You Only Live Twice, 1967. One-sheet poster from the film starring Sean Connery as James Bond. Nice art. Good condition. $90–$115

Same as above. Half-sheet. $90–$115

Same as above. Insert. Good condition. $65–$90

You Were Never Lovelier, 1942. Features potent pairing of Astaire and Hayworth in this Columbia musical vehicle. 14" × 22".
$150 (Auction)

You're Telling Me, 1934. Lobby card from the film headlining W. C. Fields. Framed. $200 (Auction)

Ziegfeld Follies, 1945. Style D, one-sheet, Tooker, stone lithographic poster presents six fabulous females in exotic chorus girl garb, autographed by director Minelli. $1,600 (Auction)

Zoo in Budapest, 1933. One-sheet, stone lithographic poster from the film starring Loretta Young and Gene Raymond, an early Young film. Fantastic artwork and colors. Very good condition. $275–$325

RESOURCES

RESOURCE GUIDE

AUCTION HOUSES

Butterfield & Butterfield, 220 San Bruno Avenue, San Francisco, CA 94103, (415) 861–7500, Carol Hay, 19th- and 20th-century works of art, 7601 Sunset Boulevard, Los Angeles, CA 90046, (213) 850–7500. Established in 1865, the largest and oldest full-service auction house in western America, with specialists in numerous areas on staff. Illustrated posters are usually in sales of fine prints and photographs.

Camden House Auctioneers, Inc., 10921 Wilshire Boulevard, #808, Los Angeles, CA 90024 (213) 476–1628, Melissa and Barry Vilkin. Specializing in motion picture and entertainment memorabilia—consignments include posters, lobby cards, props, scripts, animation cels, autographs, and costumes.

Christie's East, 219 E. 67th Street, New York, NY 10021, (212) 606–0530, Peggy Gilges, Specialist, Art Nouveau and Art Deco. Four annual Art Nouveau/Art Deco auctions, including posters. Christie's East is very well known in the collecting field for its Art Deco auctions.

Christie's South Kensington, Ltd., 85 Old Brompton Road, London, SW7 3LD, 01–581–7611, Richard Barclay, Consultant. Regularly holds poster-only auctions.

Freeman/Fine Arts Company of Philadelphia, 1808–10 Chestnut Street, Philadelphia, PA 19103, (215) 563–9275, Leslie Lynch Clinton, ASA/Marketing Director. A full-service auction and appraisal service specializing in estates, Americana, 18th- and 19-century paintings, silver, jewelry, 18th-century furniture, and real estate. Catalog subscription available yearly.

Grogan & Company, 890 Commonwealth Avenue, Boston, MA 02215, (617) 566–4100, Martha Richardson, Director of Fine Arts. Auction specialists in paintings, prints, drawings, sculpture, jewelry, silver, decorative works of art, Oriental rugs and tapestries, and furniture.

Guernsey's, 136 E. 73rd Street, New York, NY 10021, (212) 794–2280, Arlan Ettinger, President. Specializing in rare movie posters, decorative and historic American and European posters, and Buffalo Bill posters.

Oliver's, Route 1, Plaza 1, Kennebunk, ME 04043, (207) 985–3600, Susan Haley. A full-service auction company specializing in thematic sales which have produced numerous world record prices.

Phillips Fine Art Auctioneers, 406 E. 79th Street, New York, NY 10021, (212) 570–4830, Claudia Florian, Manager. Fine art auctioneers and appraisers, holding auctions in all areas of fine and decorative arts and collectibles and serving as a representative office for the London main branch.

Poster Mail Auction Company, Box 133 (#2 Patrick Street), Waterford, VA 22190, (703) 882–3574, R. Neil Reynolds, owner. Mail/telephone auction catalogs of pre-1950 original posters and related vintage graphics are issued four to five times per year. A four-issue subscription is available by first-class mail for $10.

Riba Auctions, P.O. Box 53, S. Glastonbury, CT 06073, (203) 633–3076. Posters, autographs, photography, and political items. Catalog available for $18 or $48 for the year.

Skinner, Inc., 357 Main Street, Bolton, MA 01740, (508) 779–6241, Alicia Gordon. New England's largest auction gallery, conducting over 60 auctions annually.

Swann Galleries, Inc., 104 E. 25th Street, New York, NY 10010, (212) 254–4710, Caroline Birenbaum, Director of Communications. The oldest and largest U.S. auctioneer specializing in rare books, autographs and manuscripts, photographs, Judaica, and works of art on paper; conducts some 35 sales a year. Illustrated posters are usually in sales of decorative graphics or performing arts; historical broadsides in sales of Americana or rare books. Quarterly newsletter; catalogs.

William Doyle Galleries, 175 E. 87th Street, New York, NY 10128, (212) 427–2730, Abigail Furey, Print Specialist. Semiannual auctions of Old Master and modern prints, June and December. Catalog subscriptions available, back catalogs sometimes. Call or write for details.

William J. Jenack Auctioneers & Appraisers, 18 Hambletonian Avenue, Chester, NY 10918, (914) 469-9095, FAX (914) 469-7129, William J. Jenack. Specializing in World War I, World War II, circus, travel, and specialty sales. Call for information on catalogs.

Winter Associates, 21 Cooke Street, Box 823, Plainville, CT 06062, (203) 793-0288, Linda Stamm, co-owner. Print auctions two to four times per year, some offering poster collections. Gallery specializes in estate liquidation of antiques, fine art, etc.

DEALERS

An American Collection, P.O. Box 237, Yorktown Heights, NY 10598, (914) 245-8829, Roberta and Stuart Friedman. Specializing in museum-quality American art posters by Bradley, Reed, Penfield, Dow, etc., American Art Deco posters, and 1960s' rock and roll posters. Also art books and paintings.

Anca Colbert Fine Arts., Ltd., 7278 Beverly Boulevard, Los Angeles, CA 90036, (213) 937-7573, Anca Colbert, President. European and American posters, 1865 to 1945. Specializes in performing arts subjects and exceptional images by French artists.

Antique Poster Collection, 17 Danbury Road (Route 35), Ridgefield, CT 06877, (203) 438-1836, George G. Goodstadt, owner. Art gallery and dealer—European posters featuring the Belle Epoque and Art Nouveau periods, and American posters from the mid-19th to early 20th centuries. Subjects include circus, magic, World War I and World War II, French travel, and French and American theater.

Arts of the Floating World, 270 Concord Road, Wayland, MA 01778, (508) 358-2775, Robert F. Jacobs, owner. Deals in art produced by turn-of-the-century French artists, mainly Toulouse-Lautrec, Mucha, Chéret, Steinlen, and Icart, as well as Japanese woodblock prints and paintings.

Barbara Leibowits Graphics, 80 Central Park West, New York, NY 10023, (212) 769-0105, Barbara Leibowits, President. Dealers in rare fine posters, illustrated books, prints, and drawings. Specializing in Art Nouveau, Art Deco, Russian avant-garde, De Stijl, Dada, Surrealism, and other modern movements.

Bernice Jackson, P.O. Box 1188, Concord, MA 01742, (508) 369-9088, Bernice Jackson, owner. Fine Arts Consultant specializing in posters of countries such as Austria, Holland, Switzerland, Hungary, and Poland, and offering a wide range of other posters including travel, Art Nouveau, and Art Deco.

The Chisholm Gallery, 43 Greenwich Avenue, New York, NY 10011, (212) 243-8834, Gail Chisholm. Handling decorative and rare vintage posters, 1890–1960, on a wide range of subjects, with specialties in American publishing posters, British transport, shipping, and aviation.

Chisholm Prats Gallery, 145 8th Avenue, New York, NY 10011, (212) 741-1703, Robert Chisholm. American and European posters from the 1890s to the 1950s. Exceptional collections of travel, English, American, Mexican, Spanish, Art Deco, Danish, and other specialties. Photos available, shipping arranged.

Cinemonde, 1932 Polk Street, San Francisco, CA 94109, (415) 776–9988, Jose Ma. Carpio, proprietor. Specializing in vintage posters/lobby cards of classic and popular films, both American and foreign.

Club of American Collectors of Fine Arts, Inc., One Lincoln Plaza, 20 W. 64th Street, Suite #21K, New York, NY 10023, (212) 769–1860, Jacques-Paul Athias, President. Established in 1980 by international appraiser Jacques-Paul Athias; one of the largest sources of museum-quality pieces by Lautrec, Chéret, Mucha, Steinlen, Cassandre, and other Art Nouveau and Art Deco poster artists.

Craig Flinner Gallery, 505 N. Charles Street, Baltimore, MD 21201, (301) 727–1863, Craig Flinner, owner. General line old print shop carrying a selection of posters with particular emphasis on old American ads.

DeLind Fine Art, 801 N. Jefferson Street, Milwaukee, WI 53202, (414) 217–8525, Bill DeLind. Railroad travel posters, French posters to 1938. Over 200 in inventory including well-known, unusual, and less well-known lower-priced posters.

Galerie Un. Deux. Trois, 5 Rue Muzy, Geneva, Switzerland 1207, 22/7861611, Clerc Jean-Daniel, Director. Swiss, French, Italian original posters from 1900 to 1960. Over 5,000 in stock.

Gary Borkan Antiques, Box 870, Melrose, MA 02176, (617) 662–5757, Gary Borkan, owner. General line of paper with posters on war, travel, and turn-of-the-century U.S. posters.

Graphic Expectations, Inc., 757 W. Diversey Parkway, Chicago, IL 60614, (312) 871–0957, Arthur Bernberg, Director. A modern poster gallery with total emphasis on the performing arts: Mobil posters, film, theater, dance, and music. Framed and unframed. Worldwide shipping.

Harris Gallery, 2842 Prince Street, Berkeley, CA 94705, (415) 658–6609, Stephen Harris and Sarah Stocking, owners. Specializing in European and American posters from 1885 to 1950, in all subject areas. One of the largest selections of classic original posters.

Hirschl & Adler Galleries, Inc., 21 E. 70th Street, New York, NY 10021, (212) 535–8810, Joseph Goddu. Dealer in 19th- and 20th-century American prints. Catalog for exhibition "American Art Posters of the 1890s" available for $25 postpaid.

Jane Moufflet Gallery, 8840 Beverly Boulevard, Los Angeles, CA 90048, (213) 275–3629, Bob Rehnert and Jane Moufflet. Dealing in French posters, ca. 1900–1960. Specializing in: original posters from the 1920s and 1930s; Lautrec, Mucha, and Cassandre as well as lesser names with great graphics; etchings and paintings of Louis Icart; and Foujita, Marie Laurencin, Warhol, etc.

Kate Hendrickson, 1211 N. LaSalle, Suite 703, Chicago, IL 60610, (312) 751–1932, Kate Hendrickson, owner. Specializing in European posters (1890s–1950s) with an emphasis on Italian posters.

The Kellenberger Collection, Chemin Planaz 22, Blonay/Montreux, Switzerland 1807, 011–41–21–943–4444, Eric Kellenberger. One of the world's largest selections of fine original vintage posters. More than 5,000 posters by well-known artists from all countries and all periods.

Kiki Werth Posters, 185 Westbourne Grove, London, W11 25B, England, 229–7026, Kiki Werth. Specializing in British posters of 1900–1940 and American 1950s posters. Deals in all posters pre-1970.

Larry Edmunds Bookshop, Inc., 6658 Hollywood Boulevard, Hollywood, CA 90028, (213) 463–3273, Mike Hawks, Mail Order Dept. Specializing in books on film, TV, theater. Also selling memorabilia from films such as posters, lobby cards, and fan magazines, as well as photographs from film and television programs.

The Last Moving Picture Company, 2044 Euclid Avenue, Cleveland, OH 44114, (216) 781–1821, Morris Everett, Jr., owner. Collector of posters from every known movie title. Store buys and sells all types of cinema posters, 1912 to the present. Want lists welcome.

Lucy Broido Graphics, Ltd., 908 Wootton Road, Bryn Mawr, PA 19010, (215) 527–3415, Lucy Broido, owner. Dealer to the trade only, with a very large collection of original Art Nouveau and Art Deco posters.

Luton's Theater Poster Exchange, P.O. Box 27621, 2780 Frayser Boulevard, Memphis, TN 38127, (901) 357–1649, Bill Luton, owner. Deals in all types of movie posters—from very old posters for silent movies to brand new posters, rare and expensive to B-movie and inexpensive—one-sheets, inserts, lobby cards, stills, half-sheets, three-sheets, six-sheets, window cards, etc.

Maitres De L'Affiche, Eve Phillips, 79 Chatsworth Road, London, NW2 4BH, England, 011–44–1–459–3326; Richard Barclay, 39 Inglethorpe Street, London SW6 6NS, England, 011–44–1–381–4341. European vintage posters, specializing in British Rail and other areas. Appraisals. Advisor to Christie's for European poster auctions.

Marc H. Choko, Universite du Quebec à Montreal, C.P. 8888 succ. A, Faculte de Design, Montreal, Quebec, Canada H3C 3P8, (514) 987–3913. Specializing in Canadian and Canadian-related posters.

Meehan Military Posters, P.O. Box 477, Gracie Station, New York, NY 10028, (212) 734–5683, Mary Ellen Meehan. The only poster dealer to specialize exclusively in World War I, Spanish Civil War, and World War II posters. Publish two catalogs per year (available at $5 each postpaid), containing over 500 illustrations each, including seven color plates.

Motion Picture Arts Gallery, 133 E. 58th Street, New York, NY 10022, (212) 223–1009, Ira Resnick, President. Art gallery and dealer—graphic art posters from films, silent era through 1950s, some 1960s and 1970s.

The Movie Gallery, Inc. and *Posters of the Past*, 2072 Front Street, East Meadow, NY 11554, (516) 794–0294, Nancy Lifschultz, President. In business for more than 22 years, carries more than 12,000 film posters and lobby cards from 1910 to the present. Also large quantities of foreign posters, travel posters, autographs, stills, and movie memorabilia, plus theater posters and theater memorabilia.

N. Bailly Fine Arts, 117 W. 120th Street, New York, NY 10027, (212) 866–5043, Nicolas Bailly. Specializes in rare posters by Toulouse-Lautrec, Villon, Bonnard, Cassandre, Loupot, Mucha, Chéret, Cappiello. By appointment only.

Nancy Steinbock Fine Posters and Prints, 197 Holmes Dale, Albany, NY 12208, (518) 438–1577, Nancy Steinbock, owner. Specializing in travel posters, including trains, ships, and planes; turn-of-the-century American posters; World War I and World War II posters.

Omnibus Gallery, 533 E. Cooper Street, Aspen, CO 81611, (303) 925–5567, FAX (303) 925–7805, George Sells. Specializing in rare and vintage posters, primarily dating before World War II. The extensive collection features over thirty-five different Cassandres, as well as images by Loupot, Baumberger, Chéret, Colin, Mucha and a cast of thousands.

Park South Gallery at Carnegie Hall, 885 7th Avenue, New York, NY 10019, (212) 246–5900, Laura Gold, President. Art Nouveau and Art Deco original litho posters.

Pasquale Iannetti Art Galleries, Inc., 522 Sutter Street, San Francisco, CA 94102-1102, (415) 433-2771, Silvia Pratt, Marketing Director; 946 Madison Avenue, New York, NY 10021, (212) 472-4300. Specializing in fine original prints, drawings, and other unique works by master artists from the 16th century through the contemporary era.

Pat Kery Fine Arts, 52 E. 66th Street, New York, NY 10021, (212) 734-5187, Pat Kery, owner. Specializing in rare vintage posters, Impressionist and Modern paintings, drawings, and sculpture for collectors and museums. Author of *Art Deco Graphics* and *Great Magazine Covers of the World* (see Bibliography).

Posner Gallery, 207 N. Milwaukee Street, Milwaukee, WI 53202, (414) 273-3097, Judith Posner, Director. Specializing in turn-of-the-century French posters, in excellent condition, mounted on linen.

Poster America, 138 W. 18th Street, New York, NY 10011, (212) 206-0499, Jack Banning. American and European posters, 1890-1960. Specializing in Italian, German, English posters with a design orientation.

The Poster Collector, 390 West End Avenue, New York, NY 10024, (212) 873-1893, Mark Weinbaum, Proprietor. Turn of the century through 1930s.

Posters Plus, 210 S. Michigan Avenue, Chicago, IL 60604, (312) 461-9277, David Gartler. Multi-location vintage and contemporary poster galleries with a broad selection of collectibles and a specific emphasis on American posters.

Reinhold Brown Gallery, 26 E. 78th Street, New York, NY 10021, (212) 734-7999, FAX (212) 734-7044, Susan Reinhold and Robert K. Brown, Directors. Specializing in fine, rare, 20th-century graphic design as well as classic posters by important 20th-century architects and fine artists.

Stephen Ganeles, P.O. Box 91, Prince Street Station, New York, NY 10012, (212) 674-7624. Specializing in: decorative posters and prints (1890-1950), especially from the Art Deco period; travel posters; Dutch posters, including the Amsterdam School. Catalog available for $2. Also interested in purchasing posters.

Thomas G. Boss Fine Books, 355 Boylston Street, Boston, MA 02116, (617) 421-1880, Thomas G. Boss, owner. Dealing in posters and American, English, and continental illustrated books from the Art Nouveau to Art Deco periods—1890s to 1940s. Catalogs issued.

Turner Dailey, 7220 Beverly Boulevard, Los Angeles, CA 90036, (213) 931-1185. Dealing in rare, unusual avant-garde posters, especially American, Russian, and Scandinavian. Catalogs issued.

Yaneff Gallery, 119 Isabella Street, Toronto, Ontario, Canada M4Y 1P2, (416) 924–6677, Cheryl Teron, Director. Specializing in antique French posters dating from ca. 1890 to 1925, with a large collection of Jules Chéret posters, as well as original artist and war posters.

SHOW MANAGEMENT/CONVENTIONS

Cinecon (Started in 1964). Convention for members of the National Society for Cinephiles. Held over the Labor Day weekend in a different city each year. Silent/sound films, guest stars, special events. Admission charge (includes one-year membership in the SFC). For information, contact Randy Haberkamp, Vice President, Society for Cinephiles, 978 S. Muirfield Road, Los Angeles, CA 90019.

Cinefest (Started in 1979). Held in March in Syracuse, New York, under the aegis of the Syracuse Cinephile Society. Silent/sound films, special events. Admission charge. For information, contact Phil Serling, 215 Dawley Road, Fayetteville, NY 13066–2546.

Cinevent (Started in 1977). Held over the Memorial Day weekend in Columbus, Ohio. Silent/sound films. Admission charge. For information, contact Steve Haynes, 1103 Woodrow Avenue, Columbus, OH 43207.

International Vintage Poster Fair. Loupro, Inc., produces this poster show in April and October in New York City. The October 1989 show featured 16 poster dealers from Western Europe and the United States. Admission charge. For information, contact Jack Banning or Louis Bixenbaum, Poster America, 138 W. 18th Street, New York, NY 10011, (212) 206–0499.

Sanford L. Smith & Assoc., Ltd., 68 E. 7th Street, New York, NY 10003, (212) 777–5218. Write: Sanford Smith, President, with photos of current booth and references from three dealers who currently exhibit at Sanford Smith shows. Annual shows: "Modernism 1860–1960—A Century of Style and Design" second weekend in November; "Fall Antiques Show" at the Pier, third week of October; "Art at the Armory" late November–early December; "Works on Paper" late February–early March; "Beaux Arts/The 20th Century" first week in April; and "Images and Objects" first week of October in Boston. All shows have poster dealers participating; "Works on Paper" has the greatest concentration of them.

SOCIETIES AND ASSOCIATIONS

Ephemera Society of America, Inc., P.O. Box 37, Schoharie, NY 12157. Founded in 1980 to encourage the ever-growing interest in paper collectibles, to further the special interests of the collector, and to serve as the link between collectors. The Society sponsors an annual conference and ephemera fair. Members receive *Ephemera News*, a quarterly newsletter; *The Ephemera Journal*, a scholarly review; a membership directory; and discounts on reference books from *Ephemera Books*. Membership dues begin at $25; write the above address for further information or for addresses of Ephemera Societies around the world.

National Association of Paper and Advertising Collectors (NAPAC), P.O. Box 500, Mount Joy, PA 17552, (717) 653–8240, Doris Ann Johnson, Editor of *PAC* (*The Paper and Advertising Collector*, monthly publication of NAPAC). Membership open to anyone interested in paper and advertising collecting, includes subscription to *PAC*. Fee: $12 per calendar year, $25 first-class subscription.

Society for Cinephiles, P.O. Box 290178, Fort Lauderdale, FL 33329, (305) 424–3910, R. Trent Codd, Secretary. Educational organization for film enthusiasts; sponsors annual Cinecon of film screenings and displays of film-related material.

MUSEUMS AND COLLECTIONS

Art Institute of Chicago, Michigan Avenue at Adams Street, Chicago, IL 60603, (312) 443–3660, Anselmo Carini, Associate Curator, Department of Prints and Drawings. A fine group of 19th-century French posters including almost all posters done by

Toulouse-Lautrec, plus Theophile-Steinlen and Alphonse Mucha. Hours: Mon., Wed.–Fri., 10:30–4:30; Tues., 10:30–8:00; Sat., 10:00–5:00; Sun., 12:00–5:00. Recommended admission: adults $5; students $2.50.

Baltimore Museum of Art, Art Museum Drive, Baltimore, MD 21218, (301) 396–6347, Jay M. Fisher, Curator of Prints, Drawings, and Photographs. An important collection of posters, a part of its world-renowned prints and drawings collection. Particular strengths include French 19th-century examples by Lautrec, Chéret, Steinlen, and others; turn-of-the-century Art Nouveau posters; and an extensive number of World War I and II posters. The Museum mounts occasional exhibitions utilizing this collection. Otherwise posters can be viewed by appointment in the BMA's Samuel H. Kress Foundation for Prints, Drawings, and Photographs offices. Hours: Tues., Wed., Fri., 10:00–4:00; Thurs., 10:00–9:00; Sat., Sun., 11:00–6:00. Admission: adults (18 and over) $3; under 18 free.

Beverley R. Robinson Collection, United States Naval Academy, Halligan Hall, Third Floor, Annapolis, MD 21401, (301) 267–3250, Sigrid Trumpy, Curator. Collection of war posters. Collection hours: Mon.–Fri., 8:00–5:00. (USNA Museum hours: Mon.–Sat., 9:00–5:00; Sun., 11:00–5:00.) Admission free.

Billy Rose Theater Collection, New York Public Library, 111 Amsterdam Avenue, New York,

NY 10023, (212) 870–1637, Bob Taylor, Assistant Curator. The collection of posters numbers over 25,000 and represents virtually every major field of popular entertainment: stage, cinema, circus, cabaret, etc. The collection spans the 19th and 20th centuries and includes window cards and lobby cards, as well as one-, two-, and three-sheets. Hours: Mon., Thurs., 10:00–7:45; Tues., Wed., Fri., 12:00–5:45; Sat., 10:00–5:45.

Bridgeport Public Library Historical Collections, 925 Broad Street, Bridgeport, CT 06610, (203) 576–7417, Mary K. Witkowski, Acting Department Head. Posters and broadsides include circus posters from the late 1800s to the 1940s. Call for hours.

Cooper Hewitt Museum, The Smithsonian Institution's National Museum of Design, 2 E. 91st Street, New York, NY 10028, (212) 860–6183, Gail S. Davidson, Assistant Curator of Drawings and Prints. A selection of more than one thousand American, European, and Japanese posters, mostly 20th century, with special emphasis on the posters of E. McKnight-Kauffer (1890–1954). Hours: Tues., 10:00–9:00; Wed.–Sat., 10:00–5:00; Sun., 12:00–5:00; closed Mon. Admission: adults $3; students and senior citizens $1.50; children under 12 free.

Harry Ransom Humanities Research Center, The University of Texas at Austin, Box 7229, Austin, TX 78713, (512) 471–4663, Kathleen Gee, Curator, Art Collection. Poster collection of 8,000 World War I posters (American, French, German, a few British); 600 World War II posters (primarily British, American); 250 Spanish Civil War posters; 100 Japanese occupation posters. Call for hours and admission fees.

Hood Museum of Art, Dartmouth College, Hanover, NH 03755, (603) 646–3109, Kellen Haak, Associate Registrar. Poster collection includes World War I, World War II, and American posters of 1890s. Hours: Tues.–Fri., 11:00–5:00; Sat., 11:00–8:00; Sun., 11:00–5:00; closed Mon. Admission free.

Hoover Institution Archives, Stanford University, Stanford, CA 94305, (415) 723–3563, Marilyn Kann and Carol Leadenham, Assistant Archivists. Poster collection from 1900 to 1987. Thirty thousand cataloged posters from many countries, mostly American, British, French, German, and Russian, relating to 20th-century history, including World Wars I and II and the Russian Revolution. Many are propagandistic in nature. Color slides of the posters may be purchased for $3 each. Hours: Mon.–Fri., 8:15–4:45. Open to the public.

The Jane Voorhees Zimmerle Art Museum, Rutgers University, New Brunswick, NJ 08903, (201) 932–7237, Curator of Prints. Collection includes: French posters from the mid-19th century through the 1920s, with a concentration on Chéret and lesser-known artists of the 1890s; Belgian posters from the 1890s through 1910; and a sampling of American posters of the 1890s. Call for hours and admission fees.

Jersey City Museum, 472 Jersey Avenue, Jersey City, NJ 07302, (201) 547–4514, Nina A. Jacobs, Assistant Director. Permanent collection with continuous exhibitions of contemporary art and regional history; extensive education programs for children and adults. Hours: Tues., Thurs.–Sat., 10:30–5:00; Wed., 10:30–8:00. Suggested donation: $1.

Library of Congress Prints & Photographs Division, 1st and Independence S.E., Washington, DC 20540, (202) 707–8726, Elena G. Millie, Curator, Poster Collection. A collection of approximately 100,000 posters international in scope, dating from 1830s to the present. All major countries are represented, as well as most major poster artists and styles. Hours: Mon.–Fri., 8:30–5:00. Admission is free.

Margaret Herrick Library, Academy of Motion Picture Arts and Sciences, 8949 Wilshire Boulevard, Beverly Hills, CA 90211, (213) 278–8990, Linda Harris Mehr, Director. Collection of film posters (10,000+), 1911 to the present. Of particular note are the large number of stone lithograph posters from the pre-1920 period. Available for research only.

Metropolitan Museum of Art, 1000 Fifth Avenue, New York, NY 10028, (212) 879–5500. Holdings include the Leonard A. Lauder Collection of 158 American posters of the 1890s, plus numerous other additions and gifts. Hours: Sun., Tues.–Thurs., 9:30–5:15; Fri.–Sat., 9:30–9:00; closed Mondays and Christmas Day. Suggested admission fee: adults $5; students and senior citizens $2.50. To order the museum's catalog, *American Art Posters of the 1890s*, with essays by David Kiehl, call and ask for the Museum Bookshop.

Mulholland Library of Conjuring and the Allied Arts, 10100 Santa Monica Boulevard, 5th Floor, Los Angeles, CA 90067, (213) 277–3875, Ricky Jay, Curator. A private collection open to serious scholars by application. Large holding of posters and playbills relating to magic, circus, and unusual entertainments.

Museum of the City of New York, 1220 Fifth Avenue, New York, NY 10029, (212) 534–1672. Very large collection of theater

posters and window cards, primarily from Broadway and off-Broadway theaters in New York. Also smaller numbers of ballet, opera, magic, and circus posters. Hours: Tues.–Sat., 10:00–5:00; Sun., 1:00–5:00. Admission is free, although the following contributions are suggested: adults $3; senior citizens and students $1.50; children $1; families $5.

Museum of Modern Art, 11 W. 53rd Street, New York, NY 10019, (212) 708–9756, Jennifer Carlson, Senior Press Representative. Begun in 1935, the Museum of Modern Art's graphic design collection now numbers more than 3,500 examples of poster art dating from 1880 to the present, representing outstanding artists from around the world. A small selection of the museum's poster holdings is continuously displayed at the entrance to the fourth floor Architecture and Design galleries. In 1988, the museum organized *The Modern Poster*, a survey of more than 350 examples from its collection; the accompanying catalog ($50 cloth; $25 paper) is available from the MOMA Book Store or by calling the Mail Order Department, (212) 708–9888. Hours: Fri.–Tues., 11:00–6:00; Thurs., 11:00–9:00; closed Wed. Admission: Adults $6; full-time students $3.50; senior citizens $3; children under 16 accompanied by an adult free; museum members free; Thurs. 5:00–9:00, pay what you wish.

The New York Historical Society, 170 Central Park West, New York, NY 10024, (212) 873–3400, Wendy Shadwell, Print Curator. The Society's collection includes circus and theatrical posters; Civil War, World War I, and World War II posters; and advertising posters. The Landauer Collection of Business and Advertising Art contains over one million examples of posters and other ephemera dating from 1700 to the present; selections from this collection are on view by special appointment. Hours: Tues.–Sun., 10:00–5:00; closed on Mondays and holidays. Admission: adults $3; senior citizens $2; children under 12 $1.

Peabody Museum of Salem, East India Square, Salem, MA 01970, (508) 745–1876, Paul Winfisky, Acting Curator. Extensive collection of steamship posters, part of which will be on display for the next few years in the exhibition "Steamship Travel." The Museum currently has three authorized poster reproductions in print: the *American Line*, the SS *Paris*, and the *RMS Aquitania*. Hours: Mon.–Wed., Fri., Sat., 10:00–5:00; Thurs., 10:00–9:00; Sun., 12:00–5:00. Admission: adults $4; senior citizens $3; children $1.50.

Phoenix Art Museum, 1625 N. Central Avenue, Phoenix, AZ 85004, (602) 257–1880, Gail C. Griffin, Director of Membership. Permanent collection of approximately 60 posters, mostly French, from the Belle Epoque and the 20th century. Included are Toulouse-Lautrec, Bonnard, Steinlen, Picasso, and Matisse. Hours: Tues., Thurs.–Sat., 10:00–5:00; Wed., 10:00–9:00; Sun., 1:00–5:00; closed Mondays and holidays. Admission: adults $3; senior citizens $2.50; students $1.50; children under 12 and members free.

Santa Barbara Museum of Art, 1130 State Street, Santa Barbara, CA 93101, (805) 963–4364, Barry M. Heisler, Curator of Collections. A collection of nearly three hundred turn-of-the-century American art posters which includes works in very fine condition by Penfield, Parrish, Gould, Bradley, Reed, and Rhead. The poster collection is shown on an occasional basis as gallery space allows. Hours: Tues.–Sat., 11:00–5:00; Sun., 12:00–5:00. Admission is free.

Walker Art Center, Vineland Place, Minneapolis, MN 55403, (612) 375-7600. Permanent collection includes 20th-century paintings, sculpture, prints, and other works with particular strengths in Abstract Expressionism, Pop Art, and Minimalism. The McKnight Print Study Room houses works on paper, including posters. The Center Book Shop features a wide variety of books and posters available for purchase, including catalogs published by Walker Art Center. Hours: Tues.-Sat., 10:00-5:00; Sun., 11:00-5:00; closed Mondays. Admission: Thurs., free; all other times: adults $3; young adults (12-18) and groups of ten or more $2; free to museum members, senior citizens, children under 12, AFDC cardholders.

War Memorial Museum of Virginia, 9285 Warwick Boulevard, Newport News, VA 23607, (804) 247-8523, William C. Barker, Registrar. The museum's dynamic and growing collection of posters relates primarily to the American military experience of the 20th century, with particular emphasis on the World Wars. Civil War broadsides and foreign war posters of this century are also represented. Hours: Mon.-Sat., 9:00-5:00; Sun., 1:00-5:00. Closed major holidays. Admission: adults $2; children, senior citizens, and active duty military $1.

West Point Museum, U.S. Military Academy, West Point, NY 10996, (914) 938-2203, Michael E. Moss, Director. Collection of World War I and World War II posters, mostly American, some foreign; a few Civil War and Spanish-American War posters; some post-World War II posters. Call for hours and admission fees.

PERIODICALS

Art Business News, Myers Publishing Co., Inc., 60 Ridgeway Plaza, P.O Box 3837, Stamford, CT 06905, (203) 356-1745, Jo Yanow-Schwartz, Editor. Publication to the trade—dealers, galleries, etc.—covering business news relating to art. Circulated without charge to art dealers, framers, and related businesses in the United States and Canada. Subscription rates to others $3 per copy, $20 per year.

Big Reel, Empire Publishing Co., Inc., Rt. 3, Box 83, Madison, NC 27025, (919) 427-5850. A monthly tabloid for movie memorabilia collectors. Subscription: $20 for one year; single issue $3. Free catalog available.

Classic Images, P.O. Box 4079, Davenport, IA 52808, Susan Laimans, Editor-in-Chief. Monthly newspaper covering in-depth information and articles on classic films (silent through the 1950s), film conventions, and related news. Also sells film-related books. Subscription: $25 for one year (12 issues); $14.50 for six months; foreign rates available.

Gordon's Print Price Annual, Martin Gordon, Inc., 1840 Eighth Street South, Naples, FL 33940. Professional resource for auction records on fine art prints from major auction houses around the world. Now in its 12th edition, each volume covers the one year of auctions preceding its publication and is inclusive, not selective. 1990 edition: $325 plus postage.

Journal of Decorative and Propaganda Arts, 2399 N.E. Second Avenue, Miami, FL 33137, (305) 573-9170, Lynn Lambuth. An art history quarterly on the period 1875-1945. Many back issues available with article topics including the posters of Rockwell Kent, posters in Yugoslavia, and the work of Sven Brasch.

Journal of the Print World, 1000 Winona Road, Meredith, NH 03253-9599, (603) 279-6479, Charles S. Lane, Editor. Periodical in the field of rare print collecting. Published quarterly with articles and advertisements covering six centuries of rare prints. For sample copy, write the address above.

Print Collector's Newsletter, 72 Spring Street, New York, NY 10012, (212) 219-9722, Jacqueline Brody, Editor. A bimonthly publication specializing in articles and information on works of paper of all periods.

CONTEMPORARY PUBLISHERS

Communications Workers of America, 1925 K Street N.W., Washington, DC 20006, (202) 728-2382, Marcia Pappas Devaney. A series of six prints illustrating major issues of concern to unions and their members. Commissioned in commemoration of CWA's 50th anniversary from six of the nation's foremost graphic designers, the series won *Graphic Design: USA's* 1988 "Desi 11" design competition. Posters at $5 each ($25 the set) or fine art prints at $25 each ($100 the set) are available by mail. Call for further information or rush orders.

Graphique de France, 46 Waltham Street, Boston, MA 02118, (617) 482-5066, Angela Warren. Publishes and distributes posters, notecards, and calendars depicting some of the most popular fine art, photography, and contemporary images available.

Lincoln Center for the Performing Arts, Avery Fisher Hall, Broadway at 64th Street, New York, NY 10025, (212) 580–8700, Ext. 386, Thomas Lollar, Manager, Poster/Print Dept. Since 1962 the Lincoln Center/List Art Poster and Print Program has commissioned works of art by contemporary artists to commemorate major Lincoln Center events. They have been exhibited throughout the United States and Europe and are included in over four hundred museum collections worldwide. Limited edition prints and posters are available at various prices. Posters are on view at Avery Fisher Hall;

call for information on purchasing them.

School of Visual Arts, 209 E. 23rd Street, New York, NY 10010, (212) 679–7350. Collection of posters created annually for the School of Visual Arts by New York City's most famous illustrators and graphic designers, all faculty members. Exhibited recently by the Cooper Hewitt Museum, the posters are currently on an international museum tour. Posters are for sale to benefit the student scholarship fund: $32, tax-deductible, including shipping and handling.

RESTORATION/CONSERVATION

Andrea Pitsch, Paper Conservator, 348 W. 36th Street, 11th Floor, New York, NY 10018, (212) 594–9676. Conservation treatment: evaluation of the condition of art and historic artifacts on paper including prints and drawings, posters, and documents and correction of problems. Consultation services: examination and condition reporting on artworks prior to purchase; evaluation of storage facilities, matting, framing, and condition of private and public collections and inventories.

Gillaspie Gallery, 335 W. 35th Street, 12th Floor, New York, NY 10001, (212) 695–3943, Laurance Gillaspie, owner. Conservation and restoration of artwork on

paper, specializing in posters. By appointment.

Herman Poster Mount, Inc., 250 W. 40th Street, New York, NY 10018, (212) 730–7821; 8405 2nd Avenue, North Bergen, NJ 07047, (201) 861–0825; Herman Saavedra, President. Poster restoration, linen backing. Prices based on size and condition; $40 per hour on all restoration. By appointment.

J. Fields Gallery Poster Restoration, 60 Grand Street, New York, NY 10013, (212) 966–5533, Larry Toth. Linen mounting and restoration of posters, including color touch-up and paper repairs, to the trade.

BIBLIOGRAPHY

Note: The extensive bibliography that follows is intended to give readers numerous starting points for delving further into the world of posters. More has been written about poster art than any other form of advertising, and more good resources continue to appear every year.

EXHIBITION CATALOGS

1936. *Posters by Cassandre.* Catalog by E. M. Fantl. New York: The Museum of Modern Art, 1936.

1950. *Vingt-Cing Ans d'Affiches Parisiennes.* Catalog by Georges Duthuit. Lucern: Kunstmuseum Luzern, 1950.

1967. *The American Poster.* Catalog by Edgar Breitenbach and Margaret Cogswell. New York: The American Federation of Arts in association with October House, 1967.

1968. *Toulouse-Lautrec and His Contemporaries.* Catalog by Ebvia Feinblatt. Los Angeles County Museum of Art in association with New York: Harry N. Abrams, 1968.

1970. *La Belle Epoque: Belgian Posters, Watercolors and Drawings.* Catalog by Yolande Oostens-Wittamer. International Exhibitions Foundation in association with New York: Grossman Publishers, Inc., 1970.

1971. *American Posters of Protest 1966–1970.* Cataloged and edited by David Kunzle. New York: New School Art Center, 1971.

1972. *Will Bradley: American Artist and Craftsman (1868–1962).* New York: Metropolitan Museum of Art, 1972.

1974. *American Posters of the Nineties.* Introduction by Roberta Wong. Boston: Boston Public Library, 1974.

1976. *San Francisco Rock Poster Art.* Catalog by Walter Medeiros. San Francisco: San Francisco Museum of Modern Art, 1976.

1978. *Herbert Matter: A Retrospective.* A & A Gallery, School of Art, Yale University. New Haven: Yale University, 1978.

1980. *Retrospective Jean Carlu.* Catalog edited by Alain Weill. Paris: Musée de l'Affiche, 1980.

1980. *L'Affiche en Belgique 1880–1980.* Catalog by Alain Weill. Paris: Musée de l'Affiche, 1980.

1982. *Deutsche und Europaische Plakate 1945–1959.* Munich: Munchen Stradmuseum, 1982.

1984. *Designed to Persuade: The Graphic Art of Edward Penfield.* Catalog by David Gibson. Yonkers, New York: Hudson River Museum, 1984.

1984. *Modern American Poster.* Catalog by J. Stewart Johnson. The National Museum of Modern Art, Kyoto, and The Museum of Modern Art, New York, in association with New York: New York Graphic Society Books, and Boston: Little, Brown and Co., 1983.

1984. *The 20th-Century Poster—Design of the Avant Garde.* Catalog by Dawn Ades. Walker Art Center, in association with New York: Abbeville Press, 1984.

1985. *Henri de Toulouse—Lautrec: Images of the 1890s.* Catalog edited by Riva Castelman and Wolfgang Wittrock. New York: Museum of Modern Art, 1985.

1987. *American Advertising Posters.* Catalog by David Kiehl. New York: Metropolitan Museum of Art, 1987.

1987. *Jules Chéret, Creator of the Color Lithographic Poster.* San Francisco: Pasquale Iannetti Art Galleries, Inc., 1987.

1987–1989. *The Modern Dutch Poster.* Catalog by Prokopoff, Marcel, Ed., and Franciscono, Marcel. Urbana: Krannert Art Museum, and Cambridge and London: The MIT Press, 1987.

1988. *The Modern Poster.* Catalog by Stuart Wrede. Museum of Modern Art, New York. New York: Museum of Modern Art in association with Boston: Little, Brown and Co., 1988.

1989. *The American Art Posters of the 1890s.* Catalog by Joseph Goddu. New York: Hirschl & Adler Galleries, Inc., 1989.

HISTORIC REFERENCES

MAGAZINES AND PERIODICALS

Magazines and periodicals with articles and information about the development of the poster, as well as some with tipped-in color plates of posters themselves, are included here. Pages or plates from some of the following early editions have become collectors' items in their own right.

1889–1913   *La Plume*, bi-weekly, Paris.

1894–1897   *The Chap Book*, Chicago.

1896–1897   *Bradley: His Book*, Springfield, Massachusetts.

1896   *The Poster*, New York.

1896   *Poster Lore*, Kansas City.

1896–1900   *Les Maîtres de l'Affiche*, monthly, Paris.

1897–1899   *L'Estampe et l'Affiche*, bi-weekly, Paris.

1898–1901   *The Poster and Art Collector*, London.

1899   *Poster Collector's Circular*, London.

1900   *Album d'Affiches et d'Estampes Modernes*, quarterly, Paris.

1913–1921   *Das Plakat*, Berlin, originally published from 1910–1912 as *Mitteilungen des Vereins des Plakatfreunde*.

1910–1930   *The Poster*, Chicago.

1924 to Date   *Modern Publicity*, annual, London. Originally from 1924 as *Posters and Their Designers*; from 1925 as *Art and Publicity*; and from 1926–1930 as *Posters and Publicity*.

1925–1930   *Vendre*, Paris.

1927–1939   *Arts et Métiers Graphiques*, quarterly, Paris.

1941 to Date   *Pramierte Plakate*, Zurich and Basel.

1942 to Date   *Die Besten Plakate des Jahres*, Basel, which changed its title in 1976 to *Schweizer Plakate*.

1949–1973   *International Poster Annual*, New York.

OTHER PERIODICALS

In addition to the above, numerous annual and periodical publications continue to be issued by the graphic design and advertising industries including *Biennale Plakatu Warszawa*, Warsaw, 1966 to date; *Graphis Posters*, Zurich, 1973 to date; *The Lahti Poster Biennale*, Finland, 1973 to date; *The Best in Covers and Posters*, Washington, DC, 1975 to date; and *World Advertising Review*, Eastbourne, UK, 1985 to date. See the chapter entitled "Contemporary Poster Publishers and Patrons" for additional current periodicals in the field.

BOOKS AND CATALOGS

The following entries encompass early books on posters and catalogs of posters.

Alexandre, Arsene, et al. *The Modern Poster*. New York: Charles Scribner's Sons, 1895.

Bauwens, M., et al. *Les Affiches Etrangères Illustrées*. Paris: G. Boudet, 1897.

Bolton, Charles Knowles. *A Descriptive Catalogue of Posters, Chiefly American, in the Collection of Charles Knowles Bolton*. Boston: W. B. Jones, 1895.

———.*The Reign of the Poster*. Boston: Winthrop B. Jones, 1895.

Flood, Ned Arden. *A Catalog of an Exhibition of American, Dutch, English, French, and Japanese Posters from the Collection of Mr. Ned Arden Flood*. Meadville, Pennsylvania: Flood and Vincent, 1897.

Hiatt, Charles. *Picture Posters*. London: George Bell, 1895. (Reprinted 1976.)

Maindron, Ernest, *Les Affiches Illustrées 1886–1895*. Paris: G. Boudet, 1896.

Pollard, Percival. *Posters in Miniature*. New York: R. H. Russell, 1896.

Rodgers, W. S. *A Book of the Poster*. London: Greening & Co., 1901.

Sponsel, Jean Louis. *Das Moderne Plakat*. Dresden: Gerhard Kuhtmann, 1897.

PHILLIPS AUCTION CATALOGS

1979   *A Century of Posters 1870–1970*. Catalog of the Phillips auction on November 10, 1979. Text by Jack Rennert. New York: Phillips Son & Neale, 1979.

1980   *Poster Classics*. Catalog of the Phillips auction on May 10, 1980. Text by Jack Rennert. New York: Phillips Son & Neale, 1980.

1980   *The World of Posters*. Catalog of the Phillips auction on November 15, 1980. Text by Jack Rennert. New York: Phillips Son & Neale, 1980.

1981   *Poster Pleasures*. Catalog of the Phillips auction on April 11, 1981. Text by Jack Rennert. New York: Phillips Son & Neale, 1981.

1981   *100 Poster Masterpieces*. Catalog of the Phillips auction on May 2, 1981. Text by Jack Rennert. New York: Phillips Son & Neale, 1981.

1981   *19th- and 20th-Century Posters*. Catalog of the Phillips auction on November 21, 1981. Text by Jack Rennert. New York: Phillips Son & Neale, 1981.

1983   *Rare Posters*. Catalog of the Phillips auction on November 12, 1983. Text by Jack Rennert. New York: Phillips Son & Neale, 1983.

1984   *American Circus Posters*. Catalog of the Phillips auction on May 6, 1984. Text by Jack Rennert. New York: Jack Rennert and The Circus World Museum, 1984.

BOOKS

OVERVIEWS

Ades, Dawn. *Twentieth Century Poster—Design of the Avant Garde*. New York: Abbeville Press, 1984.

Allner, Walter H. *Posters: 50 Designers Analyze Methods and Design*. New York: Reinhold, 1952.

Barnicoat, John. *A Concise History of Posters*. New York and Toronto: Oxford University Press, 1980.

Battersby, Martin. *The Decorative Twenties*. New York: Walker & Co., 1969.

Circker, Hayward. *Golden Age of the Poster*. New York: Dover Publications, 1971.

Delhaye, Jean. *Art Deco Posters and Graphics*. London: Academy Editions, and New York: St. Martin's Press, 1977, 1984.

Gallo, Max. *The Poster in History*. New York: American Heritage Publishing, 1974.

Hillier, Bevis. *Posters*. New York: Stein and Day, 1969.

———. *100 Years of Posters*. New York: Harper & Row, 1972.

Holme, Bryan. *Advertising: Reflections of a Century*. London: Heineman, 1982.

Hutchinson, Harold F. *The Poster—An Illustrated History from 1860*. New York: The Viking Press, 1968.

Kery, Patricia Frantz. *Art Deco Graphics*. New York: Harry N. Abrams, 1986.

———. *Great Magazine Covers of the World*. New York: Abbeville Press, 1982.

McKnight-Kauffer, Edward. *The Art of the Poster: Its Origin, Evolution and Purpose*. New York: Albert & Charles Boni, 1928.

Menten, Theodore. *Advertising Art in the Art Deco Style*. New York: Dover Publications, 1975.

Muller-Brockmann, Josef and Shizuko. *History of the Poster*. Zurich: ABC Verlag, 1971.

Price, Charles Matlack. *Poster Design*. New York: G. W. Bricka, 1922.

Rickards, Maurice. *The Rise and Fall of the Poster*. New York: McGraw-Hill, 1971.

Sainton, Roger. *Art Nouveau Posters and Graphics*. New York: Rizzoli, 1977.

Sheldon, Cyril. *A History of Poster Advertising*. London: Chapman and Hall, 1937.

Weill, Alain. *The Poster—A Worldwide Survey and History*. Boston: G. K. Hall & Co., 1985.

BY COUNTRY

AMERICAN POSTERS

Berman, Levi. *Posters U.S.A.* New York: American Heritage Publishing Co., 1957.

Hornung, Clarence P., Ed. *Will Bradley Posters and Graphics*. New York: Dover Publications, 1974.

Keay, Carolyn. *American Posters of the Turn of the Century*. New York: St. Martin's Press, 1975.

Kiehl, David W. *American Art Posters of the 1890s in the Metropolitan Museum of Art, Including the Leonard A. Lauder Collection*. New York: Metropolitan Museum of Art in association with Harry N. Abrams, 1987.

Ludwig, Coy. *Maxfield Parrish*. New York: Watson Guptill, 1973.

Malhorta, Ruth, Christina Thorn, et. al. *Das frühe Plakat in Europa und den U.S.A.*, Volume I, British and American Posters. Berlin: Mann Verlag, 1973.

Margolin, Victor. *American Poster Renaissance*. New York: Watson Guptill Publications, 1975.

Wong, Roberta, and Clarence P. Hornung. *Will Bradley: His Graphic Art*. New York: Dover Publications, 1974.

AUSTRIAN POSTERS

Koschatsky, Walter, and Horst-Herbert Kossatz. *Ornamental Posters of the Vienna Secession*. London: Academy Editions, and New York: St. Martin's Press, 1974.

BELGIAN POSTERS

Malhorta, Ruth, Christina Thorn, et. al. *Das frühe Plakat in Europa und den U.S.A.*, Volume II, French and Belgian Posters. Berlin: Mann Verlag, 1977.

Oostens-Wittamer, Yolande. *De Belgische Affiche 1900*. Brussels: Koningklijke Bibliotheek, 1975.

DUTCH POSTERS

Dooijes, Dick. *A History of the Dutch Poster 1890–1960.* Amsterdam: Schellema & Holkema, 1968.

ENGLISH POSTERS

Cooper, Austin, *Making a Poster.* London: The Studio, 1938.

Haworth-Booth, Mark. *E. McKnight-Kauffer: A Designer and His Public.* London: Gordon Fraser, 1979.

Hudson, Derek. *James Pride, 1866–1941.* London: Constable, 1949.

Hutchinson, Harold F. *London Transport Posters.* London: London Transport Board, 1963.

Malhorta, Ruth, Christina Thorn, et. al. *Das frühe Plakat in Europa und den U.S.A.*, Volume I, British and American Posters. Berlin: Mann Verlag, 1973.

McKnight-Kauffer, Edward. *The Art of the Poster.* London: Cecil Palmer, 1924.

Purvis, Tom. *Poster Progress.* London: The Studio, 1938.

Reade, Brian. *Aubrey Beardsley.* New York: Viking Press, and London: Studio Vista, Ltd., 1967.

Sparrow, Walter Shaw. *Advertising and British Art.* London: John Lane, 1974.

Steen, Margeurite. *William Nicholson.* London: Collins, 1943.

Strong, Ray. *London Transport Posters.* London: Phaidon, 1976.

FRENCH POSTERS

Abdy, Jane. *The French Poster: Chéret to Cappiello.* London: Studio Vista, Ltd., 1969.

Adhemar, Jean. *Toulouse-Lautrec: His Complete Lithographs and Drypoints.* New York: Harry N. Abrams, 1965.

Arwas, Victor. *Belle Epoque Posters and Graphics.* New York: Rizzoli International Publishers, 1978.

———. *Berthon & Grasset.* Paris: Denoel, 1978.

Baruch, Hugo. *Toulouse-Lautrec and Steinlen.* London: Modern Art Gallery, 1946.

Bouvet, Francis. *Bonnard: The Complete Graphic Work.* New York: Rizzoli, 1981.

Bridges, Ann, Ed. *Alphonse Mucha: The Complete Graphic Works.* New York: Harmony Books, 1980.

Broido, Lucy. *French Opera Posters.* New York: Dover, 1976.

——. *The Posters of Jules Chéret.* New York: Dover, 1980. (*Catalogue Raisonne*)

Brown, Robert K., and Susan Reinhold. *The Poster Art of A. M. Cassandre.* New York: E. P. Dutton, 1979.

Cate, Phillip, and Susan Gill. *Theophile-Alexandre Steinlen.* Salt Lake City: Gibbs Smith, 1982.

Defert, Theirry, and Lepape, Claude. *From the Ballets Russes to Vogue: The Art of Georges Lepape.* New York: Vendome Press, 1984.

Malhorta, Ruth, Christina Thorn, et. al. *Das frühe Plakat in Europa und den U.S.A.*, Volume II, French and Belgian Posters. Berlin: Mann Verlag, 1977.

Marx, Roger, Jack Rennert, and Alain Weill. *Masters of the Poster 1896–1900.* A soft-cover reproduction of all 256 plates of the *Maîtres de l'Affiche* as originally printed by Chaix 1896–1900. New York: Images Graphiques, Inc., 1977.

Mourlot, Fernand. *Les Affiches Originales des Maîtres de l'École de Paris:* Braque, Chagall, Duffy, Léger, Matisse, Miro, Picasso. Monte Carlo: A. Sauret, 1959.

Mouron, Henri. *A. M. Cassandre.* New York: Rizzoli, 1985.

Mucha, Jiri. *Alphonse Mucha.* London: Hamlyn Publishing Group, 1967.

Rennert, Jack. *100 Posters of Paul Colin.* New York: Images Graphiques, 1979.

Rennert, Jack and Alain Weill. *Mucha: The Complete Posters, and Panels.* Boston: G. K. Hall, 1984. (*Catalogue Raisonne*)

Schardt, Hermann, Ed. *Paris 1900: Masterworks of French Poster Art.* New York: Putnam, 1970.

Weill, Alain. *100 Years of Posters of the Folies-Bergère and Music Halls of Paris.* New York: Images Graphiques, 1977.

Wittrock, Wolfgang. *Toulouse-Lautrec: The Complete Prints.* 2 Vols. London: Sotheby's Publications, 1985.

GERMAN POSTERS

Malhorta, Ruth, Christina Thorn, et. al. *Das frühe Plakat in Europa und den U.S.A.*, Volume III, German Posters. Berlin: Mann Verlag, 1980.

Rademacher, Hellmut, trans. by Rhodes, Anthony. *Masters of German Poster Art.* New York: October House, 1966.

SWISS POSTERS

Margadant, Bruno, Ed. *The Swiss Poster: 1900–1983*. Basel: Birkhauser Verlag, 1983.

Rotzler, Willy, and Karl Wobmann. *Political and Social Posters of Switzerland*. Zurich: ABC Verlag, 1985.

Triet, Max, and Karl Wobmann, Eds. *Swiss Sport Posters*. Zurich: ABC Verlag, 1983.

Tschanen, Armin, and Walter Bangerter, Eds. *Official Graphic Art in Switzerland*. Zurich: ABC Verlag, 1964.

BY SUBJECT

CARE AND IDENTIFICATION OF POSTERS AND PRINTS

Dolloff, Francis W., and Roy L. Perkinson. *How to Care for Works of Art on Paper*. Boston: Museum of Fine Arts, 1985.

Gascoigne, Bamber. *How to Identify Prints*. New York: Thams and Hudson, 1986.

CINEMA POSTERS

Brown, Jay A., and the editors of *Consumer Guide*. *Rating the Movies*. Skokie, Illinois: Publications International, Ltd., 1987. (Aphabetical movie listing and capsule reviews, not a book on the posters themselves.)

Edwards, Gregory J. *International Film Poster: The Role of the Poster in Cinema Art, Advertising and History*. Topsfield, Massachusetts: Salem House Ltd., 1985.

Kobal, John. *Fifty Years of Movie Posters*. London: Hamlyn, 1973.

Morella, Joe, Edward Epstein, and Eleanor Clark. *Those Great Movie Ads*. New Rochelle, New York: Arlington House, 1972.

Rebello, Stephen, and Richard Allen. *Reel Art: Great Movie Posters from the Golden Age of the Silver Screen*. New York: Abbeville Press, 1988.

Schapiro, Steve, and David Cierichetti. *The Movie Poster Book*. New York: E. P. Dutton, 1979.

Scott, Kathryn Leigh. *Lobby Cards, The Classic Films: The Michael Hawks Collection*. London and Los Angeles: The Pomegranate Press, Ltd., 1987.

——. *Lobby Cards, The Classic Comedies: The Michael Hawks Collection, Vol. II.* London and Los Angeles: The Pomegranate Press, Ltd., 1988.

Shipman, David. *The Great Movie Stars: The Golden Years.* New York: Hill and Wang, 1979. (Guide to movies themselves, not posters.)

——. *The Great Movie Stars: The International Years.* New York: Hill and Wang, 1980. (Guide to movies themselves, not posters.)

CONTEMPORARY POSTERS

de Harak, Rudolph, Ed. *Posters by Members of the Alliance Graphique Internationale (1960–1985).* New York: Rizzoli International, 1986.

Garrigan, John (intro). *Images of an Era: The American Poster 1945–1975.* Washington, DC: Smithsonian Institution, 1975.

List, Vera, and Herbert Kupferberg. *Lincoln Center Posters.* New York: Harry N. Abrams, 1980.

MAGIC, CIRCUS, AND THEATER

Davis, Paul. *Paul Davis—Posters and Paintings.* New York: E. P. Dutton, 1977.

Fox, Charles Phillips. *American Circus Posters in Full Color.* New York: Dover, 1978.

——. *The Great Circus Street Parade in Pictures.* New York: Dover, 1978.

Haill, Catherine. *Theatre Posters.* London: Victoria and Albert Museum, 1983.

Hearn, Michael Patrick. *The Art of the Broadway Poster.* New York: Ballantine Books, 1980.

Rennert, Jack. *100 Years of Circus Posters.* New York: Darien House, 1976.

Reynolds, Charles and Regina. *100 Years of Magic Posters.* New York: Darien House, 1975.

ROCK POSTERS

Grushkin, Paul. *The Art of Rock.* New York: Abbeville Press, 1987.

King, Eric. *A Collector's Guide to the Numbered Dance Posters Created for Bill Graham and The Family Dog, 1966–1973.* Berkeley: Svaha Press, 1980.

TRAVEL AND TRANSPORTATION

Belvès, Pierre, *Cent Ans d'Affiches de Chemin de Fer*. Paris: Editions NM/La Vie du Rail, 1981.

Choko, Marc H., and David L. Jones: *Canadian Pacific Posters, 1883–1963*. Montreal: Meridian Press, 1988.

Hiller, Bevis. *Travel Posters*. New York: E. P. Dutton, 1976.

Levey, Michael F. *London Transport Posters*. Phaidon Press, Oxford, 1976.

Peignot, Jerome. *Air France: Posters 1933–1983*. Paris: Fernand Hazan, 1988.

Rennert, Jack. *100 Years of Bicycle Posters*. New York: Darien House, 1973.

Shackleton, J. T.: *The Golden Age of the Railway Poster*. Paris: New English Library, 1976.

Wobmann, Karl. *Tourism Posters of Switzerland*. Aarau: AT Verlag, 1980.

WAR AND REVOLUTION

Crawford, Anthony. *Posters of World War I and World War II in the George C. Marshall Research Foundation*. Charlottesville, Virginia: The University Press of Virginia, 1979.

Darracott, Joseph. *The First World War in Posters*. New York: Dover, 1974.

Rawls, Walton H. *Wake Up America!* New York: Abbeville Press, 1988.

Rickards, Maurice. *Posters of Protest and Revolution*. New York: Walker, 1970.

———. *Posters of the First World War*. New York: Walker, 1968.

Stanley, Peter. *What Did You Do in the War, Daddy?* Melbourne and New York: Oxford University Press, 1983.

Zeman, Zbynek. *Art and Propaganda in World War II*. London: Orbis: 1978.

WORKS PROGRESS ADMINISTRATION (WPA) POSTERS

DeNoon, Christopher. *Posters of the WPA*. Los Angeles: Wheatley Press in association with Seattle: University of Washington Press, 1987.

Prescott, Kenneth W. *Prints and Posters of Ben Shahn*. New York: Dover Publications, 1982.

———. *Complete Graphic Works of Ben Shahn.* New York: Quadrangle, 1973.

ARTICLES

Beach, Laura, Ed. "Advertising Art Climbs to a New High." *Antiques and the Arts Weekly.* May 5, 1989, Newtown, Connecticut.

———. "Gilbert and Sullivan: A Window on the Victorian World." *Antiques and the Arts Weekly.* January 26, 1990, Newtown, Connecticut.

Bohlin, Virginia. "The Illustrious Poster." Auction report on the first Phillips all-poster sale. *The Boston Globe.* November 25, 1979, Boston, Massachusetts.

Brown, Christine. "Old Wine in New Bottles." Profile of publisher Marvin Shanken and his poster collection. *Forbes.* October 16, 1989, New York, New York.

Brown, Robert K. "The Poster Art of Switzerland." *P.S.,* The Journal of the Poster Society. Spring, 1988, Upper Montclair, New Jersey. (This organization and valuable publication have unfortunately become moribund.)

Cannon, Carol. "Buying French Posters." An interview with Jacques P. Athias, President of the Club of American Collectors of Fine Art. *Antiques and Collecting Hobbies.* February 1988, Chicago, Illinois.

Choko, Marc, and David L. Jones. "Canadian Pacific Posters." *P.S.,* The Journal of the Poster Society. Spring, 1988. Upper Montclair, New Jersey.

Fusco, Tony. "Art Deco Posters." *Art New England.* July/August 1989, Boston, Massachusetts.

———. "Fabulous Freidländers: German Circus Posters of the Turn of the Century." *Collectibles Illustrated.* Nov.–Dec. 1984, Dover, New Hampshire.

———. "Fine Art Posters: Great Design, Poised for Appreciation." *Investment Vision.* January 1990, Fidelity Corporation, Boston, Massachusetts.

———. "Pulling Magic Collectibles Out of a Hat." *Collectibles Illustrated.* May–June 1982, Dover, New Hampshire.

———. "World War I American Poster Art." *Antiques & The Arts Weekly.* June 1985, Newtown, Connecticut. Reprinted in *Cape Cod Antiques Monthly.* July 1985, Falmouth, Massachusetts.

Hillier, Bevis. "Posters Revived." An early pre-Phillips auctions article on the growing popularity of posters. *Architectural Digest.* July/August 1987, New York, New York.

Jackson, Bernice. "Dutch Posters." *New England Antiques Journal.* November 1989, Ware, Massachusetts.

———. "The Vienna Secession." *New England Antiques Journal.* November 1986, Ware, Massachusetts.

Koch, Robert. "Will Bradley and the Art Nouveau Poster." *The Magazine Antiques,* 134, October 1988, p. 813, New York, New York.

Queenan, Joe. "Play it Again, Sam: Movie Posters are a Hot Collector's Item." *Barrons,* September 26, 1988, pp. 28–29, New York, New York.

Tyndall, Katie. "Art Deco Graphics' New Life as Art." *Insight.* April 6, 1987, Washington, DC.

Weaver, Jane. "Auction Offers Glimpse at Advertising's Innocent Infancy." *AdWeek,* May 8, 1989, New York, New York.

INDEX

562   *POSTERS*